Hiking
COLORADO III

Contact

Dear Readers:

Every effort was made to make this the most accurate, informative, and easy-to-use guide-book on the planet. Any comments, suggestions, and corrections regarding this guide are welcome and should be sent to:

The Globe Pequot Press
c/o Editorial Dept.
246 Goose Lane
Guilford, CT 06437
editorial@globe-pequot.com
www.falcon.com

We'd love to hear from you so we can make future editions and future guides even better.

Thanks and happy trails!

A FALCON GUIDE ®

Hiking COLORADO III

An Atlas of Colorado's
Greatest Hiking Adventures
by Maryann Gaug

FALCON®
Guilford, Connecticut
An imprint of The Globe Pequot Press

Library of Congress Cataloging-in-Publication Data is available

ISBN 0-7627-2347-5

Manufactured in the United States of America
First Edition/Second Printing

Acknowledgments

Where to begin? First let me thank Anne Robinson and Jacque Kriegel for doing several hikes with me especially the ones needing car shuttles. Because I hiked most of the trails by myself, my good friend, Keith Brown, anxiously awaited my phone calls that I was safe and not lost in the woods. A special thanks to Ken Steele of Meeker, who helped me unscrew the lug nuts to change a flat tire at East Marvine Campground, and the other man I flagged down on a lonely county road south of La Junta to loosen the fifth danged lug nut to change another flat. Needless to say, I bought new tires after that!

Pauline Stieha and I shared research information about Newlin Creek and Thompson Mountain trails with each other. She's as passionate about horseback riding as I am about hiking. Pauline, Keith, Anne, Jacque, Dave Blakeslee, Janet Jacks, Ed Adams, Joan Hutchinson, Stan Wagon, and Dale Drennan critiqued chapters for me, providing good insight and comments. Three friends who are hiking book authors provided moral support and feedback: Tom Jones, M. John Fayhee, and Mary Ellen Gilliland. Many other friends have been very enthusiastic and supportive throughout the book writing process and my frequent absences from home.

In researching my hikes and asking questions afterwards, I talked with and/or met many wonderful and interesting people who care about our public lands and work hard to maintain trails and preserve wild country. Despite the "big brother" image federal and state employees often have, these people love the backcountry and were eager to answer questions and help me. Several took time from busy schedules to review the chapter from their area and provide feedback. If I name everyone, I'll bore you to tears and would for sure accidentally forget someone. Thanks to the recreation and GIS staff at Black Canyon National Park and Grand Junction BLM for providing me with mileage information. John McCammon at the U.S. Geological Survey in Lakewood shared invaluable information about declinations and GPS settings that really helped the mapping process.

I enjoyed traveling around the state, meeting Forest Service and BLM employees with whom I've taken various classes the last five years. Seeing old friends again, while they shared their insights and advice with me, was truly a great experience!

I asked innumerable strangers in outdoor stores, libraries, grocery stores, bookstores, and visitor centers about their area. They were friendly and happy to recommend their favorite restaurant or interesting spot.

Hiking so many trails reminded me that fellow hikers are very friendly folk. I also had some interesting conversations with a mountain biker near Crested Butte and watched as he rode down a trail I thought impossible to ride. Horseback riders were friendly also. Many people wondered why I hiked with ski poles. It was fun to demonstrate my hiking poles with shock absorbers!

Thanks to Al Marlowe, former Executive Director of Rocky Mountain Outdoor Writers & Photographers, from whom I received the lead about Outside America™ (now part of the FalconGuides® series). Thanks, Scott Adams, for e-mailing the opportunity to Al and for putting up with all my questions and idiosyncrasies.

A special thanks and hug to my Mom, still living, and my Dad, long dead, for encouraging me to do what I want to do and strive for peace and happiness.

Last, but not least, thanks to you readers and fellow hikers for buying Hiking Colorado. I hope you find it useful and interesting, and may you enjoy many hours hiking the trails described between these covers.

Contents

Colorado's Long Trails: The Colorado and Continental

The Art of Hiking

HIKES AT A GLANCE

1. Homestead Trail
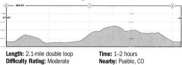
Length: 8.1-mile loop
Difficulty Rating: Moderate
Time: 3–5 hours
Nearby: Springfield, CO

2. Picket Wire Canyonlands
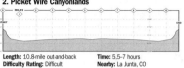
Length: 10.8-mile out-and-back
Difficulty Rating: Difficult
Time: 5.5–7 hours
Nearby: La Junta, CO

3. Arkansas Point Trail System
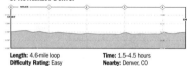
Length: 2.1-mile double loop
Difficulty Rating: Moderate
Time: 1–2 hours
Nearby: Pueblo, CO

4. Rocky Mountain Arsenal National Wildlife Refuge
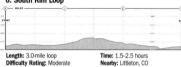
Length: 0.8–2.3-mile loops
Difficulty Rating: Easy
Time: 0.5–2 hours
Nearby: Commerce City, CO

5. Revitalized Denver
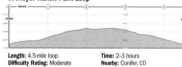
Length: 4.6-mile loop
Difficulty Rating: Easy
Time: 1.5–4.5 hours
Nearby: Denver, CO

6. South Rim Loop
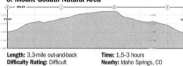
Length: 3.0-mile loop
Difficulty Rating: Moderate
Time: 1.5–2.5 hours
Nearby: Littleton, CO

7. Meyer Ranch Park Loop
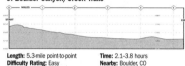
Length: 4.5-mile loop
Difficulty Rating: Moderate
Time: 2–3 hours
Nearby: Conifer, CO

8. Mount Goliath Natural Area
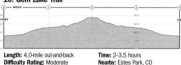
Length: 3.3-mile out-and-back
Difficulty Rating: Difficult
Time: 1.5–3 hours
Nearby: Idaho Springs, CO

9. Boulder Canyon/Creek Trails
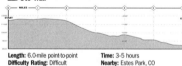
Length: 5.3-mile point-to-point
Difficulty Rating: Easy
Time: 2.1–3.8 hours
Nearby: Boulder, CO

10. Gem Lake Trail

Length: 4.0-mile out-and-back
Difficulty Rating: Moderate
Time: 2–3.5 hours
Nearby: Estes Park, CO

11. Ute Trail
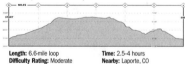
Length: 6.0-mile point-to-point
Difficulty Rating: Difficult
Time: 3–5 hours
Nearby: Estes Park, CO

12. Lulu City Trail

Length: 7.4-mile out-and-back
Difficulty Rating: Moderate
Time: 3–5 hours
Nearby: Grand Lake, CO

13. Lory State Park Loop
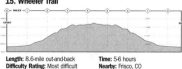
Length: 6.6-mile loop
Difficulty Rating: Moderate
Time: 2.5–4 hours
Nearby: Laporte, CO

14. Roaring Creek Trail #952

Length: 9.4-mile out-and-back
Difficulty Rating: Difficult
Time: 4–6.5 hours
Nearby: Fort Collins, CO

15. Wheeler Trail
Length: 8.6-mile out-and-back
Difficulty Rating: Most difficult
Time: 5–6 hours
Nearby: Frisco, CO

16. Hagerman Tunnel Trail
Length: 5.8-mile loop
Difficulty Rating: Moderate
Time: 3–4 hours
Nearby: Leadville, CO

17. Mount Elbert (North)

Length: 8.4-mile out-and-back
Difficulty Rating: Strenuous
Time: 6–10 hours
Nearby: Leaville, CO

18. Notch Mountain

Length: 10.8-mile out-and-back
Difficulty Rating: Most difficult
Time: 5–7 hours
Nearby: Minturn, CO

19. Mount Thomas Trail

Length: 9.4-mile out-and-back
Difficulty Rating: Difficult
Time: 4–7 hours
Nearby: Eagle, CO

20. Granite Lakes Trail

Length: 13.6-mile out-and-back
Difficulty Rating: Most difficult
Time: 8–12 hours
Nearby: Basalt, CO

21. Silver Creek Trail

Length: 11.0-mile point-to-point
Difficulty Rating: Difficult
Time: 4–6 hours
Nearby: Kremmling, CO

22. Seven Lakes

Length: 12.4-mile out-and-back
Difficulty Rating: Difficult
Time: 5–9 hours
Nearby: Walden, CO

23. Storm King Fourteen Memorial Trail

Length: 4.2-mile out-and-back
Difficulty Rating: Strenuous
Time: 2–4.5 hours
Nearby: Glenwood Springs, CO

24. Coyote and Squirrel Trails

Length: 1.8-mile loop
Difficulty Rating: Easy
Time: 1–2 hours
Nearby: Rifle, CO

25. East Marvine Trail

Length: 16.0-mile out-and-back
Difficulty Rating: Most difficult
Time: 3 days minimum
Nearby: Meeker, CO

26. Black Mountain (West Summit) Trail

Length: 6.8-mile out-and-back
Difficulty Rating: Difficult
Time: 3.5–5 hours
Nearby: Craig, CO

27. Gates of Lodore Nature Trail

Length: 1.0-mile out-and-back
Difficulty Rating: Easy
Time: 30–50 minutes
Nearby: Craig, CO

28. Buckwater Draw

Length: 10.0-mile out-and-back
Difficulty Rating: Difficult
Time: 4–7 hours
Nearby: Rangely, CO

29. Devils Canyon

Length: 6.7-mile loop
Difficulty Rating: Moderate
Time: 3–5 hours
Nearby: Fuita, CO

30. Twin Rock Trail

Length: 6.0-mile out-and-back
Difficulty Rating: Moderate
Time: 2.5–4 hours
Nearby: Florissant, CO

31. Rock Pond to Werley Ranch Loop

Length: 7.7-mile loop
Difficulty Rating: Moderate
Time: 5 hours
Nearby: Divide, CO

32. Aiken Canyon

Length: 4.0-mile loop
Difficulty Rating: Moderate
Time: 2.5–4 hours
Nearby: Colorado Springs, CO

xi

HIKES AT A GLANCE

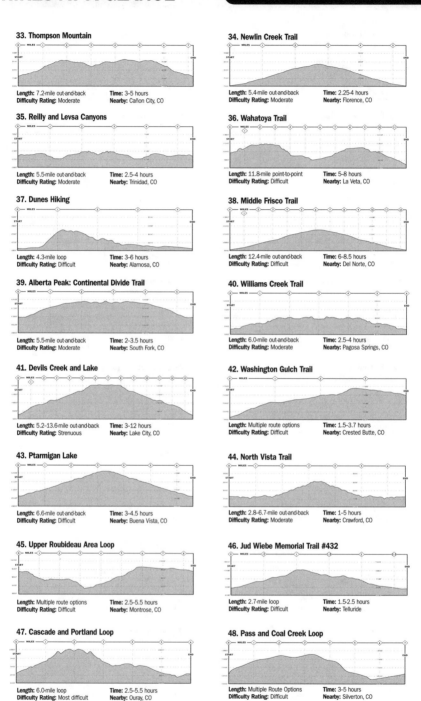

33. Thompson Mountain
Length: 7.2-mile out-and-back
Difficulty Rating: Moderate
Time: 3–5 hours
Nearby: Cañon City, CO

34. Newlin Creek Trail
Length: 5.4-mile out-and-back
Difficulty Rating: Moderate
Time: 2.25–4 hours
Nearby: Florence, CO

35. Reilly and Levsa Canyons
Length: 5.5-mile out-and-back
Difficulty Rating: Moderate
Time: 2.5–4 hours
Nearby: Trinidad, CO

36. Wahatoya Trail
Length: 11.8-mile point-to-point
Difficulty Rating: Difficult
Time: 5–8 hours
Nearby: La Veta, CO

37. Dunes Hiking
Length: 4.3-mile loop
Difficulty Rating: Difficult
Time: 3–6 hours
Nearby: Alamosa, CO

38. Middle Frisco Trail
Length: 12.4-mile out-and-back
Difficulty Rating: Difficult
Time: 6–8.5 hours
Nearby: Del Norte, CO

39. Alberta Peak: Continental Divide Trail
Length: 5.5-mile out-and-back
Difficulty Rating: Moderate
Time: 2–3.5 hours
Nearby: South Fork, CO

40. Williams Creek Trail
Length: 6.0-mile out-and-back
Difficulty Rating: Moderate
Time: 2.5–4 hours
Nearby: Pagosa Springs, CO

41. Devils Creek and Lake
Length: 5.2–13.6-mile out-and-back
Difficulty Rating: Strenuous
Time: 3–12 hours
Nearby: Lake City, CO

42. Washington Gulch Trail
Length: Multiple route options
Difficulty Rating: Difficult
Time: 1.5–3.7 hours
Nearby: Crested Butte, CO

43. Ptarmigan Lake
Length: 6.6-mile out-and-back
Difficulty Rating: Difficult
Time: 3–4.5 hours
Nearby: Buena Vista, CO

44. North Vista Trail
Length: 2.8–6.7-mile out-and-back
Difficulty Rating: Moderate
Time: 1–5 hours
Nearby: Crawford, CO

45. Upper Roubideau Area Loop
Length: Multiple route options
Difficulty Rating: Difficult
Time: 2.5–5.5 hours
Nearby: Montrose, CO

46. Jud Wiebe Memorial Trail #432
Length: 2.7-mile loop
Difficulty Rating: Difficult
Time: 1.5–2.5 hours
Nearby: Telluride

47. Cascade and Portland Loop
Length: 6.0-mile loop
Difficulty Rating: Most difficult
Time: 2.5–5.5 hours
Nearby: Ouray, CO

48. Pass and Coal Creek Loop
Length: Multiple Route Options
Difficulty Rating: Difficult
Time: 3–5 hours
Nearby: Silverton, CO

49. First Fork and Red Creek Loop

Length: 10.3-mile loop
Difficulty Rating: Difficult
Time: 4.5–7.5 hours
Nearby: Durango, CO

50. Petroglyph Point Trail

Length: 2.8-mile loop
Difficulty Rating: Moderate
Time: 1.5–3 hours
Nearby: Cortez, CO

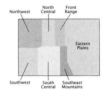

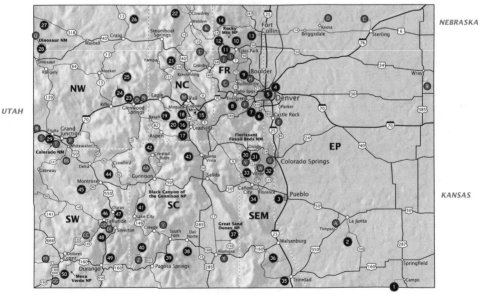

HOW TO USE THIS BOOK

Take a close enough look and you'll find that this little guide contains just about everything you'll ever need to choose, plan for, enjoy, and survive a hike in Colorado. We've done everything but load your pack and tie up your bootlaces. Stuffed with over 400 pages of useful Colorado-specific information, *Hiking Colorado* features 50 mapped and cued hikes, 33 honorable mentions, and everything from advice on getting into shape to tips on getting the most out of hiking with your children or your dog. With so much information, the only question you may have is: How do I sift through it all? Well, we answer that, too.

We've designed this Falcon Guide to be highly visual, for quick reference and ease-of-use. What this means is that the most pertinent information rises quickly to the top, so you don't have to waste time poring through bulky hike descriptions to get mileage cues or elevation stats. They're set aside for you. And yet, this guide doesn't read like a laundry list. Take the time to dive into a hike description and you'll realize that this guide is not just a good source of information; it's a good read. And so, in the end, you get the best of both worlds: a quick-reference guide and an engaging look at a region. Here's an outline of *Hiking Colorado's* major components.

WHAT YOU'LL FIND IN THIS GUIDE. Each region begins with a **Section Intro**, where you're given a sweeping look at the lay of the land. To aid in quick decision-making, we follow the Section Intro with a **Section Overview**. These short summaries give you a taste of the hiking adventures that will be featured in the section. You'll learn about the trail terrain and what surprises each route has to offer. If your interest is piqued, flip to the hike and you can read more. If not, skip to the next summary.

Now to the individual chapter. The **Hike Specs** are fairly self-explanatory. Here you'll find the quick, nitty-gritty details of the hike: where the trailhead is located, the nearest town, hike length, approximate hiking time, difficulty rating, best hiking season, type of trail terrain, and what other trail users you may encounter. Our **Getting There** section gives you dependable directions from a nearby city right down to where you'll want to park. The **Hike Description** is the meat of the chapter. Detailed and honest, it's the author's carefully researched impression of the trail. While it's impossible to cover everything, you can rest assured that we won't miss what's important. In our **Miles/Directions** section we provide mileage cues to identify all turns and trail name changes, as well as points of interest. Between this and our Route Map, you simply can't get lost. The **Hike Information** box is a hodgepodge of information. In it you'll find trail hotlines (for updates on trail conditions), trail schedules and use fees, local outdoor retailers (for emergency trail supplies), and a list of maps available to the area. We'll also tell you where to stay, what to eat, and what else to see while you're hiking in the area.

Lastly, the **Honorable Mentions** section details all of the hikes that didn't make the cut, for whatever reason—in many cases it's not because they aren't great hikes, but because they're overcrowded or environmentally sensitive to heavy traffic. Be sure to read through these. A jewel might be lurking among them.

We don't want anyone to feel restricted to just the routes and trails that are mapped here. We hope you'll have an adventurous spirit and use this guide as a platform to dive into Colorado's backcountry and discover new routes for yourself. One of the simplest ways to begin this is to just turn the map upside down and hike the course in reverse. The change in perspective is often fantastic and the hike should feel quite different. With this in mind, it'll be like getting two distinctly different hikes on each map.

For your own purposes, you may wish to copy the directions for the course onto a small sheet to help you while hiking, or photocopy the map and cue sheet to take with you. Otherwise, just slip the whole book in your backpack and take it all with you. Enjoy your time in the outdoors and remember to pack out what you pack in.

Interstate Highway	
U.S. Highway	
State Road	
County Road	
Township Road	
Forest Road	
Paved Road	
Paved Bike Lane	
Maintained Dirt Road	
Unmaintained Jeep Trail	
Singletrack Trail	
Highlighted Route	
Ntl Forest/County Boundaries	
State Boundaries	
Railroad Tracks	
Power Lines	
Special Trail	
Rivers or Streams	
Water and Lakes	
Marsh	

Airfield		Golf Course	
Airport		Hiking Trail	
Bike Trail		Mine	
No Bikes		Overlook	
Boat Launch		Picnic	
Bridge		Parking	
Bus Stop		Quarry	
Campground		Radio Tower	
Campsite		Rock Climbing	
Canoe Access		School	
Cattle Guard		Shelter	
Cemetery		Spring	
Church		Swimming	
Covered Bridge		Train Station	
Direction Arrows		Wildlife Refuge	
Downhill Skiing		Vineyard	
Fire Tower		Most Difficult	
Forest HQ		Difficult	
4WD Trail		Moderate	
Gate		Easy	

HOW TO USE THESE MAPS

1 Area Locator Map

This thumbnail relief map at the beginning of each hike shows you where the hike is within the state. The hike area is indicated by the white star.

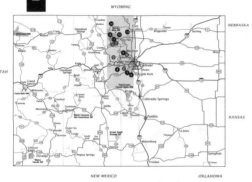

2 Regional Location Map

This map helps you find your way to the start of each hike from the nearest sizeable town or city. Coupled with the detailed directions at the beginning of the cue, this map should visually lead you to where you need to be for each hike.

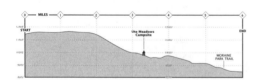

3 Profile Map

This helpful profile gives you a cross-sectional look at the hike's ups and downs. Elevation is labeled on the left, mileage is indicated on the top. Road and trail names are shown along the route with towns and points of interest labeled in bold.

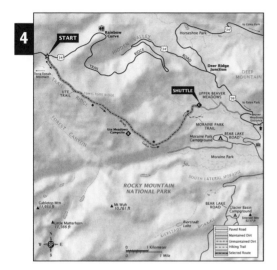

4 Route Map

This is your primary guide to each hike. It shows all of the accessible roads and trails, points of interest, water, towns, landmarks, and geographical features. It also distinguishes trails from roads, and paved roads from unpaved roads. The selected route is highlighted, and directional arrows point the way. Shaded topographic relief in the background gives you an accurate representation of the terrain and landscape in the hike area.

Hike Information *(Included in each hike section)*

🐾 Trail Contacts:

This is the direct number for the local land managers in charge of all the trails within the selected hike. Use this hotline to call ahead for trail access information, or after your visit if you see problems with trail erosion, damage, or misuse.

🕐 Schedule:

This tells you at what times trails open and close. Important winter information is also included.

💲 Fees/Permits:

What money, if any, you may need to carry with you for park entrance fees or tolls.

🅝 Maps:

This is a list of other maps to supplement the maps in this book. They are listed in order from most detailed to most general.

Any other important or useful information will also be listed here such as local attractions, outdoor shops, nearby accommodations, etc.

A note from the folks behind this endeavor...

The producers behind this latest FalconGuide® look at guidebook publishing a little differently. There's just no reason that a guidebook has to look like it was published out of your Uncle Ernie's woodshed. We feel that guidebooks need to be both easy to use and nice to look at, and that takes an innovative approach to design. You see, we want you to spend less time fumbling through your guidebook and more time enjoying the adventure at hand. We hope you like what you see here and enjoy the places we lead you. And most of all, we'd like to thank you for taking an adventure with us.

Happy Trails!

Introduc

Introduction

Colorado! The word conjures images of rugged peaks, cascading mountain streams, and crystal clear alpine lakes. Indeed the state's middle section lives up to those expectations, but the state as a whole offers so much more. Colorado's western canyon country carved by raging torrents is rich with dinosaur graveyards and artifacts and ruins of Ancestral Puebloan and Fremont Indians well worth exploring. The Eastern Plains, long thought as being too flat for anything scenic, have plenty of natural delights tucked away for the hiker. Buttes rise above the plains providing a haven for hawks and falcons while southeastern canyons cache signs of ancient inhabitants including American Indian petroglyphs and North America's largest known dinosaur tracksite.

About 355 million years ago, Colorado sat near the equator. Little crustaceans in shallow seas died and were compressed into limestone. The Ancestral Rockies were uplifted from the seas and formed part of the supercontinent Pangaea. As time progressed, the mountains eroded and coastal dunes became today's magnificent sandstone cliffs. The present Rocky Mountains were uplifted starting 70 million years ago. Volcanic activity 25 million years ago created plateaus and several mountain ranges. Then 28 to 5 million years ago the entire region began to rise 5,000 feet to its present elevation. Ice Ages took hold of Colorado (by that time around the 39th Parallel) and from 15,000 to 700,000 years ago, glaciers carved the magnificent craggy peaks and U-shaped valleys we see today.

Human history in Colorado started with hunter-gatherers followed by the Ancestral Puebloan culture that from 500 B.C. to A.D. 1300 farmed then built pueblos and magnificent cliff dwellings in the southwest corner. After A.D. 1300 other Native Americans moved into the eastern plains and mountain valleys. Spanish explorers arrived in the late 1500s followed by trappers and traders. The gold rush of 1859 was perhaps the most significant event in the state's history bringing settlers, fortune seekers, and improved transportation. The railroad companies performed engineering miracles to conquer impassable mountains and hasten the transportation of ore and the state's development. Later, equally impressive roads were built for the automobile.

Today these roads provide us with relatively easy travel to hiking trails. Hiking is one of the best ways to explore Colorado. The 50 featured hikes in this guide offer a sample of Colorado's beautiful and varied terrain, its fascinating geology, flora and fauna, and human history. Honorable Mention hikes are added to give the hiker more options in a particular region. Hikes range from easy to strenuous, from a one-mile loop around a waterfowl-filled lake to overnight backpacks. I included some classic trails and found several new ones. I especially tried to find trails in lesser-known and quieter areas. Because wilderness areas closest to Front Range metro areas are being "loved to death" and opportunities for solitude have greatly decreased, I avoided including trails in those areas.

Featured trails in this guide were hiked during 1999, 2000, and 2001. Please realize that trail locations and conditions, roads, and signage are subject to change over time. Trail mileage is as much an art as a science, even for land managers. Finding accurate historical information was sometimes interesting when different books contained conflicting information! I've included appropriate websites to assist in finding further information, but note that website addresses can change.

Henry David Thoreau said, "In wildness is the preservation of the world." Aldo Leopold added years later: "When we see land as a community to which we belong, we may begin to use it with love and respect." My wish for you is to enjoy hiking, and learn about yourself and the world around you to which we all belong. Remember, only we can preserve wild lands for current and future generations.

As you hike around our beautiful state, capture part of nature's spirit and hold it close to your own. Leave a piece of your spirit as well, so that no matter where you travel or live, the peace and beauty of Colorado's wild country, its mountains, plains, and canyons, will remain with you forever.

Weather

Difficult to forecast and prone to change quickly, Colorado's weather is a wonder in itself. The mountains often create their own weather with summer thunderstorms being a prime example. Rains may drench the Front Range and Eastern Plains while western mountains and canyons remain sunny and warm. Snow can fall in higher elevations at any time.

Spring is a great time to hike at lower elevations, renewing yourself from the chill of winter. The weather tends to be unpredictable and wet, especially in April and May. Spring runoff starts in May and typically peaks around mid-June.

Summer attempts to begin in June in the high country. June also begins thunderstorm season. As the sun heats the ground, warm air rises, cools, and releases moisture that condenses into clouds. Three problems result from thunderstorm development. One is lightning, a killer from above. The second is flash flood, which can roar out of nowhere in mountain and desert canyons. The third is more subtle: Rain in Colorado tends to be cold, and unprepared hikers can become hypothermic very quickly, even in summer. Monsoon season brings occasional gray, rainy days and increased thunderstorms from mid-July to early September.

Colorado's fall season (September to mid-October) is perhaps the best time of year to hike. Thunderstorms are less frequent and the air is crisp and cool with dazzling blue skies. Winds pick up on the mountain peaks, so be aware! Aspen trees turn gold and red about the last two weeks in September. By early October the Gambel oak and cottonwood trees are in prime color at lower elevations. Mid-October snows tend to bring an end to high altitude hiking, while lower elevations become the perfect place to hike.

Winter brings deep snow to the mountains requiring foot travel by snowshoes or skis. If you venture out on backcountry trails, take an avalanche awareness course. Colorado leads the nation in avalanche deaths. At lower elevations in the eastern and western parts of the state, year-round hiking is the norm, interrupted only by snowfalls that melt quickly.

Whatever the season, always bring layers of clothes and rain (or snow) gear. Weather can change quickly and a temperature drop of 10°F to 20°F in one hour is not unheard of. Be prepared!

An interesting rule of thumb: For every 1,000 feet of elevation gained, the temperature drops about 5.5°F. So, when Denver at 5,280 feet registers 80°F, it may only be 53°F in Leadville at 10,190 feet. Another tidbit: Research in Colorado has measured a 26-percent increase in ultraviolet radiation between 5,500 feet and 14,000 feet on a cloudless summer day.

Flora and Fauna

Colorado ranges in elevation from 3,337 feet at its lowest point in the northeastern plains to 14,433 feet at the top of Mount Elbert near Leadville. In the rain shadow of the Rocky Mountains, the Eastern Plains are high and dry with less than 15 inches of annual precipitation. Wolf Creek Pass on the Continental Divide often receives over 300 inches of snow annually. Just east of Wolf Creek Pass, the San Luis Valley is a true desert, receiving less than eight inches of moisture per year. With such extremes in a relatively short distance, Colorado has a wide diversity of flora and fauna.

At the lowest elevations, shortgrass prairie dominates the Eastern Plains while semi-desert scrub and sagebrush shrublands populate the west side. As elevation and precipitation increase, you pass from mountain shrublands into piñon-juniper forest, then ponderosa pine and Douglas fir forests. Continue to climb through lodgepole pine and aspen forests into forests of spruce-fir and limber and bristlecone pine. Mountain grasslands and wetlands punctuate the forest blanket. Finally, alpine tundra at the highest elevations supports miniature vegetation.

As you hike through these different ecosystems, notice which plants and animals live among which trees and the different soil types. For example, aspens grow in moist, protected areas. Bushes provide browse for mule deer. Grasses offer good eats for elk, who also scrape the bark off aspen in winter. Prairie dogs, mule and white-tailed deer, coyotes, and pronghorn antelope rule the plains. Little critters provide food for coyotes, foxes, eagles, hawks, and great horned owls. Elk, mule deer, and black bears live in forested areas while mountain lions prowl rocky slopes. On cliffs and rocky steeps, mountain goats and Rocky Mountain bighorn sheep somehow survive. A good place to see bighorn sheep right from your car window is along Interstate 70 near Georgetown. Long gone are the wild bison, grizzly bear, and wolf populations. Canada lynx were recently reintroduced in the San Juan Mountains amid much controversy. You can still see bison on ranches around the state.

As you gain elevation, animals and plants show their adaptations to shorter summers, less oxygen, and colder temperatures. Above treeline, you can't miss the cute little pikas scurrying around with mouthfuls of grasses and flowers or lazy marmots sunning themselves on rocks. In some heavily visited areas chipmunks, ground squirrels, and marmots will practically attack you expecting a handout. Please don't feed them, as they may not forage for themselves. Crows, magpies, blue Stellar's jays with their black crowns, and pesky Clark's nutcrackers and gray jays (nicknamed camp robbers) are easily spotted birds.

Fishing in Colorado can be superb. Native cutthroat trout are making a recovery after introduced sport fishes such as rainbow and brown trout increased competition for the food supply.

By July, wildflowers are blooming in the cool air of the high mountains. If summer has experienced normal or greater precipitation, mushrooms pop out in August and early September. Many mushrooms are poisonous while others are edible and incredibly delicious. Do not pick mushrooms unless you know what you are doing!

The dry western side of the state is covered with sagebrush, greasewood, four-winged saltbush, skunkbrush, and shadscale. Rattlesnakes, eastern fence and other lizards, coyotes, jackrabbits, and deer mice are just a few of the reptiles and mammals living in this dry country that fluctuates between extreme heat and cold.

Bristlecone pines grow in Colorado generally south of Interstate 70. These amazing trees live 1,500 to 2,000 years in our state. In the transition zone between alpine tundra and subalpine zone you can notice islands of stunted trees with a few flag trees sticking up—a pattern called krummholz. The deadwood on the windward side protects the rest of the tree island, so please don't use it for firewood.

Above treeline, each incredible tiny flower has its own particular niche, whether on windblown slopes or next to sheltering rocks. Although the terrain above treeline can appear tough or barren, it's an ecosystem distinguished by its delicate flora. Be sure to tread lightly and stay on designated trails. Just a few steps off trail can cause plant damage requiring years to repair.

Wilderness Restrictions/Regulations

Colorado's two national grasslands, six national wildlife refuges, 12 national forests, and 40 wilderness areas (not counting Wilderness Study Areas), national parks, and monuments provide numerous opportunities for hiking and backpacking in many different settings and ecosystems. Colorado also has over 40 state parks (with more coming) plus various county and city open space areas and mountain parks.

If you plan to hike or backpack in a wilderness area, contact the responsible U.S. Forest Service or Bureau of Land Management (BLM) office by phone or on the Internet for up-to-date restrictions and regulations. By law, each national forest must have a forest management plan, and each plan must be reviewed every 10 to 15 years. Several plans are in the revision process as this guidebook is being published and some regulations may change. In general, each wilderness area has specific group size limitations, usually applying to both people and pack stock. A few wilderness areas have designated campsites in heavily used areas. Presently only Indian Peaks Wilderness has a backcountry permit requirement for overnight camping. Wilderness lands closest to urban areas tend to have more regulations because of the large number of recreational users.

Non-wilderness parts of national forests and BLM lands tend to have fewer regulations. Some popular areas charge fees as part of the fee demonstration program. Eighty percent of collected fees are retained locally for improvements and maintenance. National parks and monuments charge entrance fees and require backcountry permits for camping and sometimes for hiking. State parks charge entrance fees and separate camping fees. Each county and city open space or mountain park area has its own regulations.

Leave No Trace outdoor skills and ethics are increasingly important for the preservation of Colorado's wild lands and parks. For further information, visit the website at *www.LNT.org*.

Winter Hiking

The hikes in this book were chosen for their enjoyment and adventure during snow-free times. Trails open year round are listed as such. Winter in Colorado's high country brings deep snows or wind-blown drifts that close many trailhead access roads from the time when winter gets serious (October to November) to when the snowpack melts and muddy roads dry (June to mid-July). Some snow-closed roads can be skied or snowshoed with most such roads also being used by snowmobiles.

Don't attempt to drive a snow-closed road in a 4WD vehicle. One forest ranger commented that he has seen vehicles stuck a mile down the closed road after the drivers broke through the compacted snow. Use skis, snowshoes, or snowmobiles as allowed by local regulations.

The hikes were not evaluated for avalanche danger. As noted elsewhere in this book, Colorado leads the nation in avalanche deaths. Many avalanche awareness and field clinics are offered around the state. If you venture into the high country in winter, take clinics and be prepared for variable and extreme winter conditions. The winds can blow steadily at 60 miles per hour and gust to over 100 miles per hour in higher elevations.

The Colorado Avalanche Information Center provides daily avalanche forecasts but always reminds people that conditions vary with each location and aspect. Check out their website at *geosurvey.state.co.us/avalanche/index.html*.

"Hiking" snow-covered trails in winter typically implies snowshoeing or cross country skiing. See the sidebar on those methods of transportation on page 109. Another challenge in winter is finding high country trails. Featured trails marked by blue diamonds, which denote ski touring trails (orange diamonds denote snowmobile trails), are noted. Many trails, especially those in wilderness areas, are neither maintained nor marked for winter use. Snow-covered trails can be difficult if not impossible to find. They may not be the best ski or snowshoe route either. In winter, excellent route finding skills and winter ski or snowshoe skills are mandatory. Some trails are not skier friendly because they are narrow and steep. Snowshoes are sometimes the best way to travel. And sometimes it's best to wait until summer to travel the trail. Be aware that the Forest Service may not always have up-to-date information on winter trail conditions. Check with the local land management agency for winter trail recommendations.

Hiking with Dogs

Under Canine Compatibility in the Hike Specs, the words "Controlled Dogs Permitted" means dogs can be off leash but must be under immediate voice control. If you cannot control your dog by voice command, regulations typically require the dog be leashed. This information was obtained from public land managers contacted while researching this hiking guide. According to the Colorado Division of Wildlife, harassment of wildlife (even chasing squirrels) by dogs and humans is illegal in Colorado. See The Art Of Hiking on page 381 for more information about hiking happily with dogs.

Levels of Difficulty

This rating system was developed from several sources and personal experience. These difficulty levels are meant as guidelines and may prove easier or harder depending on ability and physical fitness. Hikes are rated by having one or more of the noted characteristics.

Easy – 4 miles or less total trip distance in one day; elevation gain less than 600 feet; paved or smooth-surfaced dirt trail; less than a 6-percent grade average.

Moderate – Up to 8 miles total trip distance in one day; elevation gain of 600 to 1,200 feet; a 6- to 8-percent grade average.

Difficult – Up to 12 miles total trip distance in one day; elevation gain of 1,200 to 2,500 feet; an 8- to 10-percent grade average.

Most Difficult – Up to 16 miles total trip distance in one day; elevation gain of 2,500 to 3,500 feet; trail not well defined in places; a 10- to 15-percent grade average.

Strenuous – Mainly reserved for peak climbs or canyon descents; greater than 15-percent grade average.

Enjoy!

Times change and so do trail conditions. Remember to check with the appropriate land management agency for current fees, regulations, and trail information before heading out, then have a great hike!

Thanks for purchasing *Hiking Colorado*! Happy Hiking!

Maryann Gaug

Getting around Colorado

❶ AREA CODES

Colorado currently has four area codes: The Denver/Boulder metro area (extending out to Longmont, Idaho Springs, and Castle Rock) uses **303** and **720** (this area requires a 10-digit phone number even when calling from one house in Denver to the one next door). The **719** area code services the greater south-central and southeastern part of the state, including Colorado Springs, Pueblo, Buena Vista, Leadville, Alamosa, and Del Norte. The **970** area code services the northern Front Range, Eastern Plains, and West Slope, extending east from Craig to Sterling and south from Craig to Durango and Cortez.

❷ ROADS

For current information on statewide weather, road conditions, and closures, contact the **Colorado Department of Transportation** (CDOT) at their toll free (Colorado only) hotline 1–877–315–ROAD. Denver metro area and out-of-state callers can still access the hotline by calling 303–639–1111. The same information can also be found by visiting CDOT's website at *www.cotrip.org*.

❸ BY AIR

Denver International Airport (DIA) is 23 miles northeast of downtown Denver. Along with servicing the majority of flights into Colorado, Denver International also links flights throughout the global village. For more information, contact its website at *www.flydenver.com* or call 303–342–2000 or 1–800–AIR2DEN (247–2336).

Roughly 60 miles south of Denver lies the **Colorado Springs Airport** (COS). The Colorado Springs Airport services the southern half of the Front Range and Eastern Plains. For more information, contact its website at *www.flycos.com* or call (719) 550–1900 or 1–800–462–6774.

Servicing the northwestern towns of Steamboat Springs and Hayden, the **Yampa Valley Airport** (HDN) can be reached by calling (970) 276–3669.

The **Walker Field Airport** (GJT) in Grand Junction services Colorado and eastern Utah. Walker Field Airport features commercial carrier service with over 20 daily departures to Denver, Phoenix, and Salt Lake City, and over 500 one-stop connections to cities in the United States, Canada, Europe, and Central America. For more information, check out its website at *www.walkerfield.com* or call (970) 244–9100.

Two airports serve the towns of the central Rockies: Aspen and Eagle. **Aspen Airport** is located just north of the town of Aspen, surrounded by mountains on three sides. For information, call (970) 920–5384 or check out their website at *www.aspenairport.com*. **Eagle County Regional Airport** (EGE) lies between Vail and Glenwood Springs. Contact them at (970) 524–9490.

To the southwest lies the **Durango-La Plata County Airport** (DRO). The Durango-La Plata County Airport is located about 14 miles southeast of Durango and is served by three airlines: United Express (serving Denver with nine daily flights), America West Express (offering four daily non-stop flights to Phoenix), and Mesa Airlines (which offers five flights daily to Albuquerque). For more information, contact its website at *http://co.laplata.co.us/airport.html* or call (970) 247–8143.

To book reservations online, check out your favorite airline's website or search one of the following travel sites for the best price: *www.cheaptickets.com, www. expedia.com, www.priceline.com, www.orbitz.com, travel.yahoo.com, www.travelocity. com,* or *www.Trip.com*—just to name a few.

⊞ BY RAIL

Amtrak has two routes that travel through Colorado daily. The California Zephyr travels between Chicago and Oakland via Fort Morgan, Denver, Winter Park, Granby, Glenwood Springs, and Grand Junction. The stations in Grand Junction, Glenwood Springs, and Denver have checked baggage service. The Southwest Chief travels between Chicago and Los Angeles via Lamar, La Junta, and Trinidad. For more details, call 1–800–872–7245 or visit *www.amtrak.com* for more information.

⊟ BY BUS

Greyhound or partners serves most cities in Colorado and the major ski resorts along Interstates 25 and 70 and U.S. Highways 40, 50, and 550. Call Greyhound at 1–800–231–2222 or visit *www.greyhound.com* for more information.

Roaring Fork Transit (RFTA) runs frequent service from Glenwood Springs to Aspen, making it a convenient connection with Amtrak and Greyhound. For more information, check out the website at *www.rfta.com* or call (970) 925–8484.

Denver/Boulder Regional Transportation District (RTD) serves Boulder and Metro Denver from downtown and the airport. There is a free permit for light rail trains, and no permit required for buses. For more information contact Ken Epperson at 303–299–6000, 1–800–366–7433 or visit *www.rtd-denver.com*.

⊜ SHUTTLES

From **Denver International Airport**, taxicabs, charters, vans, and luxury limousines can deliver you to most any Colorado location by prior arrangements. Check the Denver International Airport website at *www.flydenver.com/z106.html* for a detailed listing of all available shuttle options.

❷ VISITOR INFORMATION

For general information on Colorado, visit the official website of Colorado travel: *www.colorado.com*. The site contains a wealth of vacation information.

Visitors to Colorado can find vacation information, free state maps and brochures, and clean restrooms at Colorado's welcome centers, located near most of the major highways entering Colorado. For more information, contact their website at *www.state.co.us/dtour.html*.
* **Forest Service:** *www.fs.fed.us/R2/*
* **Bureau of Land Management:** *www.co.blm.gov*
* **Colorado State Parks:** *parks.state.co.us*

The Hikes

Eastern
PLAINS

Arch Rock. *See Homestead Trail*

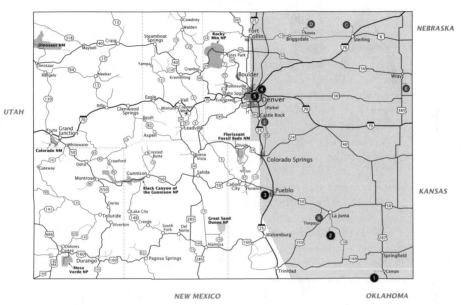

The Hikes

Homestead Trail **1.**
Picket Wire Canyonlands **2.**
Arkansas Point Trail System **3.**
Rocky Mountain Arsenal National Wildlife Refuge **4.**
Revitalized Denver **5.**

Honorable Mentions

A. Santa Fe Trail
B. Beecher Island
C. North Sterling Reservoir
D. Pawnee Buttes Trail
E. Castlewood Canyon

Eastern Plains

Almost half of Colorado lies on the Great Plains, where they bump into the Rocky Mountains. Even the lowest point in Colorado at 3,337 feet, near the Nebraska border east of Wray, is lofty compared to most of the nation. The Dust Bowl of the 1930s ended many dreams, yet it created the terrain that ultimately became the Pawnee National Grassland and Comanche National Grassland. The latter contains not only remains of pioneer settlements, but also those of Native American inhabitants who left rock carvings and an equinox marker tucked away in a cave.

Most hikers ignore the plains, thinking they are flat and boring, not to mention most of the land is private. But the plains have hidden spots every hiker should take time to explore. With most people dismissing the plains as a good hiking destination, what a great place to go for solitude!

Pawnee National Grassland lies to the north of Greeley and east of Fort Collins. The Pawnee Buttes section has a 1.5-mile hiking trail open year round. Spring brings forth beautiful flowers including prickly pear cactus, yucca, sunflowers, prairie coneflower, prairie clover, locoweed, and prairie evening primrose, to name a few. This area is popular for bird watching. Seasonal closures of the overlook and cliffs protect birds during nesting season.

Comanche National Grassland lies south of La Junta with another section south of Springfield in the southeastern corner of the state. A section of the Mountain Branch of the Santa Fe Trail can still be seen and hiked southwest of La Junta. Be sure to stop at Bent's Fort National Historic Site for a step back in time to the days of trappers and early travelers in this area. Vogel Canyon offers some loop hikes with petroglyphs and remains of old stage stops. Beyond that, a must see is the largest known dinosaur tracksite in North America in Picket Wire Canyonlands. You can hike or bike into the area or take a guided 4WD tour offered by the U.S. Forest Service. Traveling almost to Oklahoma, Picture Canyon offers several trails featuring petroglyphs, old homesteads, an arch, and a windmill.

Since Denver is the Queen City of the Plains, walks in Denver itself and trails at the Rocky Mountain Arsenal National Wildlife Refuge are included in this chapter. Rocky Mountain Arsenal produced chemical weapons and later pesticides. Nevertheless, as urban development encroached on wildlands, a variety of wildlife took refuge in the buffer zone around the manufacturing facility. Manufacturing operations ceased in 1982, and cleanup is still underway, but the new wildlife refuge offers tours and limited hiking that will be expanded in the future.

Several state parks, mainly located at reservoirs, offer hiking opportunities available virtually year round. In addition, Tamarack Ranch State Wildlife Area near Julesburg and Beecher Island Battleground south of Wray offer short trails.

Take a trip to explore the eastern half of Colorado. You'll be pleasantly surprised by the subtle beauty. Interesting geological features, wildlife and birds, and historical places await your visit. Scenic and historic byways to explore include the Santa Fe Trail, Pawnee Pioneer Trails, and the South Platte River Trail.

Section Overview

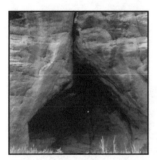

Homestead Trail

The Homestead Trail travels across a variety of landforms and human history. Rock art from 2,500 years ago to the modern era is pecked and painted onto canyon walls. An equinox carving exists in a crack on a canyon wall. Remains of homesteads from the late 1800s and early 1900s dot the landscape. A rock arch (Hells' Half Acre), numerous little canyons, springs, a windmill, windblown plains, prairie flowers and juniper trees are some sights you can see as you hike this loop. Watch for great horned owls! The trail, or lack thereof, can be challenging in spots. *(See page 16.)*

Picket Wire Canyonlands

Picket Wire Canyonlands is a trip back in time visiting early homesteads, a mission, and even farther back to dinosaurs. It is a beautiful flat, open area of rimrock, junipers, cactus, grasses, cottonwoods, and the Purgatoire River. Once down in the wide canyon, the hike is mostly gentle with a few hills. Intricately carved headstones in an old cemetery and dinosaur tracks from 150 million years ago are the highlights of this hike. The dinosaur tracksite is the largest documented in North America. *(See page 22.)*

The Homestead Trail.

Arkansas Point Trail System

The Arkansas Point Trail system takes you through history from prehistoric sea worms to modern water transportation and storage systems. The Conduit Trail creates the first 0.8-mile loop. The Arkansas Point Trail winds and climbs about 0.7 miles from the trailhead to the survey marker on Arkansas Point. The view from Arkansas Point above Lake Pueblo encompasses Colorado's plains, the Sangre de Cristo Mountains, Wet Mountains, Spanish Peaks, and Pikes Peak. Interpretive signs explain the area's history. *(See page 28.)*

Rocky Mountain Arsenal National Wildlife Refuge

Created in 1992, Rocky Mountain Arsenal National Wildlife Refuge is a work in progress. Over the years, the mile-wide buffer around the former chemical weapons plant provided a refuge for prairie animals and birds as the Denver metro area expanded. White-tailed and mule deer, eagles, prairie dogs, hawks, waterfowl, burrowing owls, and more thrive here so close to the Denver metro area. Presently the refuge is open to the public for drop-in visits only on Saturdays. A few trails are now open, with more opening in the next year or so. Check with the Arsenal for current status. *(See page 34.)*

Revitalized Denver

This walk tours lower downtown Denver and the banks of the nearby South Platte River. The area has recently received a facelift and attracts visitors and locals alike to shops, upscale restaurants, modern sports facilities, amusement parks, and museums. The South Platte Greenway provides numerous recreation opportunities close to busy downtown Denver. *(See page 40.)*

1

Homestead Trail

Hike Specs

Start: From Picture Canyon picnic ground
Length: 8.1-mile loop (9.1 miles if you include four spur trails)
Approximate Hiking Time: 3–5 hours
Difficulty Rating: Moderate due to length and route finding challenges
Elevations: 4,220–4,473 feet
Elevation Gain: 253 feet
Seasons: Best in spring and fall. Summer can be very hot and winter can bring blizzards and snow.
Terrain: Dirt trail, old ranch road, and short-grass prairie
Land Status: National grassland
Nearest Town: Springfield, CO
Other Trail Users: Equestrians, mountain bikers, motorists (on one section), hunters (in season)
Canine Compatibility: Leashed dogs permitted, but water is scarce along the trail.

Getting There

From Springfield: Drive south on U.S. 287 about 20 miles (from the intersection with U.S. 160) to Campo (very few services). Turn right onto CR J, the road the post office is on. The road shortly turns to dirt, wide and well graded, but can have washboards. The rest of the drive to Picture Canyon is on maintained dirt roads. Drive 10 miles west to CR 18 and turn left (south). Drive another 4.8 miles to the entrance to Picture Canyon and turn right on Picture Canyon Road. The picnic area is another 2.0 miles south. You can camp here also. There are three covered picnic tables and one vault toilet. It's a very pleasant area next to canyon cliffs. There's no garbage service available here—pack it out! There is also no water, so be sure to bring your own. *DeLorme: Colorado Atlas & Gazetteer:* Page 101 D6

Most people think of eastern Colorado as a flat, uninspiring expanse, but the southeastern corner bordering Oklahoma is full of interesting canyons, rock formations, wildlife, reptiles, birds, and human history.

There's evidence of people dwelling in Picture Canyon as far back as 2,000 years ago. The canyons provided their inhabitants with shelter from the elements and abundant wildlife, and supported wet bottomlands and running streams and springs, which made life in the canyons even more attractive. The first inhabitants were hunter-gatherers. By 1000 AD, farming enabled a more settled lifestyle. In Crack Cave within Picture Canyon, ancient residents carved lines onto the wall. Experts surmise the markings may have been used to help with crop planting and harvesting or to indicate ceremonies. During spring and fall equinox, the sun's rays illuminate these lines at sunrise. Because of vandalism, a locked gate now prevents the casual visitor from entering the cave, but festivals held in spring and fall allow a limited number of people to see the sunrise illumination.

About 0.5 miles from the trailhead on a side spur, numerous petroglyphs and pictographs are displayed on the canyon wall. A sea that covered much of Colorado

back in Cretaceous times (about 100 million years ago) deposited these sandstone cliffs. It's sometimes hard to tell what is old and what is new when looking at the rock art. Depictions of horses (which were introduced to North America by the Spanish) indicate that some of the artwork was done as recently as 500 years ago. Sadly, in more recent times, visitors have carved or painted initials and drawings over pre-existing artwork and made the confusion even more extreme. In one large opening, look for parallel lines carved in the rock. Some people believe these lines to be related to Ogam writing, an alphabet used in the British Isles from about A.D. 0 to 500. Some of the drawings have been interpreted as compasses and sundials, as well as equinox indicators.

Cave Spring.

MilesDirections

0.0 START at the trailhead by Picture Canyon Picnic Ground. The trail quickly joins a dirt road. ✭ 37˚00'44"N 102˚44'41"W

0.3 Road forks. Take the right branch of the road. *[Side-trip. You can turn left here to see the rock art on the canyon walls. It's about 0.4 miles out-and-back. Return the way you came and turn left on the road to continue on Homestead Trail.]*

0.5 Road forks. Take the right branch of the road. *[Side-trip. You can turn left here to see more rock art on the canyon walls. Look for the red bighorn sheep. It's about 0.1 miles out-and-back. Return the way you came and turn left on the road to continue on Homestead Trail.]* In about 250 feet the road forks again. Stay right.

0.6 The road goes left and the Homestead Trail turns right at the end of a barbwire fence. Follow the Homestead Trail, looking for wooden posts. ◆37˚00'23"N 102˚45'02"W—*[Side-trip. You can go left on the road to the base of the cliff. There are house ruins, Crack Cave, and some nice pictographs, including a huge bull or bison with horns. This spur is about 0.4 miles out-and-back.]*

0.8 Arrive at a check dam and sign pointing to Homestead and Arch Rock. Turn left and walk across the check dam. Across the check dam is a post with a black right arrow. Turn right and walk up the trail. Some juniper trees almost cover the trail, and it crisscrosses a little dry creek several times. Keep following the wooden posts.

1.0 Trail forks. The right fork is more a cattle trail but offers an interesting glimpse of Hells Half Acre. Homestead Trail goes left here and soon makes a left turn to climb up out of the canyon. Continue following wooden posts. *[Note. Watch out for yucca plants—members of the lily family—as their pointy leaves tend to hurt if you bump into them.]* The trail heads roughly 236˚ and climbs up to a flat area.

1.2 Reach the ridge top. ◆37˚00'33"N 102˚45'23"W—The wooden post may not be standing. The trail is very faint here. Follow a compass reading of 300˚ to 305˚ to the next wooden post. Then head toward a clump of juniper trees. There's a survey marker to the left of these.

1.5 Survey marker. Look for the next wooden post at about 324˚ true north. ◆37˚00'40"N 102˚45'34"W

1.6 Cross a doubletrack trail just before the next wooden post.

1.7 Arrive at a huge wooden post with no sign on it. ◆37˚00'51"N 102˚45'36"W—The trail forks here. Turn left and follow the cairns into a little slickrock canyon. (The right trail is for horses.) Continue down the little slickrock canyon. *[FYI. Toward the bottom, if there's water in a pond, look for little frogs. The nearby rocks have Indian marbles on them.]*

1.8 Junction of Homestead Trail and Arch Rock Trail. Stay left on the Homestead Trail. (It's really not another 7.5 miles for Homestead Trail as the sign says.) *[Side-trip. It's worth the 0.25-mile out-and–back hike on*

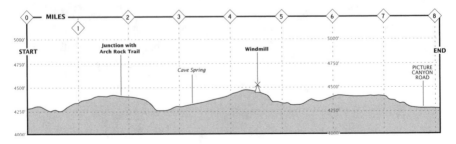

The Jicarilla Apache are known to have inhabited this area since the early 1600s and the Comanches arrived around 1700. In 1541, the Conquistador Coronado claimed this land for Spain during his search for the legendary cities of gold. By 1846, the United States declared ownership of the region. Cattle barons grazed their herds on the endless grasslands in the 1870s and 1880s. Homesteaders arrived between 1890 and 1926 in search of a new life. But making a living was tough in the arid climate. A continuous water supply was of utmost importance, and visitors today can still see the remains of rock houses close to the springs at Crack Cave and Cave Springs.

Unfamiliar with the dry climate, settlers practiced ranching and farming methods they had brought from wetter homelands. Overgrazing and plowing methods combined to damage and denude the fragile land. Several drought years in conjunction with the normally windy weather blew away the topsoil in the Dust Bowl of the 1930s. By 1938, farmers and ranchers were broke and begged the Federal Government for relief. A Federal Land Purchase program was created, and between 1938 and 1942 the government bought thousands of farms, totaling 11.3 million acres of land. The U.S. Forest Service (USFS) was assigned to manage 5.5 million of these acres, and, in 1960, four million acres were designated national grassland, where restoration efforts continue today. Presently 200 grazing allotments are managed by the USFS in Comanche National Grassland.

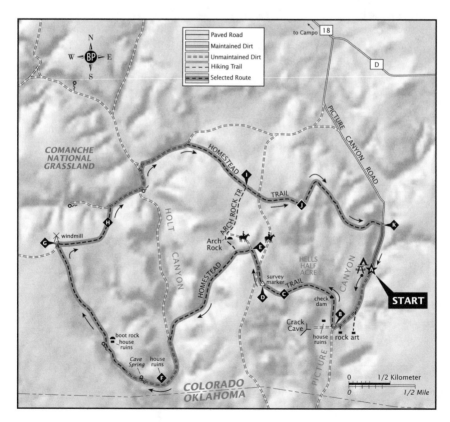

Arch Rock Trail (the right fork) to see the Arch and molar (as in tooth) rock.]

2.7 The trail intersects with a road. Turn left and walk down the road.

3.0 Rock house ruins are on the right. ✦ 37˚00'02"N 102˚46'23"W—Oklahoma border sign on the left.

3.3 Cave Spring is on your right. *[**Note.** Although the water comes from a spring, the USFS suggests treating it as a safety precaution. **FYI.** Look inside the cave for names carved in the rock and a red pictograph.]* Continue walking down the road, which turns into a singletrack soon after Cave Spring. The trail heads through a wonderful cottonwood grove then across a lush grassy area.

3.7 Arrive at a rock formation that looks like a boot. Look for the wooden post to the right of the boot. *[**FYI.** A few rocks outline an old homestead. As you climb up out of the little canyon you've been in, you'll see the top of a windmill. The trail heads there.]*

4.5 Arrive at the windmill. ✦ 37˚00'56"N 102˚47'14"W—The trail turns right here, but it's not obvious and some of the markers have fallen. Walk along some cattle paths and keep looking for posts.

5.0 There's a post leading to the canyon edge and a trail down into the next canyon. ✦ 37˚01'04"N 102˚46'48"W—Walk a little right, fol-

---

The Antiquities Act of 1906 and the Archaeological Resources Act of 1979 protect rock art and homestead ruins. Please respect the rock art by not touching it. Others arriving after you want to see original, not scarred, rock art. Touching rock art with hands, chalk, or even paper can hasten deterioration, plus it can interfere with new archaeological dating techniques.

---

low the water line down the slickrock, and then turn a little left. You'll see some cairns. Follow them down to the canyon bottom where a post along the road will be obvious.

5.1 Arrive at a dirt road and turn right, walking on the road.

5.3 The road forks. Take the left fork.

5.5 The road forks. Take the right fork.

5.9 Come to a junction with the road and Homestead Trail. Follow the trail right, up a little canyon of sorts and past some interesting rock formations. Continue following wooden posts. As you reach the high area, head a little more to the right.

6.5 Reach the junction of Arch Rock and Homestead trails. ✦ 37˚01'17"N 102˚45'40"W—Go straight (southeast); do NOT turn right. Arch and Homestead become the same trail from here back to the trailhead.

6.6 Cross a road. Keep heading southeast and look for wooden posts. The trail heads into the head of a little canyon.

6.9 Turn left up an open canyon, following the posts. ✦ 37˚01'09"N 102˚45'13"W—Once out of the canyon, walk along the high area for a while, heading generally southeast.

7.5 At this post, the trail starts heading downhill to the Picture Canyon Road. Follow the trail down a little slickrock area.

7.8 Reach the Picture Canyon Road. ✦ 37˚01'01"N 102˚44'35"W—Turn right, and walk down the dirt road.

8.1 Arrive back at the trailhead.

The prairies also attract diverse wildlife, including approximately 275 species of birds, 40 reptiles, nine amphibians, 11 fish, and 60 different mammals, including bear, mountain lion, bobcats, coyote, deer, and antelope. Watch out for rattlesnakes in the grass, rock crevices, and ruins.

This hike is often an exercise in *Where's the next trail marker?* If you follow these directions carefully and use binoculars and maybe a compass, you should be fine. Trail markers consist of juniper logs and carsonite posts (like highway reflector posts, but brown). Occasionally a marker will have fallen over, so don't panic. Four spurs are included in the hike description: the first two go to rock art panels on the canyon wall, the third to ruins and rock art by Crack Cave, and the fourth to a rock arch and rock molar.

Hike Information

🕐 Trail Contact:
Comanche National Grassland, Carrizo Unit, Springfield, CO (719) 523–6591 or *www.fs.fed.us/r2/psicc/coma/picture. htm* or *www.fs.fed.us/grasslands*

🕐 Schedule:
Open year round. Call for road and trail conditions after big snowstorms.

💲 Fees/Permits:
No fees or permits required

❓ Local Information:
Springfield Chamber of Commerce, Springfield, CO (719) 523–4061

💡 Local Events/Attractions:
Spring Equinox Festival (the first day of spring) and Fall Equinox Festival (the first day of fall), Springfield, CO (719) 523–4061 • **Kirkwell Cattle Company,** Springfield, CO (719) 324–9292 or (719) 523–4422 – *wagon train and horseback trips* • **Lesser Prairie Chicken Lek Viewing Area,** Comanche National Grassland, Carrizo Ranger District, Springfield, CO (719) 523–6591 or *www.fs.fed.us/r2/psicc* or *www. fs.fed.us/grasslands* • **Baca Little Theater,** Springfield, CO (719) 523–4061

🍴 Restaurants:
Longhorn Steakhouse, Springfield, CO (719) 523–6554 • **Main Café,** Springfield, CO (719) 523–9926 • **Bar 4 Corral,** Springfield, CO (719) 523–4065

🚶 Hike Tours:
(See the Spring and Fall Equinox festivals above.)

📖 Other Resources:
Colorado Scenic Drives, by Stewart M. Green, Helena: Falcon Press • *Petroglyphs of Southeast Colorado and the Oklahoma Panhandle,* by Bill McGlone, Ted Barker, and Phil Leonard, Salt Lake City: Publishers Press

🎒 Local Outdoor Retailers:
Gambles, Springfield, CO (719) 523–6229 – *more hunting oriented*

🅝 Maps:
USGS maps: Campo SW, CO; Tubs Springs, CO-OK

Picket Wire Canyonlands

Hike Specs

Start: From Withers Canyon trailhead
Length: 10.8-mile out-and-back
Approximate Hiking Time: 5.5–7 hours
Difficulty Rating: More Difficult due to distance
Elevations: 4,630–4,340 feet
Elevation Gain: 290 feet
Seasons: Spring and fall are best
Terrain: Dirt road, mainly doubletrack, sometimes rocky, with one steep section
Land Status: National grassland
Nearest Town: La Junta, CO
Other Trail Users: Equestrians, mountain bikers, and hunters (in season), 4WDs during tours
Canine Compatibility: Dogs permitted (must be under control)

Getting There

From La Junta: Drive south on CO 109 about 13 miles to CR 802 (David Canyon Road), at sign to Vogel and Picket Wire. Turn right onto CR 802 and drive about eight miles to CR 25 with sign to Picket Wire Canyonlands. Turn left and continue for about 6 miles to FS 500A. Turn left into the area by corrals and bulletin board. FS 500A is to the left of the bulletin board and heads southeast. Don't take the road next to the corral. Drive 3.3 miles to an open area amidst a bunch of junipers and park. Although there is supposed to be an outhouse, one may not be available. FS 500A is not maintained. In good weather, high clearance 2WD vehicles should be able to make it. If the roads are wet, 4WD vehicles will have a difficult time. You can park by the corral and hike from there, adding 6.6 miles to your overall journey. There is no camping in Picket Wire Canyonlands. A dusk to dawn closure is in effect. No facilities are available at either trailhead. Bring water. ***DeLorme: Colorado Atlas & Gazetteer:*** Page 100 B3

Although people often visualize eastern Colorado as endless and uninteresting plains, the southeastern part of the state is punctuated by canyons and juniper forests. Established in 1960, Comanche National Grassland is one of the exclamation points within the text of this land. The U.S. Forest Service manages some 435,000 acres here in Comanche National Grassland, and has since the U.S. government gave them the charge of rehabilitating the area in 1954, following a government bail-out of Dust Bowl victims whose property had been rendered virtually worthless from poor farming techniques and overgrazing. Thanks to revegetation efforts and the protection of natural grasses—still ongoing—the grassland today serves as both a wildlife habitat and a playground for human recreation. Conservation and control methods have also allowed for the reintroduction of livestock grazing.

Humans have lived in the Purgatoire Valley for perhaps as long as 10,000 years. Experts place rock art in the canyonlands between 375 to 4,500 years old. Spanish explorers first came to the area in the 1500s when the Purgatoire Valley was verdant

Remains of the Dolores mission.

and full of wildlife. Legend has it that a group of early Spanish military explorers met their death in the Purgatoire Valley, either due to exposure or conflict with the Native Americans. Either way, the men were said to have died before having their last rites administered, thus the river that courses through the canyon was named *El Rio de las Animas Perdidas en Purgatorio* (the River of Lost Souls in Purgatory). French trappers who later wandered into the canyon during the 18th Century shortened the name to Purgatoire. Settlers struggled with the French pronunciation, and the river became known as Picket Wire. (By the way, Purgatoire is pronounced *purgatory* in these parts.)

Jicarilla Apaches hunted and farmed the area for about a century, between 1620 and 1720, after which the Comanches took over control. French traders and trappers arrived prior to 1800 and hunted the plentiful beaver down to very low levels. Without a healthy beaver population to build and maintain dams, the pools and marshes of Purgatoire River disappeared into the scene you see today—a small river meandering along a broad valley between rimrock walls.

Leave the parking area and descend to a pipe gate and trail register. Please close any gates behind you. From here, the trail drops steeply through the rimrock layer of Withers Canyon, losing 270 feet in the next quarter mile. Right after the trail joins another doubletrack road in Purgatoire Canyon, ruins of an old homestead appear on the right. The trail goes up and over a few side ridges bringing you close to the cliffs. Farther upstream, remains of adobe walls rise from the ground just past the "River Water" sign. (Remember to treat any river water before drinking it.) Just a little farther are the remains of the Dolores Mission with its small cemetery. In 1871, Damacio Lopez led 12 families here, where they remained for two generations. The little head-

MilesDirections

0.0 START at parking area. ☆ 37°39'34"N 103°34'03"W

0.1 Arrive at a pipe gate and trail register.

0.9 Reach the intersection with non-motorized dirt road (doubletrack) in Purgatoire Canyon, and turn right. ◆ 37°39'44"N 103°33'42"W

1.0 Reach the remains of an old homestead.

3.4 Reach the remains of old adobe buildings. ◆ 37°38'28"N 103°34'45"W

3.8 Reach the Dolores Mission ruins and cemetery. ◆ 37°38'17"N 103°35'03"W

5.1 The road forks. Take left road branch to reach the portable toilet and the trail to the dinosaur tracksite. Turn left.

5.4 Stop and read the interpretive signs before looking for tracks along the riverbank (both sides). ◆ 37°37'03"N 103°35'47"W—Return the way you came.

10.8 Arrive back at the trailhead.

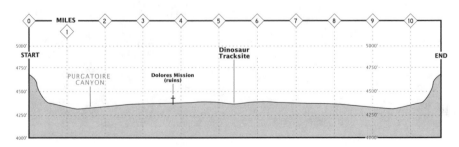

stones are intricately carved with a variety of symbols (like hearts) and inscribed with dates between 1896 and 1900. They are fragile and several are broken, so avoid touching them. A vehicle turnaround for guided tours is located here. A smoother dirt road takes you to the dinosaur tracksite another 1.6 miles upstream.

Envision yourself here 150 million years ago. Imagine a large lake of about six miles in diameter and a semiarid region. Algae, snails, minute crustaceans, fish, and horsetail plants live in and along the lake. Watch as a group of brontosaurs walk along the shore, side by side. Come another time as brontosaurs and two-legged dinosaurs use the area heavily, trampling anything underfoot. Visit yet another time to see three-toed carnivorous dinosaurs, perhaps an allosaurus, walk near the lake. Today, interpretive signs explain the fossil footprints.

By the river, three-toed footprints jump out at you. Check your foot size with theirs. Depending on the river flows, tracks can sometimes be filled with mud. The brontosaur tracks lie on the south side of the river. They extend for a quarter mile and contain about 100 different trackways with 1,300 visible footprints. Dinosaur science has not progressed enough to verify which dinosaurs created the tracks, however current speculation includes members of the brontosaur order (large terrestrial plant eaters) such as brachiosaurid, camarasaurid, and diplodocid families and the theropod order (terrestrial carnivores) such as allosaurus. Take care while here—help preserve the tracks for future generations. If you wander off trail, remember the U.S. Army's Pinyon Canyon Maneuver Site is just north of Picket Wire Canyonlands and is off-limits, besides being dangerous.

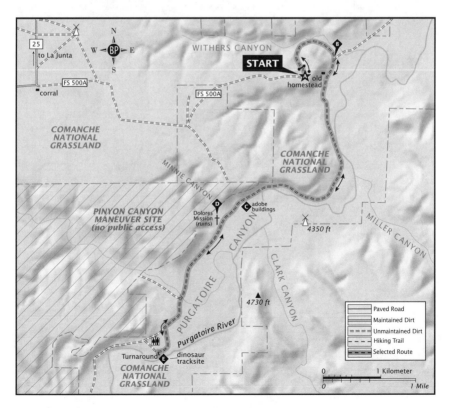

Picket Wire Canyonlands.

Hike Information

● Trail Contact:

Comanche National Grassland, La Junta, CO (719) 384–2181 or *www. fs.fed.us/grasslands*

● Schedule:

Open year round, dawn to dusk

● Fees/Permits:

No fees or permits required. Note dusk to dawn closure is in effect for Picket Wire Canyonlands.

● Local Information:

La Junta Chamber of Commerce, La Junta, CO (719) 384–7411 or *www.lajuntacochamber.com* • **Unofficial Comanche National Grasslands,** La Junta, CO *www.vipgrafx.com/misc/cng.htm*

● Local Events/Attractions:

Koshare Indian Museum, La Junta, CO 1–800–693–5482 or (719) 384–4411 or *www.koshare.org* • **Bent's Old Fort National Historic Site,** La Junta, CO (719) 383–5010 or *www.nps.gov/beol* • **Otero County Museum,** La Junta, CO (719) 384–7406 or (719) 384–7527

● Accommodations:

Vogel Canyon Picnic Ground, Commanche National Grassland, La Junta, CO (719) 384–2181 – *three picnic sites* • **KOA,** La Junta, CO (719) 384–9580 or 1–800–562–9501

● Restaurants:

Felisa's Mexican Food (good food), La Junta, CO (719) 384–4814 • **El Camino Inn,** La Junta, CO (719) 384–2871 • **Hogs Breath Saloon,** La Junta, CO (719) 384–5089

● Hike Tours:

Comanche National Grassland, La Junta, CO (719) 384–2181 – *Actually 4WD tour to Dinosaur Tracks from opposite direction. Saturdays in May, June, September, and October.*

● Organizations:

Rocky Mountain Nature Association, Comanche National Grassland, La Junta, CO (719) 384–2181

● Other Resources:

Dinosaur Lake: The Story of the Purgatoire Valley Dinosaur Tracksite Area, by Martin G. Lockley, Barbara J. Fillmore, and Lori Marquardt, Colorado Geological Survey

● Local Outdoor Retailers:

Sports World, La Junta, CO 1–800–285–0441 or (719) 384–5546

● Maps:

USGS maps: Riley Canyon, CO; Beaty Canyon, CO

Arkansas Point Trail System

Hike Specs

Start: From trailhead near Arkansas Point campground
Length: 2.1-mile double loop, optional exploration of bluff ridge
Approximate Hiking Time: 1–2 hours
Difficulty Rating: Moderate due to steep sections on Arkansas Point portion
Elevations: 4,923–5,148 feet
Elevation Gain: 225 feet
Seasons: Year round, except after big snowstorms
Trail Type: Dirt trail with some log steps, sometimes steep
Land Status: State park
Nearest Town: Pueblo, CO
Other Trail Users: Equestrians and mountain bikers
Canine Compatibility: Leashed dogs permitted. Bring plenty of water.

Getting There

From Pueblo: Drive four miles west on U.S. 50, from the junction of I-25. Turn left (south) on Pueblo Boulevard and drive four miles to Thatcher Avenue (CO 96). Turn right (west) on CO 96 and drive six miles to the park. Turn right onto the main park road. In 0.6 miles, take the left fork. Drive past the visitor center and past the entrance station for a total of 0.4 miles. Turn left onto the road to Arkansas Point Campground. The trailhead is on the right 0.1 miles up this road. Remember to pay the daily fee at the entrance station or self-serve kiosk. Water and restrooms are available at the visitors center. ***DeLorme:*** ***Colorado Atlas & Gazetteer:*** Page 73 B4

T he confluence of Fountain Creek and the Arkansas River near Pueblo has been a favorite gathering place for hundreds of years. The Plains and Ute tribes considered this neutral territory between their hunting grounds. In 1806, Lt. Zebulon Pike, commissioned by the U.S. government to explore the southwestern portion of the newly acquired Louisiana Territory, camped in the area, near present-day Pueblo, in view of the peak that would cement his place in history. (Incidentally, Pike attempted to climb the mountain from this camp, but, after encountering countless obstacles, he soon deduced that no human ever could. Today you can drive up Pikes Peak in less than three hours—or 10 minutes if you hitch a ride with a driver during the famous Pikes Peak Hill Climb.)

By 1821, fur traders started settling the area. In the fall of 1842, trader Jim Beckwourth, taking advantage of the "neutral territory" situation, constructed an adobe fortress in what he would call the town of Pueblo (meaning "town"). The settlement quickly became a major trading post, but as the settlers began moving into traditional tribal hunting grounds, and game became scarce, the Utes responded with attacks, to obtain food and horses. On Christmas Day, 1854, a band of Utes swept in, killed Pueblo's 15 male residents, and carried away a woman and two children. After the attack, the fort was abandoned. It wasn't until 1859, when the Gold Rush began in the Rockies, that Pueblo once again became a center of trade and travel.

General William Palmer brought the railroad to Pueblo in 1872 and founded the Colorado Coal & Iron Company in 1880. Coal came to Pueblo from Trinidad area mines. By 1881, Pueblo was producing the first steel west of the Mississippi. A year later, the name was changed to Colorado Fuel & Iron Company (CF&I). The interpretive sign on the Conduit Trail tells more about the company. Steel was used to make railroad rails and mining machinery. Pueblo became the smelting capital of the United States, if not the world. With four smelting plants, Pueblo was able to process more than 3,000 tons of ore per day. In 1902, Colorado's 20 smelters and reduction plants produced $48 million in gold, silver, copper, lead, and zinc. Pueblo's share of

Ridge above the Conduit Trail.

the total output was 56 percent. When the U.S. steel industry collapsed in the 1980s, so did CF&I and many jobs in Pueblo. CF&I employment decreased about 66 percent, from approximately 6,000 to 2,000 employees.

The story of Lake Pueblo is typical in Colorado. As host to the headwaters of several rivers, Colorado often finds itself with either too little or too much water. While the Eastern Plains often can't draw enough rain or snow to support agriculture or population centers, towns and cities along the Front Range can suffer millions of dollars in flood damage after intense rains in the mountains. Lake Pueblo falls in the latter

MilesDirections

0.0 START at trailhead sign for Arkansas Point Trail System near campground. ✭ 38˚15'05"N 104˚44'08"W

0.2 Reach a bench and trail junction. ⓑ 38˚14'59"N 104˚44'02"W—Turn right onto trail along what was the CF&I conduit. *[FYI. Watch for fossilized worm tunnels in rocks to the left.]*

0.4 Reach an interpretive sign and good viewpoint. ◈ 38˚14'56"N 104˚44'13"W

0.5 *[FYI. Between sign and road, watch for interesting rock features.]* At road, turn right and head toward reservoir.

0.55 Take trail to the right that goes between two rock lumps back to the trailhead. ◈ 38˚14'57"N 104˚44'17"W

0.8 Just before the trailhead, turn right to do Arkansas Point Loop. Repeat the first part of the previous loop. Hike back up to the bench.

1.0 Reach a bench and trail junction. Turn left onto trail, stay right and cross bridge over old conduit.

1.1 Reach a trail junction. Take right fork and head up hill. ◈ 38˚14'58"N 104˚43'58"

1.3 Reach the top of bluff and turn right to the

interpretive sign. ◈ 38˚14'55"N 104˚43'58"W *[Side-trip. 0.6-mile round trip along bluff to west (not included in trip mileage).]* Head east to second interpretive sign.

1.4 Reach the second interpretive sign. After reading the sign, head east and take the right fork to the post over the survey marker that marks Arkansas Point.

1.5 Reach the survey marker for Arkansas Point (5,148 feet). ◈ 38˚14'51"N 104˚43'43"W Return back to fork in the trail and turn right to head downhill on the trail.

1.6 Descend down the "crack" in the bluff via big steps.

1.8 Finish the loop. At the trail intersection, go straight and continue back on trail you came on.

1.9 Reach the trail intersection by the bench. Turn right down the trail and return to the trailhead.

2.1 Arrive back at the trailhead.

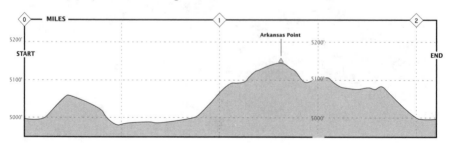

camp, created in 1921 by a three-day deluge that fell in the mountains and sent Fountain Creek and the Arkansas River on a rampage. The torrent carried away 600 houses and caused $19 million in damage (that's 1921 dollars). At least two other floods hit Pueblo in later years. In 1970, work began on the dam to create Pueblo Reservoir. As part of the Fryingpan-Arkansas Transmountain Diversion Project, this dam stores water primarily for irrigation but also provides water to municipal and industrial users along the southern Front Range. Fishermen and boaters can enjoy their sports on Lake Pueblo.

Both the Conduit and the Arkansas Point trails start near the Arkansas Point campground. Trail guides are available at the visitor center. As you hike, look for the carsonite markers (like highway reflective posts) with or

Rattlesnakes

Rattlesnakes tend to avoid humans. They will strike if surprised, threatened, or hassled. Watch where you step or put your hands on rocks or ledges. If it's really hot, snakes rest in shaded areas. In spring and fall, they try to warm up in sunny areas. If you see or hear a rattlesnake, FREEZE! That may be hard to do, but rattlesnakes strike at motion and heat. Stand still and look for the snake. Be quiet until the snake calms down, uncoils, and slithers away. If you see the snake four to five feet or more from you, back away slowly.

without numbers. The Conduit Trail is on your right just after you reach a bench. The trail follows the old CF&I conduit that carried water from the Arkansas River to the CF&I steel plant. Along the way, look on the boulders to your left for fossilized orange worm tubes. A large interpretive sign explains the conduit. As you round the end of the bluff and head downhill, look up at the different rock formations. When you come to a dirt road, turn right and head back toward the reservoir. Take a right fork in the trail to return to the trailhead.

Retrace your first steps to the intersection just past the bench and turn left for the Arkansas Point loop. Stay to the right at all trail junctions to the top of the bluff. An

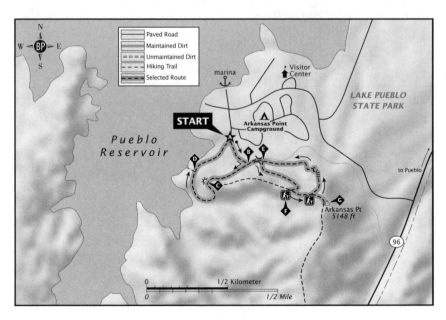

interpretive sign explains the Fryingpan-Arkansas Transmountain Diversion Project. If you continue walking on the unofficial trail heading west, there are wide-open views of the reservoir. Back at the interpretive sign, head east along the bluff to the next interpretive sign, which describes the building of the dam below you. Before descending, at the fork, take the trail to the right and walk to the post next to the survey marker indicating the high point of 5,148 feet. To return, take the trail downhill just east of the interpretive sign. The trail drops down the face of the bluff using some large steps to a trail with a guardrail. The trail continues to drop then contours back to the trailhead. Several spur trails lead to the campground to your right.

Fossilized worm tubes in rocks along Conduit Trail.

Hike Information

◐ Trail Contact:

Lake Pueblo State Park, Pueblo, CO (719) 561–9320 or *parks.state.co.us/ pueblo*

◑ Schedule:

Open year round

⑤ Fees/Permits:

Daily entrance fee or annual pass required

❓ Local Information:

Greater Pueblo Chamber of Commerce, Pueblo, CO 1–800–233–3446 or (719) 542–1704 or *www.pueblochamber.org* or *www.pueblo.org*

◑ Local Events/Attractions:

Chile & Frijole Festival, Pueblo, CO 1–800–233–3446 or (719) 542–1704 • **Prairie Princess II** (Paddle-Wheel Riverboat), Pueblo, CO (719) 547–1126 • **Pueblo Zoo,** Pueblo, CO (719) 561–9664 • **El Pueblo Museum,** Pueblo, CO (719) 583–0453 • **Pueblo City Park Carousel,** Pueblo, CO (719) 547–2082 • **Colorado State Fair,** Pueblo, CO 1–800–444–FAIR

◑ Accommodations:

Lake Pueblo State Park campgrounds, Pueblo, CO (719) 561–9320 – *400 sites* • **Pueblo KOA,** Pueblo, CO (719) 542–2273 or 1–800–562–7453

◑ Restaurants:

Nacho's Restaurant, Pueblo, CO (719) 544–0733 • **Gaetano's** (Italian), Pueblo, CO (719) 546–0949 • **La Renaissance,** Pueblo, CO (719) 543–6367 • **Latronica's,** Pueblo, CO (719) 542–1113

◑ Clubs and Organizations:

Colorado Mountain Club – El Pueblo Group, Pueblo, CO (303) 279–3080

◑ Other Resources:

Exploring Colorado State Parks, by Martin G. Kleinsorge, University Press of Colorado • *Colorado State Parks A Complete Recreation Guide,* by Philip Ferranti, The Mountaineers • *A Colorado History,* by Carl Ubbelohde, Maxine Benson, and Duane A. Smith, Pruett Publishing Co. • *Colorado Byways A Guide Through Scenic and Historic Landscapes,* by Thomas P. Huber, University Press of Colorado • *NOLS Wilderness First Aid,* by Tod Schimelpfenig and Linda Lindsey, NOLS Publications

◑ Local Outdoor Retailers:

Great Divide Ski Bike & Hike, Pueblo, CO (719) 546–2453 • **Edge Ski Paddle & Pack,** Pueblo, CO (719) 583–2021 or *www.edgeskiandpaddle.com*

Ⓝ Maps:

USGS maps: Northwest Pueblo, CO; Southwest Pueblo, CO

Rocky Mountain Arsenal National Wildlife Refuge

Hike Specs

Start: From trailheads near visitor center

Length: Loop trails from 0.8 to 2.3 miles

Approximate Hiking Time: 0.5–2 hours, varies with each hike

Difficulty Rating: Easy due to flat terrain and Americans with Disabilities Act (ADA) compliant surfaces.

Elevations: 5,200–5,300 feet

Elevation Gain: Varies with each hike

Seasons: Year round, except after big snowstorms; summer can be very hot

Terrain: Aggregate, ADA compliant, dirt road, and boardwalk

Land Status: National wildlife refuge

Nearest Town: Commerce City, CO

Other Trail Users: Hikers only

Canine Compatibility: Dogs not permitted

Getting There

From Denver: Take Exit 278 off I-70 onto Quebec Street and head north. You can also head north on Quebec Street from I-270. From I-70 and Quebec Street, travel north 3.6 miles to East 72nd Avenue and turn right (east). There's a large sign for Rocky Mountain Arsenal National Wildlife Refuge at the corner. The welcome center is immediately on your left. Turn and park here. A shuttle will take you to the visitor center. Eventually a new visitor center will be built closer to Quebec Street. Always check with the Rocky Mountain Arsenal National Wildlife Refuge for the latest information about public hours. Also ask about events—they offer various programs from eagle watches to coyote calling to bike riding. Water, restrooms, and a bookstore are located in the visitor center. **DeLorme: Colorado Atlas & Gazetteer:** Page 40 B3

The Arsenal lands were originally shortgrass prairie grazed by deer, antelope, and bison. Homesteaders arrived in the late 1800s, built houses, grew crops, dug irrigation ditches, and planted non-native trees. The bombing of Pearl Harbor in 1941 changed the fate of this 27-square-mile (17,000 acres) area. The U.S. Army bought the farmers' lands and built a chemical weapons manufacturing complex, the Rocky Mountain Arsenal. After World War II, the Army leased some facilities to private companies to manufacture pesticides. Part of the Arsenal became highly contaminated, threatening the health of nearby residents. The Arsenal was declared a Superfund site in 1987.

Amazingly, people discovered a large animal population thriving in the Arsenal's buffer zone. With the discovery of a communal roost of bald eagles, the U.S. Fish & Wildlife Service (USFWS) became involved in the area. In 1992, Congress created the Rocky Mountain Arsenal National Wildlife Refuge. Exhibits in the visitor center and interpretive signs at trailheads relate the historic and natural details.

The USFWS offers numerous environmental education classes to schoolchildren. During one class, teachers and students gathered near a prairie dog town to observe these little critters. While they watched, a young badger grabbed a prairie dog for its lunch. Nothing like seeing nature in action!

During your first visit, take a tram tour for a great overview of the refuge. Then take a hike! The following trails are, or soon will be, open on Saturdays only.

Trails Open in 2001:

Lake Mary. The Lake Mary Trail highlights wetlands. Trail guides are available at the visitor center. The loop is one mile long, starting near the visitor center. After passing a prairie re-vegetation effort, the trail circles Lake Mary. Part of the trail is a boardwalk across a section of lake, providing a more intimate look at the wetlands. Two piers take you out over the water.

USFWS educator with a red-tailed hawk.

In mid to late 1965, earth tremors occasionally jolted Denver's citizens. This was strange, as Denver had been quite stable during recorded history. A connection was made between earth tremors and waste being pumped into a deep (12,000-foot) well at the Rocky Mountain Arsenal northeast of Denver. It seems the wastewaters hit an old fault in the earth and lubricated it. Once the pumping stopped, the tremors interestingly enough ended.

Locust Loop. Start at the visitor center and head northeast to the trailhead. The loop is about 0.8 miles round trip. This trail highlights the history of the Arsenal, from the Egli farmhouse (the only one remaining) to the South Plants, one of the closed chemical manufacturing facilities. Notice the two groves of New Mexico locust along what was the driveway to the Egli's house. The Eglis only planted two trees, one on each side of the road. Locust trees, like aspens, spread by underground suckers, and the trees multiplied over the years. Cottontails and deer now benefit from their shelter.

Lake Ladora. A trail leads from the east side of Lake Mary to a road. Follow the road to the trail next to Lake Ladora. This trail is closed seasonally to protect the bald eagles that love to perch in the cottonwoods along the lake's south shore. Ducks, great blue herons, various shore birds, and oth-

Stepping stones on Wetlands Trail.

ers can be seen on the lake. Watch for cormorants with their outspread wings. This trail continues toward restrooms and interpretive signs where you can turn around or loop back via the road. Fishing is allowed in the lake by permit only. Another trail will connect the Lake Ladora Trail to the Quad Trail. A loop from Lake Mary along the shores of Lake Ladora to the restrooms and back along the road is about 1.3 miles.

Future Trails Planned to Open in Spring 2002:

Quad Trail. Starting near the south shore of Lake Ladora, the Quad Trail makes a 1.75-mile rectangle through an old homestead area. Cottonwoods line abandoned lanes while elms, fruit trees, white poplars, New Mexico locusts, and even a ponderosa pine reveal a long ago human touch. White-tail deer, a woodland species, roam freely here. Interpretive signs convey the farming history of the area.

Wetlands Trail. Presently (2001) open only for environmental education classes, the 1.5-mile Wetlands Trail wanders past three human-created wetlands and provides a good glimpse at a natural prairie. On a clear day, views of the Front Range are spec-

Hike Information

● Trail Contact:
Rocky Mountain Arsenal National Wildlife Refuge Visitor Center, Commerce City, CO (303) 289-0930 or www.pmrma.army.mil

● Schedule:
Open Saturdays only, year round, except after big snowstorms

● Fees/Permits:
No fees or permits required for hiking. Restricted hours.

● Local Information:
Aurora Chamber of Commerce, Aurora, CO (303) 344-1500 or www.aurora chamber.org • Denver Metro Convention & Visitors Bureau, Denver, CO 1-800-233-6837, (303) 892-1505 or www.denver.org

● Local Events/Attractions:
Rocky Mountain Arsenal National Wildlife Refuge, Commerce City, CO (303) 289-0232 or www.pmrma. army.mil – For activities, call or visit their website. Among the events are Eagle Fest and National Wildlife Refuge Week.

• Denver Museum of Nature & Science, Denver, CO 1-800-925-2250 or (303) 322-7009 or www.dmnh.org • Denver Zoo, Denver, CO (303) 376-4800 or www.denverzoo.org

● Restaurants:
Mountain Man Steak House & Saloon, Commerce City, CO (303) 287-9771 • La Casa del Rey, Commerce City, CO (303) 287-7480

● Clubs and Organizations:
Rocky Mountain Arsenal Wildlife Society, Commerce City, CO (303) 289-0820 or www.rmawildlifesociety.org

● Other Resources:
When Nature Heals. The Greening of Rocky Mountain Arsenal, by Shattil/Rozinski/Madson, Boulder: Roberts Reinhart, Inc., in cooperation with the U.S. Fish & Wildlife Foundation

● Local Outdoor Retailers:
There are countless in Denver and Aurora.

● Maps:
USGS map: Montbello, CO

tacular! A shuttle carries hikers to and from the trailhead. This loop includes the stepping-stones, which keep your feet dry while crossing Avocet Shallows (seasonal). Bullfrog Pond has a concrete ramp to help children and wheelchairs get in the water for sampling. Chorus Frog Marsh is viewable from the distance. Down a spur trail not far from the trailhead, an observation blind overlooks the marsh. Watch for big-eyed mule deer watching you from their hiding places in the grass.

Due to ongoing cleanup at the Rocky Mountain Arsenal, public access is well controlled for safety reasons. As cleanup progresses, more areas will open to the public, and new trails will be developed. The Arsenal will be a great source of new discovery and enjoyment for many years to come!

MilesDirections: Lakes Mary and Ladora Loops

0.0 START at the trailhead by the interpretive signs southwest of the Visitor Center.

0.1 Come to a fork and turn left to head to the lake. Come to a second fork next to some interpretive signs. Walk left to signs then continue to left and walk over the boardwalk.

0.3 Come to a fork and go to the left for the Lake Ladora Loop. Follow the trail as it switchbacks up to the road. Please respect any seasonal trail closure signs.

0.6 Trail junction with road. ⓑ 39˚49'04"N 104˚51'38"W—Turn right and walk down the road about 200 feet then turn left onto trail to Lake Ladora.

0.7 Come to a fork and go right. (The left branch goes toward the lake and ends there.) Come to another fork and turn right for the loop. (The left will connect to the Quad Trail in the future.)

0.9 Restrooms and Lake Ladora interpretive

signs. Turn right past the signs to the road, and walk back along the road to the trail to Lake Mary.

1.4 Turn left onto trail back to Lake Mary.

1.7 Turn left onto trail circling Lake Mary.

1.8 The South Amphitheater is to the right. The little birdhouses on poles along the trail are for tree swallows.

2.1 Come to a fork. ◈ 39˚49'09"N 104˚51'49"W— Turn right to continue around the lake. A viewing platform over the lake is immediately to the right. A picnic shelter with tables is to your left a little beyond.

2.15 Another viewing/fishing platform over the lake is immediately to the right.

2.2 You've completed the loop. Turn left and return the way you came to the trailhead and the visitor center.

2.3 Arrive back at the trailhead.

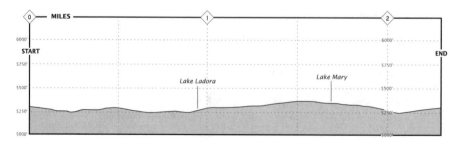

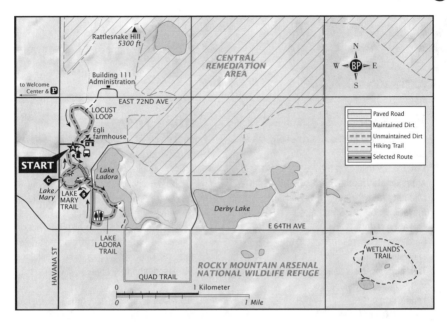

MilesDirections: Locust Loop

0.0 START at the trailhead northeast of the visitor center. ★ 39°49'18"N 104°51'46"W—The Egli farmhouse is to the right.

0.06 Cross over dry Sand Creek lateral (ditch) that used to carry water from the Highline Canal via the lakes.

0.1 Come to a fork and go right.

0.3 Come to a fork and go left to complete the loop back to the visitor center. Some good views of the Front Range.

0.7 Come to a fork and go right to go back to the visitor center.

0.8 Arrive back at the trailhead.

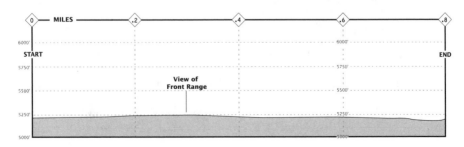

5

Revitalized Denver

Hike Specs

Start: From the northeast corner of 14th and Larimer streets

Length: 4.6-mile loop trip

Approximate Hiking Time: 1.5–4.5 hours

Difficulty rating: Easy

Elevations: 5,180–5,210 feet

Elevation Gain: 30 feet

Seasons: Year round, except after a major snowstorm

Terrain: Concrete and asphalt sidewalks, bike paths, and a few stairs

Land Status: City

Nearest Town: Denver, CO

Other Trail Users: Pedestrians, joggers, cyclists, and rollerbladers

Canine Compatibility: Leashed dogs permitted

Getting There

From Denver: This walk through the lower downtown area and Platte River Greenway near Spear Boulevard can start anywhere on the loop. The challenge is to find parking at reasonable prices, which means avoiding game days for the Broncos, Rockies, Avalanche, and Nuggets. The hike description starts at the corner of 14th and Larimer Streets. As Denver changes, some buildings in this description may change.

Public Transportation: Numerous RTD regional bus routes stop at the Market Street Station, which is at mile 0.3 of this hike. RTD light rail runs from Littleton to downtown frequently, 20 hours a day. Get off the train at the stop at 14th and California Streets. Walk north on 14th Street to Larimer Street to begin this hike. *DeLorme: Colorado Atlas & Gazetteer:* Page 40 B3

As with much of Colorado's European history, Denver's roots began with the discovery of gold near the confluence of the South Platte River and Cherry Creek. Denver was established in November 1858. Auraria had already been founded across Cherry Creek. By April 1860, Auraria was absorbed by Denver. Because of a lack of wood, settlers made bricks from area clay deposits to construct their buildings. The railroad arrived in 1870 connecting Denver to the East and later with the prosperous mountain mining districts to the west. William Henry Jackson, the photographer for the Hayden Survey, was in Denver before departing on the survey in the summer of 1873. He noted: "Larimer Street, running east and west through the heart of the city, was by far the most heavily trafficked, the widest, and had the finest shops. Beginning in old Auraria, across the creek, and extending westward, streets lettered from A to H bisected Larimer and composed the booming city's 'downtown.' Throughout its length, Larimer Street had fine wooden sidewalks with hitching posts before each house and business establishment. Gas lights illuminated the thoroughfare at night." The area around Larimer Street to Union Station is now affectionately called LoDo, for Lower Downtown.

The Sherman Silver Act of 1893 took its toll on Denver's prosperity. Building in LoDo virtually ceased. After World War II, the area further declined with the popu-

larity of the automobile. LoDo became skid row where bums roamed amid flophous-es. Luckily part of Larimer Street was designated an historic district in 1973. Entrepreneurs saw an opportunity and began to renovate and revitalize the historic buildings. Their endeavors paid off and by 2000 the area had blossomed with reno-vations and new buildings designed to draw people to the neighborhood.

This walk passes many of the renovated and newly built facilities; it also meanders along the Platte River Greenway and the Cherry Creek Bikeway. On some buildings, plaques offer a glimpse into Denver's history. The following descriptions explain plaques and buildings along this tour of revitalized Denver.

The Granite Building (1882). Southeast corner of 14th and Larimer streets. In this vicinity Denver was founded when General William H. Larimer, Jr. staked out a town and named it after James Denver, the Territorial Governor of Kansas. Walk inside to check out historical Denver photographs in the lobby.

Tabor Center (1984). Northeast corner of 16th and Larimer streets. The Tabor Center was the last of the great oil-boom projects that changed the face of downtown Denver in the early 1980s. The first two floors along the 16th Street Mall house a glass-enclosed galleria of specialty shops and restaurants. Offices, a hotel, and con-vention center fill the rest of the building,

Historical plaque at the Regional Transportation District (RTD) building. Northeast corner of 16th and Blake streets. The plaque on the west wall relates Denver's transportation history.

Coors Field.

MilesDirections

0.0 START at the northeast corner of 14th and Larimer streets. ★39˚44'51"N 104˚59'57"W— Walk northeast on Larimer Street.

0.1 Corner of 15th and Larimer Streets and the Granite Building. Visit the Granite Building on the southeast corner then continue northeast on Larimer Street.

0.2 Corner of 16th and Larimer Streets. Tabor Center and 16th Street Mall. Turn left and walk along the mall.

0.3 Regional Transportation District's (RTD) Market Street Station.

0.4 Corner of 16th and Blake Streets. Turn right and walk northeast on Blake on the right side of the street. Stop to read the historic plaques on RTD's building and the Crocker Cracker Factory building at 19th and Blake streets.

0.7 Corner of 20th and Blake Streets. ◆ 39˚45'16"N 104˚59'38"W—Cross diagonally left to the Coors Field sidewalk. Walk along the stadium, then down the stairs to the pedestrian mall.

0.9 Turn left on the little pedestrian mall with the baseball arch. Stay on the right side when the mall becomes Wynkoop Street.

1.1 Union Station. Walk inside and see the historic display. Outside again, cross Wynkoop Street to the left side and continue southwest to 16th Street.

1.2 Mercantile Building and Tattered Cover Book Store on the corner of 16th and Wynkoop Streets. Turn left onto 16th Street, then right onto Wazee Street.

1.4 Corner of 15th and Wazee Streets. Turn right onto 15th Street and head northwest staying on the right side of the street. After crossing Delgany Street, stay to the left following the pedestrian path on the right side of the street. Walk under the first two overpasses, past two murals.

1.7 At the third mural, walk up the stairs, turn left at the top, and cross 15th Street on the pedestrian bridge. Turn right and continue following 15th Street.

1.8 Just past the power substation, turn left onto the pedestrian path that goes along the South Platte River. Cross the bridge over Cherry Creek, then turn right, heading toward the South Platte. You're at Confluence Park. Turn left along the river.

1.9 Kayak viewing area. Turn right at the bridge and cross the South Platte River. ◆ 39˚45'16"N 105˚00'30"W

1.9+ REI's Denver Flagship Store complete with a Starbuck's. Turn left onto the Platte River Greenway path.

2.2 Path to Ocean Journey. You can stop and visit or continue southeast along the South Platte.

2.6 Path to Children's Museum of Denver. You can stop and visit or continue along the concrete path (not the dirt trail) past Gates Crescent Park. Follow the path as it curves left across the trolley tracks then back along the river and under the I-25 viaduct.

2.8 Turn left and walk across the pedestrian

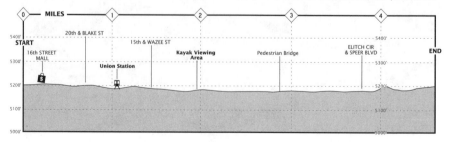

Historical plaque on the Crocker Cracker Factory building (1887). Northeast corner of 19th and Blake Streets. Take a few moments to read the plaque about the Windsor Farm Dairy Building (1918) across Blake Street and the Crocker Cracker Factory building.

Coors Field (1995). Northwest corner of 20th and Blake Streets. Coors Field is the home of the Blake Street Bombers as the Colorado Rockies baseball team is often

---

bridge over the South Platte River. ◆ 39˚44'35"N 105˚00'57"W Turn left, walk under the I-25 viaduct again, and continue onto the pedestrian path that heads northeast along the South Platte past Six Flags Elitch Gardens.

3.6 Turn right onto the pedestrian path just past Elitch's fence at the start of Centennial Park. Turn right at Little Raven (by the bus stop), then left at Elitch's water park fence.

3.7 Turn left at Elitch Circle and walk up to Speer Boulevard. Stop in Elitch's first if you'd like.

3.8 Corner of Elitch Circle and Speer Boulevard. Turn right and walk on the pedestrian path along Speer.

4.0 Corner of Chopper Circle and Speer

Boulevard. The Pepsi Center is to your right. Turn left and cross Speer Boulevard on Chopper. Across the street, turn slightly left and follow the pedestrian path that heads to a pedestrian bridge. There are two bridges here: the one you'll cross and the one next to it with the fake train. Walk across the bridge over Cherry Creek, turn left and walk downhill to the pedestrian path along Cherry Creek.

4.1 Turn left onto the pedestrian path on the northeast side of Cherry Creek.

4.5 Turn left at the Indian "rock art" or "kachina" type figures and climb the steps to Larimer Street. Turn right and walk one block.

4.6 Arrive back at the corner of 14th and Larimer Streets.

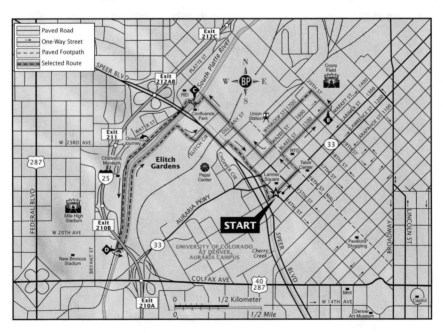

called. Principal designer Brad Shrock designed the ballpark to reflect the historic buildings in the surrounding neighborhood. The clock above the entrance is over 10 feet in diameter.

Ice House (1903). Between 18th and 19th Streets on Wynkoop Street. This historic building was recently remodeled to restaurants, shops, and residential lofts.

Union Station (1881). 17th and Wynkoop Streets. The train station once hosted over 80 arrivals and departures daily. Step inside for a look at an interesting historical display about railroad history and transportation in Denver. Notice the ornate details on the outside of the building.

C.S. Morey Mercantile Building (1896). Southeast corner of 16th and Wynkoop Streets. A plaque describes this historic building, renovated in 1994 and now home to the Tattered Cover Book Store.

REI Denver Flagship store (1901). Southeast corner of 15th and Platte Streets. Inside this powerhouse once belonging to the Denver Tramway Company, steam turbines generated electricity to drive Denver's streetcar system. The Forney Transportation Museum moved into the old powerhouse in the late 1960s. The building was sold to Recreational Equipment Inc. in 1998. The REI Denver Flagship store opened on April 28, 2000 in the remodeled building. The Forney Transportation Museum opened in its new quarters in north Denver in 2001.

Ocean Journey (1999). Water Street. Featuring the Colorado River's 500-mile journey to the Sea of Cortez and the Kampar River in Indonesia and the Pacific Ocean, Ocean Journey displays fish, birds, mammals, and other animals from these watersheds and seas.

Children's Museum (1984). The Children's Museum was founded in 1973 to "promote the value of childhood by using the arts and sciences to educate, support and nurture children." Exhibits and programming focus on children, ages infant through eight, and the adults who care for them.

Downtown Denver and the South Platte River.

Six Flags Elitch Gardens (1995). The Elitch family moved their amusement park from Lakewood, CO to its new home on the banks of the South Platte River just west of downtown Denver. The park was then acquired by Six Flags Theme Parks, Inc.

Pepsi Center (1999). Chopper Travaglini Boulevard. This 675,000 square foot, five-level arena is home to the Denver Nuggets basketball and Avalanche hockey teams as well as host to many concerts.

Hike Information

ⓢ Fees/Permits:
Parking fees

❷ Local Information:
Denver Metro Convention & Visitors Bureau, Denver, CO 1–800–233–6837 or (303) 892–1505 or *www.denver.org* • **Historic Denver,** Inc., Denver, CO (303) 534–5288 or *www.historicdenver.org*

◕ Local Events/Attractions:
Six Flags Elitch Gardens, Denver, CO (303) 595–4386 or *www.sixflags.com/ elitchgardens* • **Ocean Journey,** Denver, CO (303) 561–4450 or *www.ocean journey.org* • **Children's Museum,** Denver, CO (303) 433–7444 or *www. cmdenver.org* • **Platte Valley Trolley,** Denver, CO (303) 458–6255 • **Coors Field,** Denver, CO (303) 762–5437 or *rockies.mlb.com* • **Larimer Square,** Denver, CO (303) 685–8143 or *www. larimersquare.com* • **Pepsi Center,** Denver, CO (303) 893–1999 or *www.pepsi center.com* • **Tabor Center,** Denver, CO (303) 572–6868 • **Invesco Field**, Denver, CO

● Accommodations:
Most accommodations in Denver are quite expensive. **Hostelling International-Denver,** Denver, CO (303) 861–7777

⍾ Restaurants:
Del Mar Crab House, Denver, CO (303) 825–4747 • **Wynkoop Brewing Company,** Denver, CO 1–888–WYNKOOP – *one of the largest brewpubs in the world* • **Little Russian Café,** Denver, CO (303) 595–8600

• **Broker Restaurant,** Denver, CO (303) 292–5065 – *shrimp bowl with dinner*

↻ Other Resources:
Tattered Cover Book Store, Denver, CO (303) 436–1070 or *www.tattered cover.com*

↻ References:
Quest of the Snowy Cross, by Clarence S. Jackson and Lawrence W. Marshall, Denver: University of Denver Press • *The Lower Downtown Historic District,* by Barbara Gibson, Denver: Historic Denver, Inc. • *Denver: The Modern City,* by Michael Paglia, Rodd L. Wheaton, and Diane Wray, Denver: Historic Denver, Inc.

⛹ Clubs and Organizations:
Historic Denver, Inc., Denver, CO (303) 534–5288 or *www.historicdenver.org*

⛷ Hike Tours:
Denver Metro Convention & Visitors Bureau, Denver, CO 1–800–233–6837 or (303) 892–1505 or *www.denver.org*

⛫ Local Outdoor Retailers:
Recreational Equipment, Inc. (REI), Denver, CO (303) 756–3100 or *www.rei.com* • **Patagonia,** Denver, CO (303) 446–9500 or *www.patagonia.com* • **Grand West Outfitters,** Denver, CO (303) 825–0300

Ⓝ Maps:
USGS map: Commerce City, CO; Arvada, CO; Fort Logan, CO; Englewood, CO

Honorable Mentions

Eastern Plains

Compiled here is an index of great hikes in the Eastern Plains region that didn't make the A-list this time around but deserve recognition. Check them out and let us know what you think. You may decide that one or more of these hikes deserves higher status in future editions or, perhaps, you may have a hike of your own that merits some attention.

(A) Santa Fe Trail

You can still walk a three-mile section of the Mountain Branch of the Santa Fe Trail southwest of La Junta. Trade between the United States and Santa Fe in what was then Mexico prospered via this route in the mid 1800s. Settlers followed, spreading across Colorado and northern New Mexico. Spanish Peaks, a landmark for those long ago travelers, is visible from this section of trail. From La Junta, drive south on U.S. 350 for about 13 miles. Turn right onto CO 71 for about 0.5 mile then turn left into the Sierra Vista Overlook parking lot. Hike up to the overlook for an overview of the surrounding territory. The trail is marked by stone posts and ends three miles southwest at the Timpas Picnic Area. If you have two cars, leave one at the picnic area, which is an additional three miles down U.S. 350. Turn right at CR 16.5, cross the railroad tracks, then turn right into the parking lot. A 0.5-mile nature loop leads from the picnic area to Timpas Creek and back. The creek was a welcome relief, for it was the first water source after leaving the Arkansas River in a very dry country. You can also reach the trailheads from Trinidad, with Sierra Vista Overlook at 56 miles and the town of Timpas at 53 miles. Spring and fall are the best times to hike; summer can be really hot. Make sure to bring water with you. For more information, contact Comanche National Grassland at (719) 384–2181 or visit their website at *www.fs.fed.us/r2/psicc/coma/index.htm*. *DeLorme: Colorado Atlas & Gazetteer:* Page 100 A3

(B) Beecher Island

Beecher Island is the site of a battle between the Cheyennes and the U.S. Cavalry in 1868. A group of soldiers held out for ten days on an island in the Arikaree River while being besieged by the Cheyennes. The all-black 10th Cavalry Regiment came to their rescue. The Beecher Island Memorial Association owns the land. A 0.8-mile easy loop hike takes you from the parking lot along the Arikaree River then up Roman Nose Ridge. (Roman Nose was the Cheyenne chief.) The bluff overlooks the Arikaree River Valley and the battle site south of the river. From Wray, drive south on U.S. 385 and follow the signs for 15 miles to the Beecher Island Community Center on KK Road. Park in the lot closest to the river. For more information contact the Wray Museum at (970) 332–5063 or the Wray Chamber of Commerce at (970) 332–3484. *DeLorme: Colorado Atlas & Gazetteer:* Page 102 A4

Ⓒ North Sterling Reservoir

Shortgrass prairie and cottonwoods surround North Sterling Reservoir, originally called Point of Rocks Reservoir. Chimney Canyons' chalk cliffs lie to the north. Monuments commemorate the Battle of Summit Springs between the Cheyennes and the U.S. Cavalry while a large boulder saved from construction contains the fossilized jawbone of an archaic plains mammal. The South Shoreline Trail is new and is a seven-mile out-and-back trail along the south shore. Balanced Rock, Sunset Point Overlook and Quarry Loop trails are each 0.25-mile long leading from Chimney View and Inlet Grove Campgrounds. These trails provide a sampling of northeastern Colorado. From Main Street and North 7th Avenue (which becomes CR 39 and wiggles through a few more county road designations) in Sterling, drive north on North 7th Avenue to CR 46 and turn left to go to the park's south entrance. Total distance is about 12.5 miles. For further information, contact North Sterling State Park at (970) 522–3657 or visit their website at *www.parks.state.co.us/north_sterling*. **DeLorme: Colorado Atlas & Gazetteer:** Page 95 A4

Ⓓ Pawnee Buttes Trail

The Pawnee Buttes reach toward the sky 300 feet above the surrounding plains. The shortgrass prairie is home to many birds including great horned owls, American kestrels, eagles, hawks, killdeer, mountain plover, and rock doves, to mention a few of the 296 species that have been spotted in Pawnee National Grassland. Coyotes, foxes, deer and elk, mountain lions, pronghorns, and an assortment of mice, voles, rabbits, prairie dogs, and even bats call this special place home. Spring fills the prairie with colorful wildflowers. A 3.0-mile out-and-back hike takes you to the base of West Pawnee Butte. From Fort Collins, drive about 45 miles east on CO 14 through Briggsdale to the sign for Keota at CR 103. Turn left and drive about 4.5 miles to Keota. The road jigs and jogs a little near Keota until you end up on CR 105. Drive north on CR 105 another three miles to CR 104, turn right and drive another three miles to CR 111. Turn left and drive 4.5 miles to FS 685 which heads north from a left curve. You can also take FS 807, which loops with FS 685. You'll reach the trailhead in less than a mile. The trail is open year-round except after a big snowstorm. Summers can be extremely hot, so spring and fall are best for hiking. Bring water with you. Please obey any seasonal closures and avoid disturbing nesting birds. Hawks and falcons nest in the cliffs while others nest in the grasses. Rattlesnakes live in this area too, so keep an eye and ear open for them. For further information contact Pawnee National Grasslands at (970) 353–5004 or visit their website at *www.fs.fed.us/r2/psicc/coma/index.htm*. **DeLorme: Colorado Atlas & Gazetteer:** Page 94 A2

(E) Castlewood Canyon

Castlewood Canyon lies in the Black Forest on the high plains. Views of Pikes Peak and the Front Range are spectacular. This canyon once held a dam, which was built in 1890 to store irrigation water from Cherry Creek. Its collapse in 1933 caused two deaths and about $1 million damage. This state park is day use only, open from sunrise to sunset. Dogs must be on leash. Elevations range from 6,300 to 6,500 feet. About 6.5 miles of trails allow you to explore this interesting canyon. The Inner Canyon–Lake Gulch Loop is a moderate two-mile hike. For a slightly longer hike that has some steep sections, try the Dam–Creek Bottom–Rim Rock Loop hike at 3.9 miles. Two 15-foot-long caves can be explored from Cave Trail, a steep hike. From I-25 at Castle Rock, drive east on CO 86 for six miles to Franktown. Turn right (south) onto CO 83 (South Parker Road) for about five miles to the park entrance. For more information, contact Castlewood Canyon at (303) 688–5242 or visit their website at *www.parks.state.co.us/castlewood*. **DeLorme: Colorado Atlas & Gazetteer:** Page 51 B4

Front
RANGE

Looking east from the Front Range toward the Denver skyline.

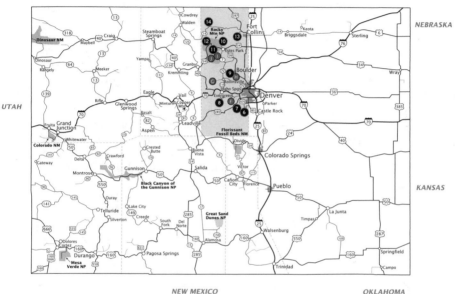

Front Range

The easternmost spine of mountains in Colorado running from the Wyoming border to Colorado Springs is known as the Front Range. Rising first in foothills, then in high mountains, they provided a formidable barrier and foreboding of what was yet to come to any explorer or pioneer trying to cross the North American Continent. Five of Colorado's 54 peaks over 14,000 feet, including Longs Peak and Mount Evans, are located in this region. Another famous Front Range peak, Pikes Peak, can be seen from three featured hikes in the Southeast Mountains section.

The Front Range foothills contain fun hiking trails and interesting geology. A rock feature known as the Flatirons protrudes like standing irons from the foothills in the Boulder area. Another great example of these tilted rocks created from the Fountain formation can be seen in Red Rocks Park and Roxborough State Park. A real gem, Roxborough has received numerous state and national designations for its tilted geology, and rich natural and human history. Dinosaur Ridge, a National Natural Landmark west of Denver, preserves dinosaur tracks from eons ago in the Dakota Hogback. Foothills canyon topography creates a perfect funnel for flash floods. Learn about Boulder's devastating floods while hiking the Boulder Creek Path.

About 75 percent of Colorado's population lives in the metropolitan areas just east of the Front Range. Within a short driving distance, recreational opportunities abound. With altitudes between 5,000 and 14,264 feet, hikers can enjoy their sport nearly year round. As summer temperatures rise beyond 90°F in the foothills, backcountry trails to mountain peaks and lakes offer a great respite.

Rocky Mountain National Park is one of the crown jewels of the national park system with its glacially sculpted peaks and high alpine lakes. Trail Ridge Road, the highest continuous automobile road in the United States, takes you to the "land above the trees," the alpine tundra. An interesting land of small microclimates, the land is very fragile. Rocky Mountain Nature Association offers great classes in all aspects of the region's natural history, including this remarkable ecosystem. The western part of Rocky Mountain National Park holds the headwaters of the Colorado River and offers wonderful wildlife viewing. Rocky, as locals call the park, contains an incredible number of hiking trails to lakes, historic sites, mountaintops, and even across the Continental Divide. Backpacking permits are required here and guarantee you a spot, often secluded from others.

Although several wilderness areas have been designated in the Front Range, the trails are not included in this guide because of their popularity and high volume of hikers. Should you hike in these wilderness areas, be careful to keep impact at an absolute minimum.

Many Front Range cities and counties have open space programs, and those parks along with state parks offer a great variety of hiking venues. Boulder started its open space program in 1967 when citizens passed a 0.4 percent sales tax to acquire and manage open space. Boulder City and Boulder County have preserved many acres between them. In spring while the mountain trails are still buried in the white stuff, trails in the Boulder Mountain Parks provide an excellent way to get in shape for summer hiking. Green Mountain, South Boulder Peak, and Bear Peak offer some steep terrain featuring trails with 1,620+ feet of elevation per mile.

Jefferson County citizens approved a sales tax in 1972 to acquire, maintain, and preserve open spaces. As of April 2001, Jefferson County operated 16 parks, a nature center, one museum, and several other open space properties.

Scenic and historic byways winding through this area include Cache La Poudre-North Park, Guanella Pass, Trail Ridge Road, Peak to Peak, and Mount Evans.

Front Range

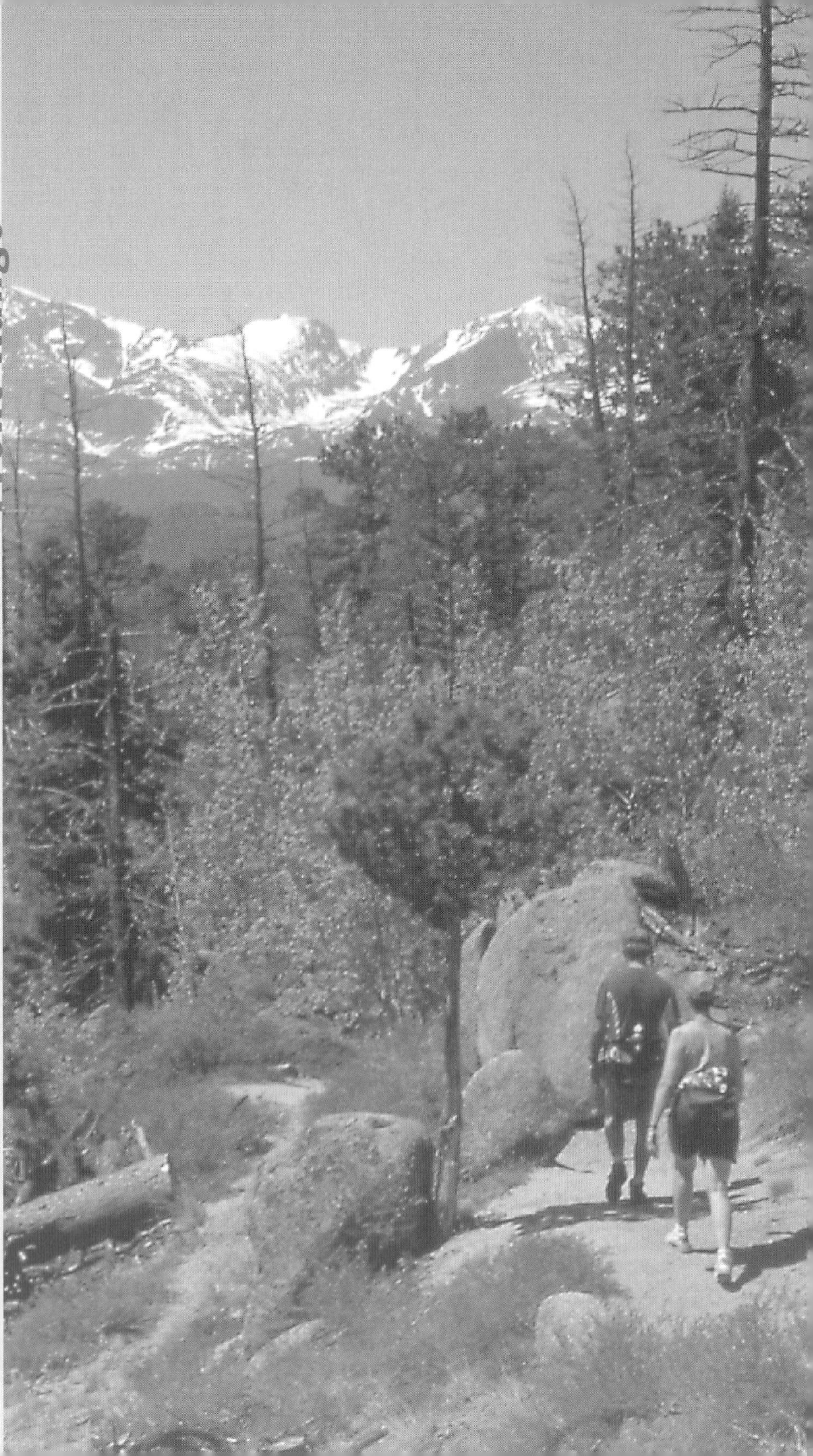

Section Overview

South Rim Loop

Roxborough State Park is a land of red rock slabs jutting up from the ground like upside down spear points. The South Rim Loop Trail circles the south end of Roxborough first winding through Gambel oak past some of the huge rocks. Crossing over grassland and past ponderosa pine forest, the trail ascends a ridge for an almost aerial view of the interesting rock formations. The geology is easy to see and examine from up here. On clear days, skyscrapers to the north form a contrasting backdrop to the natural towers of tilted rocks. *(See page 58.)*

Meyer Ranch Park Loop

Meyer Ranch Park offers numerous loop trails appropriate for hikers of all abilities. Mountain bikers, joggers, and equestrians also enjoy the park. Typical of the Front Range foothills, various grasses, lodgepole and ponderosa pines, aspens, Douglas firs, and spruces cover the hills. Picnic tables are available along Owl's Perch trail and under a shelter where Old Ski Run Trail heads uphill. This hike follows west side trails to the top of the park and back along east side trails. Near the top you can get a nice view of Mount Evans to the west. *(See page 64.)*

Mount Goliath Natural Area

The Bristlecone Pine Loop Trail and Alpine Garden near the nature center are recent additions adjacent to the Mount Goliath Natural Area. This hike explores the new trails then continues up Pesman Trail #50 through an ancient bristlecone pine forest and alpine tundra with its fantastic tiny wildflowers. (Peak bloom is mid-July.) An illustrated flower brochure is available at the nature center. To return, hike a little higher on Alpine Garden Loop #49 for great 360-degree views, then rejoin the Pesman Trail down to the nature center. Much of this hike is above treeline so plan your trip to avoid thunderstorms and lightning. *(See page 68.)*

55

Boulder Canyon/Creek Trails

This hike follows an old railroad grade through lower Boulder Canyon. The dirt path is wide and used by a variety of non-motorized visitors. Boulder Pioneer Trail interpretive signs along this section enlighten users about Boulder's colorful past. Walking along Boulder Creek below the canyon walls provides a different perception than driving. Rock climbers can be seen scaling popular routes just off the trail. The path becomes paved and exits the canyon through Eben G. Fine Park then continues along past various public buildings, Central Park, the Dushanbe Teahouse, and Old Main on the University of Colorado campus. (See page 74.)

Gem Lake Trail

At 8,830 feet, Gem Lake lives up to its name. Granitic boulders, ledges and cliffs surround this small rain fed jewel. The trail travels along south and east facing slopes wandering in and out of a couple narrow canyons between granitic outcroppings. Interesting rock formations inspire the imagination. Several sections offer great views of Estes Park, Twin Sisters, Longs Peak, and the Continental Divide in Rocky Mountain National Park. Colorful wildflowers grace the trail from mid-June to early July. This trail is a good early and late season hike in Rocky Mountain National Park. (See page 80.)

Ute Trail

The Ute Trail gains 200 feet, then loses 3,200 feet of elevation over its six-mile course. Make sure your knees are in good shape or bring hiking poles with you! The hike starts above treeline and crosses alpine tundra along Tombstone Ridge. It then drops steeply into Windy Gulch, which is filled with limber pine trees. The views are beautiful, and the changes from one ecosystem to another as you descend to Upper Beaver Meadows are fascinating. Make sure to leave the upper

trailhead before any thunderstorms or whiteouts develop. The first two miles are very exposed and high. (See page 86.)

Lulu City Trail

Follow traces of an old wagon road to the Shipler Mine and Cabins and the Lulu City site. Lodgepole pine and spruce-fir trees line this family-friendly trail. Hiking early in the morning or in the evening, you are likely to see elk, deer, moose, chipmunks, and birds (especially camp robbers). The infant Colorado River winds through the Kawuneeche Valley on its long journey to Mexico. Lulu City was a lively mining town from 1880–1884. The Grand Ditch, which still carries water from the Colorado River watershed to the Cache la Poudre River drainage to the north, is visible for much of the hike. *(See page 92.)*

Lory State Park Loop

Lory State Park is a hiker's dream with many trails designated "foot only." Situated next to Horsetooth Reservoir, trails climb into the nearby Montane foothills with ponderosa pine and Douglas fir forests. Wild turkeys hide, mule deer browse, and Abert's squirrels and cottontail rabbits frolic. Lory even has six backcountry campsites available by permit. At a lower elevation, this is a perfect place to satisfy early season hiking and camping urges. Arthur's Rock protrudes above the park providing views of the Fort Collins area. This hike makes a loop using sections of four different trails. *(See page 98.)*

Roaring Creek Trail #952

Roaring Creek Trail climbs steeply up a south-facing slope through sagebrush, juniper, Douglas fir, and huge ponderosa pine. Roaring Creek roars even when the water is low and becomes quite thunderous when full with spring runoff. Views of Poudre Canyon are great hiking up this steep slope. After the first mile, the trail levels and continues along the creek lined with willows through a lodgepole pine forest. Occasionally an interesting rock outcropping punctuates the scenery. Native greenback cutthroat trout live in the creek, and moose or elk are sometimes seen at the upper end. Enjoy a pleasant hike near Fort Collins! *(See page 104.)*

South Rim Loop

Hike Specs

Start: From Roxborough State Park Visitor Center

Length: 3.0-mile loop trail

Approximate Hiking Time: 1.5–2.5 hours

Difficulty Rating: Moderate due to length and trail condition

Elevations: 6,080–6,320 feet

Elevation Gain: 240 feet

Seasons: Year round, except after a big snowstorm (open for snowshoeing or cross country skiing)

Terrain: Dirt trail, closed dirt roads, paved walk, and parking lot

Land Status: State park

Nearest Town: Littleton, CO

Other Trail Users: Hikers only

Canine Compatibility: Dogs not permitted in park

Getting There

From Littleton: Head south on Santa Fe Drive (U.S. 85) from CO 470 for about 4.3 miles to Titan Road (CR 7). Turn right (west) onto Titan Road. In about 3.1 miles Titan Road curves left and becomes North Rampart Range Road. After the curve, drive another 3.6 miles to Roxborough Park Road and turn left. Turn right in less than 0.1 mile and follow the road into the park. Stop at the entrance station to pay the fee, or if it is unattended, stop at the self-serve station. The visitor center parking lots are about 2.1 miles from the last turn. Water and restrooms are available at the visitor center. *DeLorme: Colorado Atlas & Gazetteer:* Page 50 A2

Roxborough State Park has received many designations over and above state park: Colorado Natural Area, National Historic District, National Natural Landmark, and National Archaeological District. Once you arrive, you will understand why so many titles have been bestowed upon this area. The tilted red slabs of sandstone immediately catch your eye, but look around and you will discover other geologic formations that have developed over 500 million years. The area also exemplifies the transition zone between prairie and mountains. Around and between the towering rocks, many natural microcosms provide a home for very diverse vegetation such as yucca and Gambel oak, ponderosa pine, aspen, wild roses, and marshes. With a variety of food available, mule deer, foxes, rock squirrels, coyotes, and black bears populate the area, with an occasional visit from a mountain lion. Raptors soar above the ridges.

Colorado Natural Areas preserve special sites that meet at least one of four criteria of statewide significance: native plant communities, geologic formations or processes, paleontological localities, and habitat for rare plants or animals. Roxborough Park's different designations require conservation of this special land for present and future generations. Emphasis is placed on protecting the total park resource. For example, assuring grasses grow undisturbed by humans means the local

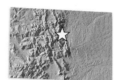

mice and other little critters have enough to eat. These small mammals are an important food source for the area's many raptors, including golden eagles.

Everyone can help preserve the uniqueness of Roxborough by staying on the trails, not feeding or disturbing wildlife, and leaving what you find. With so many visitors, hiking off trail can lead to vegetation damage and destruction. Collecting samples of vegetation and rocks only robs others of the chance to see nature at its best. Picking flowers or fruits deprives wildlife of needed nutrients. One autumn day, a woman visiting the park loudly challenged the various regulations. People later observed her

View of Roxborough State Park from South Rim Trail.

leaving with some bright red branches, presumably for home decoration. Imagine her surprise upon discovering she had an armful of poison ivy!

The George O'Malley Visitor Center contains excellent exhibits and displays. A new geology exhibit was installed at the end of 2000. Various naturalist-guided activities are available year round. Numerous events help children explore and learn about the natural world close to a major metropolitan area. The park provides many opportunities for volunteers to become naturalists, guide tours, and maintain trails. Check with the visitor center or Roxborough's website for events and volunteer opportunities.

To truly experience this unique area, visit Roxborough at various times of year. Towering rocks wet from melting snow contrast sharply against a brilliant blue Colorado sky and snow-draped hills and trees. Spring brings fragrant blossoms and colorful flowers with changing variety throughout summer. Gambel oaks turn blazing red in fall while aspens don regal gold. Lucky visitors might catch a glimpse of a new fawn or fledgling spreading its wings. No matter the season, something is always new for the observant hiker!

A word about names: when Colorado State Parks became a separate entity under the Division of Natural Resources, George O'Malley was named its first director. Henry Persse, owner of much of the land that is now the park, suggested renaming

MilesDirections·

0.0 START at the Visitor Center west patio and walk northwest to the trailhead for Willow Creek Loop, South Rim Loop, and Carpenter Peak trails. ★ 39°25'46"N 105°04'08"W

0.5 Reach a junction with Willow Creek Loop. Stay to the right on South Rim Loop.

0.6 Reach a junction with Carpenter Peak Trail and stay to the left on South Rim Loop. ◆ 39°25'27"N 105°03'55"W—*[**Side-trip.** The Carpenter Peak Trail leads 2.9 miles to 7,800-foot Carpenter Peak, the highest point in the park. The trail is steep in spots and gains about 1,000 feet, but the summit rewards the willing with a spectacular panoramic view.]* You'll soon cross Willow Creek.

1.7 You've arrived at the top of the ridge with an interesting perspective of the standing rocks and points north, south and east. ◆ 39°25'17"N 105°03'36"W

2.4 Junction with Willow Creek Loop. Continue straight down Willow Creek Loop.

2.6 Cross the entrance road to the trail on the north side to return to the visitor center. ◆ 39°25'45"N 105°03'50"W—You'll end up walking through parking lots.

3.0 Arrive back at the visitor center.

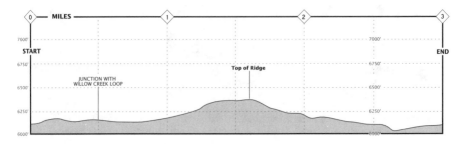

the area "Roxborough," after his family's estate in Ireland. Originally called Washington Park (see if you can find the rock that looks like George Washington), confusion with Denver's Washington Park necessitated the name change.

A Willow Creek Loop Trail Guide will enhance your hike. While walking you can learn about geology and plants and animals living in the grasslands and Gambel oak. At the large fountain formation slabs take in the "feel small" perception. Poison ivy and rattlesnakes live here, so be careful not to tangle with either. The trail climbs gently past ponderosa pines, eventually gaining a ridge (rim) with a unique perspective of the park's standing rock formations. On a clear day, the view includes the outlying plains to the east and tall buildings in the south metro area. Dropping down from the ridge, switchback to a junction with the Willow Creek Loop Trail, and stay to the right. The trail crosses a bridge over Willow Creek. Return to the visitor center via a trail north of the entrance road. Enjoy the special features of Roxborough State Park and return to watch the seasons change!

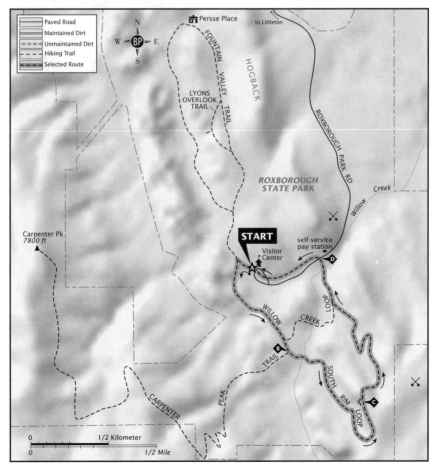

Tilted rocks along Willow Creek Trail.

Hike Information

◐ Trail Contact:
Roxborough State Park, Littleton, CO (303) 973–3959 or *parks.state.co.us/ roxborough*

◐ Schedule:
Open year round. Roxborough is a day-use only park. The park is open from 8:00 A.M. to 5:00 P.M. daily, until 8:00 P.M. in the summer. Call or check the website for exact hours as they can change monthly. The Visitor Center hours also change with the season. Park gates are locked at closing!

⑤ Fees/Permits:
Entrance fee or annual pass required.

❷ Local Information:
South Metro Denver Chamber of Commerce, Littleton, CO (303) 795–0142 or *www.bestchamber.com*

❾ Local Events/Attractions:
Chatfield State Park, Littleton, CO (303) 791–7275 or www.*parks.state.co.us/ chatfield* • **Waterton Canyon** (Colorado Trail northeast trailhead), Pike National Forest, South Platte Ranger District, Morrison, CO (303) 275–5610 or *www.fs.fed.us/r2/psicc*

⊟ Accommodations:
There are many accommodations in the south metro area. **Chatfield State Park campgrounds,** Littleton, CO (303) 791–7275 or *parks.state.co.us/chat field*

⑩ Restaurants:
There are many restaurants in the south metro area.

⑱ Clubs and Organizations:
Friends of Roxborough, Littleton, CO (303) 973–3959 • **Colorado Mountain Club,** Golden, CO (303) 279–3080 or 1–800–633–4417 (Colorado only) or *www.cmc.org* • **Colorado Trail Foundation,** Golden, CO (303) 384–3729, ext. 113 or *www.colorado trail.org*

❽ Hike Tours:
Roxborough State Park, Littleton, CO (303) 973–3959 or *parks.state.co.us/ roxborough*

⏎ Local Outdoor Retailers:
Recreational Equipment, Inc. (REI), Englewood, CO (303) 858–1726 or *www.rei.com* • **EMS,** Littleton, CO (303) 790–0760 or *www.ems.com*

◉ Maps:
USGS maps: Kassler, CO • **Trails Illustrated® map:** #135 – Deckers/ Rampart Range

Meyer Ranch Park Loop

Hike Specs

Start: From Meyer Ranch Park trailhead

Length: 4.5-mile loop trail

Approximate Hiking Time: 2–3 hours

Difficulty Rating: Moderate due to distance and elevation gain

Elevations: 7,880–8,700 feet

Elevation Gain: 820 feet

Seasons: Year round, except after a big snowstorm

Terrain: Dirt road and dirt trail

Land Status: Open space

Nearest Town: Conifer, CO and Aspen Park, CO

Other Trail Users: Equestrians and mountain bikers

Canine Compatibility: Leashed dogs permitted. Little to no water along the trail.

Getting There

From Englewood: Head west on U.S. 285. After crossing CO 470, continue 11.3 miles through Turkey Creek Canyon to the southwest end of South Turkey Creek Road. Exit right and turn left under the overpass onto South Turkey Creek Road. The trailhead entrance is about 0.1 miles on your right. There are no facilities at the trailhead but there is a composting toilet about 0.2 miles up the trail and a water pump a little farther. The Meyers family still live in the historic Victorian house on the north side of U.S. 285. Please respect their privacy! *DeLorme: Colorado Atlas & Gazetteer:* Page 40 D1

The historic Victorian house across the highway from Meyer Ranch Park was built about 1890. The Meyers moved here in 1950, when local residents were either ranchers, old-timers, or people who owned summer cabins. For baby boomers growing up in Denver in the 1960s, a trip to Fairplay or beyond meant driving through Turkey Creek Canyon with three interesting attractions. Tiny Town, a miniature town, came first just off U.S. Highway 285 on South Turkey Creek Canyon Road. The Victorian Meyer Ranch house, complete with an airplane in the yard, was the next landmark. And not to be forgotten was the hot dog stand in Aspen Park that really looked like a hot dog! Amazingly all three landmarks still exist in 2001.

Most of the park trails were originally game (deer and elk) trails later used and improved by the Meyers. The upper trail is called Old Ski Run Trail. Back in the early to mid 1940s, a small ski area operated here in a sheltered little bowl. Owners Hopkins and Kuster built a substantial frame shelter house complete with wood burning cookstove and warming stove. A horse-drawn sled carried people up to the ski run. A rope around a wheel powered by a Buick chassis towed people to the top of the run. Gas rationing during World War II ended the life of the little ski area since people were unable to drive up from Denver. The building is now gone and nature is slowly reclaiming the old ski run.

By the mid 1980s, developers started to lean on the Meyers to sell the land for a housing development. Not wanting to see houses and roads on the pretty mountain across the highway, Mr. Meyer investigated turning his land into open space. After three years of negotiations, the land was transferred to Jefferson County Open Space in 1987. Meyer Ranch Park now offers an escape from expanding development and our motorized world.

Meyers' private house near the park.

Hike Information

🗨 Trail Contact:

Jefferson County Open Space, Golden, CO (303) 271–5925 or *www.co.jefferson. co.us*

🕐 Schedule:

Open year round. Snowshoes may be necessary in winter.

💲 Fees/Permits:

No fees or permits required

❓ Local Information:

Conifer Chamber of Commerce, Conifer, CO (303) 838–0178 or *www.conifer chamber.com*

💡 Local Events/Attractions:

Tiny Town, northeast end of South Turkey Creek Road, near Indian Hills, CO (303) 697–6829 – *a miniature town, open May through October* • **Conifair,** Conifer, CO (303) 838–0178 or *www.coniferchamber.com*

🍴 Restaurants:

The Coney Island, Aspen Park, CO (303) 838–4210 – *hot dog stand in shape of a hot dog*

👥 Clubs and Organizations:

Jeffco Open Space Foundation, Arvada, CO (303) 403–2430

🥾 Hike Tours:

Jefferson County Open Space, Golden, CO (303) 526–0594 or *www.co.jefferson. co.us*

🎒 Local Outdoor Retailers:

Frontier Adventure & Supply Conifer, CO (303) 838–4508 – *hiking, backpacking, and rock climbing equipment*

🅝 Maps:

USGS map: Conifer, CO

The Jefferson County Open Space program began in 1972, when citizens initiated and approved a 0.5 percent county sales tax to fund planning, procuring, maintaining, and preserving open space lands. The program has expanded with voter approval. In June 1996, Jefferson County Open Space received the first Trail Town U.S.A. award from the American Hiking Society and the National Park Service. For most county residents, a trail is located within one mile of their homes. Active interpretive and volunteer programs keep local residents involved in understanding and protecting the land.

Starting at the bulletin board, the hike follows Owl Perch Trail past the vault toilet and around the west side of the picnic area. The trail intersects Lodgepole Loop near a grassy meadow. Soon you enter a forest with common juniper, ponderosa pine, and spruce. Climbing a little higher, you will find aspen and lodgepole pine. As you ascend Old Ski Run Trail, take in the wonderful views of Mount Evans and the Aspen Park area. Shadier areas shelter Douglas firs and mosses.

MilesDirections

0.0 START at the Meyer Ranch Trailhead. Stop and read the bulletin board for interesting area information. The first part of the trail is a gravel road, closed to public vehicles. ☆ 39˚32'45"N 105˚16'19"W

0.2 Arrive at the composting toilet. From here, follow the sign to the picnic tables to find the Owl's Perch Trail loop.

0.25 The trail forks here at the Owl's Perch Trail loop. Start by taking the right branch.

0.4 The trail comes to a T-intersection. Turn right onto Lodge Pole Loop Trail.

1.1 Arrive at the intersection of Lodge Pole Loop and Sunny Aspen Trail. Turn right onto Sunny Aspen Trail.

1.4 A picnic shelter is on your left and Old Ski Run heads uphill to the right. ◆ 39˚32'13"N 105˚16'46"W—Turn right here.

2.0 At the half log bench, look to the west for a view of Mount Evans.

2.2 The trail forks here. ◆ 39˚32'07"N 105˚16'26"W—Take the left branch.

2.3 A little trail goes to the left and up some boulders. Not a great view, but a nice warm sunny spot for lunch or a snack.

2.6 High point on trail. ◆ 39˚32'02"N 105˚16'20"W

2.7 End of the upper loop. Turn left and head downhill.

3.4 Arrive back at the upper picnic shelter. Turn right and head down Sunny Aspen Trail.

3.9 The upper part of Lodge Pole Loop Trail comes in from the left. Stay to the right heading downhill.

4.1 The lower part of Lodge Pole Loop Trail comes in from the left. ◆ 39˚32'31"N 105˚16'30"W—Stay to the right and head downhill.

4.2 Owl's Perch Trail comes in from the left. Continue downhill back to the composting toilet.

4.5 Arrive back at the trailhead.

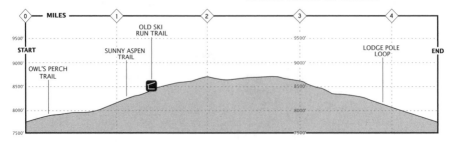

To distinguish the various coniferous trees from each other, look at the needles. The easiest one is common juniper, which is a low growing shrub. For pines, firs, and spruces, remember a little saying about their needles: "Pines are prickly and come in packets, spruces are sharp and square, firs are flat and friendly." Ponderosa pines have long needles, usually with three in a packet. The bark is reddish and fairly thick. Smell the bark – some people say it smells like vanilla. Ponderosas tend to grow in sunny, dry areas. Lodgepole pines usually have skinny trunks, used for lodge poles by Native Americans. Their needles are shorter than ponderosa needles and come in packets of two. Spruce and fir needles each grow separately, not in packets, from the branch. Spruce needles are sharp and square and roll between your fingers. Fir needles are soft and pliable and flat in shape.

An occasional trail marker provides guidance at the few confusing spots on the loop. Benches made of big half logs provide rest stops on Old Ski Run Trail. On the upper loop, you can enjoy a sun stop on some big boulders. A stone picnic shelter is located at the intersection of Sunny Aspen and Old Ski Run Trails, which makes for a nice shady break spot.

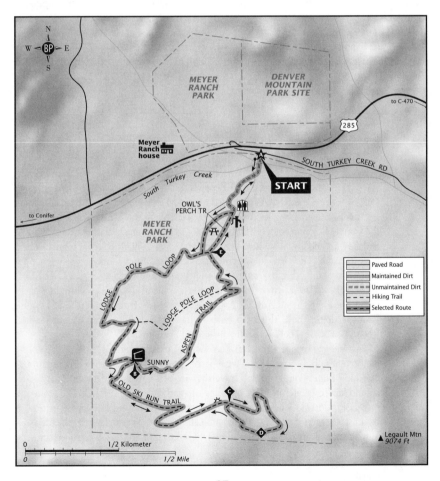

Mount Goliath Natural Area

Hike Specs

Start: From lower Mount Goliath trailhead by the nature center

Length: 3.3-mile out-and-back trail with two little half loops

Approximate Hiking Time: 1.5–3 hours

Difficulty Rating: Difficult due to altitude and rocky trail in spots

Elevations: 11,540–12,152 feet

Elevation Gain: 612 feet

Seasons: Best from late June through September; Mount Evans Road must be open

Terrain: Dirt trail with some rocks

Land Status: National forest

Nearest Town: Idaho Springs, CO

Other Trail Users: Hikers only

Canine Compatibility: Leashed dogs permitted

Getting There

From Idaho Springs: Take Exit 240 off I-70 onto CO 103. Drive up CO 103 about 13 miles to CO 5 (Mount Evans Scenic Byway) by Echo Lake Lodge. Turn right here and drive to the entrance station and pay the fee. Continue driving up the twisty road about three more miles to the lower trailhead and Mount Goliath Nature Center (construction started in 2001). Restrooms, but no water, are available at the nature center. *[Option. If you have two cars, you can leave one here and drive to the upper trailhead, another 1.8 miles up Mount Evans Road. Very small parking lot.] DeLorme: Colorado Atlas & Gazetteer: Page 39, C-6*

The Mount Evans area harbors a very large stand of bristlecone pine trees. Some of these twisted and contorted trees are over 1,600 years old! The U.S. Forest Service (USFS) set aside 160 acres of this ancient forest as a Research Natural Area (RNA) many years ago. The RNA is protected from development and most human activity enabling scientists to study a relatively untouched area. In the 1950s, the Denver Botanic Gardens (DBG) developed a program of "planned altitude units" and surveyed potential areas. The area near Mount Goliath RNA appeared to be a perfect match. The DBG approached the USFS, and they formed a partnership for the Alpine Unit. A trail was built along the flank of Goliath Peak (12,216 feet) allowing people to see the bristlecone pines and the abundant alpine tundra flowers along the route. In August 1962, the DBG and USFS dedicated the M. Walter Pesman Alpine Trail. About 0.5 miles of the trail is in the RNA. Mount Goliath RNA was also designated a Colorado Natural Area in 1980.

M. Walter Pesman arrived in Fort Collins, Colorado in 1908. A native of the Netherlands, he earned his Bachelor of Science degree in Horticulture from Colorado State College (now University) in 1910. Although his career revolved around landscape architecture, he loved the native flora of Colorado. He wrote the first Colorado wildflower identification book geared toward lay people instead of botanists. In *Meet the Natives*, he separated flowers by colors and also by the life zones in which they were usually found. The DBG's Board of Trustees decided to name the

trail at Mount Goliath in Pesman's honor in appreciation of his many years of teaching the general public about natural landscapes and native plants.

Over time the Pesman Trail deteriorated as a result of the elements and general use. In 1996, the Garden Club of Denver made a three-year commitment to repair the trail and to develop guided tours. Volunteers for Outdoor Colorado (VOC) pitched in with manual labor to fix the trail. The USFS trail crew worked on the more difficult sections. The groups created a plan for a nature center for Mount Goliath to be located in the lower parking lot. A new trail was built through the first part of the bristlecone forest—a fairly level and easy dirt trail, usable by wheelchair users and others unable to hike the Pesman Trail.

Bristlecone pine with Mount Evans Road in the background.

The DBG is also planting an alpine garden at the lower trailhead. This garden will contain alpine tundra plants found along the Pesman Trail, allowing those who cannot hike to see these amazing plants. Receipts from the Mount Evans fee demonstration project were combined with funds raised by the DBG and the Garden Club to pay for these projects. The Friends of Mount Goliath, a group of people who care deeply about the Pesman Trail and Mount Goliath RNA, will assure the trail is maintained. Construction of the new nature center is slated for 2001, with interpretive displays to be completed in winter 2001–2002.

Begin the hike by the interpretive signs on the Bristlecone Pine Loop Trail to the left, which soon joins the Pesman Trail. Continue up the Pesman Trail through the bristlecone forest. Engelmann spruce trees also live here with colorful yellow cinquefoil, bright red Indian paintbrush, fuzzy purple fringe, white chickweed, and blue Jacob's ladder. As you climb toward treeline, small bristlecone pines next to the trail provide a closer glimpse of needles and cones. Plants display tiny flowers at this elevation. Please stay on the trail because the tundra is very fragile. Plants may grow only 0.25 inches in one year and can be easily damaged. The yellow sunflowers, large by alpine standards, are called old-man-of-the-mountain. Purple sky pilot, yellow cinquefoil, white American bistort, alpine phlox, and lots of little sage line the trail. Occasionally look behind you for a view of the eastern plains south of Denver.

MilesDirections

Note. These directions are for the out-and-back hike.

0.0 START at the lower Mount Goliath trailhead by the Mount Goliath Nature Center. Start hiking on the Bristlecone Pine Loop to the left. ☆ 39˚38'34"N 105˚35'34"W

0.2 Trail intersection with Pesman Trail 50. Turn left and head uphill.

0.6 Look behind you for good views of the eastern plains of Colorado.

1.3 You're basically above treeline here.

1.5 Trail junction with Alpine Garden Loop 49. ● 39˚38'8"N 105˚36'12"W—Continue to the left to the upper trailhead.

1.7 Arrive at upper trailhead. ● 39˚37'58"N 105˚36'14"W—On your return, hike up Alpine Garden Loop 49 to the left of the Interpretive Sign.

1.9 Reach the top of the ridge and look at the great 360˚ view. ● 39˚38'7"N 105˚36'16"W

2.0 Trail junction with Pesman Trail 50. Turn left and head downhill the way you came.

3.2 Trail junction with Bristlecone Pine Loop. Continue straight down the trail.

3.3 Arrive back at the trailhead.

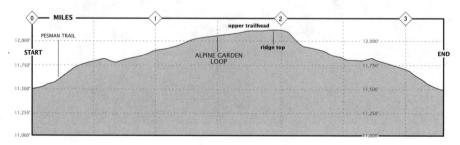

Bristlecone pine cones.

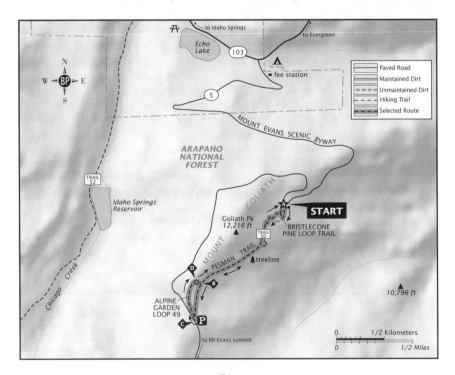

Once above treeline you are exposed to the ever-present wind. Make sure to bring extra layers, as it is mighty chilly at 12,000 feet. The trail also becomes rougher and rockier above treeline. After reaching the upper trailhead, return via the Alpine Garden Loop #49 to the left of the interpretive signs. The trail gently ascends between rock outcroppings where you get a great 360-degree view, including Mount Evans (14,264 feet). Dropping down, rejoin the Pesman Trail. Remember to take a walk around the Alpine Garden at the lower trailhead. Come often to this trail as various weather conditions change the feel of the area.

Old-man-of-the-mountain.

Bristlecone Pine

Bristlecone pine, Pinus aristata, can witness many happenings in its 1,500- to 2,000-year lifespan. Contorted by wind and often polished on one side by ice crystals and blowing dirt, it is hard to imagine how the trees survive. Bristlecone pines grow in windy areas in coarse, rocky soils. They thrive where the slope is sunny and dry, well drained, and prone to cold temperatures and frost. Bristlecones are reasonably easy to spot, sporting fairly dense needles that grow in packets of five. The needles are no longer than two inches and are usually coated with sticky resin drops. The thick clusters produce a brush-like effect, thus the name bristle. Purplish-brown female cones with prickles grow near the tip of a branch. Male cones are small, oval, and dark orange, growing in clusters near the branch tips. During tough years, bristlecones may shut off nutrients to a branch or two, killing the branch to save the rest of the tree. They also survive with much of their bark blasted off, although enough has to be left to carry nutrients. Another survival secret is slow-growth, which produces very dense wood to protect the tree from fire, insects, and disease. A living tree may consist of both live and dead parts. Even after death, the twisted, contorted ghost tree attracts photographers and artists with its interesting shapes and gray to brown to black hues. Several trails in this book pass through bristlecone pine stands. Take a moment to be quiet with these trees that have seen so many changes in their lives. Think about the survival mechanisms that allow them such longevity. Be kind and do not damage them—let them continue to live, much longer than any one human ever will.

Hike Information

◐ Trail Contact:
Arapaho National Forest, Clear Creek Ranger District, Idaho Springs, CO (303) 567–3000 or *www.fs.fed.us/r2/arnf*

◐ Schedule:
Open year round

◐ Fees/Permits:
Fee demonstration project for the Mount Evans Road (daily fee, annual pass, Golden Eagle, Golden Age, or Golden Access pass required)

❓ Local Information:
Clear Creek County Tourism Board, Idaho Springs, CO (303) 567–4660 or 1–800–882–5278 or *www.clearcreek county.com* • **Mount Evans website:** *www.mtevans.com* • **Idaho Springs Visitor Center,** Idaho Springs, CO (303) 567–4382 or 1–800–685–7785 or *www.idahospringschamber.com*

◐ Local Events/Attractions:
Mount Evans Scenic Byway, Idaho Springs, CO (303) 567–4660 • **Argo Gold Mill,** Idaho Springs, CO (303) 567–2421 or *www.historicargotours.com* • **Phoenix Gold Mine,** Idaho Springs, CO (303) 567–0422 • **Indian Hot Springs,** Idaho Springs, CO (303) 989–6666 or *www.indianspringsresort.com* • **George-town Loop Railroad,** Georgetown, CO (303) 569–2403 or 1–800–691–4386

Accommodations:
National Forest Campgrounds, Arapaho National Forest, Clear Creek Ranger District, Idaho Springs, CO (303) 567–3000

◐ Restaurants:
Echo Lake Lodge, Idaho Springs, CO (303) 567–2138 • **Beau Jo's Pizza Restaurant,** Idaho Springs, CO (303) 567–4376 • **Tommyknocker Brewery & Pub,** Idaho Springs, CO (303) 567–2688 • **The Buffalo Restaurant & Bar,** Idaho Springs, CO (303) 567–2729 • **Two Brothers Delicatessen,** Idaho Springs, CO (303) 567–2439

◐ Other Resources:
Gingerbread Bookstore, Idaho Springs, CO (303) 567–2304 • *Green Thumb* (2 issues: 1957 and 1964) from the Denver Botanic Gardens

◐ Clubs and Organizations:
Denver Botanic Gardens, Denver, CO 720–865–3500 or *www.botanic gardens.org* • **Garden Club of Denver,** Denver, CO – *call the Denver Botanic Gardens for current contact* • **Friends of Mount Goliath,** Denver, CO – *call the Denver Botanic Gardens for current con-tact*

◐ Hike Tours:
Denver Botanic Gardens, Denver, CO 720–865–3500 or *www.botanicgardens. org*

◐ Local Outdoor Retailers:
Outback Outfitters, Idaho Springs, CO (303) 567–0850 • **Morin Custom Boots,** Idaho Springs, CO (303) 567–4854

◐ Maps:
USGS map: Idaho Springs, CO • **Trails Illustrated® map:** #104 – Idaho Springs/Loveland Pass

Boulder Canyon/ Creek Trails

Hike Specs

Start: From Park-N-Ride at Four Mile Canyon and CO 119

Length: 5.3-mile point-to-point (can start via bus)

Approximate Hiking Time: 2.1–3.8 hours

Difficulty Rating: Easy due to graded dirt path and paved path

Elevations: 5,725–5,340 feet

Elevation Loss: 385 feet

Seasons: Year round, except after a big snow-storm

Terrain: Dirt path and paved path

Land Status: City and county

Nearest Town: Boulder, CO

Other Trail Users: Bikers, joggers, rock climbers, anglers, and skateboarders

Canine Compatibility: Leashed dogs permitted

Getting There

From Boulder:

With Shuttle: From Canyon and Broadway, head north on Broadway one block to Walnut, turn right, and drive 2.5 blocks. You can park in the parking building by the Boulder Transit Center (fee). This option also works if you want to shuttle via bicycle (free). To reach the trail, head south on Broadway and turn right on Canyon Boulevard. Travel west on CO 119 about three miles to the Park-N-Ride on the left just past Four Mile Canyon Road. • **Without Shuttle:** From Canyon and Broadway travel west on CO 119 about three miles to the Park-N-Ride on the left just past Four Mile Canyon Road.

Public Transportation: From the Downtown Denver RTD Market St Station take RTD B line/Boulder Express to the Boulder Transit Center and transfer RTD Regional bus route N Line to the Four Mile Canyon Park and Ride. Check the schedule before heading out as route N runs only four to six trips a day. The RTD has an excellent trip planner on their website at *www.rtd-denver.com. DeLorme: Colorado Atlas & Gazetteer:* Page 29 D7 (start point); 30 D1 (shuttle point)

Hopeful miners, led by Tom Aikins, camped near the mouth of Boulder Creek in 1858. Chief Niwot of the Southern Arapaho tribe warned them to leave. The Horse Creek Treaty of 1851 had guaranteed the great plains of Colorado as Native American land. Unable to defend his tribe's interests against the superior weapons of the white men, Niwot sensed the future demise of Arapaho holdings. The Arapaho held their final antelope hunt near Valmont, east of Boulder, in 1860. The Aikins group eventually found gold, and in 1859, the Boulder City Town Company was formed. Members divided 1,280 acres into 4,044 lots at $1,000 each versus the $1.25 per acre for homestead lands. From the very beginning the town of Boulder had a reputation as expensive!

Town founders envisioned building a university and received approval in 1861 to build one. They realized that dream 16 years later. Boulder became a supply town for the nearby mines. By late 1859, the town had 70 cabins. Pearl Street filled with mud and garbage and droppings from horses, mules, chickens, and pigs. Flies were ram-

Rock climbers on The Dome in Boulder Canyon.

MilesDirections

0.0 START at the Four Mile Canyon Park-N-Ride. ⭐ 40˚00'54"N 105˚19'29"W

0.3 Cross under CO 119.

1.0 Come to the Boulder Pioneer Trail interpretive sign.

1.3 Look ahead for rock climbers.

2.2 Reach the Eben G. Fine Park. ❻ 40˚00'47"N 105˚17'48"W—Take a side trip to the left to Settlers Park.

2.4 Return to Eben G. Fine Park. Turn left on path along creek.

2.6 Start of Boulder Creek Path at rock with "0 km" on it. Turn left and cross bridge. Watch for dirt trail to right. You can either stay on concrete path or use dirt trail.

2.9 Boulder County Justice Center on your left. ◆ 40˚00'51"N 105˚17'18"W

3.0 At the fork, stay on the lower path that goes under the 6th Street bridge.

3.1 Reach the Evert Pierson Kids' Fishing Pond.

3.2 Stay on path that goes under the 9th Street bridge.

3.3 Path passes under the Boulder Public Library walkway. Unless you want to go into the library, stay on the path that goes straight ahead.

3.5 Path passes under Broadway bridge. The path actually seems lower than the creek here.

3.6 Central Park, with train and bandshell, is on your left. [**Side-trip.** Go straight ahead to at

least look at the Boulder Dushanbe Teahouse just past Central Park.] Return to the fork near the train and turn left to continue down the Boulder Creek Path.

3.7 At the fork, stay right and go under the Arapahoe Avenue bridge along the creek.

3.8 At the fork, stay left. The path to the right will be the one you'll loop back on to this location.

3.9 Boulder High School soccer and football fields and school building. Stay right to continue on Boulder Creek Path.

4.0 At the fork, take the right path up to 17th Street. Turn right on 17th and head uphill to CU campus. At 17th Street and University Avenue, jog to the left to go onto CU campus instead of going west on University Avenue.

4.1 Turn right onto Pleasant Street and go past Macky Auditorium and Old Main, the first building on CU campus. ◆ 40˚00'33"N 105˚16'22"W

4.3 Turn right onto the bike path and head downhill to Canyon Boulevard. This bike path parallels Broadway.

4.8 Turn left at the fork with the Boulder Creek Path and go to Broadway. Turn right onto the sidewalk next to Broadway, cross Canyon Boulevard, and go to Walnut.

5.2 Turn right onto Walnut and walk two blocks to the RTD transit station at 14th and Walnut.

5.3 Arrive at RTD transit station. Pick up your vehicle or bike.

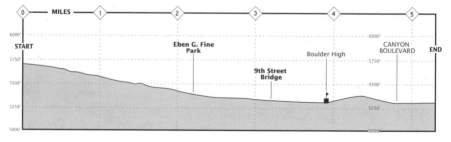

pant. Early settlers tried to farm, but grasshoppers often ruined their crops. Being a semiarid area, lack of good spring rains posed problems for crops. Irrigation canals were built to remedy the latter situation. Mud and filth still posed problems in the 1870s. Carriages often became mired in the muck. Citizens finally approved a bond issue in 1895 to build the first sewer system.

In 1894 came the big flood. The winter had been long, cold, and snowy. By the end of May, warm spring rain fell and rapidly melted the large snowpack. After 60 hours of rain in the mountains west of town, Boulder Creek, enlarged by its tributaries, inundated Boulder. The flood destroyed mountain roads, bridges, and some mines. Even the 4th Street railroad bridge disappeared, leaving behind a semicircle of tracks. Railroad Engine #155 sunk, stuck in mud and debris. The center of Boulder became a lake with a few islands. Amazingly, no one died. Miners dynamited debris caught along the creek to free the water. An interpretive sign near Arapahoe Avenue along the Boulder Creek path has pictures of the 1894 and more recent floods. In 1908, Boulder hired Frederick Law Olmstead, Jr., a Harvard-trained landscape architect, to study Boulder. His recommendations for dealing with floods included designating the lands along Boulder Creek as parklands throughout the city. He visualized walkways, benches, and playing fields. Olmstead's vision resulted in the present trail.

Starting at Four Mile Canyon Park-N-Ride, the Boulder Canyon Trail heads downhill. It crisscrosses the creek several times through the lower part of the canyon and crosses under CO Hghway 119. After the first mile, the Boulder Pioneer Trail interpretive signs start. The hike covers these backward, but each stands on its own. The history of roads, canals, and railroads are explained while viewing remains from the past. Various vegetation lines the trail: Douglas fir, ponderosa pine, juniper, willows, horsetails, and berry bushes to name a few. About 1.25 miles along, rock climbers scale the canyon walls like so many flies.

The trail turns from dirt to concrete 1.4 miles in. In another 0.5 miles, the trail treads on the remains of old Arapahoe Avenue. The street was rerouted when the Boulder Creek Path was extended up the canyon. At the west end of Eben G. Fine Park, take a side trip to the left to Settlers Park. The Boulder Pioneer Trail official trailhead is here (this hike was done in reverse), and you can walk about 100 feet uphill to see the supposed site of Aikins' camp.

Head back to Eben G. Fine Park and continue east on the Boulder Creek path. Just east of 6th Street, dirt trails parallel the paved one and make for more pleasant walking closer to the creek. Continue along to Central Park and check out the historic narrow gauge train. Walk one block straight ahead to the Boulder-Dushanbe Teahouse, a gift from Boulder's Sister City in Tajikistan. The hike leaves

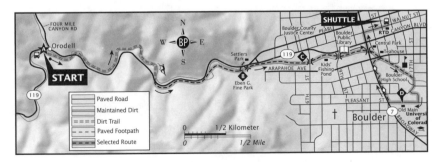

the Boulder Creek path, heading uphill at 17th Street to wander past Old Main, the first building on the University of Colorado campus, opened in 1877. Merging with a bike path, head down Broadway, cross Canyon Boulevard, turn right on Walnut Street, and walk two blocks back to the RTD Transit Station to either your waiting vehicle or bike.

Old railroad abutments now support water pipes.

Hike Information

◐ Trail Contacts:

Boulder County Open Space, Boulder, CO (303) 441–3950 or *www.co.boulder. co.us/openspace* • **City of Boulder Open Space,** Boulder, CO (303) 441–3440 or *www.ci.boulder.co.us/ openspace*

◑ Schedule:

Open year round

⑤ Fees/Permits:

Permit required for groups of 25 or more

❓ Local Information:

Boulder Chamber of Commerce, Boulder, CO (303) 442–1044 or *www.chamber.boulder.co.us/front.html* • **Boulder Historical Society,** Boulder, CO (303) 449–3464 or *bcn.boulder.co. us/arts/bmh/bmhintro.htm* • **Regional Transportation District (RTD),** Denver, CO (303) 299–6000 or 1–800–366–7433 or *www.rtd-denver.com – covers metro area including Boulder*

❓ Local Events/Attractions:

Bolder Boulder, Boulder, CO (303) 444–7223 or *www.bolderboulder.com* • **Boulder Creek Festival,** Boulder, CO (303) 449–3825 or *www.bouldercreekfestival.com* • **Boulder Mountain Parks/ Flatirons,** Boulder, CO (303) 441–3408 or *www.ci.boulder.co.us/openspace* • **Colorado Shakespeare Festival,** Boulder, CO (303) 492–0554 or *www.colorado shakes.org* • **Colorado Music Festival** (music at Chautauqua), Boulder, CO (303) 449–1397 or *www.colorado musicfest.org* • **Celestial Seasonings Tour of Tea,** Boulder, CO (303) 581–1204 or *www.celestialseason ings.com* • **Leanin' Tree Museum of Western Art,** Boulder, CO (303) 530–1442 or *www.leanintree.com*

🏠 Accommodations:

Boulder Mountain Lodge (campground), Boulder, CO (303) 444–0882

🍴 Restaurants:

Mustard's Last Stand, Boulder, CO (303) 444–5841 • **The Walnut Brewery,** Boulder, CO (303) 447–1345 • **Boulder Broker,** Boulder, CO (303) 449–1752 • **Himalayas Restaurant,** Boulder, CO (303) 442–3230 • **Ras Kassa's Ethiopian Restaurant,** Boulder, CO (303) 447–2919 • **Boulder Dushanbe Teahouse,** Boulder, CO (303) 442–4993

ⓛ Other Resources:

For information about the train in Central Park: *www.narrowgauge.net/bcrhs*

ⓛ References:

A Look at Boulder From Settlement to City, by Phyllis Smith, Boulder: Pruett Publishing Co.

🏢 Clubs and Organizations:

Colorado Mountain Club – Boulder Group, Boulder, CO (303) 554–7688 or *bcn.boulder.co.us/recreation/bcmc*

🏕 Local Outdoor Retailers:

Neptune Mountaineering, Boulder, CO (303) 499–8866 • **Mountain Sports,** Boulder, CO (303) 443–6770 • **Eastern Mountain Sports,** Boulder, CO (303) 442–7566 • **North Face,** Boulder, CO (303) 499–1731

Ⓝ Maps:

USGS map: Boulder, CO

10

Gem Lake Trail

Hike Specs

Start: From Gem Lake trailhead on Devil's Gulch Road
Length: 4-mile out-and-back
Approximate Hiking Time: 2–3.5 hours
Difficulty Rating: Moderate due to several steep sections
Elevations: 7,740–8,830 feet
Elevation Gain: 1,090 feet
Seasons: Best from May to November, depending on snowfall, avoid hot summer days
Terrain: Dirt trail with some steeper sections that have log or stone steps
Land Status: National park
Nearest Town: Estes Park, CO
Other Trail Users: Equestrians and joggers
Canine Compatibility: Dogs not permitted

Getting There

From Estes Park: From the intersection of U.S. 34 and U.S. 36 in Estes Park, take U.S. 34 west about 0.5 mile to MacGregor Avenue. (also called Devil's Gulch Road). Turn right and travel 3.4 miles to the large right curve. Continue around the curve and down the road another 0.8 mile. On the right will be a stone driveway entrance with an address of 1261. An unsigned parking lot on the left is trailhead parking. There are no facilities at the trailhead. *DeLorme: Colorado Atlas & Gazetteer:* Page 29 A6

When people think of Rocky Mountain National Park, visions of craggy peaks, shimmering lakes, tumbling streams, and alpine tundra come to mind. The eastern part of the park, however, offers a very different landscape called Lumpy Ridge. Large granitic domes take on various shapes and extend above the surrounding hills. Glaciers that carved the high peaks to the west did not reach this area.

The first part of the trail makes right angles between fences surrounded by private property. Soon you enter a shady canyon and forest of ponderosa pine, Douglas fir, and aspen. The trail starts climbing with water bars and long steps. After turning right on the trail at the intersection with Twin Owls Trail, you arrive at several big granitic boulders. Look northwest for a good view of Twin Owls.

Eons ago a sea covered this area. As sediments washed into the sea and accumulated, they compacted into sandstone and shale. Later, under great pressure, the sandstone and shale were heated and transformed into gneiss and schist. Then about 300 million years ago, the Ancestral Rocky Mountains rose from a shallow sea. Uplifting created cracks into which molten magma oozed, cooling into granite.

About 70 to 45 million years ago, geologic forces uplifted the present Rocky Mountains. Erosion wore the mountains down to a sloping arch. From about five to 28 million years ago, the entire area was uplifted about 5,000 feet. As steeper streams quickened erosion, old metamorphic rocks and granitic intrusions were exposed. Lumpy Ridge contains many exposed intrusions. When erosion uncovers granite, the

rock expands, and parallel or spherical joints or fractures form along large exposed surfaces. Repeated freeze-thaw cycles cause the joints to expand and contract. Eventually rock surfaces break off, much like peeling layers off an onion. The granite erodes into fascinating shapes.

As the trail continues to climb, flat horizontal rocks on the left then on the right offer expansive views of the Estes Park area. Human history in this area starts around 11,000 years ago. Hunters found abundant game in summer, but abandoned the area during long, cold winters. Various explorers came near or through the area, but none stayed. In 1859, while searching for gold, Joel Estes entered a grassy area surrounded by mountains (called a "park" in Colorado). A year later he moved his family to his newly claimed land. Estes decided to harvest the abundant elk and deer and sell meat to the growing Denver market. In 1864, William N. Byers, founder of Denver's *Rocky Mountain News*, hiked up to visit Estes and named the area Estes Park.

The dominant peak rising to the southwest with its sheer east face is Longs Peak, named after Major Stephen H. Long, who explored parts of Colorado in 1820. Major John Wesley Powell, the Grand Canyon explorer, and Byers along with several others were the first white men to record a climb of Longs Peak (14,255 feet) on August 23, 1868. As later told by Arapaho elders, Native Americans climbed the peak to catch eagles to extract their feathers for ceremonies. Englishwoman Isabella L. Bird visited the area in 1873 and wrote a book about her adventures. *A Lady's Life in the Rocky Mountains* spread word of the beautiful Estes Park area. Albert Bierstadt's (1830–1902) paintings conveyed its beauty to the world's eyes.

Some early settlers realized they could make more money by entertaining tourists than by ranching and built tourist lodges. By 1875, a toll road operated up North

Gem Lake.

81

Saint Vrain Canyon with a road up Big Thompson Canyon completed in 1904. Five years later F.O. Stanley, of Stanley Steamer fame, and B.D. Sanborn opened the Stanley Hotel, complete with the first electricity in Estes Park. (This grand hotel, now expanded into a conference center, is visible from the road on the way to the trailhead.) At the urging of residents such as Enos Mills and F.O. Stanley, Congress created Rocky Mountain National Park in 1915.

The trail enters a nice aspen grove, then a narrow canyon between granitic outcroppings. The trail narrows and climbs numerous short switchbacks supported by rock retaining walls. There's a great place to stop and catch your breath by an interesting rock formation. Some people call it Paul Bunyan's boot, while others might see a modern art sculpture. From here the trail proceeds up a series of water bar steps. The cliff on the left resembles a badly assembled LEGO® structure. Through the trees a white rocket ship form appears. This "rocket" is really an outhouse.

In a few more steps you reach Gem Lake. Explore all sides of the lake, especially the view to the south from the north end. Many of the trees around the lake are limber pine. Keep an eye on the ground squirrels as they may try to make off with your lunch or hiking poles!

MilesDirections

0.0 START the hike at the Gem Lake Trailhead. ★ 40°23'39"N 105°30'26"W— Information is posted on the bulletin board on the left a few steps down the trail.

0.7 Enter Rocky Mountain National Park. The trail junction with the Twin Owls Trail is just a little farther. ◆ 40°24'07"N 105°30'42"W—At the junction, turn right on the trail to go to Gem Lake.

0.8 Big granitic boulders on your right provide great views and a nice place to stop. The trail stays to the left.

1.0 [*FYI. Views of Longs Peak with its diamond-shaped east face, Mount Meeker, Estes Park, Twin Sisters, and the Continental Divide open up to the west and south along this area. The trail enters a nice aspen grove.*]

1.2 The trail opens onto a broad spot with views of interesting rock formations to the east and a little north. The trail turns north here and loses a tiny bit of elevation.

1.6 Several interesting rock formations, including Paul Bunyan's Boot, provide a good place to rest before the next steep section. ◆ 40°24'31"N 105°30'18"W

1.9 Reach the outhouse spur. Please use the outhouse instead of the area around Gem Lake.

2.0 Reach Gem Lake. Return the way you came. ◆ 40°24'39"N 105°30'11"W

4.0 Arrive back at the trailhead.

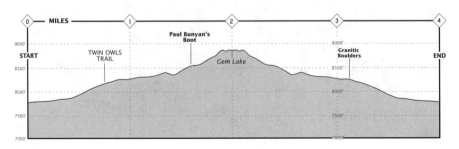

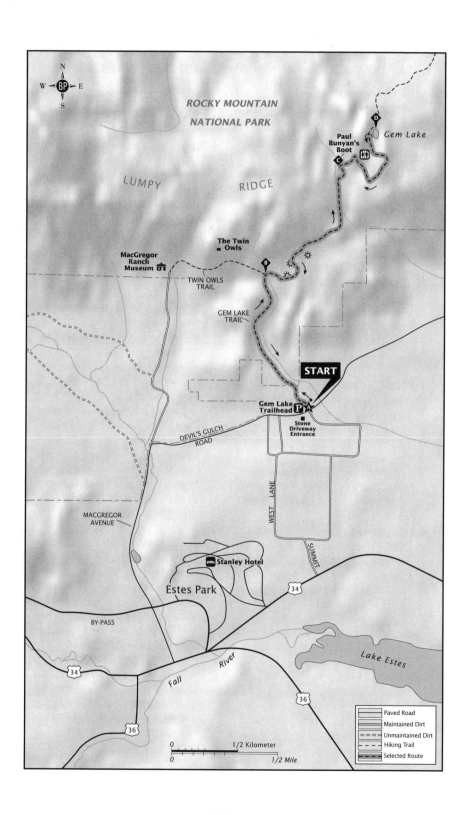

N
W — (BP) — E
S

ROCKY MOUNTAIN

NATIONAL PARK

LUMPY   RIDGE

Gem Lake

Paul
Bunyan's
Boot
C

D

The Twin
Owls

MacGregor
Ranch
Museum

B

TWIN OWLS
TRAIL

GEM LAKE
TRAIL

START

Gem Lake
Trailhead

Stone
Driveway
Entrance

DEVIL'S GULCH
ROAD

MACGREGOR
AVENUE

WEST LANE

SUMMIT

Stanley Hotel

Estes Park

34

BY-PASS

34

Lake Estes

Fall   River

36

36

0   1/2 Kilometer

0   1/2 Mile

	Paved Road
	Maintained Dirt
	Unmaintained Dirt
	Hiking Trail
	Selected Route

Hike Information

🟤 Trail Contact:
Rocky Mountain National Park, Estes Park, CO (970) 586–1206 or (970) 586–1333 or *www.nps.gov/romo*

🕐 Schedule:
Open year round

💲 Fees/Permits:
No fees for using this part of Rocky Mountain National Park. Backpacking permit required for overnight camping.

❓ Local Information:
Estes Park Chamber Resort Association, Estes Park, CO (970) 586–4431, 1–800–443–7837 or *www.estesparkresort.com* • **eWelcome Center** website: *www.estes-park.com*

📍 Local Events/Attractions:
Estes Park Area Historical Museum, Estes Park, CO (970) 586–6256 • **MacGregor Ranch Museum,** Estes Park, CO (970) 586–3749 • **Longs Peak Scottish Highland Festival,** Estes Park, CO 1–800–903–7837 • **Stanley Hotel Museum,** Estes Park, CO 1–800–976–1377 or (970) 586–3371

🛏 Accommodations:
YMCA of the Rockies, Estes Park, CO (970) 586–3341 • **Rocky Mountain National Park,** Estes Park, CO – *Reservations only: Glacier Basin and Moraine Park (1–800–365–2267). First-come, first-served at Longs Peak (tents only) and Aspenglen.* • **KOA,** Estes Park, CO 1–800–KOA–1887 or (970) 586–2888

🍴 Restaurants:
Wild Basin Smorgasbord, Allenspark, CO (303) 747–2545 or *www.wildbasin lodge.com* • **Sweet Basilico,** Estes Park, CO (970) 586–3899 • **Mama Rose's,** Estes Park, CO (970) 586–3330

• **The Other Side,** Estes Park, CO (970) 586–2171 • **Nicky's Restaurant,** Estes Park, CO (970) 586–5376

🔵 Other Resources:
Macdonald Book Shop, Estes Park, CO (970) 586–3450 • **Rocky Mountain National Park Visitor Center/ Headquarters,** Estes Park, CO • **Moraine Park Museum,** Estes Park, CO – *located in Rocky Mountain National Park* • **Alpine Visitor Center,** Estes Park, CO – *located in Rocky Mountain National Park*

🔵 References:
Colorado's Best Wildflower Hikes: The Front Range, by Pamela D. Irwin, Westcliffe Publishing • *Roadside History of Colorado,* by James McTighe, Johnson Books • *Estes Park A Quick History,* by Kenneth Jessen, First Light Publishing • *Early Estes Park,* by Enos Mills, A.B Hirshield • *A Lady's Life in the Rocky Mountains,* by Isabella L. Bird, Ballantine Books • *Rocky Mountain National Park Natural History Handbook,* by John C. Emerick, Roberts Rinehart Publishers • *Physical Geology Earth Revealed,* by David McGeary and Charles C. Plummer, Wm. C. Brown Publishers

🏔 Clubs and Organizations:
Colorado Mountain Club – Longs Peak Group, Longmont, CO at *www.cmc.org* – *Contact CMC's state office at (303) 279–3080 or 1–800–633–4417 (Colorado only) for the group's current phone number.* • **Rocky Mountain Nature Association,** Estes Park, CO (970) 586–0108 or 1–800–816–7662 or *www.rmna.org/home.html* • **Rocky Mountain National Park Associates,** Estes Park, CO (970) 586–0108 or *www.rmna.org/donations.html*

🚶 Hike Tours:

Rocky Mountain National Park, Estes Park, CO (970) 586–1206 • **Rocky Mountain Nature Association,** Estes Park, CO (970) 586–0108 or 1–800–816–7662 • **Colorado Outward Bound,** Denver, CO (303) 837–0880 or 1–800–477–2627 or *www.cobs.org* • **Estes Park Mountain Shop,** Estes Park, CO (970) 586–6548 or 1–800–504–6642 • **Colorado Mountain School,** Estes Park, CO (970) 586–5758 or *www.cmschool.com* – *backpack trips*

🏕 Local Outdoor Retailers:

Estes Park Mountain Shop, Estes Park, CO (970) 586–6548 or 1–800–504–6642 • **Outdoor World,** Estes Park, CO

(970) 586–2114 or *www.RMConnection. com* • **The Hiking Hut, Inc.,** Estes Park, CO (970) 586–0708 • **Komito Boots,** Estes Park, CO (970) 586–5391 or 1–800–422–2668 • **The Warming House,** Inc., Estes Park, CO (970) 586–2995

Ⓝ Maps:

USGS map: Estes Park, CO • *Trails Illustrated®* map: #101, Cache La Poudre/Big Thompson or #200, Rocky Mountain National Park park maps and additional hiking trail information are available from the visitor centers or by calling the park.

Geology Babble

metamorphic rock – *A rock formed when high heat or intense pressure cause one type of rock to be transformed into another type of rock.*

gneiss – *A metamorphic rock with light and dark bands (think "nice" lines).*

schist – *A metamorphic rock, usually dark-colored, with lots of mica (a shiny mineral).*

igneous rock – *A rock formed when magma (molten rock) cools.*

granite – *A light colored igneous rock formed when magma cooled under the earth's surface, usually in rock cracks, often with pink minerals and quartz imbedded.*

erosion – *The process of losing material, usually due to water, wind, or glacial ice.*

freeze-thaw cycle – *When water freezes in a rock crack it expands; when the ice thaws, the water takes less space, and the crack contracts. The repeated process can eventually break a rock apart.*

joint – *A fracture or crack in rock.*

glacier – *A flowing, compacted mass of ice that moves because of its own weight on a sloping surface.*

Ute Trail

Hike Specs

Start: From Ute Crossing along Trail Ridge Road
Length: 6.0-mile point-to-point
Approximate Hiking Time: 3–5 hours
Difficulty Rating: Difficult due to steep downhill section
Elevations: 11,640–8,440 feet
Elevation Loss: 3,200 feet
Seasons: Best from July to September, Trail Ridge Road must be open
Terrain: Dirt trail, sometimes steep with loose rocks
Land Status: National park
Nearest Town: Estes Park, CO
Other Trail Users: Equestrians (on last 1.5 miles)
Canine Compatibility: Dogs not permitted

Ute Trail in Windy Gulch.

Getting There

With Shuttle:
From Estes Park: Set up a car shuttle. Drive west on U.S. 36. Pay the entrance fee at the Beaver Meadows entrance station, just past park headquarters and visitor center. Drive another 0.7 miles to a big right curve and turn left onto the dirt road marked Upper Beaver Meadows. It's easy to miss this road as it's in the middle of the curve. The trailhead parking lot is about 1.5 miles at the end of the dirt road. Leave one car here. Return to U.S. 36, turn left and continue on Trail Ridge Road past Deer Ridge Junction to about two miles west of Rainbow Curve (last restroom). The trailhead is on the left side of the road at a very small parking area. The land is rather flat here after climbing up from Estes Park and before continuing to climb on the road.

Without Shuttle: (12-mile out-and-back Most Difficult hike)
From Estes Park: Set up a car shuttle. Drive west on U.S. 36. Pay the entrance fee at the Beaver Meadows entrance station, just past park headquarters and visitor center. Drive another 0.7 miles to a big right curve and turn left onto the dirt road marked Upper Beaver Meadows. It's easy to miss this road as it's in the middle of the curve. The trailhead parking lot is about 1.5 miles at the end of the dirt road. *DeLorme: Colorado Atlas & Gazetteer:* Page 29 A5

The first part of Ute Trail crosses alpine tundra with spectacular views of peaks carved by long ago glaciers along the Continental Divide. At the trailhead look right to see the rounded top and sheer northeast side of Terra Tomah Mountain (12,718 feet). Glacial movement created its steep side and the pointy peaks to the south. The last glacial period extended from about 35,000 to 12,000 years ago. A slow moving glacier carved the depths of Forest Canyon, located between the trailhead and the Continental Divide. Glaciers mainly occurred on east facing slopes because winds from the west deposited snow there, just as they do today.

Despite all the nearby glacial activity, the gently rolling land at the beginning of this hike was not covered by a glacier. Notice how rocky the area is. Recurring freeze-thaw cycles pushes these rocks up from the bedrock. Carefully rock hop to look at some of the tundra plants. Some grow only 0.25 inches per year, and a few footsteps can severely damage them, requiring 20 years or more to recover. Look around for lit-

Hiking the Ute Trail.

tle depressions, noticing the different types of plants that grow. Alpine tundra consists of many micro-communities. Some plants only grow where 100 mile-per-hour winter winds keep the ground free of snow. Others thrive where snow is deeper and lingers longer in spring.

While hiking this first gentle part, keep alert for marmots sunning themselves and playing around. The tiny pika, a mouse-like creature that is a member of the rabbit order of mammals, busily runs around collecting grass and flowers for its hay piles. Because pikas do not hibernate, they store food piles in the rocks for the long winter. Elk love this area in summer, and it's possible to see a lone bull or even an entire herd. If you are lucky, you may see bighorn sheep. Bees and flies pollinate the tiny alpine flowers, ten grasshopper species hop around, and butterflies color the air. The rustling of a well-camouflaged white-tailed ptarmigan may startle you. Its mottled feathers allow it to blend perfectly into the rocky background.

About 1.3 miles in, a rock formation called Tombstone Ridge rises to your left. When dropping into Windy Gulch, be careful of loose, ball bearing-like stones. Watch closely for human created rock piles called cairns marking the way. Stop at each cairn and look for the next one before continuing down. Limber pine, which loves windy, rocky places, prevails here. When you first see it, notice how it spreads along the ground with only a few flag trees brave enough to grow a few feet high. This type of tree growth is called *krummholz* meaning "crooked wood." Trees take this shape in the transition area between alpine and subalpine life zones. Keeping low to the ground helps them survive extremely high winter winds.

MilesDirections

0.0 START at the trailhead at Ute Crossing along Trail Ridge Road. ★ 40°23'35"N 105°41'42"W

1.3 Tombstone Ridge is on the left.

1.9 Ute Trail drops steeply into Windy Gulch.

3.3 Reach the Ute Meadows campsite. ◈ 40°21'48"N 105°39'01"W—Notice that the trail signs have different mileage than indicated in this guide.

4.0 The creek you've been following drops steeply to the right. Stay on trail to the left.

4.5 Come to an intersection with a longer trail to Upper Beaver Meadows. Stay on the right branch.

5.5 Reach the intersection with Moraine Park trail. Stay on trail to the left.

5.9 Several trails go to the parking lot. Stay on the left branch.

6.0 Arrive at Upper Beaver Meadows trailhead, the end of the trip if you are treating this hike as a shuttle. ◈ 40°22'23"N 105°36'49"W

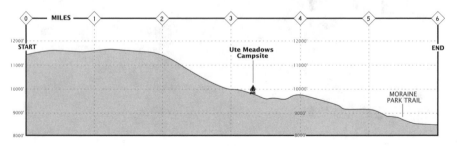

Windy Gulch continues to descend steeply for about 1.3 miles. The farther you descend, the taller the limber pines grow. Around 10,000 feet where the trail becomes more gentle, lodgepole pine, Englemann spruce, subalpine fir, and common juniper mix with the limber pine. The flower display is incredible! Look for cinquefoil, varieties of paintbrush, dandelions, and many-rayed goldenrods.

Ute Meadows campsite is located about 3.3 miles from Trail Ridge Road. Beyond there, the creek in Windy Gulch flows regularly, and the trail winds along a lush riparian community. The creek then drops into a narrow, shallow canyon. Watch carefully for the trail here. Where the creek plunges down a steep area, the trail curves to the left, up and over some rocks. Do not follow the creek down the cliffs as it can be dangerous.

The trail contours around, almost at the edge of a ledge, then heads up to easier ground. A boggy area displays a wealth of different flowers including cow parsnip and big sunflowers. Ponderosa pines, Douglas firs, and aspens replace subalpine trees. Just past the trail junction with the longer trail to Upper Beaver Meadows is an overlook on the right. Longs Peak (14,255 feet) and Moraine Park bordered by South Lateral Moraine are most prominent. A little farther the trail passes a crop of antelope bit-

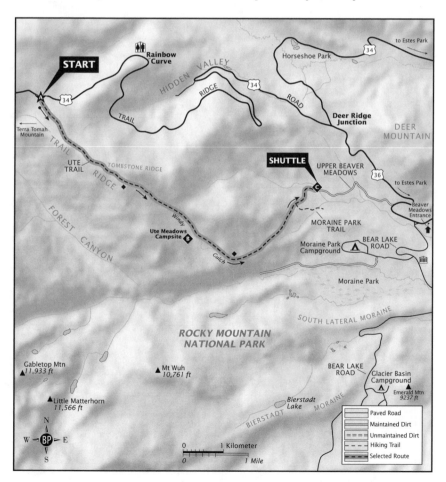

terbrush, commonly called "mule deer ice cream" because they really enjoy it. Occasionally glimpses of Upper Beaver Meadows can be seen below. Stay left at the next trail junction and hike about 0.5 miles to your waiting vehicle.

Although there is some dispute about this trail originally being used by Utes, parts of it probably were. The miners also crossed Trail Ridge going from Lulu City to Estes Park. The Park Service rerouted the trail below Windy Gulch sometime in the past 40 years; however, the U.S. Geological Service (USGS) topographical map does not show the new section. No matter what its history, the Ute Trail offers an interesting introduction to the various ecosystems of Rocky Mountain National Park.

When hiking the 11,000-plus-foot high Ute Trail, be sure to wear sunscreen and sunglasses. Even if it is overcast, ultraviolet light from the sun can burn skin and eyes very quickly.

View of Continental Divide from the start of the Ute Trail.

Hike Information

🌢 Trail Contact:

Rocky Mountain National Park, Estes Park, CO (970) 586–1206 or (970) 586–1333 or *www.nps.gov/romo*

🕐 Schedule:

Trail Ridge Road closed by snow in winter so upper trailhead not accessible. Lower access road to Upper Beaver Meadows is closed by snow 1.5 miles from trailhead but is hikeable. The first part of the trail is also used in winter. Middle and upper part of the trail not marked for winter use. Wind can blow 200 mph above treeline in winter. Call for trail and road conditions October through June.

💲 Fees/Permits:

Entrance fee, annual pass, Golden Eagle, Golden Access, or Golden Age Pass required

❓ Local Information:

(See Hike 10: Gem Lake Trail.)

💡 Local Events/Attractions:

(See Hike 10: Gem Lake Trail.)

🛏 Accommodations:

(See Hike 10: Gem Lake Trail.)

🍴 Restaurants:

(See Hike 10: Gem Lake Trail.)

📖 References:

Land Above the Trees, A Guide to American Alpine Tundra, by Ann H. Zwinger and Beatrice E. Willard, Johnson Printing. 1991 • **A Sierra Club Naturalist's Guide to The Southern Rockies,** by Audrey DeLella Benedict, Sierra Club Books • **High Country Names Rocky Mountain National Park and Indian Peaks,** by Louisa Ward Arps and Elinor Eppich Kingery, Johnson Books

🚶 Clubs and Organizations:

(See Hike 10: Gem Lake Trail.)

🏃 Hike Tours:

(See Hike 10: Gem Lake Trail.)

🛍 Local Outdoor Retailers:

(See Hike 10: Gem Lake Trail.)

🅝 Maps:

USGS maps: Trail Ridge, CO; McHenrys Peak, CO; Longs Peak, CO • **Trails Illustrated®** map: #101, Cache La Poudre/Big Thompson or #200, Rocky Mountain National Park • **Park maps** and additional hiking trail information are available from the visitor centers or by calling the park.

Lulu City Trail

Hike Specs

Start: From Colorado River Trail trailhead
Length: 7.4-mile out-and-back
Approximate Hiking Time: 3.0–5.0 hours
Difficulty Rating: Moderate due to length
Elevations: 9,010–9,480 feet
Elevation Gain: 470 feet
Seasons: Best from mid June to mid October
Terrain: Dirt trail
Land Status: National park
Nearest Town: Grand Lake, CO
Other Trail Users: Equestrians and anglers
Canine Compatibility: Dogs not permitted

Getting There

From Grand Lake: Drive 1.8 miles north on U.S. 34 to the entrance station to Rocky Mountain National Park and pay the entrance fee. (The Kawuneeche Visitor Center, at mile 1.3, is an excellent place to start your visit.) From the entrance station, drive another 9.4 miles to the Colorado River Trail trailhead entrance, on the left. The parking lot is another 0.1 miles. There are vault toilets and picnic tables. Drinkable water is available at Timber Creek campground 1.7 miles south or at the visitor center. *DeLorme: Colorado Atlas & Gazetteer:* Page 28 A4

On the way to the Colorado River Trail trailhead, notice the broad valley through which you're driving. This U-shaped valley was carved by the 20-mile-long Colorado River Glacier, which melted about 12,000 years ago. We now call this the *Kawuneeche* (Kah-wu-nee-chee) Valley, an Arapaho term for "valley of the coyote." Coyotes still flourish here, as do deer and elk. In 1978, moose were reintroduced into North Park—northwest across the Continental Divide—and have found a home in the wet valley meadows. Mountain lion also live here—so hike in groups and keep children close. The hike continues up the Kawuneeche Valley along the North Fork of the Colorado River. Several high peaks to the west show the steep, sharp crags and cliffs formed by glacial carving.

At about mile 0.6, you cross a large meadow where the Lulu City Trail intersects with the Red Mountain Trail. In 1907, Tober Wheeler (a.k.a. Squeaky Bob due to his high-pitched voice) built a tent resort in this meadow to showcase the area's beautiful scenery and trophy hunting and fishing. In the mid 1920s, Lester Scott bought the place and renamed it Phantom Valley Ranch—after the ghosts of Native Americans, miners, and others whose presence he felt. In the 1960s, the Park Service bought and tore down the old ranch to let the land revert to a wild state. When hiking here in the fall, watch for elk scat along the trail and imprints of elk beds in the grass and listen for their eerie bugle.

After passing the mine tailings from the Shipler Mine, you come across the remains of two cabins at the edge of a meadow. One of these cabins was built in 1876 by Joel Shipler, a prospector who just a few years later would discover a silver lode on the mountain that bears his name. Word of Shipler's strike spread, and miners quickly arrived in the upper part of the North Fork of the Grand River valley. By

A meadow on the trail to Lulu City.

A gold-mantled ground squirrel surveys the Lulu City site.

MilesDirections

0.0 START at the Colorado River Trail trailhead. ☆ 40˚24'7"N 105˚50'53"W11

0.2 Top a little knoll after two switchbacks.

0.6 The trail forks. Red Mountain Trail is to the left. This is the site of Phantom Valley Ranch. Stay on trail ahead and sort of right. **Ⓑ** 40˚24'30"N 105˚50'55"W

1.1 The trail is next to Colorado River for a little while.

1.6 The trail passes through boulderfield. [*FYI. Watch for raspberries among the rocks. The tiny fruits are edible, but please take no more that one out of 10 berries because animals, like bears, depend on the berries for winter fat.]*

1.8 Arrive at the Shipler Mine tailings. **Ⓒ** 40˚25'40"N 105˚50'57"W—[*FYI. Look down to left to see an old ore cart.]*

2.2 Arrive at the Shipler Cabin ruins. **Ⓓ** 40˚25'52"N 105˚51'0"W—[**Option.** *For a shorter 4.4-mile out-and-back hike, you can turn around here and return the way you came.]*

2.6 Reach Crater Creek bridge.

2.9 Trail curves to right and heads uphill more steeply.

3.1 Trail curves to left and wiggles and undulates along the side of Specimen Mountain.

3.5 Trail junction with Lulu City and La Poudre Pass trails. **Ⓔ** 40˚26'38"N 105˚50'43"W—Take the left fork and head downhill to Lulu City.

3.7 Arrive at the Lulu City site. (Old cabin ruins are on the right.) **Ⓕ** 40˚26'46"N 105˚50'49"W—[*FYI. Left trail goes to the Colorado River. Right trail continues through Lulu City site to the outhouse, which is approximate 0.06 miles from here, and Thunder Pass.]* Return the way you came.

7.4 Arrive back at the trailhead.

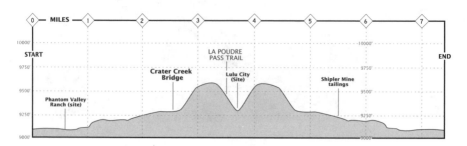

June 1880, plans were laid for a town in the valley, to be called Lulu City—exactly who Lulu was remains a question.

Lulu City boasted a clothing store, a barbershop, an assay shop, a hardware store, a grocery, and liquor stores. Stagecoaches connected the town with Fort Collins and Grand Lake. A fine hotel and bank gave the little community a civilized air, while the red light district, which operated a little north of town, satisfied the rowdier element. Two sawmills provided lumber for buildings and mines. Unfortunately, the extracted ore proved to be low-grade and not worth much money. By 1884, the death knell sounded for Lulu City.

Joel Shipler, however, continued to live in his cabins until about 1914. The Shipler Mine only penetrated about 100 yards into the mountain and probably didn't support his family very well. Still, Shipler reported abundant game in the area, knee-high grass, and catching "as many as 583 trout in one day." The leader of a Colorado Mountain Club outing in 1914 claimed to have caught 127 brook trout near Squeaky Bob's place.

After Shipler Cabins, the trail gradually climbs through thick forest, then turns east and heads uphill for about 0.2 miles. It then undulates along the side of Specimen Mountain. At the intersection with La Poudre Pass Trail, you drop somewhat steeply along a few switchbacks down into the valley, and ultimately to the Lulu City site. The log cabin ruin on the right is all that remains of the town. Wildflowers brighten the meadow, and ground squirrels might beg for lunch. Hike down to the river on a spur trail or farther north on the trail to Thunder Pass. An outhouse is north across a little branch named Lulu Creek.

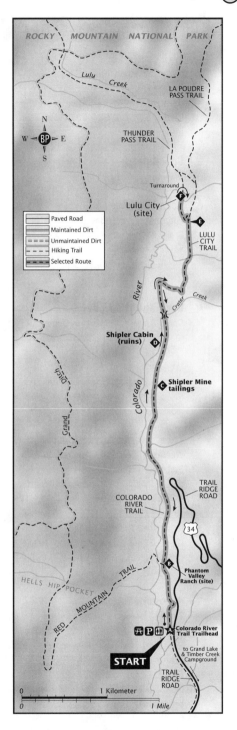

Hike Information

Trail Contacts:
Rocky Mountain National Park, Estes Park, CO (970) 586–1206 • **Kawuneeche Visitor Center,** Grand Lake, CO (970) 627–3471 or *www.nps.gov/romo*

Schedule:
Open year round

Fees/Permits:
Entrance fee or annual pass, Golden Eagle, Golden Access, or Golden Age pass required. Backpacking permit required for overnight camping (fee required).

Local Information:
Grand Lake Chamber of Commerce, Grand Lake, CO 1–800–531–1019 or (970) 627–3402 or *www.grand lakechamber.com* • **Websites:** *www. grandlakecolorado.com* or *www.explore-rocky.com* or *www.mtnds.com/hikes/ main.asp*

Local Events/Attractions:
Western Week & Annual Buffalo Barbecue Celebration, Grand Lake, CO (970) 627–3402 • **Grand Lake Regatta & Lipton Cup Races,** Grand Lake, CO (970) 627–3377 • **Rocky Mountain Repertory Theatre,** Grand Lake, CO (970) 627–3421 • **Kauffman House and Museum,** Grand Lake, CO (970) 627–3421

Accommodations:
Timber Creek Campground, Rocky Mountain National Park • **Arapaho-Roosevelt National Forest,** Sulphur Ranger District, Granby, CO (970) 887–4100 or *www.fs.fed.us/r2/arnf* • **Grand Lake Lodge (National Historic Landmark),** Grand Lake, CO (970) 627–3967

Restaurants:
Mountain Inn, Grand Lake, CO (970) 627–3385 • **Pancho & Lefty's,** Grand Lake, CO (970) 627–8773 • **Grand Lake Lodge,** Grand Lake, CO (970) 627–3185 • **Daven Haven Lodge,** Grand Lake, CO (970) 627–8144

References:
High Country Names Rocky Mountain National Park and Indian Peaks, by Louisa Ward Arps and Elinor Eppich Kingery, Johnson Books

Books:
Rocky Mountain National Park A History, by C.W. Buchholtz, University Press of Colorado • *Rocky Mountain National Park Natural History Handbook,* by John C. Emerick, Roberts Rinehart Publishers • *National Parkways Photographic and Comprehensive Guide to Rocky Mountain & Mesa Verde National Parks,* edited by Michael D. Yandell, National Parks Division of World-Wide Research and Publishing Co. • *Lulu City Colorado River Trail,* by Glen Kaye, Rocky Mountain Nature Association

Clubs and Organizations:
Rocky Mountain Nature Association, Estes Park, CO (970) 586–0108 or 1–800–816–7662 or *www.rmna.org/ home.html* • **Rocky Mountain National Park Associates,** Estes Park, CO (970) 586–0108 or *www.rmna.org/dona-tions.html*

Hike Tours:
Rocky Mountain National Park, Kawuneeche Visitor Center, Grand Lake, CO (970) 627–3471 or *www.nps. gov/romo* • **Rocky Mountain Nature Association,** Estes Park, CO (970)

586–0108 or 1–800–816–7662 or *www.rmna.org*

Local Outdoor Retailers:
Never Summer Mountain Products, Grand Lake, CO (970) 627–3642 • **Rocky Mountain Sports,** Grand Lake, CO (970) 627–8124

N Maps:
USGS maps: Fall River Pass, CO • *Trails Illustrated®* maps: #200, Rocky Mountain National Park

The Grand Ditch Project

To the west of Lulu City, along the Never Summer Range, is a long, manmade scar in the earth known as Grand Ditch. As people settled Colorado's dry Eastern Plains, the region's natural water supply proved insufficient to satisfy the developing cities, ranches, and farms. Colorado's West Slope receives more moisture, but it drains west into the Colorado River, so people soon devised schemes to divert water from the west side to the east. The Larimer City Ditch Company was formed in 1881 to divert water toward Fort Collins and the eastern plains. By October 1890, the first section of the Grand Ditch brought water from the Never Summer Range over La Poudre Pass to Long Draw Creek to the Cache La Poudre River, which flows near Fort Collins. By 1936, the Grand Ditch extended to Baker Creek, a total of 14.3 miles. Built by Swedish, Japanese, Mexican, Chinese, and other laborers with little more than picks, shovels, and wheelbarrows, the ditch captures water from high alpine basins of the Never Summer Range. At its widest point, the ditch is 20 feet wide by six feet deep.

Water diversion helps humans, no question, but often it adversely impacts wildlife, forests, and ecosystems. Arguments have raged over the years, and continue today, over the issue of moving water from one side of the Continental Divide to the other.

Grand Ditch was named after the river whose waters it diverted. Grand River was the original name of the Colorado River, within Colorado. Not until the Grand joined with the Green River in Utah did it become the Colorado River. In 1921, after some sneaky politics by Colorado Congressman Edward Taylor, President Harding signed a bill into law that renamed Grand River the Colorado River from its source high in Rocky Mountain National Park.

13

Lory State Park Loop

Hike Specs

Start: From the Well Gulch Nature Trail trailhead by the South Eltuck Picnic Area

Length: 6.6-mile loop trail

Approximate Hiking Time: 2.5–4 hours

Difficulty Rating: Moderate due to length and some steep spots

Elevations: 5,480–6,760 feet (Arthur's Rock is 6,780 feet)

Elevation Gain: 1,280 feet (1,300 feet with Arthur's Rock)

Seasons: Year round, except after a big snowstorm

Terrain: Dirt trail, sometimes steep and rocky, sometimes gentle

Land Status: State park

Nearest Towns: Laporte, CO and Fort Collins, CO

Other Trail Users: Parts open to mountain bikers and equestrians, hunters in season

Canine Compatibility: Leashed dogs permitted. Little to no water along the trail.

Getting There

From Fort Collins: Take U.S. 287 north from Fort Collins, turn left onto CR 54G through Laporte, then in about three miles turn left to Rist Canyon (CR 52E). Turn left after one mile onto CR 23N, drive 1.4 miles south, and then turn right onto CR 25G. Drive another 1.6 miles to the park entrance. Pay the entrance fee here and stop in the new visitor center to check out the interpretive displays. Restrooms and water are available at the visitor center. Drive one mile south to the South Eltuck Picnic Area, across from the Well Gulch Nature Trail trailhead. There are restrooms but no water here. Bring water with you as there's usually none on the trails. *DeLorme: Colorado Atlas & Gazetteer:* Page 20 D1

Human activity in this area can be traced back 15,000 years. The Folsom culture lived and hunted here starting about 11,000 years ago. The term "Folsom culture" comes from archeological evidence first found near Folsom, New Mexico, in 1926 that distinguished this group's tools and culture from those of other ancient Native Americans. More modern tribes of the area included Arapaho, Cheyenne, and Ute.

In the early 1800s, fur traders came to the area in search of pelts. In 1836, a party of trappers climbed into the foothills west of the Fort Collins area. Their supplies became too heavy and they decided to hide them. The supposed location of this *cache* was near today's Bellvue. Because the cache included gunpowder, the river near their cache became known as the Cache la Poudre.

One of the party members, Antoine Janise, returned a few years later to settle down. Janise saw his opportunity for success after gold was discovered near Denver. Near present-day Laporte, he established a settlement called Colona in 1859, after receiving permission from the local Arapaho tribe. Prospectors began combing all the tributaries of the South Platte River including the Cache la Poudre. Settlers continued to arrive establishing farms to feed themselves and the miners.

Trees are not overly plentiful on the plains of Colorado, so the town of Fort Collins grew with stone. Colorado's first commercial quarry opened in 1873 near Stout located

at the mouth of Spring Canyon. Over 1,000 Swedish and Italian laborers quarried sandstone for sidewalks and buildings. A railroad spur arrived in 1882 from Fort Collins to Bellvue then to Stout. When Portland cement replaced the need for building stone, the quarry closed. Stout now lies beneath the waters of Horsetooth Reservoir.

The plains and foothills of Colorado are known to be dry, and early farmers looked to the Poudre River for relief. G.R. Sanderson built the first irrigation ditch in northern Colorado, diverting water from the Poudre above Bellvue. By 1933, irrigation took much water from the Poudre and the Big Thompson River to the south. The U.S. Bureau of Reclamation started the Colorado–Big Thompson Project to divert West Slope water to the thirsty farms and growing population of the east. A 9.75-foot diameter tunnel, up to 3,600 feet underground, was drilled under the Continental Divide. The Alva B. Adams Tunnel transports water from Grand Lake on the west to Mary's Lake near Estes Park on the east. Water from Mary's Lake flows through various reservoirs, ultimately to Horsetooth Reservoir, which was completed in 1949.

The 2,400 acres of Lory State Park are part of a 3,600-acre ranch formerly owned by John Howard. As Fort Collins and the surrounding area quickly expanded, Lory Park's role in

Geology 101

Arthur's Rock (6,780 feet) is composed of granite pegmatite, which is estimated to be 1.7 billion years old. Pegmatite forms from thick magma, which cools very slowly allowing large crystals to develop. The red Fountain formation by Horsetooth Reservoir was created by sediments eroded from the Ancestral Rockies about 300 million years ago. East of Horsetooth is Dakota sandstone formed about 100 million years ago in the Cretaceous Seaway that covered much of Colorado. This formation was then folded into the Dakota Hogback during the rise of today's Rockies, starting about 65 million years ago.

Arthur's Rock.

MilesDirections

0.0 START at Well Gulch Nature Trail trailhead by South Eltuck Picnic Area. ★ 40°34'41"N 105°10'42"W—Stop at the bulletin board for information and a Well Gulch Self-Guided Nature Trail brochure. Directly after the bulletin board, reach an intersection with Valley Trail. Continue straight on Well Gulch Nature Trail.

0.5 Come to an intersection with Well Gulch Nature Loop and Well Gulch Trail. Turn right onto Well Gulch Trail to reach Timber Trail.

1.0 Reach a T-intersection with Timber Trail. ◆ 40°34'45"N 105°11'28"W—Turn left onto Timber Trail and head uphill. Trail switchbacks up an open, south-facing slope.

1.3 Trail swings left, from a south-facing to a north-facing slope. *[FYI. Check out the change in vegetation with the change in slopes.]*

2.0 Reach the intersection with Westridge Trail, and stay to the left on Timber Trail. ◆ 40°34'34"N 105°12'01"W—*[FYI. The flat ponderosa-filled area is a nice place for a little break. You'll be passing by the designated campsites on this section.]*

2.7 Reach the campsite #1 sign. Walk up the little ridge to the right for views to the west. As you continue along the trail, Arthur's Rock is ahead. Signs are lacking here.

3.0 Come to the intersection with Arthur's Rock Trail. *[Side-trip. A trail goes straight ahead and winds around to a point where you can scramble to the top of Arthur's Rock for great views. ◆ 40°34'06"N 105°11'15"W]* Turn right and head downhill on the trail called Arthur's Rock Trail (versus the side trail to the rock itself). In a few feet the trail forks again. Turn left onto the upper branch of Arthur's Rock Trail. Signs are lacking here. The trail switchbacks and drops down along the side of Arthur's Rock. *[FYI. Good view of what 1.7-billion-year-old rock looks like.]*

3.4 Stay on the trail to the right as it drops below the ridge at the end of Arthur's Rock.

3.7 Intersect with the lower branch of Arthur's Rock trail. Continue on the trail to the left heading downhill.

4.0 Intersect with the Mill Creek Link. Turn left at this fork.

4.4 Intersect with the Overlook Trail. ◆ 40°33'48"N 105°10'41"W—Turn left and follow Overlook Trail back to Well Gulch Nature Trail. Overlook Trail meanders up and down at the edge of forest but eventually plains out.

5.8 Come to the intersection of Overlook Trail and Well Gulch Nature Trail. Turn right and follow Well Gulch Nature Trail toward Homestead Picnic Area.

6.3 Reach the intersection of Well Gulch and Valley trails. Turn left and walk along the Valley Trail, past Homestead Picnic Area, heading mostly north.

6.5 Reach the intersection of Valley Trail and Well Gulch Nature Trail. Turn right and return to South Eltuck Picnic Area.

6.6 Arrive back at the Well Gulch Nature Trail trailhead where you started.

Note. *At most junctions the trails are posted but a few areas are a little confusing.*

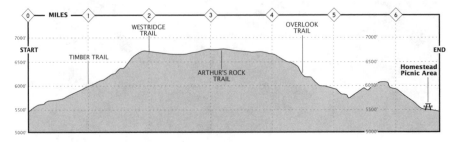

wildlife preservation became even more important. Recreational opportunities within in Lory State Park, Horsetooth Mountain Park, and Horsetooth Reservoir also provide welcome relief from the fast pace of our modern world.

This hike starts at the Well Gulch Nature Trail trailhead near the South Eltuck Picnic Area. Following Well Gulch through yucca, wooly mullein, and shortgrass prairie, the trail enters ponderosa pine and Douglas fir forests. Watch out for poison ivy along this trail. It then joins the Timber Trail and climbs steadily and sometimes steeply to a ridge. As the trail turns from south to north facing slopes, notice how the vegetation changes in response to a slightly cooler and wetter climate. At various points excellent views to the Eastern Plains and Fort Collins open up.

At the ridgeline, numbered poles mark campsites. Near campsite #1, climb a little ridge to the right for views to the west. Back on Timber Trail, Arthur's Rock rises straight ahead. A short trail scrambles to the top for even better views. Return to the main trail and continue to join the upper section of Arthur's Rock Trail, which drops and twists below granitic cliffs. Continue down Arthur's Rock Trail to the Overlook Trail. This trail travels the edge of forest and plains, climbing and dropping across drainages before finally emerging onto the prairie for the last leg of the loop.

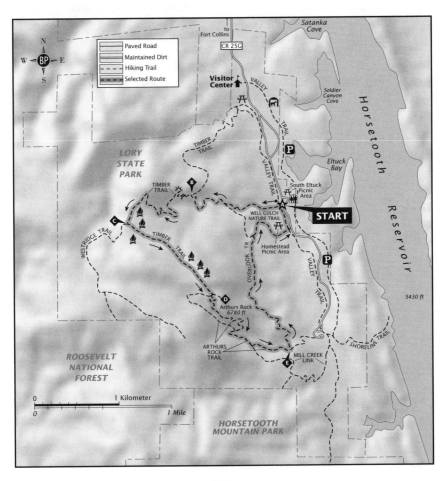

Hike Information

Trail Contact:
Lory State Park, Bellvue, CO (970) 493–1623 or *parks.state.co.us/lory*

Schedule:
Open year round. Call for trail conditions in winter.

Fees/Permits:
Daily fee or annual parks pass required. Permit required for backpacking (overnight camping at designated campsites).

Local Information:
Convention & Visitor Bureau, Fort Collins, CO (970) 482–5821 or *www.ftcollins.com* • Fort Collins Chamber of Commerce, Fort Collins, CO (970) 482–3746 or *www.fcchamber.org* • City of Fort Collins, Fort Collins, CO (970) 221–6500 or *www.ci.fort-collins.co.us*

Local Events/Attractions:
Fort Collins Museum, Fort Collins, CO (970) 221–6738 • Anheuser-Busch Brewery, Fort Collins, CO (970) 490–4691 or *www.budweisertours.com* • Rocky Mountain Raptor Center, Fort Collins, CO (970) 491–0398 or *www.fort net.org/RMRP* • Discovery Center Science Museum, Fort Collins, CO (970) 472–3990 or *www.dcsm.org*

Accommodations:
Edwards House Bed & Breakfast, Fort Collins, CO (970) 493–9191 or 1–800–281–9190 or *www.edwards house.com* • Helmshire Inn, Fort Collins, CO (970) 493–4683

Restaurants:
The Rainbow, Fort Collins, CO (970) 221–2664 – *vegetarian* • Coppersmith's

Pub & Brewing, Fort Collins, CO (970) 498–0483 • Rio Grande Mexican Restaurant, Fort Collins, CO (970) 224–5428 • Sri Thai, Fort Collins, CO (970) 482–5115 – *Thai food* • Avogadro's Number, Fort Collins, CO (970) 493–5555 • Panhandler's Pizza, Fort Collins, CO (970) 221–4567 • Beau Jo's Pizza Restaurant, Fort Collins, CO (970) 498–8898 • Taj Mahal Restaurant, Fort Collins, CO (970) 493–1105 – *voted best Indian in Fort Collins* • Deli Works, Fort Collins, CO (970) 226–4308 • Egg & I, Fort Collins, CO (970) 223–5271 or (970) 223–8022 – *Voted best breakfast. Serves break and lunch.* • Bisetti's Italian Restaurant, Fort Collins, CO (970) 493–0086

Other Resources:
A Quiet Corner Bookstore & Coffeehouse, Fort Collins, CO (970) 416–1916

References:
Fort Collins: The Post – The Town, by Guy Peterson, Old Army Press • *Exploring Colorado State Parks,* by Martin G. Kleinsorge, University Press of Colorado • *Colorado State Parks A Complete Recreation Guide,* Philip Ferranti, The Mountaineers • *Wilderness Medicine* (4th Edition), by William Forgey, M.D., ICS Books, Inc.

Clubs and Organizations:
Friends of Lory Trails, Bellvue, CO (970) 493–1623 • Colorado Mountain Club (Fort Collins group) website: *members. aol.com/FortCMC/index.html – see website for current contact phone numbers.*

Hike Tours:

Colorado Mountain Club (Fort Collins group) website: *http://members.aol.com/FortCMC/index.html*

Local Outdoor Retailers:

The Mountain Shop, Fort Collins, CO (970) 493–5720 • JAX Outdoor, Fort Collins, CO (970) 221–0544 • Fort Collins Outdoor World, Fort Collins, CO (970) 442–1732 or (970) 221–5166 •

Recreational Equipment, Inc. (REI), Fort Collins, CO (970) 223–0123 or *www.rei.com* • Eastern Mountain Sports (EMS), Fort Collins, CO (970) 223–6511 or *www.easternmountainsports.com*

Maps:

USGS maps: Horsetooth Reservoir, CO

The Wood Tick

Colorado has relatively few poisonous or irritating plants, insects, and reptiles. Be aware, however, of the wood tick, Demacentor andersoni. The small insect is about 1/8 of an inch long, with a flat body. Ticks are active from late March into early July and live in grassy, woody, or brushy areas, waiting for a warm-blooded body. Humans and dogs can easily pick up ticks by brushing against vegetation. The tick embeds itself head first into your flesh, with its body sticking out. Unlike mosquitoes, ticks feed on the host's blood for hours. An anchor below their mouths keeps them attached.

The wood tick may carry one of two infections threatening to human hosts. If the tick bite goes undetected, a person may develop the virus Colorado Tick Fever. Symptoms appear within three to six days after the bite and include head and body aches, lethargy, nausea, vomiting, and abdominal pain. The illness lasts for five to 10 days. These wood ticks also carry the bacterium causing Rocky Mountain Spotted Fever. In two to four days, symptoms appear, to include fever, spotted rash, headache, nausea, vomiting, and abdominal and muscle pain. If Rocky Mountain Spotted Fever is suspected, seek medical attention immediately as this illness can be life threatening.

While hiking during tick season, check yourself (skin, hair, clothes) often to remove any ticks before they can transmit disease. Applying DEET- and permethrin-based repellants on skin and clothes can help. Wear light clothing so you can see ticks more easily. Tuck loose clothing into your socks and pants. If you find a tick embedded, grasp the tick as close as possible to the skin with a pair of tweezers and gently pull it straight out. Remove the tick intact. Do NOT leave the head and neck in your skin. Other removal methods, such as covering the insect with alcohol, fingernail polish, or oil, may cause the tick to regurgitate and pass the infection on to its host. If you cannot effectively remove the tick, seek medical attention.

Roaring Creek Trail #952

Hike Specs

Start: From Roaring Creek Trail (Trail 952) trailhead
Length: 9.4-mile out-and-back
Approximate Hiking Time: 4–6.5 hours
Difficulty Rating: Difficult due to length and one steep section
Elevations: 7,750–9,820 feet
Elevation Gain: 2,070 feet
Seasons: Best from June to November, south face open during winter
Terrain: Dirt trail with some creek crossings
Land Status: National forest
Nearest Towns: Fort Collins, CO and Rustic, CO
Other Trail Users: Equestrians, mountain bikers, and hunters (in season)
Canine Compatibility: Controlled dogs permitted

Getting There

From Fort Collins: Drive north on U.S. 287 to Ted's Place. Turn left here onto CO 14 and drive west up Poudre Canyon about 40.5 miles. The trailhead is on the right, just before mile marker 82 and about 1.2 miles west of Big Bend Campground. There are no facilities at the trailhead. *DeLorme: Colorado Atlas & Gazetteer:* Page 19 C5

A series of slow-moving glaciers over the past 100,000 years carved a U-shaped valley along the upper part of the Cache la Poudre River. They didn't scour the entire canyon, but stopped west of Rustic. The glaciers sculpted beautiful, jagged peaks to the west, while the river cut a narrow canyon to the east. Poudre Canyon has been recognized for its beauty through the designation of CO Highway 14 as the Cache la Poudre–North Park Scenic Byway. Additionally, the upper stretch was designated a Wild & Scenic River in 1986. Thousands of people visit and play in this area each year. Kayaking, fishing, hiking, camping, hunting, cross-country skiing, snowmobiling, and wildlife viewing are just a few popular activities. Facilities in the canyon have been upgraded recently to include more vault toilets, new campgrounds, interpretive signs, and better parking. Cooperative efforts among the U.S. Forest Service (USFS), Scenic Byway Council, the Colorado State Historical Society, and others created these improvements.

During a 1986 land trade, the USFS acquired Arrowhead Lodge, two miles west of Rustic. Because the lodge had become a community center over the years, area residents did not want the building torn down. With community assistance, the Forest Service obtained a National Historic Places designation with supporting grants, and Arrowhead Lodge became a visitor center.

During the 1990s, Colorado's population boomed, as did the number of backcountry visitors. Unfortunately, the USFS's recreation budget decreased significantly—

Roosevelt National Forest's budget dropped from $12 million to $6 million—resulting in staff reductions and other cutbacks. In 1995, a seasonal USFS ranger, Chuck Bell, noticed that the influx of visitors was beginning to degrade the trails and campsites, as well as previously pristine areas. In talking with trail users, who were generally unaware of Leave No Trace techniques, Bell came up with the idea of having volunteers educate backcountry users. The USFS enthusiastically welcomed his plan. With the help of friends, the Poudre Wilderness Volunteers (PWV) became a reality.

View up the Cache la Poudre from Roaring Creek Trail.

In the first year, 200 people applied for volunteer jobs with the PWC, and 80 people were chosen. Each successful applicant attended training and committed to at least six days of service, either on horseback or on foot. The official mission of PWV is "to protect the region's pristine wilderness and backcountry areas through public education." PWV volunteers wear uniforms, talk with backcountry users, help with minor first aid and lost hikers, and provide accurate usage statistics to the USFS. The group supports itself through grants and the support of Fort Collins area businesses.

Roaring Creek Trail is an excellent place to see numerous ecosystems on one hike. Beginning on a dry south-facing slope, you hike past trees and plants that enjoy warm, dry conditions. Juniper, Douglas fir, ponderosa pine, and sagebrush are a few obvious residents. Aspen grow in moister areas. The change in vegetation is particularly obvious when the trail zigs close to Roaring Creek, then zags back into the open. Following switchbacks up the steep slope, you're actually hiking up a lateral (side) moraine left by the glacier. At the top of the ridge, where the trail descends a little, is the top of the moraine. Home Moraine, about three miles east of the trailhead, marks the farthest the glacier advanced. While sweating your way uphill, cool down with thoughts of the ice that created the slope!

MilesDirections

0.0 START at the Roaring Creek Trail (Trail 952) trailhead. ★40˚42'51"N 105˚44'04"W

0.2 Cross the bridge over East Fork.

1.0 *[FYI. There's a nice view of Poudre Canyon through the aspen trees.]*

1.3 The trail comes close to creek and becomes more level.

2.1 The trail forks; stay on the trail to the right.

3.1 Come to a big granitic rock outcropping with a boulder field to the right.

3.6 The trail heads uphill slightly. Stay on the trail that heads to the left of the big rock outcropping. Ignore the trails heading up to the right. The trail and creek merge for a few feet here. ◈ 40˚44'52"N 105˚46'16"W—Use the logs

or rocks to walk along the right edge of the creek. The trail continues to the right of the creek past the outcrop. *[Note. Do not cross to the left side of the creek here!]*

4.0 The trail curves right, up a little ridge next to some nice cascades. Up the ridge, the trail heads left along the right side of the creek again.

4.6 The trail crosses a little creek. Roaring Creek is still to the left, lazing through a willow patch.

4.7 *[FYI. This is a nice spot for lunch near some big ponderosa pine trees.]* ◈ 40˚45'48"N 105˚45'56"W—Turn around here and return the way you came.

9.4 Arrive back at the trailhead.

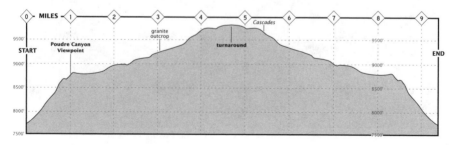

Once up the steep section, the trail drops slightly and then stays level or gently climbing. Willows line the creek to the left and lodgepole pines dominate the woods. (Native Americans used the skinny trunks for lodge poles, hence the name.) Keep an eye open for grouse, deer, and garter snakes. The trail is relatively obvious, except in one place. At a large rock outcropping, trails go in several directions. The correct trail and the creek are actually the same here. Hop across logs or rocks to reach the trail continuing on the same side of the creek, just on the other side of the rock outcropping. Spruce and fir trees mix in with lodgepole pines now. After ascending a little ridge, the trail enters a wider valley. It continues to the South Bald Mountain jeep road, but just before the road there is a beautiful little meadow with huge ponderosa pines that makes a perfect lunch spot and turnaround point.

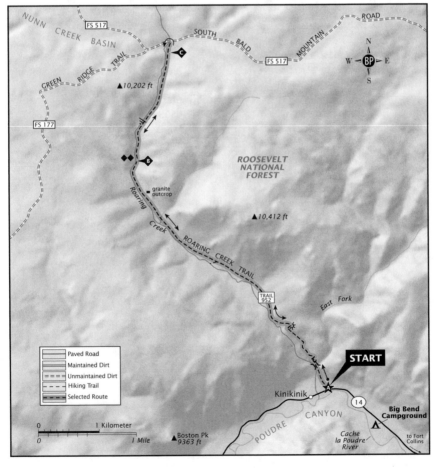

Hike Information

Trail Contact:
Roosevelt National Forest, Canyon Lakes Ranger District, Fort Collins, CO (970) 498–2770

Schedule:
Open year round. First slope often snow-free. After first mile, may need snow-shoes in winter.

Fees/Permits:
No fees or permits required

Local Information:
Arrowhead Lodge Visitor Center, Rustic, CO (970) 498–2770 • **Convention & Visitors Bureau,** Fort Collins, CO (970) 482–5821 or *www.ftcollins.com*

Local Events/Attractions:
Arrowhead Lodge Visitor Center, Rustic, CO (970) 498–2770

Accommodations:
Rustic Resort, Rustic, CO (970) 881–2179 or *www.caccl.com/rustic resort* • **Glen Echo Resort,** Rustic, CO (970) 881–2208 • **National Forest Campgrounds,** (970) 498–2770

Restaurants:
Rustic Resort, Rustic, CO (970) 881–2179 • **Glen Echo Resort,** Rustic, CO (970) 881–2208

Clubs and Organizations:
Poudre Wilderness Volunteers website: *www.fortnet.org/pwv* • **Colorado Mountain Club** (Fort Collins group) web site: *members.aol.com/FortCMC/index. html – see website for current contact phone numbers*

Hike Tours:
No permitted outfitter/guides on this trail. • **Colorado Mountain Club** (Fort Collins group) website: *members.aol. com/FortCMC/index.html*

Local Outdoor Retailers:
(See Hike 13: Lory State Park.)

Maps:
USGS maps: Kinikinik, CO; Boston Peak, CO; Deadman, CO • **Trails Illustrated®** maps: #112, Poudre River; #111 Red Feather Lakes

Winter Hiking

When winter brings a blanket of snow to Colorado's mountains, don't hibernate! **Cross-country skis** and **snowshoes** open a new world to summer hikers. Many trails are still used in the winter, and ski trails are often marked with blue diamonds. Orange diamonds denote snowmobile routes. Be aware that unmarked trails may be extremely hard to find as a snow-blanketed forest looks very different than in summer. Also be aware of and avoid avalanche danger.

The type of equipment you buy depends on how you are going to use it. Lightweight, small snowshoes are great on packed trails, but sink in deep, off-trail snow where larger snowshoes work better. Snowshoeing is like walking with wide and long feet. Hiking or ski poles can help with balance.

Colorado hosts numerous Nordic centers and guest ranches with groomed trails where skinny track and skating skis or snowshoes are the mode of travel. For where to go, check the website *www.colorado-xc.org*. If you've never cross-country skied before, take a couple of lessons at one of these centers. You'll learn correct technique which will make backcountry skiing more enjoyable. It's also easier to learn on groomed trails.

Backcountry skiing comes in three varieties: touring, telemarking, or downhill. Wider skis are used in the backcountry, but several styles are available. For novices or spring skiing, waxless skis are the way to go. As you gain skill, Colorado's snow is great for waxing skis. Waxes grip the snow so you don't slide backwards while going uphill but let you slide downhill. Waxless skis work the same but are usually less efficient. Skins placed on the bottom of your skis can help you climb interestingly steep or hard-packed hills (remember avalanche danger though). Then you need to decide if you are just touring or entering the downhill world of telemarking or randonée. Touring and telemarking require free-heel bindings while randonée depends on a binding that allows the heel to lift on the uphill but clamps down for parallel turns on the downhill.

Colorado has fantastic backcountry hut systems. Traveling to these huts requires good winter backcountry and route finding skills and equipment. Trails may not be obvious and many a skier has camped overnight outdoors without finding the hut.

Summer hiking trails may or may not be the best ski trails in winter. Check with local forest service, BLM, state, or local parks for recommended winter trails.

Then have a great winter "hike" on your snowshoes or skis!

Honorable Mentions

Front Range

Compiled here is an index of great hikes in the Front Range region that didn't make the A-list this time around but deserve recognition. Check them out and let us know what you think. You may decide that one or more of these hikes deserves higher status in future editions or, perhaps, you may have a hike of your own that merits some attention.

Ⓕ Alderfer/Three Sisters Park

Located up Buffalo Park Road out of downtown Evergreen, Alderfer/Three Sisters Park offers almost 11 miles of hiking trails. Roughly half the miles are located in the northern half, which features the Precambrian rock formations called "The Three Sisters" and "The Brother." A great view of the surrounding area can be had by hiking to the top of "The Brother." Various families owned the present park lands, raising cattle, horses, silver fox, and hay. A sawmill even operated on the property. A number of loop hikes of various lengths and levels of difficulty can be created from the different trails. From downtown Evergreen, travel south on CO 73. Turn west (right) on Buffalo Park Road, then drive approximately one mile to the east parking lot. A second parking lot is located another 0.5 miles along Buffalo Park Road. Dogs must be on leash. For more information contact Jefferson County Open Space at (303) 271–5925 or visit the park's webpage at *www.co.jefferson.co.us/ dpt/openspac/alderfer.htm*. *DeLorme: Colorado Atlas & Gazetteer:* Page 39 D7

Ⓖ Heart Lake

Located west of Rollinsville and the Moffat Tunnel, Heart Lake is a pleasant hike through forest along South Boulder Creek to a heart-shaped lake above treeline sitting below the Continental Divide. The trail starts about 9,200 feet and gains about 2,120 feet to the lake. You can also reach nearby Rogers Pass Lake or climb to the Divide at Rogers Pass at 11,860 feet. South Boulder Creek begins at these two lakes. The trip to Heart Lake is seven miles out-and-back. Being above treeline, watch out for thunderstorms and lightning. From South Boulder Creek Trail 900 you can also access the trails to Crater Lakes, Arapaho Lakes, and Forest Lakes. To reach the trailhead, drive to Rollinsville then turn west onto CR 16 (Rollins Pass Road). Drive about 8 miles to the East Portal of the Moffat Tunnel and park in the parking area observing any restrictions. The trailhead is on the south side of the tunnel entrance. For further information, contact Roosevelt National Forest at (303) 444–6600 or visit their website at *www.fs.fed.us/r2/arnf*. *DeLorme: Colorado Atlas & Gazetteer:* Page 39 A5

(H) Green Mountain West Ridge and Boulder Mountain Parks

The west ridge of Green Mountain is a fairly easy way to conquer the peak for great panoramic views of the plains and Boulder back around to the Indian Peaks. The first part of the trail meanders along somewhat flat terrain but then starts switch-backing and climbing up the west side of the mountain. The trail starts at about 7,680 feet and travels about 1.5 miles to the summit at 8,144 feet. From Boulder starting at Baseline Road and Broadway, drive west on Baseline Road about 6.1 miles up Flagstaff Mountain to a small parking area on the right side of the road. The trail starts on the left side. For more information and current dog regulations, contact Boulder Mountain Parks (Parks & Recreation Dept.) at (303) 441-3408 or visit their website at www.ci.boulder.co.us/bmp/oriented.htm.

The Boulder Mountain Parks offer great hiking opportunities and some steep trails for early season training before the snow melts in the high country. Try Mount Sanitas northwest of downtown Boulder off of Mapleton Avenue at the beginning of Sunshine Canyon. Other good leg burners include Fern Canyon to Bear Peak, Shadow Canyon, Mallory Cave, and Royal Arch. The website has fantastic topographical shaded image maps to help you create hiking loops of various lengths and elevation gains. Please check the website above for current dog regulations and which trailheads have parking fees. DeLorme: *Colorado Atlas & Gazetteer:* Page 40 A1

(I) Flattop Mountain

Flattop Mountain trail starts at Bear Lake and climbs steadily up through aspen, spruce-fir-lodgepole, krummholz, then across the alpine tundra to the Continental Divide. You can actually hike down to the Grand Lake area from the top. The Flattop Trail is about 9.0 miles out-and-back and ranges from 9,475 to 12,324 feet for a Most Difficult hike. Be aware of thunderstorms and lightning when nearing treeline. The trail passes overlooks of Dream and Emerald Lakes far below and Tyndall Glacier next to the trail. The views are forever. To reach the trailhead from Estes Park, drive west on U.S. 36. Pay the entrance fee at the Beaver Meadows entrance. Just past the entrance station, turn left on Bear Lake Road. Remember to start early to avoid thunderstorms. You may be required to take a shuttle – follow the signs. Otherwise, continue to the Bear Lake Parking lot. Facilities are available here. Follow the Flattop signs at trail intersections. Dogs are not allowed on the trails. For more information, contact Rocky Mountain National Park at (970) 586-1206 or visit their website at *www.nps.gov/romo*. *DeLorme: Colorado Atlas & Gazeteer:* Page 29 B5

Longs Peak and Gem Lake.

(J) Rocky Mountain National Park

Rocky Mountain National Park offers some of the best hiking in the Front Range. You can choose hikes that follow a river or lead to beautiful alpine lakes nestled in trees. Some trails lead to waterfalls while others lead to peaks or the top of the Continental Divide. A few trails take you over the Divide, traversing the width of the park. Several hikes are featured in this book, and Flattop Mountain makes the Honorable Mention list. That doesn't take away from the other fantastic hikes in the park! Check out the different areas. Wild Basin near Allenspark offers hikes to waterfalls, lakes, and to the Grand Lake area. Longs Peak trailhead leads to Longs Peak (a long climb requiring some mountaineering skills) or an easier, but still "difficult" hike to Chasm Lake at the base of the diamond of Longs Peak (plus others). Twin Sisters, an old fire lookout, stands by itself south of Estes Park and is a cool trail to hike up a mountain with great views, especially of Longs Peak. The Lily Lake area has some newer trails. The Bear Lake/Glacier Gorge area is extremely popular, and you may be required to take a shuttle to the trailheads. Alpine lakes, Flattop Mountain, and some loops are available out of this base. Devils Gulch trailheads lead to Twin Owls, Gem Lake, and other trails in the Lumpy Ridge area, quite a contrast in terrain with the glaciated peaks of the main part of the park. The west side of the park has several trailheads along the Colorado River or up to more lakes nestled in trees or to cross the Divide to Bear Lake or Glacier Gorge. Lesser-known trailheads off Devils Gulch Road in the northeast part of the park lead to lakes in the Mummy Range. Backpacking is a delight in the park. You can choose from designated campsites to backcountry zones. You must have a permit to backpack in the park, and a fee is charged to help administer costs. The positive side is a known campsite or area without hordes of people as in some parts of Colorado. Check out Rocky—it's the greatest! Dogs are not allowed on trails. For more information, contact Rocky Mountain National Park at (970) 586–1206 or visit their website at *www.nps.gov/romo*. ***DeLorme: Colorado Atlas & Gazetteer:*** Page 29 B6

North
CENTRAL
MOUNTAINS

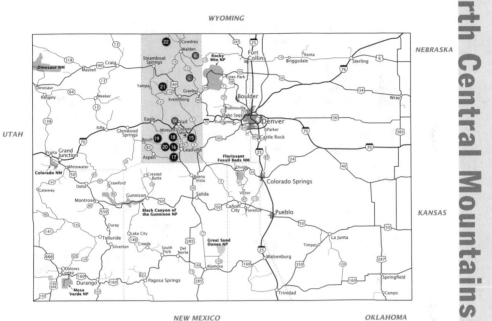

The Hikes

Wheeler Trail **15.**
Hagerman Tunnel Trail **16.**
Mount Elbert (North) **17.**
Notch Mountain **18.**
Mount Thomas Trail **19.**
Granite Lakes Trail **20.**
Silver Creek Trail **21.**
Seven Lakes **22.**

Honorable Mentions

K. Kelly Lake
L. Parkview Mountain
M. North Vail Trail System

North Central Mountains

North Central Colorado is a land of sharp social and landscape contrasts. Ranching still provides the livelihood in most of the northern half of this region. From North Park—a huge valley between the Medicine Bow, Rabbit Ears, and Park mountain ranges—the North Platte River begins its journey to the Missouri River and on to the Gulf of Mexico via the Mississippi. Bison once grazed here; now cattle and wildlife munch the tall grasses. The Yampa River and its tributaries also support the ranching community keeping the Old West spirit alive and well. Steamboat Springs keeps one foot on each side—one with ranching, the other with tourists, a ski resort, and hot springs. The southern half of this region contains the highest peaks in the state along with much of the high-priced real estate. The two highest peaks, Mount Elbert and Mount Massive, raise their lofty heads above Leadville, once home to rich mine owners such as Horace Tabor.

North Park, near Walden, hides interesting treasures including sand dunes, Colorado's largest herd of moose, great hiking, and a yurt system. Walden is the gateway to less used areas of the Mount Zirkel Wilderness and Colorado State Forest State Park. The Arapaho National Wildlife Refuge provides nesting habitat for waterfowl and other migratory birds. Moose were reintroduced to the area in the late 1970s. Elk, pronghorn, mule deer, and sage grouse also take advantage of the refuge's shrubland.

Most public lands in the southern half of this region are contained in the White River National Forest, a 2.25 million-acre parcel of rugged mountains, beautiful streams and lakes—a true hiker's paradise. It is consistently rated among the top five national forests in the United States for total recreation use. World-renowned ski resorts such as Aspen, Vail, Beaver Creek, Copper Mountain, Breckenridge, and Keystone are located here along with several smaller ski areas. As ski areas develop into year-round resorts, and golf courses continue to pop up, this region is becoming a resort-lover's dream. Don't let that scare you away. All or parts of 10 wilderness areas plus trails throughout national forest lands can keep you in new hiking terrain for many years. Fifteen of Colorado's 54 peaks over 14,000 feet are located in this region.

It's hard to believe Mount Elbert (14,433 feet) is the tallest point of the state when its peak only rises 4,243 feet above the plains near Leadville (10,190 feet). Mount Elbert's false summits drive hikers crazy as does the rarefied air. Still, the view from the top is worth the effort! Colorado's high point lies in mining country that stretches from Aspen to the gold fields of Breckenridge. The incredible Hagerman Tunnel on the old Colorado Midland Railroad is only one of many engineering feats accomplished by men desperate for gold, silver, and promised fortunes.

Colorado scenic and historic byways for exploring the North Central area include Colorado River Headwaters, Flat Tops Trail, Cache La Poudre–North Park, West Elk Loop, and Top of the Rockies.

Summit of Mt Elbert (14,433 feet).

North Central Mountains

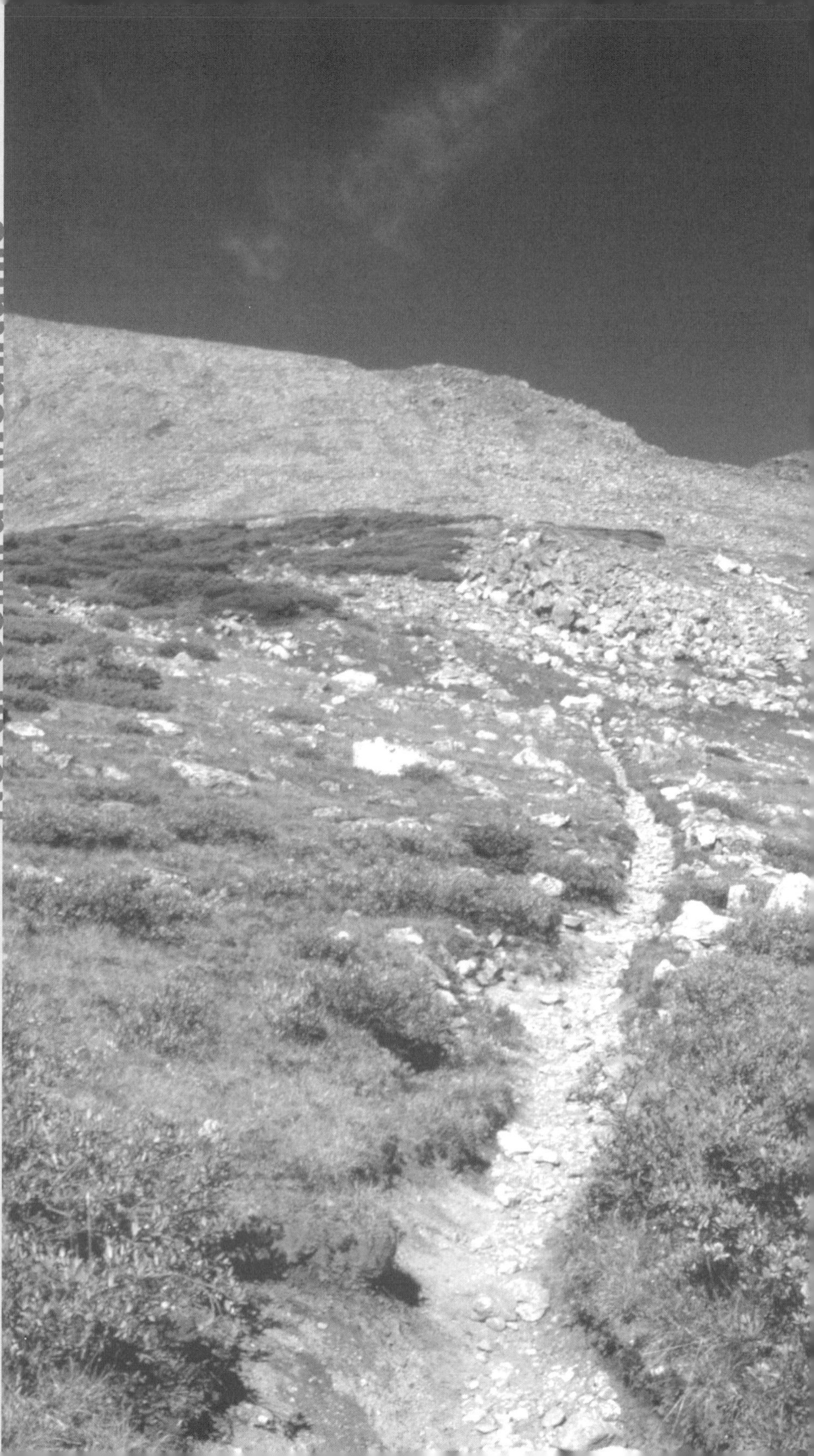

Section Overview

Wheeler Trail

This trail to the top of Wheeler Pass (unofficial name) is part of both the Wheeler National Recreational Trail and the Colorado Trail. It climbs steadily through spruce-fir and lodgepole forest on the western slope of the Tenmile Range. Views of the Gore Range, Copper Mountain, Breckenridge, French Gulch, and the Front Range are fabulous! Because this trail goes to a ridge above treeline, be sure to get an early start to avoid afternoon thunder and lightning storms. *(See page 122.)*

Hagerman Tunnel Trail

Take a pleasant walk along the abandoned Colorado Midland Railroad grade through spruce-fir forest. The site of Colorado's longest railroad trestle can be visited before heading up an old wagon road to the ruins of Douglass City, which once housed laborers working on the Colorado Midland Railway. The trail continues up to Opal Lake, site of the old steam boiler that provided power to build the Hagerman Tunnel. The trail continues as a hiking trail up to the railroad bed and shortly to the entrance of the Hagerman Tunnel, which in its time was considered a tremendous engineering feat. The return trip follows the railroad grade back through several old snowsheds (only one has some timbers left) and past another trestle site. *(See page 128.)*

Mount Elbert (North)

Mount Elbert is the highest point in Colorado and second highest in the Lower 48. The North Mount Elbert trail climbs steeply through lodgepole then spruce-fir forest and across alpine tundra. The worst parts of hiking Mount Elbert are its false summits and wind. The best parts include tremendous views and a feeling of great accomplishment. It's imperative to leave no later than 6:30 A.M. to avoid thunderstorms and lightning. Allow at least four to six hours for the hike up. Bring plenty of water and energy food. *(See page 134.)*

Notch Mountain

This hike takes you to the stone shelter on Notch Mountain for a fantastic view of Mount of the Holy Cross. The trail starts gently through spruce-fir forest with occasional glimpses of the notch in Notch Mountain. Eventually the trail climbs to treeline, then through tundra and boulder fields via switchbacks. Watch for pikas, white-tailed ptarmigans, marmots, and beautiful alpine wildflowers. The switchbacks make the hike easier than most trails up 13,000-foot peaks. Remember to leave early to reach the summit by 11 A.M. so you can head back by noon and avoid thunderstorms. *(See page 140.)*

Mount Thomas Trail

The Mount Thomas summit, a bump on Red Table Mountain, offers spectacular 360-degree views of the central Colorado Rockies! Overwhelming views stretch from the Maroon Bells and Elk Mountains in the southwest, circling northwest to the Flat Tops then Interstate 70 north of Eagle. The Gore Range rises in the northeast with the Sawatch Mountains towering in the east and southeast. Cattle still graze on some of the grassy southern slopes. Beautiful alpine wildflowers decorate the upper ridges. The trail crosses open areas for about 1.6 miles, so be sure to make the summit and be heading down before thunderstorms hit. *(See page 146.)*

Granite Lakes Trail

The Granite Lakes Trail first wanders along the Fryingpan River, meandering up and down through thick forest and around some interesting granite formations. The first 3.3 miles are fairly gentle. Turning up the Granite Creek drainage, the trail climbs steadily, and often steeply, to Lower Granite Lake tucked in a bench above Granite Creek. Upper Granite Lake is about 0.75 miles farther along a fairly gentle path. Once in the subalpine, the wildflowers and views are beautiful. Backpack in and take an extra day or two to explore this beautiful and quiet area. *(See page 152.)*

Silver Creek Trail

Silver Creek Trail starts out on closed logging roads, rising slightly to the Sarvis Creek Wilderness boundary. From here the trail mostly heads downhill, with a few uphills for variety. Silver Creek is a sparkling, crystal clear stream, very worthy of its name. Interesting granite formations appear occasionally on the north side of the trail. Lodgepole pine, Englemann spruce, subalpine fir, aspen, and eventually ponderosa pine trees line the trail. This area is great for a quiet getaway, except during hunting season, which starts at the end of August. *(See page 158.)*

Seven Lakes

The Big Creek Trail starts on the gentle Red Elephant Nature Trail through lodgepole, spruce, and fir forest. Turning west, it climbs gently to the Mount Zirkel Wilderness boundary near Big Creek Falls. The trail wanders along Big Creek then climbs a very steep section with many switchbacks. Excellent views of Big Creek Lakes can be seen from several viewpoints. The next section goes through old growth forest and into flower-filled meadows just below Seven Lakes. The lakes are in a high, open area with views of Red Elephant Mountain and the Continental Divide. The lakes are a peaceful backpacking destination. *(See page 164.)*

15

Wheeler Trail

Hike Specs

Start: From Wheeler Flats trailhead
Length: 8.6-mile out-and-back
Approximate Hiking Time: 5–6 hours
Difficulty Rating: Difficult due to elevation gain
Elevations: 9,680–12,400 feet
Elevation Gain: 2,720 feet
Seasons: Best from late June to mid-October
Terrain: Dirt trail climbs steadily with some small creek crossings, rocks, and roots
Land Status: National forest
Nearest Town: Frisco, CO
Other Trail Users: Equestrians, mountain bikers, and hunters (in season)
Canine Compatibility: Controlled dogs permitted

Getting There

From Frisco: Head west on I-70 to Exit 195 (Copper Mountain and Leadville, CO 91). Exit and take CO 91 over I-70. Come to the entrance to Copper Mountain Resort (on the right). Turn left here onto an unnamed road, and drive past the gas station. It's 0.4 mile to the parking lot at Wheeler Flats trailhead. (The gas station has restrooms, food, and water.) *DeLorme: Colorado Atlas & Gazetteer:* Pages 38 D1

M any summer moons ago, Ute Indians camped in this area and hunted bison, deer, elk, antelope, and mountain sheep in the surrounding high open areas. In 1879, Judge John Wheeler purchased 320 acres, now part of Copper Mountain Resort, and started a hay ranch. The next year silver miners arrived, and the ranch became a town known by various names: Wheeler's Ranch, Wheeler Station, Wheeler's, Wheeler, and Wheeler Junction. Wheeler prospered with a hotel, saloons, a post office, and several sawmills. The sawmills provided lumber for the numerous mines along Tenmile Creek from Frisco to the top of Fremont Pass. Despite its status as a mining town, tourists came to Wheeler for the beautiful scenery and excellent fishing. In 1884, the Colorado & Southern Railroad finished laying tracks to Wheeler on the east side of Tenmile Creek. The railroad station at Wheeler was named Solitude Station. On the other side of the creek, the Denver & Rio Grande railroad built their line with a station called Wheeler's. The Denver & Rio Grande railroad serviced this area from 1880 to 1911. The Colorado & Southern ended its rail service around 1937.

The trail is mostly flat the first mile while it follows part of the old Colorado & Southern Railroad route, now covering a gas pipeline. In one place the trail seems lower than the creek! After a mile, you reach a junction. Turn left up the trail to access Wheeler Pass. Judge Wheeler used this trail to take his stock from Wheeler to his ranch in South Park. The trail now ends near Hoosier Pass, south of Breckenridge. It was designated a National Recreational Trail in 1979.

In about 3.4 miles, the trail exits the forest for a view of Climax Molybdenum Mine's settling ponds. Several prosperous mining towns, including Robinson and

SKY Avalanche Chutes on the Tenmile

In the first 1.5 miles of the Wheeler Trail, several little creeks fall steeply down gullies devoid of tall trees. These gullies are winter avalanche chutes. When seen from eastbound Interstate 70 between Vail Pass and Copper Mountain, several chutes in this area (with the help of a little imagination) spell the word "SKY."

Tenmile Creek and the Tenmile Range.

Kokomo of Wheeler's era, are buried there. Watch and listen for marmots. As the trail contours left into another drainage, you can see the ridge of the Tenmile Range and cairns marking the trail. From here the trail winds in and out of forest, meadow, and willows. Colorful wildflowers line the trail. Trees become twisted krummholz near treeline and finally give up. The trail is sometimes smothered by willows, but is passable. Three cairns built of good-sized logs mark the way; the second one, however, is not on the trail, so stay alert. Finally when your breath is short from elevation and the steep trail, the summit cairn comes into view.

That is, until you reach it and realize the trail continues farther up. Notice the vegetation along the trail. Willows and little red elephants grow in shallow depressions containing snow and water. The drier areas contain sedges and grasses, old-man-of-the-mountain, paintbrush, American bistort, chickweed, and alpine avens. The tundra is fragile. If you must go off trail, step on rocks as much as possible. When in a group, spread out.

The sign at the top of Wheeler Pass reports an elevation of 12,460 feet, but the topo map clearly indicates just under 12,400 feet. Be sure to hike to the little rocky knob on the left (12,408 feet) for the best easterly views. Breckenridge, French Gulch, and part of Breckenridge ski area are on the east side; Copper Mountain and the Gore Range are to the northwest.

Founded in 1859 by General Spencer, Breckenridge was named after U.S. Vice President John Cabell Breckinridge to ensure the new town would receive a post office. During the Civil War, John Breckinridge joined the Confederate Army. Upset Breckinridge residents changed the "i" to "e" spelling the name "Breckenridge." Other stories indicate the town was named after Thomas E. Breckenridge, a member

MilesDirections

0.0 START in the parking lot. ★ 39˚30'33"N 106˚08'30"W—Cross the wooden bridge over West Tenmile Creek, turn right down the paved bike path and in less than 0.1 miles come to a bridge over Tenmile Creek. Veer right and walk across the gravel-topped bridge.

1.0 Reach a trail junction and turn left, heading uphill on the Colorado Trail. ◆ 39˚29'48"N 106˚08'05"W—*[FYI. One trail (along the gas pipeline) goes straight along the creek and the other goes right to CO 91.]*

2.8 Trail junction with Miners Creek Trail. ◆ 39˚28'38"N 106˚06'56"W—Go right on Wheeler Trail.

4.3 Top of Wheeler Pass. ◆ 39˚27'40"N 106˚06'19"W—Return the way you came.

8.6 Arrive back at the trailhead.

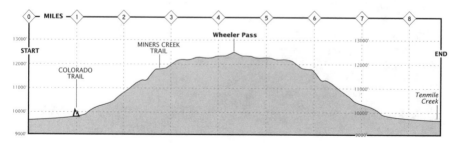

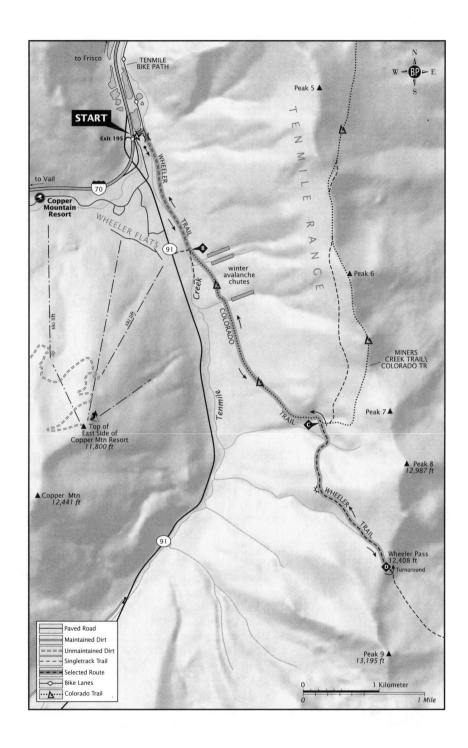

to Frisco

TENMILE
BIKE PATH

Peak 5 ▲

START

Exit 195

to Vail

70

**Copper
Mountain
Resort**

WHEELER FLATS

WHEELER

TRAIL

91

B

winter
avalanche
chutes

COLORADO

Creek

Tenmile

TEN MILE RANGE

Peak 6 ▲

MINERS
CREEK TRAIL\
COLORADO TR

Peak 7 ▲

TRAIL

ski lift

ski lift

▲ Top of
East Side of
Copper Mtn Resort
11,800 ft

▲ Copper Mtn
12,441 ft

▲ Peak 8
12,987 ft

WHEELER

TRAIL

91

Wheeler Pass
12,408 ft
D Turnaround

Peak 9 ▲
13,195 ft

N
W ⊕BP E
S

	Paved Road
	Maintained Dirt
	Unmaintained Dirt
	Singletrack Trail
	Selected Route
	Bike Lanes
	Colorado Trail

0   1 Kilometer

0   1 Mile

of the original mining party. At one time, men panning gold in the Blue River and French Gulch could earn as much as $12 to $20 a day each! Dredge boats came later to scoop up more gold, and mines were burrowed into the hills. The largest gold nugget ever found in Colorado came from this area. At 13 pounds, it was called "Tom's Baby." *(See "The Mystery of Tom's Baby" below.)*

Today both Breckenridge and Copper Mountain Resort are known for their popular ski areas. Ski lifts at each area can be seen from various points along the trail. Skiing, other forms of outdoor recreation, and vacation homes have replaced mining in a new "gold rush" to the Rockies.

The Mystery of Tom's Baby

Tom Groves and Harry Lytton mined the area near Breckenridge known as Farncomb Hill. On July 23, 1887, Tom knocked down a clump of dirt and went to toss it in a dirt pile. The clump seemed heavier than usual, so he opened it with his shovel. Inside was a huge hunk of gold, or more precisely, crystallized gold. The two men ran down to Breckenridge, with Tom cradling the nugget as if it were a baby. Thus the name "Tom's Baby." The little darling weighed in at 160 ounces, which at 12 troy ounces per pound, put it at 13.3 pounds. After washing it off, it still weighed a respectable 136 ounces. From here a mystery developed – what happened to Tom's Baby?

In 1973, Reverend Mark Fiester finished writing a book, Blasted, Beloved Breckenridge. He had spent many hours researching the whereabouts of Tom's Baby. Since the nugget was supposedly Colorado's largest, it would have brought more money from being displayed than being melted. On July 5, 1965, The Denver Post revealed that a phony "Tom's Baby" had been created. Without clues of the whereabouts of the real one, Rev. Fiester suspected it had become part of John Campion's gold collection. Campion was associated with Tom Groves and the mine's owners. Finally, after the book's publication, the Denver Museum of Natural History, which had no record of Tom's Baby, found a box from John Campion's gold collection in their vault. The box contained a large collection of crystallized gold, including a big hunk. Tom's Baby had finally been found!

Hike Information

🗨 Trail Contact:

White River National Forest, Dillon Ranger District, Silverthorne, CO (970) 468–5400

🕐 Schedule:

This trail crosses several avalanche chutes in the winter. It is neither maintained nor marked for winter use. Call for avalanche forecast.

💲 Fees/Permits:

No fees or permits required

❓ Local Information:

Copper Mountain Resort Chamber, Copper Mountain, CO (970) 968–6477 or *www.copperchamber.com* • **Summit County Chamber of Commerce,** Frisco, CO 1–800–530–3099 or *www.summit chamber.org* • **Breckenridge Resort Chamber,** Breckenridge, CO (970) 453–6018 or 1–877–864–0868 or *www.gobreck.com* • **Frisco Chamber of Commerce** website: *www.frisco colorado.com*

💡 Local Events/Attractions:

Country Boy Mine, Breckenridge, CO (970) 453–4405 • **Sunset at the Summit Concert Series** (free), Dillon, CO (970) 262–3400 • **Colorado Barbecue Challenge,** Frisco, CO (970) 668–5276

🛏 Accommodations:

Alpen Hutte (youth hostel), Silverthorne, CO (970) 468–6336 • **National Forest campgrounds,** Dillon Ranger District, Silverthorne, CO (970) 468–5400 • **Summit County Int'l Hostel,** Dillon, CO (970) 468–2886 • **Fireside Inn B&B,** Breckenridge, CO (970) 453–6456

🍴 Restaurants:

Creekside Pizzeria & Deli, Copper Mountain, CO (970) 968–2033 • **Backcountry Brewery,** Frisco, CO (970) 668–2337 • **El Rio Cantina & Grill,** Frisco, CO (970) 668–5043 • **Silverhead at the Ore House,** Frisco, CO (970) 668–0345 • **Ti Amo,** Frisco, CO (970) 668–1993

🕐 Other Resources:

Summit Historical Society, Breckenridge, CO (970) 453–9022 • *Summit A Gold Rush History of Summit County,* Colorado, by Mary Ellen Gilliland, Alpenrose Press • *Echoes of the Past: Copper Mountain,* Colorado, by Janet Marie Clawson, Waldo Litho • *Blasted Beloved Breckenridge,* by Mark Fiester, Pruett Publishing Co. • *Ghosts of Summit County,* by John K. Aldrich, Centennial Graphics • *"The Legend of Tom's Baby,"* by Mark Craddock, Summit Sentinel, May 1, 1987, page 1B

👥 Clubs and Organizations:

Friends of the Eagles Nest Wilderness, Frisco, CO (970) 453–9056

🎒 Local Outdoor Retailers:

Wilderness Sports, Frisco, CO (970) 668–8804 • **Antlers Ski & Sport,** Frisco, CO (970) 668–0248 • **Frisco Mountaineer,** Frisco, CO (970) 668–0889 • **Mountain Outfitters,** Breckenridge, CO (970) 453–2201

Ⓝ Maps:

USGS maps: Breckenridge, Copper Mountain, Vail Pass, CO • *Trails Illustrated®* map: #109 Breckenridge/Tennessee Pass; #108 Vail

16

Hagerman Tunnel Trail

Hike Specs

Start: From the Colorado Midland Centennial Trail parking area

Length: 5.8-mile loop

Approximate Hiking Time: 3–4 hours round trip

Difficulty Rating: Moderate due to length

Elevations: 10,940–11,530 feet

Elevation Gain: 590 feet

Seasons: Best from late June to mid-October

Terrain: Gentle old railroad grade, old wagon road, and steep, narrow hiking trail, sometimes rocky

Land Status: National forest and wilderness area

Nearest Town: Leadville, CO

Other Trail Users: Mountain bikers (on some sections) and hunters (in season)

Canine Compatibility: Leashed dogs permitted

Getting There

From Leadville: Head south on U.S. 24 to mile marker 177 to McWethy Drive/CR 4 (across from the road to Colorado Mountain College). Turn right, drive past the high school, and continue about 3.1 miles staying right to the entrance to Turquoise Lake Recreation Area. Drive another 4.2 miles, across Turquoise Lake Dam to FS 105/Hagerman Pass Road. This dirt road is actually straight ahead as the paved road curves to the right. The road is usually passable by most passenger cars. It has many potholes and is only one car wide in spots. After 3.6 miles there is a large parking area on the right with two trailheads on the left. The closed Carlton Tunnel entrance is near this parking area. The road becomes a little rougher so you may want to park here and walk along the road. You can drive the remaining mile to the little parking area on the right across the road from the Colorado Midland Centennial Trail sign. This sign is fairly large, but is almost hidden by willows. No facilities are available at the trailhead. *DeLorme: Colorado Atlas & Gazetteer:* Page 47 B6

I nadequate and slow transportation often hindered mining operations during mining's heyday through the 1870s and 1880s. Various railway companies staged a battle to provide transportation to remote mines and towns. Steep mountains and curving routes necessitated the use of narrow gauge railways with only three feet between rails. The Colorado Midland Railway (CMR) was incorporated in November 1883 to construct a standard gauge railroad from Colorado Springs through South Park to Leadville and then to Aspen. This railroad would be the first standard gauge (four feet 8.5 inches between rails) to negotiate these mountains. In 1885, James John Hagerman was elected CMR's President. He had moved to Colorado the year before in hopes of recuperating from tuberculosis. While his health was improving, he bought a silver mine near Aspen and valuable coal deposits near Glenwood Springs. He needed transportation more efficient than pack animals and wagons to transport supplies and ore.

CMR chose W. A. Douglass & Co. of Leadville to build 25 miles of rail from Leadville to the mouth of the Roaring Fork and Fryingpan rivers, including a tunnel

under the Continental Divide. Construction on the Hagerman Tunnel, one of railroad engineering's greatest feats, began in mid May 1886. Laborers cut about 100 feet of rock per week, finishing the tunnel bore in June 1887. A 1,084-foot long curving trestle, the longest in Colorado, was another major accomplishment.

The hike starts where the present Hagerman Pass road separates from the old CMR railroad bed. For the first 1.4 miles the trail follows the old railroad, climbing gently from 10,940 feet to about 11,120 feet. Spruce-fir forest dominates this area. Original cinders are still evident along the railbed. Many road cuts and fills were required to keep the railroad grade moving steadily uphill across undulations in the hillside.

After 1.4 miles, the trail switchbacks right to Douglass City. Before turning, continue straight ahead a few yards to where the trestle crossed a gully to the other side. It's an impressive distance even without the trestle. Return to the trail and continue up the switchback. The trail climbs more steeply now, curving left and into a meadow, the former site of Douglass City. Remains of numerous log cabins dot the landscape for the next 0.3 miles. The town housed Italian laborers who toiled on the tunnel and trestles. With eight saloons and a dance hall, the city was noted for its wildness and ladies of the evening. The trail meanders on, through meadows, forest,

Trail approaching Douglass City site.

and past three-foot tall tree stumps. Trees were often cut in winter when moving large logs was easier over snow than over the rough, rocky ground of summer.

The trail swings to the northeast and passes small Opal Lake. On the far end lie the remains of the old steam boiler building. The boiler-powered air compressors provided fresh air to the tunnel and ran drills. A few air pipes remain. From here you can see the railroad grade above and the ridge of the Continental Divide pierced by the tunnel.

The trail climbs steeply to the railroad grade. Turn left and proceed 0.1 miles to the tunnel entrance. Remember: Do not enter old tunnels as they are filled with water and bad air. The snowshed that once protected the tunnel entrance is in ruins, and many boulders have fallen from the sides onto the old railbed. After looking into

MilesDirections

0.0 START at the trailhead to the right of the Colorado Midland Centennial Trail sign. ☆ 39°15'34"N 106°27'32"W—Walk along the old railroad grade. *[FYI. The first part may have some running water on it.]*

1.2 The Carlton Tunnel entrance is 240 feet below to the left. Cross a little creek.

1.4 The trail switchbacks to the right off of the railroad grade. ❸ 39°14'49"N 106°28'34"W—Turn here after looking at the expanse that the curved trestle crossed. The old trestle site is just ahead.

1.6 The trail crosses the old railroad grade. ❹ 39°14'59"N 106°28'28"W—This intersection is the start of the loop part of the hike. You'll return via the railroad grade on your right. Follow the trail sign ahead of you.

1.7 Reach the site of Douglass City.

2.0 Arrive at Opal Lake and the old steam boiler building ruins.

2.2 Reach the railroad grade and turn left.

2.3 Reach the Hagerman Tunnel. ❶ 39°15'08"N 106°29'00"W—*[Option. From here you can reverse directions for a 4.6-mile out-and-back hike.]* Continue back along the old railroad grade as follows.

2.4 On the return, the trail you ascended to the old railroad grade is on your right. For a shorter trip, return the way you came. To hike the loop, continue straight ahead on the old railroad grade.

3.1 Hagerman Lake and remains of old snowshed. ❺ 39°15'31"N 106°28'10"W

3.3 Come to another trestle site.

3.9 Roger's Spur forks off to the left. Continue straight on the old railroad grade.

4.2 Turn left onto trail that you came up on from the old railroad grade. Return the way you came.

4.4 Turn left onto railbed.

5.8 Arrive back at the trailhead. *[Please note. The USFS lists this hike as 5.5 miles, but I get roughly 5.8 by pedometer and map measurer.]*

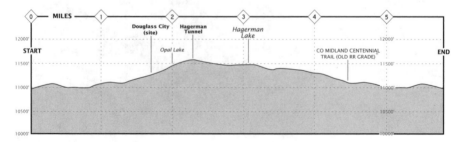

the tunnel and enjoying the views, continue back along the railbed instead of returning to Opal Lake. Before the first rock outcropping, notice the wooden remains of snowsheds down to the right. At 3.1 miles, you arrive at Hagerman Lake. Just past the lake in a rock cut are some huge timbers from a snowshed. Scramble over these noticing the square spikes and jointed wood. When you come into the open again, the railbed comes to another trestle location. Either drop gently to the right or walk to the edge and down the steeper area. Hike up the other side to the railbed. At another rock cut, the railbed splits. Stay to the right. The left branch is Roger's Spur, part of the original railway plan that was abandoned. At 4.2 miles, drop off another trestle location, cross the creek, and arrive back at the singletrack trail you came up. Turn left and return to the railbed near the curved trestle location. Turn left again returning to the trailhead.

The Hagerman Tunnel was only used from August 30, 1887 to December 13, 1893, and then again from October 31, 1897 to June 20, 1899. The "high line" proved too costly to maintain and keep free of snow. The Carlton Tunnel, the entrance to which you passed a mile below the trailhead, replaced the Hagerman Tunnel. By July 1900, the Hagerman "high line" had been dismantled.

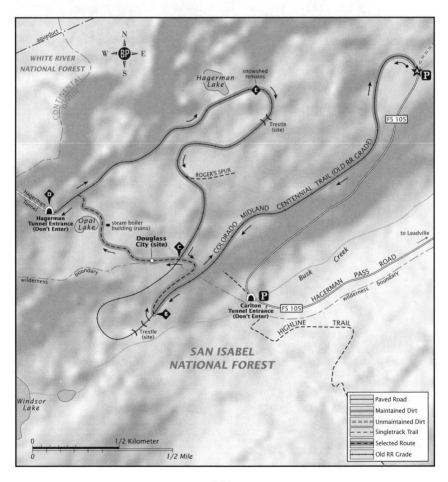

Old Colorado Midland Railroad Grade
(trail to Hagerman Tunnel).

Hagerman Tunnel east entrance.

Hike Information

☎ Trail Contact:
San Isabel National Forest, Leadville Ranger District, Leadville, CO (719) 486–0749 or *www.fs.fed.us/r2/psicc*

⏱ Schedule:
Open year round, but best from July to September

$ Fees/Permits:
No fees or permits required

❓ Local Information:
Leadville/Lake County Chamber of Commerce, Leadville, CO 1–800–933–3901 or (719) 486–3900 or *www.leadvilleusa.com*

📍 Local Events/Attractions:
Healy House & Dexter Cabin, Leadville, CO (719) 486–0487 • **Heritage Museum & Gallery,** Leadville, CO (719) 486–1878 • **Leadville, Colorado and Southern Railroad Company,** Leadville, CO (719) 486–3936 or *www.leadville-train.com* • **Matchless Mine** (Baby Doe Tabor Museum), Leadville, CO (719) 486–3900 • **National Mining Hall of Fame & Museum,** Leadville, CO (719) 486–1229 • **Tabor Opera House,** Leadville, CO (719) 486–8409

🛏 Accommodations:
The Delaware Hotel, Leadville, CO (719) 486–1418 or 1–800–748–2004 or *www.DelawareHotel.com* • **Leadville Hostel & Inn,** Leadville, CO (719) 486–9334 or *www.leadvillehostel.com* • **National forest campgrounds,** San Isabel National Forest, Leadville Ranger District, Leadville, CO (719) 486–0749

🍴 Restaurants:
Golden Burro Café & Lounge, Leadville, CO (719) 486–1239 • **The Grill Bar & Café,** Leadville, CO (719) 486–9930 – Mexican • **Quincy's Steak & Spirits,** Leadville, CO (719) 486–9765 • **Wild Bill's Hamburgers & Ice Cream,** Leadville, CO (719) 486–0533

📖 Other Resources:
The Book Mine, Leadville, CO (719) 486–2866 • *Colorado Midland Railway,* by Dan Abbott, Sundance Publications, Ltd.

👥 Clubs and Organizations:
Colorado Mountain College, Timberline Campus, Leadville, CO (719) 486–2015

🥾 Hike Tours:
About Wilderness, Inc., Silverthorne, CO 1–888–810–7249 or (970) 468–6219 – *women's backpacking trips on the Colorado Trail* • **Colorado Outward Bound,** Leadville, CO (719) 486–2052 • **Paragon Guides,** Vail, CO 1–877–926–5299 or (970) 926–5299 or *www.paragonguides.com – llama trekking*

🚴 Local Outdoor Retailers:
Buckhorn Sporting Goods, Leadville, CO (719) 486–3944 • **Bill's Sports Shop,** Leadville, CO (719) 486–0739

Ⓝ Maps:
USGS map: Mount Massive, CO; Homestake Reservoir, CO • *Trails Illustrated®* map: #127, Aspen/Independence Pass; #126, Holy Cross/Ruedi Reservoir

Mount Elbert (North)

Hike Specs

Start: From the Mount Elbert trailhead near Elbert Creek Campground

Length: 8.4-mile out-and-back

Approximate Hiking Time: 6–10 hours

Difficulty Rating: Strenuous because of steepness and elevation

Elevations: 10,040–14,433 feet

Elevation Gain: 4,393 feet

Seasons: Best from July through September

Terrain: Dirt trail, mostly steep, rocky in a few areas

Land Status: National forest

Nearest Town: Leadville, CO

Other Trail Users: Colorado Trail section only: equestrians, mountain bikers, and hunters (in season)

Canine Compatibility: Controlled dogs permitted

Getting There

From Leadville: Drive south out of Leadville on U.S. 24 (Harrison Avenue in Leadville) about four miles. Turn right onto CO 300, a well-marked road (just past a big left curve) with signs to Halfmoon Campground. In 0.7 miles, turn left onto CR 11 that again is well-signed to Halfmoon. In another 1.3 miles, turn right onto dirt FS 110. Continue on for about 5.1 miles to the Mount Elbert trailhead parking lot on the left. The trailhead is 0.1 miles off of FS 110. The dirt road is less than two cars wide, so be watchful for oncoming cars, especially around curves. It's passable by most vehicles, the worst problems being a few potholes and washboard sections. Some dispersed camping is available along the road (please camp at least 100 feet away from roads and streams to help with restoration efforts). Halfmoon and Elbert Creek Campgrounds are also nearby. A vault toilet but no water at the trailhead. Make sure to bring a lot of water with you. **DeLorme: Colorado Atlas & Gazetteer:** Page 47 C6

When first seeing Mount Elbert from afar, you might wonder about its *highest in Colorado* status. Looming above the Arkansas Valley that already lies at 10,000 feet, the elevation gain does not seem dramatic. North of Mount Elbert across Halfmoon Creek, the aptly named Mount Massive (14,421 feet) stands a mere 12 feet lower. Mount Elbert's long, smooth ridges make it a good first Fourteener to climb. The magnificent views are reason enough to return.

French Mountain, Casco Peak, and Frasco form the foreground for summits to the west. Five of Colorado's Fourteeners pierce the western sky: Capitol Peak (14,130 feet) with its distinctive knife edge ridge, white-faced Snowmass Mountain (14,092 feet), Maroon Bells (Maroon Peak (14,156 feet) and North Maroon Peak (14,014 feet)), and Pyramid Peak (14,018 feet). To the south lies La Plata Peak (14,336 feet) in the Sawatch Range. To the north, Mount Massive, Mount of the Holy Cross (14,005 feet), and Notch Mountain (13,237 feet) dominate with the Gore Range in the distance. The mighty Mosquito Range that made Leadville a mining center rises to the east. You can see all the way to Pikes Peak (14,110 feet)

and the Sangre de Cristo Range. Down below lie the South Halfmoon and Arkansas valleys and Twin Lakes.

When the current Rockies arose from the earth about 65 million years ago, mineral-rich liquid oozed into faults and cracks in the stressed rock. As the liquid cooled, rich ores formed. The Leadville area, located at the north end of the Arkansas Valley, has produced over $500 million in silver, lead, zinc, gold, and other minerals. The Arkansas Valley is actually part of the Rio Grande Rift, a slice of land that stayed in place when the rest of Colorado rose about 5,000 feet around 28–5 million years ago. Glaciers later formed the cirque on Elbert's east side while glacial moraines dammed Lake

The Colorado Fourteeners Initiative (CFI) started in 1994 when people realized the damage being caused by the alarming popularity of climbing Colorado's Fourteeners. An estimated 200,000 people climb Fourteeners annually, a 300 percent increase in 10 years! CFI forms partnerships with land agencies, hiking groups, and sponsoring companies to protect and preserve both natural and recreational resources. Volunteers are greatly appreciated!

Mount Elbert summit (14,433 feet).

Creek creating Twin Lakes. Mount Elbert itself is formed of 1.7 billion year old rock of gneiss and schist.

Mount Elbert stood guardian as Leadville boomed first with gold, then with silver. In 1860, Abe Lee hit the first major gold strike. In 1874, as the gold dwindled, miners extracted silver-rich lead carbonate. The silver rush started, turning Leadville and surroundings into a large city, second to Denver. Enjoying prosperity, Leadville built a magnificent ice palace during the winter of 1896. It covered over three acres with two 90-foot Norman towers. Inside lighted dining rooms and an ice rink provided hours of entertainment. Ice sculptures of miners and prospectors decorated the palace.

The Hayden Survey of 1874 recorded the first ascent of Mount Elbert. The peak was named after Samuel Hitt Elbert. Elbert first held the position of territorial secretary until the governor seized the state seal from him. Elbert resigned and left Colorado in 1866 only to return in 1873 as territorial governor. He held this post for one year before being appointed to the Colorado Supreme Court. Elbert was instrumental in formulating visionary conservation and irrigation concepts.

Hiking Mount Elbert is invariably an adventure. Snow falls at any time of year and the temperature seldom exceeds 50°F. The wind always seems to blow. Plan ahead and be prepared for adverse conditions. Weekends find the trail filled with people. Yet there is nothing like standing at the top of Colorado, beholding an endless horizon of

MilesDirections

0.0 START at Mount Elbert trailhead near Elbert Creek Campground. ★ 39°09'06"N 106°24'43"W

0.1 Reach the junction where the trail from parking lot joins the Colorado Trail. Take the left branch "to climb Mount Elbert."

0.6 Reach the top of a little ridge and descend slightly.

0.9 Reach the junction of the Colorado Trail and the North Mount Elbert Trail. ● 39°08'39"N 106°24'28"W—Take the right fork.

1.9 Reach the northeast ridge.

2.4 Reach the treeline. ● 39°07'59"N 106°25'31"W

3.7 Come to a false summit. ● 39°07'20"N 106°26'21"W Two smaller false summits to go.

4.2 You're on top! ● 39°07'04"N 106°26'41"W —Return the way you came.

8.4 Arrive back at the trailhead.

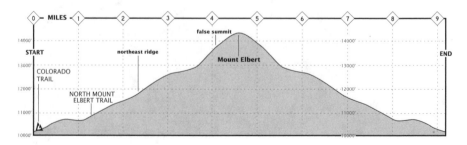

mountains. The first section follows part of the Colorado Trail, which traverses almost 500 miles of the state. About 0.9 miles into the hike you come to a juncture. Turn right onto the North Mount Elbert Trail.

In the next trail section small groups of skinny lodgepole pines stand right in the middle of the trail, reminiscent of pictures with ski tracks each going on opposite sides of a tree. From here, the trail climbs steeply to a ridge. The U.S. Forest Service rerouted this section in 1992, a great improvement over the old trail. Along the ridge, a glimpse of the top comes to view. But it's really a false summit at about 13,880 feet—the real summit rises 550 feet higher.

Once above treeline around 11,900 feet, the trail climbs through beautiful alpine tundra. The tiny plants are extremely fragile, so please stay on the trail. Yellow alpine avens, old-man-of-the-mountain with its large sunflower head, various paintbrushes, and blue-purple sky pilot brighten the surroundings. If stopping for a break here, watch out for marmots who might try to swipe your snack. The trail is steepest along the right side of the false summit. Loose rocks and some big rock steps make this sec-

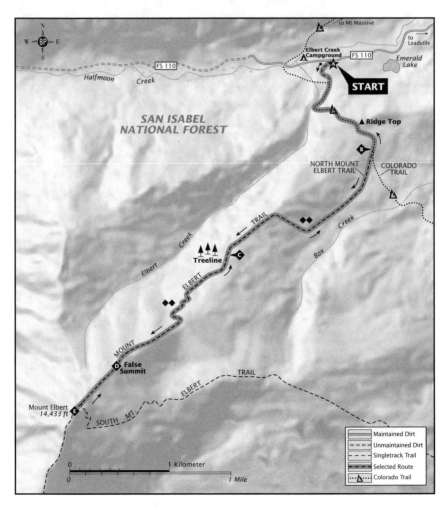

Mount Elbert from U.S. Highway 24.

Tips for Climbing 14,000-Foot Peaks in Colorado

The first and foremost rule is to leave early enough to reach the summit and return to treeline before thunderstorms and lightning start. Thunderstorms can build quickly as the day warms. A good rule of thumb is to summit by 11 A.M. and head back by noon. If the weather looks iffy at any time, turn back. The peak will be there another day. Know your party's abilities and plan accordingly. One mile per hour or less is not an unreasonable estimate.

Hiking Fourteeners takes energy. In the cool, dry air, your body loses moisture from breathing and sweating. Drink a few mouthfuls of water every 15 minutes or so to keep your body hydrated. Eating small amounts of food while drinking will keep your body fueled. A hydrated body also helps ward off altitude sickness indicated by headache, nausea, and/or dizziness. Moving to a lower altitude cures the problem.

Bring layers of non-cotton clothes for wind, cold, and wet. Bring a winter hat—as much as 50 percent of one's body heat can be lost through the top of the head. Pack a pair of gloves, too. Wear appropriate boots for the terrain. Snow and hail are common, and the winds usually blow above treeline. Cherish any summit with sun and no wind!

Carry topo maps and a compass and know how to use them. A GPS could be useful. Every year hikers need to be rescued because they lose their way coming down.

Tread lightly in high elevations. Fragile plants are critical to the land. Do not litter – a piece of trash covering a plant can kill it in a few weeks! Check the Colorado Fourteener Initiative website for additional guidelines when traveling in the "land above the trees." Your actions, compounded by those of thousands of other visitors, determine the health of our natural environment.

tion challenging. After this part, the trail becomes gentler. The summit lies beyond the next rock hump. The last 0.1 miles crosses a somewhat skinny ridge where the wind can blast with fury. Finally the summit appears, complete with short rock walls to shelter hikers from the winds. Remember to sign the peak register. Enjoy the view and the top of Colorado!

Hike Information

Trail Contacts:
San Isabel National Forest, Leadville Ranger District, Leadville, CO (719) 486–0749 or *www.fs.fed.us/r2/psicc* • **Colorado Trail Section: Colorado Trail Foundation,** Golden, CO (303) 384–3729, ext. 113 or *www.coloradotrail.org*

Schedule:
Open year round. Access road closed by snow in winter about 4.8 miles from the trailhead. Trail neither marked or maintained for winter use. Winds can blow over 100 mph above treeline.

Fees/Permits:
Groups of 10 or more people must get a permit from the Forest Service in Leadville before the trip.

Local Information:
(See Hike 16: Hagerman Tunnel.)

Local Events/Attractions:
(See Hike 16: Hagerman Tunnel.)

Accommodations:
(See Hike 16: Hagerman Tunnel.)

Restaurants:
(See Hike 16: Hagerman Tunnel.)

Other Resources:
The Book Mine, Leadville, CO (719) 486–2866 • *A Climbing Guide to Colorado's Fourteeners,* by Walter R.

Borneman and Lyndon J. Lampert, Pruett Publishing Co. • *Guide to the Colorado Mountains,* by Robert M. Ormes, Cordillera Press, Inc. • *Roadside History of Colorado,* by James McTighe, Johnson Publishing Co. • *Roadside Geology of Colorado,* by Halka Chronic, Mountain Press Publishing Co. • *Leadville, Colorado's Magic City,* by Edward Blair, Pruett Publishing Co.

Clubs and Organizations:
Colorado Mountain College, Timberline Campus, Leadville, CO (719) 486–2015 • **Colorado Fourteeners Initiative,** Golden, CO (303) 278–7525 ext. 115 or *www.coloradofourteeners.org* • **Colorado Trail Foundation,** Golden, CO (303) 384–3729, ext. 113 or *www.coloradotrail.org*

Hike Tours:
None up Mount Elbert

Local Outdoor Retailers:
(See Hike 16: Hagerman Tunnel.)

Maps:
USGS maps: Mount Elbert, CO; Mount Massive, CO • **USFS maps:** San Isabel National Forest map • *Trails Illustrated®* map: #127 Aspen/Independence Pass

18

Notch Mountain

Hike Specs

Start: From the Fall Creek Trail trailhead
Length: 10.8-mile out-and-back
Approximate Hiking Time: 5–7 hours
Difficulty Rating: Most difficult due to length and elevation gain
Elevations: 10,320–13,100 feet
Elevation Gain: 2,780 feet
Seasons: Best from late June to mid-October
Terrain: Dirt trail, rocky in spots
Land Status: National forest and wilderness area
Nearest Towns: Minturn, CO, and Vail, CO
Other Trail Users: Equestrians (Fall Creek Trail section) and hunters (in season)
Canine Compatibility: Leashed dogs permitted

Getting There

From Minturn: Drive south on U.S. 24 toward Leadville about three miles (5.1 miles from the junction of I-70 and U.S. 24). Just past mile marker 48, turn right onto Tigiwon Road. This road provides National Forest access. Drive 8.4 miles up this dirt road to the trailhead. The dirt road is extremely bumpy with rocks and potholes. One section, just past the Tigiwon Community House and Campground, has some big rocks. Most passenger cars can make the trip with care. The road is narrow, so be careful when rounding curves. The parking lot gets crowded early as the trailhead for Mount of the Holy Cross is also here. There are no facilities at the trailhead. The small campground near the trailhead is for people climbing Mount of the Holy Cross. *DeLorme: Colorado Atlas & Gazetteer:* Page 47 A6

I n the 1800s various stories about a mountain with a "snowy cross" circulated around Colorado. In 1869, William H. Brewer reported seeing Mount of the Holy Cross (14,005 feet) from the summit of Grays Peak (14,269 feet). As part of the Hayden Survey in the 1870s, William Henry Jackson photographed various areas of Colorado. The Hayden Survey was one of four great surveys of the West sponsored by the U.S. government between 1867 and 1878. From 1873 to 1875, leader Ferdinand V. Hayden concentrated on Colorado.

The 1873 Survey set a goal to find this mysterious peak. Jackson climbed Grays Peak and also spotted the cross from the summit. By August the survey group arrived near present day Minturn. For three days they attempted in vain to find a route on Notch Mountain (13,237 feet) from which to view and photograph the "cross." Fallen trees and thick willows made the going too rough for pack animals, and the group ended up carrying Jackson's 100 pounds of photographic gear on foot. Jackson used a wet glass plate camera. Not only was the "film" made of glass, which had to be handled carefully, but also it needed to be developed soon after exposure. Jackson carried a portable darkroom tent with all necessary chemicals and supplies with him. Finally finding an approach, the still difficult hike took two days with little food and no shelter. (They thought they could do it in one day.) Finally atop Notch Mountain, fog decreased visibility to a few feet. Luckily, the fog broke briefly, giving Jackson a glimpse of the infamous cross across the valley. The next morning dawned clear and

still giving him a beautiful shot of the cross. He took several pictures, which caused a sensation across the country as people believed the snow-filled cross to be a sign from God.

The devout began to make annual pilgrimages to Mount of the Holy Cross in 1927. The U.S. Forest Service (USFS) issued a special use permit in 1928 to Mount of the Holy Cross Pilgrimage Association allowing the construction and maintenance of community houses and a semi-public campground. President Herbert Hoover proclaimed 1,392 acres around Mount of the Holy Cross as a National Monument in 1929. Survey crews laid out an automobile route from U.S. Route 24 to Tigiwon, and with help from citizens, Eagle County government, and F. G. Bonfils, a road was completed to Tigiwon in 1932.

The Civilian Conservation Corps (CCC) improved the road in 1933, extending it to the

Keeping dogs leashed on the trail benefits you, your pet, other visitors, and wildlife. Dogs will surely come out the loser in a bout with the porcupines and mountain lions that live in these areas. Bears have also been known to chase dogs back to their owners. Freely roaming dogs can cause serious damage to delicate ecosystems. A leashed dog can also help you become more aware of wildlife as dogs can easily detect smells and movement that would go unnoticed by humans.

Mount of the Holy Cross and Notch Mountain shelter.

present trailhead. The CCC also constructed the Notch Mountain Trail, the large community house at Tigiwon, and the stone shelter on Notch Mountain. The present Notch Mountain Trail with its many switchbacks stands as testimony to the excellent work done by the CCC. This trail was originally used by packhorses as well as hikers. Pilgrimages ceased in the early 1940s, presumably because of World War II. The U.S. Army actually controlled much of this area between 1938 and 1950. Nearby Camp Hale was a training ground for the famous 10th Mountain Division troops.

The cross is created by a 1,500-foot vertical gully and a 750-foot horizontal rock bench on the mountain's eastern face. Collected snow causes the formation to stand out against the mountainside. The right arm deteriorated due to rockslides, and access remained difficult even after the CCC's work. In 1950, President Harry Truman retracted national monument status and returned the land to the USFS. Even slightly damaged, a cross of snow still forms. The Tigiwon Community House, after years of disrepair, has been mostly restored and is occasionally used for weddings. The

MilesDirections

0.0 START at the Fall Creek Trail trailhead (versus the Half Moon Trail trailhead). ☆ 39˚30'02"N 106˚25'57"W—Cross a creek on a bridge and take the right fork in the trail (head south).

1.4 The trail traverses a landslide area.

1.5 Cross a wide creek on boulders. ❸ 39˚28'52"N 106˚26'17"W—*[**Note.** The crossing may be easier or harder depending on water volume. Be careful.]*

2.4 Reach the trail intersection with Notch Mountain Trail. ❸ 39˚28'15"N 106˚26'28"W—This is a good place for a break. Turn right onto the Notch Mountain Trail.

3.2 *[**FYI.** Look on the left for a stick figure with human decorations, locally called the Praying Man. It sometimes changes or falls over, so don't always expect it to be there.]*

3.5 Start to enter the land above the trees.

*[**Note.** Turn back if thunderstorms are imminent.]*

4.2 Switchbacks increase in number up to the ridge. Depending on where you start counting, you'll zigzag up 27 switchbacks in 780 feet. *[**FYI.** Please do not shortcut the switchbacks. Shortcutting causes environmental damage and erosion that does not heal quickly at this elevation. Also, don't attempt this trail during whiteouts or low visibility. If you miss any of four particular switchbacks, you'll be freefalling over a cliff.]*

5.4 Reach a stone shelter on Notch Mountain with a breathtaking view of Mount of the Holy Cross. ❹ 39˚28'10"N 106˚27'31"W—*[**Note.** The shelter is meant for protection from lightning–no overnight camping allowed.]* Return the way you came.

10.8 Arrive back at the trailhead.

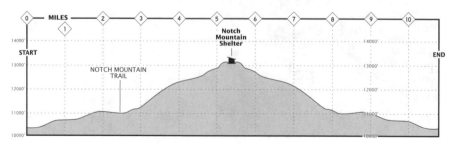

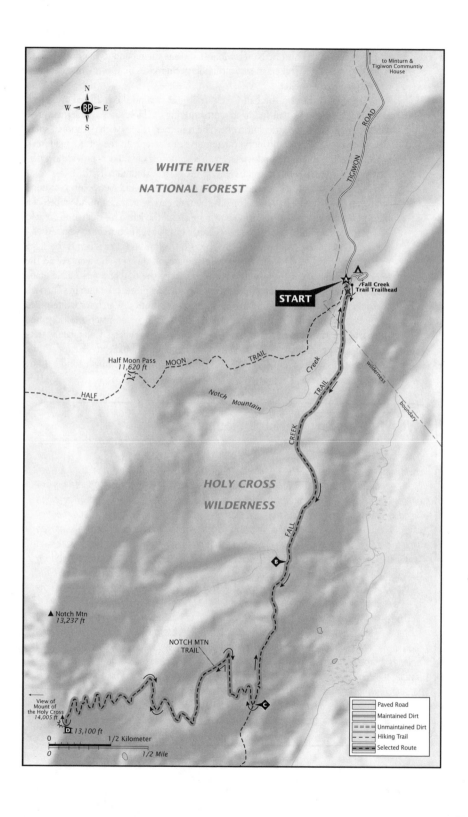

to Minturn &
Tigiwon Communtiy
House

N
W ᴮᴾ E
S

WHITE RIVER

NATIONAL FOREST

TIGIWON ROAD

Fall Creek
Trail Trailhead

START

Half Moon Pass
11,620 ft

MOON   TRAIL

HALF

Notch Mountain

Creek

Wilderness

Boundary

CREEK   TRAIL

HOLY CROSS

WILDERNESS

FALL

B

▲ Notch Mtn
13,237 ft

NOTCH MTN
TRAIL

C

View of
Mount of
the Holy Cross
14,005 ft

D 13,100 ft

0   1/2 Kilometer

0   1/2 Mile

| Paved Road |
| Maintained Dirt |
| Unmaintained Dirt |
| Hiking Trail |
| Selected Route |

USFS maintains the historic Notch Mountain stone shelter and its lightning rods to provide protection for hikers in case a thunderstorm moves in. Overnight camping is not allowed in the shelter.

Make sure to start on the Fall Creek Trail. Just beyond the trailhead and creek crossing, take the right trail and head south entering the Holy Cross Wilderness area. The first mile is fairly gentle, but rocky. The trail then climbs with occasional small elevation drops. Continuing along the terrain drops steeply to the left to Fall Creek below. After 2.4 miles the trail widens with a scattering of boulders providing a perfect spot for a break before turning right up the Notch Mountain Trail.

From the rest spot, it's another 3.0 miles to the shelter and viewpoint. Not quite a mile up the Notch Mountain Trail, as the trail curves around a meadow below a hillside, keep your eyes open for the praying man on the left. This human-decorated stick has been around a while, but may change or fall over from year to year. After a few switchbacks, the trail begins to pass through treeline and zigzags across the slope to the summit. Over 27 switchbacks help you ascend the last 780 feet. Avoid the temptation to shortcut the switchbacks as they keep the trail at a reasonable grade (which makes for easier hiking in the thinning air) and protect the terrain. Through this area marmots and pikas zip around with amusing antics. Watch for white-tailed ptarmigan moms followed by a line of little chicks. Once you reach the ridge and stone shelter, Mount of the Holy Cross looms large directly ahead. Camp below treeline. The alpine wildflowers grow thick and beautiful in July and early August. White arctic gentians signal summer's end. Please walk carefully on the fragile tundra, using rocks for steps as much as possible.

Wildlife Watching on Notch Mountain

Notch Mountain is a good area to see alpine animals and birds, particularly marmots, pikas, and white-tailed ptarmigan.

In summer ptarmigan blend in perfectly with the mottled rocks, making them hard to see. Members of the grouse family, the males live in the alpine all year. Ptarmigan mate for life, although after breeding the couple goes their separate ways until the next spring. Ptarmigan blend in so well, it's possible to almost step on one before noticing it's there. In summer tiny chicks line up to follow around after mom. When threatened the mother will fake a broken wing to draw predators away from her offspring. In winter ptarmigan plumage turns white with feet and legs heavily feathered for warmth and flotation on the snow. Willows, which produce next year's buds in the fall, provide food for ptarmigan during long, cold winters. The birds might dive into a snowdrift, especially around willows, to stay warm on cold nights—a ptarmigan version of an igloo. Look for piles of ptarmigan droppings near willows while hiking.

The pika lives in the alpine and subalpine year round living in rock piles. Active during winter as well as summer, it eats hay piles it busily collects during the summer. The pika alert reverberates through the rocks. The small mouse-like creature with the short tail belongs to the rabbit order. Look closely or you might miss the busy critter as it scurries among the rocks. A mouthful of grass and flowers whizzes by as the pika stores its hay. Researchers have discovered that pikas will steal each other's piles. Watch for big white splotches on boulders along the trail. The splotches indicate pika restrooms. Bright orange lichen often grows near the splotches, energized by the nitrogen rich fertilizer.

Hike Information

Trail Contact:

White River National Forest, Holy Cross Ranger District, Minturn, CO (970) 827–5715 or *www.fs.fed.us/r2/white river*

Schedule:

Open year round. Access road closed by snow about 7.5 miles from the trailhead. Road used by snowmobilers and cross-country skiers. Trail neither maintained nor marked for winter use.

Fees/Permits:

No fees required. Group size limited to a combination of 25 people and stock. As this book goes to print, the White River National Forest Plan is undergoing revision. Group sizes and other regulations may change in this process.

Local Information:

Vail Valley Tourism & Convention Bureau, Vail, CO 1–800–525–3875 or *www.visitvailvalley.com* • **The Chamber of Commerce,** Avon, CO (970) 949–5189 or *www.vailvalleychamber.com*

Local Events/Attractions:

Camp Hale, between Leadville and Minturn, CO (970) 527–8715 or *www.camphale.org – WWII training ground of the 10th Mountain Division troops* • **Bravo! Vail Valley Music Festival,** Vail, CO (970) 827–5700 or *www.vailmusicfestival.org* • **Top of the Rockies Scenic and Historic Byway,** Holy Cross Ranger District, Minturn, CO (970) 827–5715

Accommodations:

National Forest campgrounds, Holy Cross Ranger District, Minturn, CO (970) 827–5715

Restaurants:

The Turntable Restaurant, Minturn, CO (970) 827–4164 • **Poppyseeds,** Vail, CO (970) 476–5297

Other Resources:

Holy Cross – The Mountain and the City, by Robert L. Brown, The Caxton Printers, Ltd. • **Roadside History of Colorado,** by James McTighe, Johnson Publishing Co. • **From Grassland to Glacier,** by Cornelia Fleischer Mutel and John C. Emerick, Johnson Books • **Land Above the Trees A Guide to American Alpine Tundra,** by Ann H. Zwinger and Beatrice E. Willard, Johnson Books

Clubs and Organizations:

Colorado Mountain Club – Gore Range Group, Avon, CO – *Call the state offices at (303) 279–3080 or 1–800–633–4417 (Colorado only) for current contact information or visit www.cmc.org.*

Hike Tours:

Trailwise Guides, Red Cliff, CO (970) 827–5363 or 1–800–261–5364 or *www.trailwiseguides.com* • **Paragon Guides,** Vail, CO (970) 926–5229 or 1–877–926–5299 or *www.paragonguides.com*

Local Outdoor Retailers:

Gore Range Mountainworks, Vail, CO (970) 476–7625 or (970) 476–4223 • **Mountain Quest Sports,** Edwards, CO (970) 926–3867 • **Ptarmigan Sports,** Edwards, CO (970) 926–8144

Maps:

USGS maps: Mount of the Holy Cross, CO; Minturn, CO • **Trails Illustrated®** map: #126 Holy Cross/Ruedi Reservoir

19 Mount Thomas Trail

Hike Specs

Start: From the top of Crooked Creek Pass

Length: 9.4-mile out-and-back

Approximate Hiking Time: 4–7 hours

Difficulty Rating: Difficult due to elevation gain and distance

Elevations: 10,000–11,977 feet

Elevation Gain: 1,977 feet

Seasons: Best of late June to mid-October

Terrain: Dirt road and dirt trail with some steep sections and a boulder field

Land Status: National forest

Nearest Town: Eagle, CO

Other Trail Users: Dirt bikers, equestrians, mountain bikers, hunters in season

Canine Compatibility: Dogs permitted (must be under control)

Getting There

From Eagle: From I-70 (Exit 147), head south about 0.3 miles to U.S. 6 and turn right. Drive 0.2 miles and turn left onto Broadway at the Central Business District and Sylvan Lake sign. In 0.2 miles turn left onto Fifth Street, then in 0.1 miles turn right onto Capital. You're now on CR 307 that goes up Brush Creek. When in doubt on turns, follow the Sylvan Lake signs. CR 307 becomes FS 400. After turning onto Capital in Eagle, drive about 10.1 miles to the fork in the road. Take the right branch, again to Sylvan Lake. Drive another 10 miles, staying on FS 400 past Sylvan Lake State Park, to the top of Crooked Creek Pass. Park in the dirt area to the right. There are no facilities or water available. With a 4WD, you can drive another 0.7 miles to the actual trailhead, but there is very limited parking under the power lines. *DeLorme: Colorado Atlas & Gazetteer:* Page 47 A4

Mount Thomas (11,977 feet) was named after the head of the St. Louis & Colorado Smelting Company. Thomas (the rest of his name apparently lost to history) started a smelter along the Colorado Midland Railroad in the Fryingpan Valley around 1890. The town that grew nearby, Thomasville, also bears his name. He became involved in some mining ventures north of town in the Lime Creek drainage. He did not have much luck—the mines produced little ore and his unprofitable smelter closed in 1892. A little peak on the ridge between Lime and Brush creeks commemorates his involvement in the area. The ridge itself is known as Red Table Mountain.

Grassy meadows provide good grazing for cattle in the Lime Creek drainage. When settlers arrived in Colorado in the late 1800s, cattle and sheep grazed freely on public lands. Ranchers and sheepherders ran as much stock as possible damaging many acres across the West from overgrazing. The Taylor Grazing Act of 1934 created grazing districts to minimize the degradation of public lands. Today the U.S. Forest Service (USFS) grants grazing permits on the lands under its management. A rancher may hold several grazing allotments in an area. With guidance from the USFS, the rancher moves his herd at designated times rotating cattle to different areas. Rotation has several benefits. The cattle continue to have fresh grass to eat. The grass in any

Elk Mountains from Mount Thomas Trail.

given area is not totally consumed and has time to recover and stay healthy. Fences help keep cattle in designated areas. The rancher holding the grazing allotments is responsible for maintaining the fences. In the Lime Creek area, "lay down" fences are common. After the cattle leave the high country in the fall, the rancher lets the fences down. This practice prevents snow damage. In spring trees downed by winter snows and winds are removed from the fence line, the fences are set up again, and cattle are brought back to the grassy slopes. The rancher also helps maintain the hiking and other trails, which his cattle use.

MilesDirections

0.0 START at the top of Crooked Creek Pass. ☆ 39˚26'28"N 106˚41'04"W

0.4 Reach the junction with FS 431. Follow the road to the left.

0.6 The Mount Thomas Trail (Trail 1870) trailhead is up the road to the right under some power lines. ◆ 39˚26'11"N 106˚40'59"W—Walk up the road to a somewhat flat area and look to the left for the trail. Follow what looks like a road to the power pole but turns into a singletrack there.

1.0 The trail enters a meadow. *[FYI. Beautiful views of Lime Creek drainage.]*

1.6 The trail starts to switchback up the ridge.

2.0 *[FYI. Great views into Brush Creek to Eagle and Sylvan Lake.]*

2.2 The trail crosses some meadows. Cairns mark the trail.

2.8 Encounter a steep climb up a ridge section. Red boulder fields lie on both sides of the trail.

3.1 The trail is now above treeline. The trail is fairly easy to find, and is marked by cairns.

3.3 The trail crosses a hump on Red Table Mountain and descends a little from here. ◆ 39˚25'29"N 106˚43'20"W—*[FYI. Awesome views of the Maroon Bells to the southwest.]*

3.9 The trail leaves the ridge to traverse along the south side through a boulder field.

4.6 Ascend to a ridge and turn right up the ridge to the summit of Mount Thomas. There's no trail, but there are some open areas between the krummholz (stunted trees) to walk on. Continue up a boulder field to the top.

4.7 Reach Mount Thomas summit. ◆ 39˚25'11"N 106˚44'35"W—Return the way you came.

9.4 Arrive back at the trailhead.

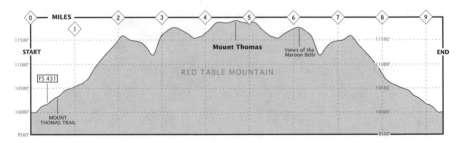

During the hike, you may come across herds of cattle. They will not bother you and will just move up or off the trail as you approach. Please restrain dogs and do not harass the herd.

From Crooked Creek Pass the hike follows a 4WD road, climbing steadily up to the trailhead located under some power lines. The trailhead is not marked, so follow the cues carefully. A deep thick spruce-fir forest surrounds the trail creating a dark primeval atmosphere where the appearance of elves and gnomes would hardly be surprising. Slip past the forest spirits into an open meadow with an airy view of the Lime Creek drainage. The trail winds between small stands of conifers and open, flower covered meadows.

The trail continues up to a ridge and follows the north side. Below, the town of Eagle sits in the distance with Sylvan Lake in the foreground. Catch a breather in this level area through the trees before negotiating an interesting skinny ridge. Red boulder fields drape the ridge to the north and south. The trail is tricky here with a slippery climb up the next ridge. As the trail enters open meadow at treeline, the views are incredible. Maroon Bells (Maroon Peak and North Maroon Peak), Pyramid, Snowmass, and Capitol rear their 14,000-foot heads to the southwest.

The trail traverses below the ridge to the south side. After attaining the ridge again, turn right and hike to the red rock Mount Thomas summit. The rocks are the Maroon formation, the same rocks that comprise the famous Maroon Bells near Aspen. This formation eroded from the ancestral Rockies in western Colorado. As sediments were buried by streams, a rust-like stain formed creating the red color. There is no official trail to the top, but it's easy to find the way. Views in every direction include the Gore Range, the Flat Tops, Mount Sopris near Carbondale, the Holy Cross Wilderness, and the peaks mentioned above. Keep an eye out for thunderstorms. The ridge is no place to be if lightning is flashing or approaching. Enjoy a picnic lunch and return the way you came!

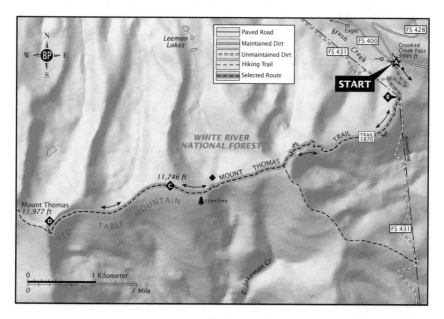

Red Table Mountain from FS 400.

Guardian Dogs

Should you come across a herd of sheep while hiking, be on the lookout for one or two guardian dogs. These dogs do not herd the sheep, but instead protect them from predators such as coyotes, mountain lions, bears, and other dogs. Interestingly enough, coyotes and domestic dogs are the main predators of sheep in the United States. Guardian dogs are typically Great Pyrenees, Akbash, or Komondor breeds. This concept has become more popular as the practices of hunting and poisoning predators have lost favor and effectiveness. Guardian dogs may also be used with herds of cattle.

If you see sheep with a guardian dog, keep your distance from the flock and keep your own dog leashed. Determine a good way to move past without disturbing the sheep or the dog. If a guardian dog approaches, stay calm. Do not throw anything at it, but instead command it to go back to the sheep. Move slowly. The main objective here is to not pose, or appear to pose, a threat to the flock. The dog's job is to protect the sheep. If you do not threaten the herd, the dog will leave you alone. Do not let your dog(s) chase any sheep or approach the guardian dog. Although not all hikers approve of livestock grazing on public lands, sheep and cattle ranchers hold grazing permits in many areas that are designated multi-use. Please respect and understand that they have a right to be there, just as we hikers do.

Hike Information

📞 Trail Contacts:

White River National Forest, Eagle Ranger District, Eagle, CO (970) 328–6388 or *www.fs.fed.us/r2/white river* • **Sopris Ranger District,** Aspen, CO (970) 963–2266

🕐 Schedule:

Open year round. Access road closed by snow just past Sylvan Lake State Park, 5.5 miles from the trailhead. Road used by snowmobilers and cross-country skiers. Trail neither maintained nor marked for winter use.

💲 Fees/Permits:

No fees or permits required

❓ Local Information:

Eagle Valley Chamber Of Commerce, Eagle, CO (970) 328–5220 or *www.eagle valley.org*

💡 Local Events/Attractions:

Sylvan Lake State Park, Eagle, CO (970) 625–1607 or *parks.state.co.us/sylvan* • **Eagle County Historical Society's Visitor Center** (museum), Eagle, CO (970) 328–6464 • **Glenwood Canyon National Recreation Trail,** Glenwood Springs, CO 1–888–445–3696 or (970) 945–6589 or *glenscape.com/glncyn. htm* • **Eagle Flight Days Celebration,** Eagle, CO (970) 328–5220

🛏 Accommodations:

Sylvan Lake State Park campground, Eagle, CO (970) 625–1607 or *parks. state.co.us/sylvan* • **Prairie Moon Inn,** Eagle, CO (970) 328–6680

🍴 Restaurants:

Jackie's Old West Restaurant (breakfast), Eagle, CO (970) 328–7297 • **Mi Pueblo,** Eagle, CO (970) 328–5156 • **The Eagle Diner,** Eagle, CO (970) 328–1919

📖 Other Resources:

Eagle Library, Eagle, CO (970) 328–6273 • *Roaring Fork Valley,* by Len Shoemaker, Sage Books – *a discussion with a rancher who holds the Lime Creek grazing allotment*

🎒 Local Outdoor Retailer:

Eagle Pharmacy "The Nearly Everything Store," Eagle, CO (970) 328–6875

🗺 Maps:

USGS maps: Crooked Creek Pass, CO • *Trails Illustrated®* maps: #126, Holy Cross/Ruedi Reservoir

151

Granite Lakes Trail

Hike Specs

Start: From the Granite Lakes Trail (Trail 1922) trailhead

Length: 13.6-mile out-and-back

Approximate Hiking Time: 8–12 hours (recommended 2–3 day backpack)

Difficulty Rating: Difficult due to elevation gain, length, and altitude

Elevations: 8,760–11,600 feet

Elevation Gain: 2,840 feet (2,120 feet is gained in last 3.5 miles)

Seasons: Best from late June to mid-October

Terrain: Dirt trail, sometimes steep

Land Status: National forest and wilderness area

Nearest Towns: Basalt, CO and Meredith, CO

Other Trail Users: Equestrians, anglers, and hunters (in season)

Canine Compatibility: Leashed dogs permitted

Getting There

From Basalt: Drive east on the Fryingpan River Road (FS 105) about 31 miles (paved all the way) to a sign on the right side that says Nast Lake, Granite Lakes Trail trailhead. Turn right and drive down a dirt road about 0.9 miles and cross the Fryingpan River bridge. On the other side of the bridge to the right is a parking area and the trailhead. Be sure to park here and do not drive any farther. There are no facilities here. Water from streams and lakes must be treated. Walk down the road to the Fryingpan Ranch—the trail continues on the left past the mailboxes. Please stay on the trail and respect private property. *DeLorme: Colorado Atlas & Gazetteer:* Page 47 B5

Several stories recount the naming of the Fryingpan River. In one version, several miners ran across the mountains from a river drainage to escape angry Utes, only to find more Utes camped on the other side. One miner commented that it was like "jumping from the frying pan into the fire." The river from which they ran became known as the Fryingpan. Another account reports trappers being attacked by Utes, with only two trappers surviving. One left his wounded companion in a nearby cave and hung a frying pan in a tree so he could find his buddy when he returned with help. Henry Gannet, one of the leaders of the Hayden Survey, officially named the river.

For many years, the Ute Indians hunted game in the Fryingpan and Roaring Fork River valleys. As miners swarmed over the area and homesteaders established ranches and farms, the Utes were forced from their cherished homelands. Mines were located near Meredith and Thomasville around 1882, but the ore soon played out. Other mines near Aspen were booming, but transportation proved to be an expensive nightmare. A race developed between railroad companies to provide rail service to Aspen and Glenwood Springs. The Colorado Midland Railway Company decided to build a railroad from Colorado Springs through Leadville and on to Aspen. The route tunneled through the Sawatch Range and down the Fryingpan River to its intersection with the Roaring Fork River. (Read about the Hagerman Tunnel in Hike 16.) By November 1887, the railroad arrived at Aspen Junction, presently the town of Basalt.

As settlers moved into the area, they harvested its many resources. Some people provided elk and deer meat to the railroad workers and miners. By 1890 eight sawmills reportedly operated along the Fryingpan River, supplying lumber for building railroads, homes, buildings, and mine tunnels.

Even back in the 1890s the Fryingpan valley earned the reputation as a sportsman's paradise with large herds of elk and deer and abundant trout in lakes and streams. In the early 1900s, Arthur Hanthorn and James Morris built a tourist resort with a large lodge and several other buildings near the Nast railroad siding.

The mountains in the Fryingpan valley area became part of the Holy Cross Forest Reserve in 1905. Len Shoemaker served as a forest ranger in the area for about 20 years and in 1958 wrote a book, *Roaring Fork Valley*, in which he relates interesting

> In the late 1800s and early 1900s, hunting reached epic proportions all over Colorado. Buffalo vanished and elk disappeared in many areas. Elk actually had to be reintroduced in the early 1900s and were heavily protected until herds were large enough for limited hunting.

Lower Granite Lake.

historical tidbits. In 1918, the last Colorado Midland Railroad train ran the Fryingpan route. The sawmills closed soon thereafter, and the Fryingpan River valley returned to a quieter existence.

MilesDirections

0.0 START at the Granite Lakes Trail (Trail 1922) trailhead by Nast Lake. Please sign the trailhead register and read up-to-date regulations on the bulletin board. ★ 39°17'53"N 106°36'20"W

0.2 Arrive at Fryingpan River Ranch. Walk on the road to the left past the mailboxes for Mountain Nast Community.

0.3 Granite Lakes Trail turns left off the road. Follow the trail to the left along the river. ◆ 39°17'42"N 106°36'09"W

1.2 Reach the wilderness boundary sign.

1.5 The trail comes very close to a U-curve on the Fryingpan River.

2.3 The trail wanders through various granitic boulders and rock formations. Watch out for cairns marking the trail in rocky areas.

3.3 Reach a junction with Fryingpan Lakes Trail. ◆ 39°16'03"N 106°33'44"W—This is a good place for a break. Turn right onto Granite Lakes Trail and head uphill. Trail starts to switchback steeply not too far from here. Elevation is 9,480 feet.

4.3 *[FYI. To the left is a water slide down smooth granite.]*

5.0 The trail comes to a beautiful meadow and goes downstream a little to Granite Creek crossing over big boulders. *[Note. Creek*

crossing can be tricky.] ◆39°15'06"N 106°33'53"W—In a few feet you'll cross another little creek. Continue across the meadow, staying right of a big boulder in the meadow. There's a cairn near the trees.

5.1 Cross Granite Creek again. You now leave Granite Creek and climb uphill to a bench above the drainage. The trail switchbacks steeply in spots (again).

5.7 The trail climbs more gently through some wetter areas and more open areas.

6.0 The trail crosses a little creek. Turn right at the cairn. *[Note. Remember this spot on the way back as it's easy to miss.]* Reach Lower Granite Lake. ◆ 39°14'30"N 106°34'13"W

6.2 Come to a meadow with view. Cross a little flat area.

6.4 Come to a creek crossing with lots of tree stumps. The trail is a little hard to find, but there are some cairns. Keep heading across open area, slightly uphill. *[FYI. Look behind for a good view of the Sawatch Range.]* Come to a little flat area. The trail will drop down to the upper lake.

6.8 Reach Upper Granite Lake. ◆ 39°13'52"N 106°34'09"W—Return the way you came.

13.6 Arrive back at the trailhead.

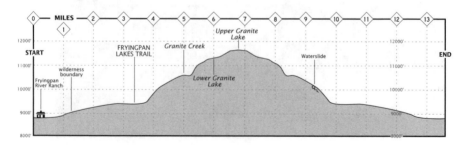

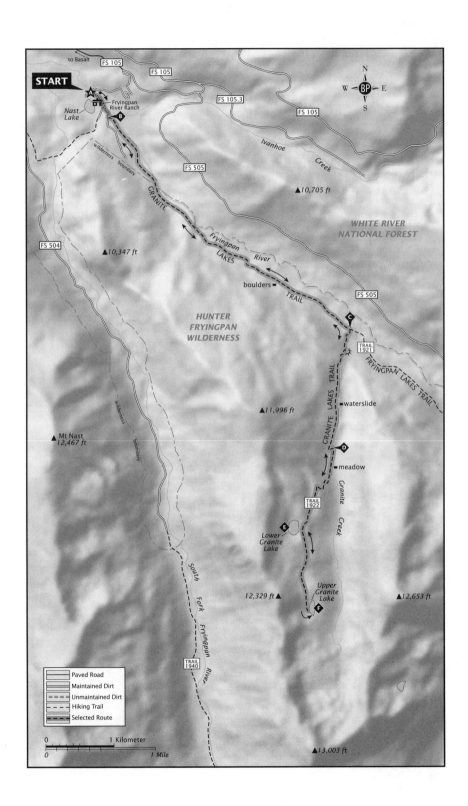

START

to Basalt

FS 105

FS 105

FS 105.3

FS 105

Nast Lake

Fryingpan River Ranch

B

wilderness boundary

GRANITE

FS 505

Ivanhoe Creek

▲10,705 ft

WHITE RIVER NATIONAL FOREST

FS 504

▲10,347 ft

Fryingpan River

LAKES

boulders ■

TRAIL

FS 505

C

TRAIL 1921

FRYINGPAN LAKES TRAIL

HUNTER FRYINGPAN WILDERNESS

wilderness boundary

▲11,996 ft

■ waterslide

GRANITE LAKES TRAIL

D

■ meadow

Granite Creek

TRAIL 1922

▲ Mt Nast 12,467 ft

E

Lower Granite Lake

South Fork Fryingpan River

12,329 ft ▲

Upper Granite Lake

▲12,653 ft

F

TRAIL 1940

▲13,003 ft

N W E S BP

Paved Road
Maintained Dirt
Unmaintained Dirt
Hiking Trail
Selected Route

0   1 Kilometer

0   1 Mile

In 1978, Congress created the Hunter-Fryingpan Wilderness, named after two of its drainages. When the area around Mount Massive (14,421 feet) was considered for wilderness designation, Congress intended to include it in the Hunter-Fryingpan. An oversight, however, created a separate Mount Massive Wilderness in 1980. The Spruce Creek drainage was added to the Hunter-Fryingpan in 1993 for a total of 82,729 acres.

The first part of the hike crosses Mountain Nast Community, home to the private Fryingpan River Ranch and several summer cabins. Please respect the rights of property owners by staying on the trail. You'll pass through a few meadows, sometimes close to the creek, then enter thick forest. The trail crosses many small creeks while weaving up and down around various granite formations. The U.S. Forest Service (USFS) recently worked on the trail with the help of Colorado Rocky Mountain School and others. Take time to appreciate their work across boggy areas. Part of the task of keeping an area pristine involves maintaining trails to avoid environmental damage. Volunteer and youth groups play an important role by helping the USFS with trail projects.

In about 3.3 miles the trail intersects the Fryingpan Lakes Trail. Taking a right turn, the Granite Lakes Trail climbs steeply out of the valley. The trail occasionally levels out, giving you a chance for a breather. Granite Creek cascades nearby forming small waterfalls and interesting water slides. At 5.0 miles, the trail enters a beautiful meadow with sweeping views up the valley. After crossing Granite Creek twice, you begin climbing again.

Upper Granite Lake.

Granite Lakes are nestled in a bench above Granite Creek. Trout jump and swim in the clear waters of Lower Granite Lake. The trail to the upper lake crosses flower-filled meadows. If you're backpacking, remember to camp at least 100 feet away from the lakes, streams, and trail. By making yourself less obvious, you and others can fully enjoy the peace and solitude.

Hike Information

🕭 Trail Contact:
White River National Forest, Sopris Ranger District, Carbondale, CO (970) 963–2266 or *www.fs.fed.us/r2/white river*

🕔 Seasons:
Open year round. Trail neither maintained nor marked for winter use.

💲 Fees/Permits:
No fees required. Maximum group size in the Hunter-Fryingpan Wilderness is 25 people and/or stock.

❓ Local Information:
Basalt Chamber of Commerce, Basalt, CO (970) 927–4031 or *www.basalt.com*

💡 Local Events/Attractions:
Basalt River Days, Basalt, CO (970) 927–4701 • **Strawberry Days,** Glenwood Springs, CO (970) 945–6589 • **Latin American Festival,** Carbondale, CO (970) 945–4060 • **Carbondale Mountain Fair,** Carbondale, CO (970) 963–1680 • **Aspen Music Festival,** Aspen, CO (970) 925–9042 or *aspen musicfestival.com*

🍴 Accommodations:
National Forest Campgrounds, Sopris Ranger District, Carbondale, CO (970) 963–2266 or 1–877–444–6777

🍴 Restaurants:
Two Rivers Café, Basalt, CO (970) 927–3348 • **Bucky's Rotisserie,** Basalt, CO (970) 927–4773

🕮 Other Resources:
Roaring Fork Valley, by Len Shoemaker, Sage Books. • *The Complete Guide to Colorado's Wilderness Areas,* by John Fielder and Mark Pearson, Westcliffe Publishers, Inc.

👥 Clubs and Organizations:
Roaring Fork Outdoor Volunteers, Basalt, CO (970) 927–8241, (877) 662–5220 or *www.rfov.org* • **Colorado Mountain Club – Aspen Group,** Aspen, CO – *For current contacts, call (303) 279–3080 or 1–800–633–4417* • **Colorado Rocky Mountain School,** Carbondale, CO (970) 963–2562 or *www.crms.org* • **Aspen Wilderness Workshop,** Aspen, CO (970) 963–8684

🏃 Hike Tours:
Aspen Alpine Guides, Aspen, CO (970) 925–6618 or *www.aspen.com/aspen alpine*

🕸 Local Outdoor Retailers:
Bristlecone Mountain Sports, Basalt, CO (970) 927–1492

🅝 Maps:
USGS maps: Nast, CO; Mount Champion, CO • *Trails Illustrated®* maps: #126, Holy Cross/Ruedi Reservoir; #127, Aspen/Independence Pass

21

Silver Creek Trail

Hike Specs

Start: From east Silver Creek Trail (Trail 1106) trailhead on Red Dirt Road

Length: 11.0-mile point-to-point (with opportunities for camping and an out-and-back return)

Approximate Hiking Time: 4–6 hours

Difficulty Rating: Difficult due to length

Elevations: 7,960–9,860 feet

Elevation Gain: 70 feet (1,900-foot elevation loss)

Seasons: Best from mid-June through October

Terrain: Old logging roads closed to motorized use and dirt trail

Land Status: National forest and wilderness area

Nearest Towns: Kremmling, CO, and Yampa, CO

Other Trail Users: Equestrians and hunters (in season)

Canine Compatibility: Controlled dogs permitted

Getting There

With Shuttle

From Yampa: Set up a car shuttle. These directions assume you would like to hike mostly downhill. Drive about eight miles north of Yampa on CO 131 to CR 14. Turn right onto CR 14 and drive about 3.2 miles to CR 16. Turn right onto CR 16, following the Lynx Pass signs. Drive 1.6 miles then turn left by some condo buildings to stay on CR 16. In another 1.2 miles, turn right. Continue on CR 16 for another 5.4 miles. The trailhead is past mile marker 8.0, on the left side. There is parking on the right. Leave one car here. Continue south about 13.5 miles on CR 16, which becomes FS 270, to Gore Pass Road (CO 134). Turn left on CO 134 and drive about three miles east to FS 250. Turn left onto FS

250. At the first fork, stay left. In 3.1 miles, turn left at the fork. In another 3.6 miles, the road forks again—turn left. There's yet another fork in another 1.4 miles, but this time turn right. Red Dirt Road (FS 100) is in another 2.9 miles. The last mile here is a little rough, and low clearance vehicles should go very slowly. Turn left onto Red Dirt Road (FS 100). Drive 5.0 miles north. The trailhead is on the left side of the road, past mile marker 11.0. You can camp near the east trailhead—remember to stay at least 100 feet from streams, trails, and the road. There are no facilities at either trailhead.

Without Shuttle

From Kremmling: These directions assume you would like to hike mostly downhill. Drive west and north on U.S. 40 about six miles to CO 134, Gore Pass Road. Turn left onto Gore Pass Road and drive about 10.3 miles west to Red Dirt Road (FS 100). At the first two forks, stay right. At the third fork at FS 101 (also CR 191) around mile 4.8, stay left. In another 1.7 miles, reach FS 250 and stay right. Follow the signs "Buffalo Park." The trailhead is on the left side of the road, about 11.5 miles from Gore Pass Road (CO 134). You can camp near the east trailhead—remember to stay at least 100 feet from streams, trails, and the road. There are no facilities at either trailhead.

DeLorme: Colorado Atlas & Gazetteer: Page 26 C3 (shuttle point), Page 27 C5 (start point)

Silver Creek Trail traverses the southern part of Sarvis Creek Wilderness. This wilderness is unique because it is not composed of "rocks and ice" like so many other national forest wilderness areas in Colorado. Although heavily forested, its pristine and primitive nature qualified it for wilderness status. This distinction recognizes the biological diversity philosophy of wilderness designation—to preserve different types of ecosystems. Congress designated this area as wilderness in 1993.

The Silver and Service creeks cut through the Sarvis Creek Wilderness. Old-timers insist the area's original name was Sarvis. Some mapmaker, however, decided that "sarvis" was a common mispronunciation of the word "service" and placed the name "Service Creek" on the map. The wilderness area designation tried to right the incorrect spelling by reclaiming the Sarvis name. The Sarvis Timber Company harvested trees in the Service Creek area in the mid 1910s using portable mills.

The Civilian Conservation Corps (CCC) built much of the Silver Creek Trail. After the 1929 stock market crash and subsequent depression, 13.6 million Americans were unemployed by 1933. That year Congress passed the Emergency Conservation Work Act creating what became known as the CCC. Young, unemployed, unmarried men between the ages of 18 and 25 were eligible to join. Conservation of natural resources—reforestation, forest fire fighting, erosion control, trail building and maintenance, development of state parks, and other public works—became the CCC's mission. The U.S. Army built camps, the government furnished food and clothing, and the Departments of the Interior and Agriculture provided work projects and leadership. Each man earned $30 per month of which $25 was sent home to his family.

View into Morrison Creek near west trailhead.

The CCC is credited with building 46,854 bridges, 3,116 fire lookout towers, and 318,076 dams to help with erosion control, plus numerous buildings and trails. By 1937, the CCC employed over 500,000 young men, working on projects all over the United States. The Army operated more than 2,500 camps to house all the workers.

The men of the CCC performed excellent work. The CCC-built trail up Notch Mountain in the Holy Cross Wilderness still carries thousands of visitors to view Mount of the Holy Cross each year. According to U.S. Forest Service personnel, the CCC workers who built the Silver Creek Trail created one that is easy to maintain.

MilesDirections

0.0 START at the east Silver Creek Trail (Trail 1106) trailhead, by the bulletin board. ★ 40˚11'52"N 106˚36'22"W—Walk back to road, turn left and walk up road over creek to trail.

0.1 Silver Creek Trail starts to the left of the road at the big mounds of dirt that are used to close the old logging road to motorized vehicles. Hike up the dirt mound to the doubletrack Silver Creek Trail 1106.

0.3 The trail forks; turn right and walk up that old logging road.

1.4 The trail forks; turn left and walk up that old logging road.

1.5 The trail forks; turn left and walk up that old logging road.

1.6 Reach the wilderness boundary sign. ◆ 40˚12'22"N 106˚37'28"W

2.4 Cabin remains are on the left. ◆ 40˚12'11"N 106˚38'22"W

3.5 Round a ridge with a good view down Silver Creek drainage.

6.9 The trail forks; go up the main trail to the right.

7.5 Cross Silver Creek. ◆ 40˚12'51"N 106˚43'30"W—*[**Note.** Be careful in early summer when the creek runs high. The boulders may be underwater and the current swift.]*

8.8 There's a nice view down and across Silver Creek.

9.2 Reach the wilderness boundary sign. ◆ 40˚13'01"N 106˚45'05"W

10.3 Top a ridge and begin the final descent to the west trailhead.

10.6 The trail forks; stay to the left (actually go straight downhill as there's a viewpoint off to the left).

10.9 Silver Creek west trailhead bulletin board. If you're coming up this direction, please stop to read up-to-date area information. *[**Note.** From here you'll be on private property. The Forest Service has permission for the trail to cross here. Please respect the private property!]*

11.0 Arrive at the west Silver Creek Trail trailhead. ◆ 40˚13'20"N 106˚46'45"W

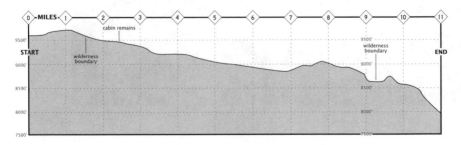

Shiprock along Silver Creek Trail.

It has great drainage, rolling dips, and cribbed walls. Moss now covers the rock walls making them difficult to see.

From the east trailhead, the hike follows several old logging roads, now closed to motorized travel. The trail gradually gains elevation to the wilderness boundary, which is nearly the highest point of the trail. From here you drop into the Silver Creek drainage, with marshy meadows hidden behind trees to the south. The granitic rocks along the trail take on some interesting shapes. Look for Kissing Rocks on the right. After crossing a marshy section, the remains of a log cabin rest on the left. The former occupants are unknown, but the notched logs still show careful work by the cabin's builder. Shiprock sticks up its prow to the right a little farther down the trail. Colorful aspens frame the boulders in the fall. The hike specs indicate this trail is mostly downhill, but there is a little uphill section coming soon. As you round a ridge, check out the view down the drainage. The various lumps and cliffs of rock are composed of Precambrian granite (quartz monzonite). Precambrian rocks formed over 600 million years ago when molten magma oozed up into other rocks, cooled slowly, and became the granite you see today. Granite tends to erode like an onion peels, hence some of the rounded shapes.

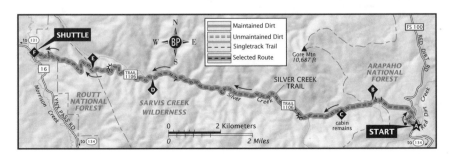

Sometimes Silver Creek runs swiftly down a tiny canyon, leaping over little cascades. Other times it broadens and sparkles in the sun. Deep pools attract fish—sit and watch for a while. Some good campsites can be found up on low ridges to the north of the trail—an appropriate 200-plus feet from the trail and creek, but close enough to fetch water easily. While you hike and camp, remember to use your zero-impact skills!

About two-thirds of the way into the hike, the trail crosses Silver Creek at a wide spot. Hop across on nice boulders. The trail then swings away from the creek and eventually traverses a very steep slope leaving the creek far below. After topping the ridge, you drop down on south and west facing slopes. The vegetation changes here with dryness and heat. Ponderosa pines, Gambel oaks, sagebrush, and grasses replace the lodgepole and spruce-fir forest.

This area is very popular during hunting season. Bow and black powder hunters are plentiful during September. Be considerate and wear some blaze orange clothing.

Cabin remains along Silver Creek Trail.

Hike Information

🦶 Trail Contact:

Medicine Bow – Routt National Forest, Yampa Ranger District, Yampa, CO (970) 638–4516 or *www.fs.fed.us/r2/mbr/ ya/yawel.htm* or *www.fs.fed.us/mrnf/ mbrwild/sarvis.htm*

🕐 Schedule:

Open year round. Trail neither maintained nor marked for winter use.

💲 Fees/Permits:

No fees or permits required. Group size may not exceed a combination of 25 people and livestock, with the maximum number of people being 15. Camping and campfires are prohibited within 100 feet of all streams and trails.

❓ Local Information:

Kremmling Visitor Center, Kremmling, CO (970) 724–3472 or 1–877– 573–6654 or *www.kremmlingchamber. com* • **South Routt County** website: *www.southrouttedc.org*

🌟 Local Events/Attractions:

Kremmling Days, third weekend in June, Kremmling, CO (970) 724–3472 – *celebration of town's history* • **Middle Park Fair & Rodeo,** third weekend in September, Kremmling, CO (970) 724–3472 • **Kremmling's Annual Roadkill Chile Supper,** in October, Kremmling, CO (970) 724–3472 • **Montgomery's General Merchandise,** Yampa, CO (970) 382–2563

🛏️ Accommodations:

National Forest Service campgrounds, Medicine Bow - Routt National Forest, Yampa, CO (970) 638–4516 • **Not on the Beaten Path Bed, Breakfast & Barn,** Yampa, CO (970) 273–9668 or *www.bbonline.com/co/noton/index.html*

• **Historic Hotel Eastin,** Kremmling, CO (970) 724–3261 • **Cliffside Inn,** Kremmling, CO (970) 724–9620 or 1–877–254–3374

🍽️ Restaurants:

Cliffside Pizza Factory & Pub - Home of the Cow Pie Pizza!, Kremmling, CO (970) 724–9219 • **Quarter Circle Saloon,** Kremmling, CO (970) 724–9601 • **Antler's Café & Bar,** Yampa, CO (970) 638–4555 • **Lombardi's Café,** Yampa, CO (970) 638–0446

🕯️ Other Resources:

CCC information on the web: *www.parks.wa.gov/civilian.htm*, *www.usgw.org/ms/perry/Ccc.htm*, or *pages.prodigy.com/reunion/history.htm* • **The Complete Guide to Colorado's Wilderness Areas,** by John Fielder and Mark Pearson, Westcliffe Publishers, Inc.

👥 Clubs and Organizations:

Yampatika, Steamboat Springs, CO (970) 871–9151 or *www.yampatika.org*

🏔️ Local Outdoor Retailers:

Montgomery's General Merchandise, Yampa, CO (970) 382–2563 – *limited supplies* • **Wilderness Sports,** Silverthorne, CO (970) 468–5687 – *may pass on the way to the hike* • **Ski Haus,** Steamboat Springs, CO (970) 879–0385 – *may pass on the way to the hike* • **Mountain Quest Sports,** Edwards, CO (970) 926–3867 – *may pass on the way to the hike*

🗺️ Maps:

USGS maps: Gore Mountain, CO; Tyler Mountain, CO; Green Ridge, CO • *Trails Illustrated®* maps: #119, Yampa/Gore Pass

Seven Lakes

Hike Specs

Start: From Big Creek Trail (Trail 1125) trailhead near Big Creek Lakes Campground
Length: 12.4-mile out-and-back
Approximate Hiking Time: 5–9 hours (recommended 2–3 day backpack)
Difficulty Rating: Difficult due to length and one steep section
Elevations: 9,000–10,733 feet
Elevation Gain: 1,733 feet
Seasons: Best from mid-June to mid-October
Terrain: Dirt trail with some flat sections, occasional rocks and mud, and one section of many steep switchbacks
Land Status: National forest and wilderness area
Nearest Town: Walden, CO
Other Trail Users: Equestrians, anglers, mountain bikers (not within the wilderness boundary), and hunters (in season)
Canine Compatibility: Controlled dogs permitted

Getting There

From Walden: Drive north a little over nine miles on CO 125 to Cowdrey. Turn left onto CR 6W. The road becomes gravel in about five miles. Drive a total of 18.8 miles from Cowdrey to FS 600/CR 6A. Turn left. The road narrows as it enters the national forest. Be careful of oncoming vehicles as the road is not wide enough for two cars. Drive about five miles to the junction with FS 689. Turn left, staying on FS 600. In about mile 0.8, enter the Big Creek Lakes Campground—stay right at the campground entrance. Follow the hiker signs. There's a bulletin board with campground check-in and rules 0.4 mile from the entrance. Continue another 0.2 miles and turn left at the Big Creek Trail (Trail 1125) trailhead. The parking lot is right there. Water and a vault toilet are nearby. *DeLorme: Colorado Atlas & Gazetteer:* Page 17 A5

T
he Mount Zirkel Wilderness was one of the original five Colorado wilderness areas designated by Congress in the Wilderness Act of 1964. This area around Big Creek Falls and Seven Lakes was added in 1993.

In 1867, Congress authorized a geological and natural resource survey along the fortieth parallel. Clarence King, just five years out of the Sheffield Scientific School at Yale, was appointed Geologist in Charge of the Geological Exploration of the Fortieth Parallel. King hired two assistant geologists, three topographic aides, two collectors, a photographer, and support men. He chose well-educated scientists, who had studied at Yale or Harvard, and the geologists had even completed advanced studies in German universities. One geologist was Ferdinand Zirkel, who developed a common classification system for American and European rocks. For his contribution to science, a peak in the Park Range was named after him in 1874.

The Park Range forms the backbone of the Mount Zirkel Wilderness area. As the range stretches north toward Wyoming, it becomes known as the Sierra Madre. Part of the Sierra Madre near Seven Lakes produces the Encampment River, which flows north into the North Platte River. On the other side of the Continental Divide, the

Boardwalk on Red Elephant Nature Trail.

Elk River drains many of the high valleys, feeding its water into the Yampa River, and eventually the Colorado. The Park Range is composed mainly of Precambrian metamorphic rocks like gneiss and schist with some granite interspersed. These rocks are around 1.7 billion years old. Glaciers covered the area at various times, and Seven Lakes are probably one result.

This area escaped the miners' shovels and road building. The land has not been altered or changed by humans as much as in other parts of Colorado. The Continental Divide by Seven Lakes appears to be a gentle ridge. The area hosts a spectacular display of July wildflowers including paintbrushes, red elephants, pussytoes, penstemons, blue gentians, and varieties of yellow composites. Red Elephant Mountain (11,569 feet) raises its head watching the entire trail to Seven Lakes. This peak apparently reminded someone a long time ago of an elephant head and trunk. Can you see it?

The first part of the trail follows the Red Elephant Nature Trail. Pick up a nature guide at the trailhead. As you hike, notice how some areas are filled with deadfall while other areas have hardly any. A forest fire swept through in the 1920s and the resulting lodgepole forest has little deadfall compared to the older, moister spruce-fir

MilesDirections

0.0 START at Big Creek Trail (Trail 1125) trailhead near Big Creek Lakes Campground. ☆ 40˚55'53"N 106˚37'10"W—Head up Big Creek Trail. The Red Elephant Nature Trail shares the trail. (Pick up a nature guide at the trailhead.)

1.2 The Red Elephant Nature Trail breaks left. ⓑ 40˚54'59"N 106˚37'20"W—Stay right, continuing on Big Creek Trail.

2.5 Reach the wilderness boundary sign. Big Creek Falls is off to the left. ◆ 40˚54'32"N 106˚38'15"W

3.5 Come to a creek crossing over a dilapidated bridge. Cross on rocks and logs on upstream side.

4.4 Reach the top of steep climb, with switchbacks.

5.2 Come to a nice meadow on left, followed by an old-growth spruce forest.

5.8 Come to a trail junction with Buffalo Ridge Trail (Trail 1151). Stay to the left and head uphill.

6.1 Come to a trail junction with Big Creek Trail and the trail to Seven Lakes. Stay to the left (more straight ahead) and hike another 0.1 miles to the lakes.

6.2 Reach the first of the Seven Lakes. *[**Side-trip.** Hike an additional 0.25 miles to view the biggest of Seven Lakes.* ◆ 40˚53'47"N 106˚40'59"W] Otherwise, return the way you came.

12.4 Arrive back at the trailhead.

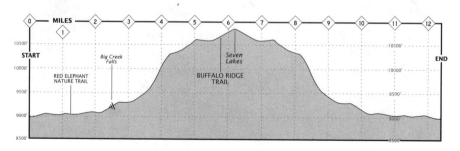

forest. Fire is important to the natural health of the forest, creating different vegetation pockets that support various plants and animals. In several places, nice plank bridges cross wet areas. A lily pad–covered pond lies nestled in a cradle of trees.

After the trail turns west to follow Big Creek, an open area provides good views of Upper Big Creek Lake. A prominent cliff face towers above the wilderness boundary. Just beyond, down a little trail to the left is Big Creek Falls. Not overly huge, they are still impressive. Take a break and enjoy the cool creek and falls before heading on. The trail stays close to Big Creek for a while, then gradually climbs up a flower-filled section of trail with numerous seeps. Cow parsnip, pearly everlasting and alder line the trail. A dilapidated bridge crosses an unnamed creek. Cross the creek on rocks and logs on the upstream side if the bridge is still in bad shape, unless you want to practice balancing skills! Take a quick break since the trail climbs steeply from here. More than 15 switchbacks take you up 750 feet in a half-mile. The trail then levels out and rolls gently through a nice old growth forest past some beautiful meadows. A final climb threads through flower-filled meadows and on to Seven Lakes.

Follow the faint trail to the left of the first lake to reach the biggest lake, which is stocked yearly with native trout. There is a nice campsite above the largest lake, at an appropriate distance from the water. The U.S. Forest Service requests that all camps must be located at least 100 feet away from lakes, other water sources, and trails and that no new campfire rings be built. Use existing fire rings, make a mound fire, or preferably use a stove. Be aware of lightning danger in open areas.

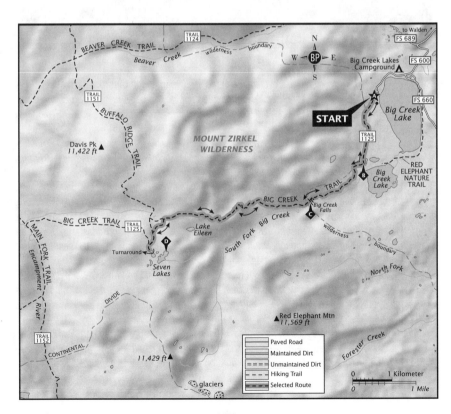

Two of the Seven Lakes and Red Elephant Mountain.

Building a Mound Fire

Many people enjoy an evening campfire for camaraderie, warmth, storytelling, and even security. From other perspectives, fires can damage the vegetation underneath as well as leave ugly scars on ground and rock. However, there are ways to have your fire and prevent damage, too.

A mound fire is an ecological and aesthetic way to build a fire and prevent both damage to the environment and ugly scars. First, make sure no fire bans are in effect and that you are below treeline. Next, find a big level rock imbedded in the ground, make a rock base out of "flat" rocks, or find exposed soil with less than three inches of plant remains. Make sure not to build your fire right under tree branches. Find some "mineral soil" along a creek or by an uprooted tree. Mineral soil is dirt and/or sand that has minimal organic matter such as pine needles, leaves, or twigs in it. Put enough soil on a large plastic garbage bag to make a flat-topped mound about six to eight inches thick and about 18 inches or less in diameter. Carry the garbage bag and soil to your chosen spot and shape the mound.

To gather firewood, spread out and pick up downed and dead wood that's no larger than your wrist. Gather the wood from various places on the ground so as not to remove all dead wood in an area. Birds use dead branches on trees, so please don't break any off. Build your fire on the mound within 1 inch of the edges. Enjoy!

When finished, let the fire cool to white ash. Scatter the cold ash and any unused wood over a large area. That way no one will see that you had a fire. Return the soil to where you found it. If the garbage bag has no burn holes, you passed the mound fire test!

Hike Information

🔦 Trail Contact:

Medicine Bow–Routt National Forest, Parks Ranger District, Walden, CO (970) 723–8204 or *www.fs.fed.us/r2/mbr/ mbrwelcome.htm*

🕐 Seasons:

Access road closed about 13 miles from the trailhead in winter. Snowmobile or cross-country ski on the road. Trail neither maintained nor marked for winter use.

🅢 Fees/Permits:

There is a day-use fee. Check with the campground host on your way to the trailhead for information about parking while backpacking or hiking as the rules may change from year to year. Mount Zirkel Wilderness has a group size limit of a combination of 25 people and livestock with a maximum of 15 people.

❓ Local Information:

Walden Chamber of Commerce, Walden, CO (970) 723–4600 or *www.northpark coc.com*

💡 Local Events/Attractions:

Arapaho National Wildlife Refuge, Walden, CO (970) 723–8202 or *http://mountain-prairie.fws.gov/ refuges/arapaho* • **North Park Museum,** Walden, CO (970) 723–8371 or *www.northpark.org/town/ history-main.htm* • **Outhouse Tour,** Jackson County • **Friends of the Library,** Walden, CO (970) 723–4600 • **The North Park Fair,** Walden, CO (970) 723–4298 • **Colorado State Forest,** Walden, CO (970) 723–8366 or *www.parks.state.*

co.us/state_forest • **McCallum Field (Oil & Gas) Auto Tour,** BLM Kremmling Resource Area, Kremmling, CO (970) 724–3437

⊜ Accommodations:

National Forest campgrounds, Parks Ranger District, Walden, CO (970) 723–8204 or *www.fs.fed.us/r2/mbr/ colcamp.htm*

🍴 Restaurants:

The Coffee Pot, Walden, CO (970) 723–4670 • **Moose Creek Cookhouse & Saloon,** Walden, CO (970) 723–8272 • **Elkhorn Bar & Café,** Walden, CO (970) 723–9996

🖉 Other Resources:

Roadside Geology of Colorado, by Halka Chronic, Mountain Press Publishing Co. • *A Sierra Club Naturalist's Guide to The Southern Rockies,* by Audrey DeLella Benedict, Sierra Club Books • **Four Great Surveys of the West from USGS website:** *pubs.usgs.gov/circular/ c1050/surveys.htm*

🚲 Local Outdoor Retailer:

Outdoor stores in this area mainly cater to fishermen and hunters. Maps and limited backpacking supplies are available. **Sportsman's Supply,** Walden, CO (970) 723–4343 or *www.sportsmans supply.xtcom.com*

Ⓝ Maps:

USGS maps: Pearl, CO; Davis Peak, CO • *Trails Illustrated*® maps: #116, Hahn's Peak/Steamboat Lake

North Central Mountains

Compiled here is an index of great hikes in the North Central region that didn't make the A-list this time around but deserve recognition. Check them out and let us know what you think. You may decide that one or more of these hikes deserves higher status in future editions or, perhaps, you may have a hike of your own that merits some attention.

(K) Kelly Lake

Kelly Lake is snuggled in a cirque at 10,805 feet on the west side of the Medicine Bow Mountains in Colorado State Forest State Park. This state park offers a yurt system and cross-country skiing and snowshoeing in winter, too. The trail climbs about 1,200 feet in six miles for a difficult hike. To reach the trailhead, drive east from Walden on CO 14 to the park entrance (about 20 miles). Turn left at the KOA campground and follow the signs to the entrance station and pay the fee. You'll be on CR 41. Stay right at the first fork. Stay to the left at the junction to Bockman Campground and continue about five miles to the trailhead. For further information, contact Colorado State Forest State Park at (970) 723–8366. *DeLorme: Colorado Atlas & Gazetteer:* Page 18 C3

(L) Parkview Mountain

Parkview Mountain at 12,296 feet is the high point of the Rabbit Ears Range and offers incredible views of the Flat Tops, Never Summer, Gore, Tenmile, Collegiate, Mosquito, and Front Ranges. This most difficult 9.2-mile out-and-back trail starts at the top of Willow Creek Pass (9,620 feet) and follows the Continental Divide Trail (CDT) to the summit. The trail itself stays mainly to the south of the Continental Divide. Follow the CDT signs and cairns. Willow Creek Pass is located northwest of Granby or southeast of Walden on CO 125. Parkview Mountain is above treeline, so watch out for thunderstorms and lightning! For more information contact Arapaho National Forest at (970) 887–4100 or visit their website at *www.fs.fed.us/r2/arnf/* (Sulphur Ranger District). *DeLorme: Colorado Atlas & Gazetteer:* Page 28 B2

Ⓜ North Vail Trail System

The U.S. Forest Service and Town of Vail worked together to design and build a trail on the north side of I-70 for residents and visitors of Vail to use—a "close-to-home" trail. The system goes from the west side of Vail eventually to Spraddle Creek. Some new trail was built, while existing trail and dirt roads were linked. For a moderate 5.5-mile point-to-point hike, start in West Vail by driving west past Wendy's on the Frontage Road. There's a parking area on the right side of North Frontage Road West. Park here and check the bus shelter for information about catching the bus back from Buffehr Creek Road. Walk a little farther west to the trailhead, which starts where the road curves right to become Arosa Drive. The trail switchbacks up the side of a ridge to a fence and road (Davos Trail) at the top. Go through the gate, remembering to close it behind you, turn right on the road and head downhill. After curving around a drainage, you'll find a trail coming in sharply from the left. Turn left here (or return to town on the right to Cortina Road). Assuming you're continuing on the trail, it climbs and traverses around a ridge, coming into open meadows with good views of town and the ski area. Watch for deer. The aspen are pretty nice in this area, too. The trail eventually switchbacks down through an area of Gambel oak that burned in 1999. When you reach a T-intersection, turn right to head down to Buffehr Creek Road. Left continues on the North Vail Trail to Red Sandstone Road (you can leave a car there, but it's a long walk back to the bus if you only have one car). Once at Buffehr Creek Road, turn right and walk down to the bus stop to catch a bus back to your car. Dogs must be on leash. Please honor seasonal wildlife closures on this trail from May 15 to June 15. For more information, contact the Town of Vail at (970) 479-2158 or the White River National Forest at (970) 827-5715. *DeLorme: Colorado Atlas & Gazetteer:* Page 37 C6

Northwest

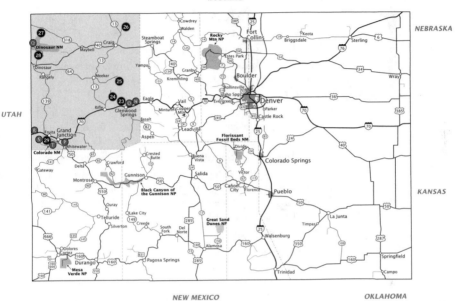

Northwest

L ying where the Rocky Mountains meet the Colorado Plateau, the northwest section of Colorado is a mixture of mountains, plains, plateaus, and canyons. Dinosaurs roamed the western edge where several trails (e.g. Trail Through Time—see page 222) and museums in Grand Junction and Fruita show the ancient beasts both in the ground and assembled. Although not in Colorado, be sure to visit Dinosaur National Monument's Dinosaur Quarry located about seven miles north of Jensen, Utah (21 miles west of Dinosaur, Colorado) where bones still lie in the tilted rock, forming one wall of the quarry building.

John Wesley Powell floated through this region on his way to the Grand Canyon, losing a boat on the wild Green River after passing through Gates of Lodore. Both the Yampa and Green Rivers have accomplished the seemingly impossible—they have downcut through mountains, creating steep and beautiful canyons. Early human inhabitants also left their mark with petroglyphs carved in rock walls in Dinosaur National Monument and at Canyon Pintado south of Rangely. Later inhabitants included outlaws such as Butch Cassidy, the Sundance Kid, and Matt Rush, who hid out in Brown's Park. Be sure to stop at the Brown's Park store for some interesting history. For a little high wire excitement drive over the one lane swinging bridge across the Green River on County Road 83.

Volcanic flows imprinted by an icecap created the Flat Tops, one of Colorado's wilderness areas. Home to the largest elk herd in Colorado, the Flat Tops still contains old growth forest. The Elkhead Mountains northeast of Craig provide a getaway from the more popular Colorado hiking areas.

The Grand Junction area offers a variety of hiking experiences within short distances. Beautiful canyons and monoliths of Wingate sandstone dazzle the eyes and spirits. One of Colorado's newest wilderness areas, Black Ridge Canyons, contains not only spectacular canyons, but also the second largest collection of arches in the country after Arches National Park. Colorado National Monument shows off spectacular rock formations. The nearby Bookcliffs and areas north are home to wild horse herds. The mighty Colorado River flows through the area, providing irrigation for peach and apple orchards, vineyards, and Colorado's wineries, not to mention other tasty vegetables. Grand Mesa, one of the world's largest flat-topped mountains, rises east of Grand Junction.

Northwest Colorado is a dry area, mainly covered by sagebrush rangeland and piñon-juniper-Gambel oak forests. Storm King Mountain, west of Glenwood Springs, was the site of a wildland firefighting tragedy in 1994. Fourteen men and women fire-fighters died when the fire blew up and overtook them. After a long day hiking, have a soak in Glenwood Springs hot springs pool. Volcanoes may no longer erupt, but the earth still heats water for hot springs across western and central Colorado. Limestone caves are common in this area, and Glenwood Caverns offers tours of one.

The Flat Tops Trail, Grand Mesa, and Dinosaur Diamond are the Colorado scenic and historic byways to explore in Northwest Colorado.

Storm King Mountain.

Boulder field on Black Mountain
(West Summit) Trail

Section Overview

Storm King Fourteen Memorial Trail

This trail built by volunteers is a memorial to fourteen firefighters who lost their lives on Storm King Mountain in July 1994. Interpretive signs explain wildland firefighting and this unfortunate disaster. You can stop at the observation point to look across to the ridge where the firefighters died or hike farther to the memorial sites. The trail is a journey into a burned land, now recovering. The steep trails give you a brief insight into and feeling for the work of those who fight wildland fires. *(See page 180.)*

Coyote and Squirrel Trails

Coyote Trail winds past limestone caves, through a lush riparian and forested area, then above for a bird's-eye view of Rifle Falls. Kids of all ages will love exploring the caves. Bring a flashlight for the largest one. Squirrel Trail crosses East Rifle Creek and winds through Gambel oak forest to the base of a red sandstone cliff. The trail continues along the Grass Valley Canal that takes water to Harvey Gap Reservoir. Hiked together, the trails make a lopsided figure-8 through a naturally and historically interesting area along East Rifle Creek. *(See page 186.)*

East Marvine Trail

The hike description takes you to the top of the White River Plateau in the Flat Tops Wilderness. From here, choose your own destination for a multi-day backpacking trip. The public resource and wilderness preservation history in this area is significant. Part of the hike travels through dense spruce-fir forest conveying a primeval feeling. Once on the plateau, the land rolls along in subalpine meadows and alpine tundra punctuated by clumps of trees and short peaks. Small lakes and ponds abound up here. Take time to climb Big Marvine Peak or explore the various lakes on your own. Camping is available below the plateau and on top. *(See page 192.)*

Black Mountain (West Summit) Trail

This hike climbs to the west summit of Black Mountain, a volcanic plateau in the Elkhead Mountains. The trail first winds through an aspen forest with vegetation so thick at times that you might feel the need for a machete. The trail can also be muddy after heavy rains. The trail proceeds into lodgepole and spruce-fir forests where the soil allows for a drier trail. Once up the plateau, a spur trail takes you to a raptor viewing area complete with an interpretive poster and views west toward Dinosaur National Monument and Utah. *(See page 198.)*

Gates of Lodore Nature Trail

Gates of Lodore Nature Trail takes you through semi-desert shrubland to a viewpoint near the Gates of Lodore. Here the Green River cuts through the Uinta Mountains creating the Canyon of the Lodore, a spectacular gorge with towering 2,000-foot vermilion cliffs. Take time to read the nature trail guide. Then sit for a while on the sandstone looking down the canyon. Listen to the breeze, the crickets, and watch the dragonflies. Look for raptors soaring above. Think back to a time when John Wesley Powell passed here in 1869 at the beginning of his first journey down the Colorado River through the Grand Canyon. *(See page 204.)*

Buckwater Draw

This hike drops down into the solitude of the Bull Canyon Wilderness Study Area on an old ranch road now closed to public motorized use. Cattle still graze here. The trail starts in sagebrush then enters a nice juniper forest. As you lose elevation, beautiful views of slickrock cliffs appear. After four miles, this hike follows Buckwater Draw upstream for one mile via cattle paths and creek bottom into a canyon that shrinks to very steep, tight walls. This last part is subject to flash floods so keep an eye on the weather. The return is uphill so be sure to have enough water! *(See page 208.)*

Devils Canyon

This hike takes you into an easily accessible canyon in the new Black Ridge Canyons Wilderness area. The trail first crosses open high desert country of rabbitbrush, junipers, and other thorny plants. It then makes a loop in Devils Canyon below huge walls of Wingate sandstone and interesting rock formations. Part of the loop follows the creek bottom and should be avoided during thunderstorms. Hiking beneath immense sandstone cliffs and past amphitheaters in a colorful canyon is a real treat! Keep an eye out for desert bighorn sheep and rattlesnakes. *(See page 214.)*

Storm King Fourteen Memorial Trail

Hike Specs

Start: From Storm King Fourteen Memorial Trail trailhead
Length: 2.0 miles (4.2 miles if you include the out-and-back to observation points)
Approximate Hiking Time: 2–4.5 hours
Difficulty Rating: Most Difficult due to steepness
Elevations: 5,660–6,360 feet
Elevation Gain: 700 feet
Seasons: Best from April through November.
Terrain: Dirt trail mainly on south and southwest facing slopes; short and fairly steep; slippery when wet; open ridge near observation point
Land Status: BLM land
Nearest Town: Glenwood Springs, CO
Other Trail Users: Hunters (in season)
Canine Compatibility: Leashed dogs permitted. No water on trail.

Getting There

From Glenwood Springs: Take I-70 west to Exit 109, Canyon Creek. Turn right then immediately right again onto the frontage road. Head back east past Canyon Creek Estates about 0.9 miles to a dead end with a parking lot. The trail starts by several interpretive signs at the east end of the lot. There is presently a portable toilet but no water at the trailhead. *DeLorme: Colorado Atlas & Gazetteer:* Page 35 D6

On July 2, 1994, a very natural event occurred. A lightning strike started a small fire in a piñon-juniper-Gambel oak forest on Storm King Mountain (8,793 feet). Several large wildland fires were already burning across Colorado, strapping firefighting resources. The small fire received low priority. By July 5, the fire covered five acres and crews arrived to build fire lines. But, Mother Nature had other plans. By mid-afternoon July 6, a dry cold front passed through the region causing very strong winds, which fanned the fire into a roaring inferno traveling much faster than any human could run, especially uphill. The fire soon consumed over 2,100 acres. Fourteen firefighters could not escape the 100-foot-high flames racing toward them. Thirty-five others escaped either by hunkering down in their fire shelters or by escaping down an eastern gully to the highway.

Although forest fire is a natural and important process, a fire on Storm King Mountain could endanger homes and businesses in West Glenwood to the east or Canyon Creek Estates to the west. The trees on Storm King also provided essential erosion control. Storm King and surrounding mountains are a combination of red sandstone and shale, called Maroon formation deposited over eons by inland seas. When shale gets wet, mudslides often result.

Volunteers built this trail in 1995 to honor wildland firefighters nationwide and to provide an insight into their experiences. The trail begins with several interpretive

Memorial crosses on Storm King.

signs about the July 1994 fire. They invite you to imagine being a firefighter, hiking up steep slopes and carrying 30 to 60 pounds of equipment.

The trail climbs steeply along the south side of a ridge, through rabbitbrush, wild roses, Mormon tea, and cheatgrass with numerous log steps to hike up. Where the trail turns to follow the west side of a ridge, a small sign relates the camaraderie of firefighters and gives you a chance to take a few deep breaths. The Colorado River roars below as does Interstate 70. The trail continues to climb through piñon-juniper forest. The steepness of the trail is tiring even with a light pack. About 0.2 miles up, a sign announces entry into Bureau of Land Management (BLM) lands. Switchbacks take you steadily uphill. A bench provides a handy place to check out the western

MilesDirections

0.0 START at the trailhead east of Canyon Creek Estates. ★ 39°34'26"N 107°26'02"W Take a few minutes to read the interpretive signs. *[**Note.** The first part of the trail crosses private property, which the BLM has permission to use for this trail. Please respect the owners' property.]*

0.2 Reach the BLM boundary sign.

0.3 Reach a bench and interpretive sign on the right side of the trail. Good place to catch your breath and enjoy the view down the Colorado River.

0.6 Gain a ridge with views of Storm King Mountain and the burned area. ◈ 39°34'32"N 107°25'38"W

1.0 Arrive at the observation point with interpretive signs. *[**Turnaround Point:** You can turn around here for a shorter, easier hike]*

1.1 Reach the bottom of the first gully, contour around into the second gully, and start climbing up to the next ridge.

1.6 The trail comes to a T-intersection. ◈ 39°34'40"N 107°24'56"W Take the left trail to the helitack crew memorial site.

1.9 Arrive at the helitack crew memorial site. ◈ 39°34'51"N 107°24'48"W Look across the deep little gully near a rock outcropping to see the crosses. Head back toward the T-intersection.

2.2 Arrive back at the T-intersection. Proceed ahead to the other 12 memorial sites.

2.3 The trail switchbacks downhill past the memorial sites that are marked with signs along the trail. *[**Note:** Please remember to stay on the trail that switchbacks and do not walk straight down between the crosses. The area between crosses is extremely steep and prone to erosion.]*

2.4 The trail ends below the 12 memorial sites. ◈ 39°34'36"N 107°25'05"W Walk to the end to read the poem. Return the way you came.

2.6 Back at the T-intersection. Turn left to head downhill to return to the observation point.

4.2 Arrive back at the trailhead.

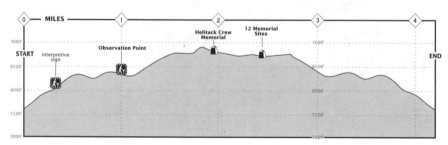

view and catch your breath. Down valley, Interstate 70 twists like a serpent, following the river's contours. The Grand Hogback and Coal Ridge form the horizon to the south.

At 0.6 miles, the trail reaches a ridge at 6,280 feet. Storm King Mountain with scorched sticks and green Gambel oak comes into view. You can see how the fire raced up gullies to different ridges. The trees to the right of the trail are blackened snags of their former selves. To the left, most trees are green and alive. Narrow-leaved penstemon and blue flax flowers grow among the ghostly trunks. Across the gully, Gambel oak is returning to the slopes, although junipers and piñon pines may take 40 to 100 years to reestablish themselves.

The trail follows a mostly flat ridge 0.4 miles to the observation point. Three large interpretive signs explain the events of the fateful July day. With a pair of binoculars, you can see the slope that 12 firefighters scrambled up trying to reach safety. Look closely for the pair of crossed skis marking one memorial site. You can turn around here or continue to the memorial sites.

To reach the memorial sites on the next ridge, continue on the trail left of the interpretive signs. If you hike this trail, be aware several sections are very steep with loose footing. Once on that ridge, a trail to the left leads to where two helitack crewmembers died across a steep little gully by a rock outcropping. The trail to the right leads to the slope where nine members of the Prineville, Oregon, Hotshots crew and three smokejumpers died. To reach the 12 sites, walk about 0.1 miles to a trail that switchbacks down the west slope. Memorial sites are noted with the firefighters' names. The BLM and families request that you stay on the trail and do not walk straight down between the crosses. The area between crosses is extremely steep and prone to erosion. Look around, see and feel the steepness of the slope. Imagine what it would be like to have a fire chasing you up that hill. Read the poem at trail's end below the memorial sites and be thankful for people who give their lives to protect the lives and property of others.

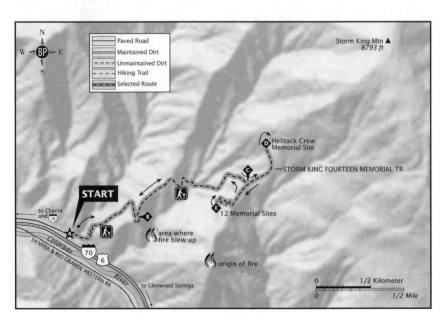

183

Other Items of Interest about Storm King

Two Rivers Park in Glenwood Springs contains a memorial to the 14 firefighters who died on Storm King Mountain. A bronze sculpture depicting three wildland firefighters is surrounded by a garden, pictures, and information about each of the lost firefighters.

To reach Two Rivers Park from Storm King Fourteen Memorial Trail, take Interstate 70 eastbound. Exit at West Glenwood and turn left under the highway. Then turn right onto U.S. Route 6 eastbound. Go 1.8 miles to Devereux Drive and turn right. Drive 0.3 miles, crossing over Interstate 70, and look for the park on the left. Turn left into the park. The memorial garden is straight ahead.

The story of the Storm King Mountain Fire (mistakenly reported as being in South Canyon) is captured in the book Fire on the Mountain *by John N. McLean, published in 1999. Many interesting articles, including the report of the investigation team, can be found via the Internet.*

View of trail to memorial sites from the observation point.

Hike Information

📞 Trail Contact:

Bureau of Land Management, Glenwood Springs Field Office, Glenwood Springs, CO (970) 947–2800 or *www.co.blm.gov/gsra/gshome.htm*

🕐 Schedule:

Open year round. Call first for trail conditions December through March.

💲 Fees/Permits:

No fees or permits required

❓ Local Information:

U.S. Forest Service, White River National Forest, Glenwood Springs, CO (970) 945–2521 or (970) 945–3249 or *www.fs.fed.us/r2/whiteriver* • **Glenwood Springs Chamber Resort Association,** Glenwood Springs, CO (970) 945–6589 or *www.glenscape.com/home.htm* • **Frontier Historical Society,** Glenwood Springs, CO (970) 945–4448

💡 Local Events/Attractions:

Glenwood Hot Springs Pool, Glenwood Springs, CO (970) 945–6571 or 1–800–537–7346 or *www.hotsprings pool.com* • **Glenwood Caverns,** Glenwood Springs, CO (970) 945–4228 or 1–800–530–1635 or *www.glenwoodcaverns.com* • **Strawberry Days,** Glenwood Springs, CO (970) 945–6589 • **Doc Hollidays,** Glenwood Springs, CO (970) 945–6589 • **Fall Arts Festival,** Glenwood Springs, CO (970) 945–6650

🛏 Accommodations:

Hotel Colorado (historic), Glenwood Springs, CO 1–800–544–3998 or *www.hotelcolorado.com* • **Hot Springs Lodge** (historic), Glenwood Springs, CO

(970) 945–6571 or 1–800–537–7946 or *www.hotspringspool.com* • **Glenwood Springs Hostel,** Glenwood Springs, CO (970) 945–8545 or 1–800–946–7895

🍴 Restaurants:

Smokin' Willies, Glenwood Springs, CO (970) 945–2479 • **Glenwood Canyon Brewing Co.,** Glenwood Springs, CO (970) 945–1276 • **Wild Rose Bakery,** Glenwood Springs, CO (970) 928–8973 • **Italian Underground,** Glenwood Springs, CO (970) 945–6422 • **Sapphire Grille,** Glenwood Springs, CO (970) 945–4771

⏱ Other Resources:

Fire on the Mountain, by John N. McLean, William Morrow and Company, Inc. • *Smoke Jumpers,* by Paul Freeman, Baskerville Publishers, Inc. – *inspired by the Storm King Mountain fire*

👥 Clubs and Organizations:

Colorado Mountain Club – Aspen Group, Aspen, CO – *For current contacts, call the state office at (303) 279–3080 or 1–800–633–4417 (Colorado only) or visit www.cmc.org/cmc.*

🏃 Hike Tours:

None for Storm King area

🎒 Local Outdoor Retailer:

Summit-Canyon Mountaineering, Glenwood Springs, CO 1–800– 360–6994 or (970) 945–6994 or *www.summit canyon.com*

🅝 Maps:

USGS maps: Storm King Mountain, CO • *Trails Illustrated®* maps: #123, Flat Tops SE/Glenwood Canyon

Coyote and Squirrel Trails

Hike Specs

Start: From the Rifle Falls State Park picnic ground

Length: 1.8-mile loop

Approximate Hiking Time: 1–2 hours

Difficulty Rating: Mostly easy with some steep sections

Elevations: 6,440–6,600 feet

Elevation Gain: 100 feet

Seasons: Year round except after snowstorms

Terrain: Paved road, dirt road, and dirt trail

Land Status: State park

Nearest Town: Rifle, CO

Other Trail Users: Wheelchair users (on first part of Coyote), anglers, and mountain bikers

Canine Compatibility: Leashed dogs permitted

Getting There

From Rifle: From I-70 Rifle Exit, head north on CO 13 through town. In about four miles, turn right onto CO 325 and drive another four miles to Rifle Gap Reservoir. Stay on CO 325, which turns right and goes over the dam. Drive another 5.6 miles to Rifle Falls State Park entrance. Pay the fee here or at the self-serve kiosk. Turn left and drive 0.2 miles through the campground to the picnic area. Park here. A vault toilet and water are available. *DeLorme: Colorado Atlas & Gazetteer:* Page 34 C4

L ined with red sandstone and limestone cliffs Rifle Falls State Park is a showplace with a 60-foot triple waterfall, lush riparian and forested areas, wildlife habitat, and a nice picnic area and campground. Two trails, named after local inhabitants, wander through the park for a complete tour. Interpretive signs along Coyote Trail explain the natural and social history of the area.

The original configuration of Rifle Falls consisted of one wide sheet of water, with some early pictures showing multiple ribbons of water. In 1908, the Rifle Light, Heat, and Power Company was incorporated to provide electricity to the town of Rifle. This group built the first hydroelectric plant in Colorado by diverting part of East Rifle Creek through a pipe descending the cliff at Rifle Falls. As a result, Rifle Falls became two ribbons of water plus the pipeline. Thirteen miles of transmission cable linked Rifle with the power plant. In town, eight miles of wires, 25 streetlights, and wiring for most buildings were installed. Rifle received its first electricity from the power plant on December 31, 1909. The company merged with Public Service Company in 1926. Public Service sold their property to the Colorado Game and Fish Department in 1959, at which time the plant was closed. The stone power plant was torn down in 1971. With the removal of the pipe, the falls have reverted to three streams of water.

The cliffs that create the falls are made of calcium carbonate from underground creeks in limestone deposits upstream. Thousands of years ago, the creek ran over some obstacle, which geologists believe was a giant beaver dam. The water left deposits that developed into today's cliffs. You can approach the falls from various sides, getting sprayed no matter which way you choose. To the right of the falls,

Coyote Trail winds past limestone caves, created by water eroding the cliff from the inside out. Some are shallow while one is large enough (90 feet) to need a flashlight to explore. Bats live in these caves, so be respectful if they are hanging out. The caves contain interesting formations such as flowstone, popcorn stone, and stalactites hanging from the ceiling. Watch your head as you hike from cave to cave. One place in particular has very low clearance.

> Various stories exist about how Rifle Creek was named. Most stories develop the theme of someone leaving or finding a rifle leaning against a tree along the creek. Another legend refers to a custom of cowboys firing their rifles at a roundup ground near the confluence of the three creeks.

Rifle Falls.

187

Outside the caves, cottonwoods, box elders, chokecherry trees, hawthorns (emphasis on thorns), coyote willows, and a little stream line the trail. Blue Steller's jays squawk overhead. The trail curves around and up until you are on top of the cliff. A trail to the Rifle Fish Hatchery branches to the north just before the falls. The hatchery was completed in 1954 as the largest trout hatchery in the state. Old metal pipes and wooden water diversions still remain from the hydroelectric plant days. The quickly flowing water disappears over the cliff in a white froth as it takes the plunge. Observation decks hang beyond the cliff for a bird's eye view and a potential vertigo adrenaline rush. The trail down is steep, but stairs make the trek a little easier. The riparian area around the falls creates wildlife watching opportunities.

After arriving back at the picnic area, walk through the main campground past the fee kiosk to Squirrel Trail. This trail takes you to the Grass Valley Canal, built between 1891 and 1894. At the same time, a dam was being built about five miles away (as the crow flies) across a gap in the Grand Hogback. This tilted ridge is the western Colorado version of the Dakota Hogback east of Denver. The canal brings

MilesDirections

0.0 START at the picnic ground at the closed pipe gate on the paved road. ☆ 39˚40'35"N 107˚41'55"W Head north toward Rifle Falls on the Coyote Trail.

0.1 View the Rifle Falls area and interpretive signs. ◆ 39˚40'40"N 107˚41'53"W *[**Note.** You might get sprayed by the falling water mist.]*

0.2 Reach the start of the limestone caves.

0.4 Come to the intersection with the trail to the fish hatchery. Go straight ahead to the falls overlook.

0.6 The trail drops downhill, sometimes steeply down concrete steps, back to the picnic area.

0.8 Arrive back at the paved road in the picnic area. Continue south on the paved park road until you reach the Squirrel Trail trailhead.

1.0 Reach the Squirrel Trail trailhead. ◆ 39˚40'24"N 107˚41'56"W

1.2 Stay to right at Campsite #20, drop down, and cross East Rifle Creek on a swinging bridge.

1.3 The Squirrel Trail climbs steeply and comes to a T-intersection. ◆ 39˚40'15"N 107˚41'53"W First climb up the ladder to the right to see one end of the canal tunnel. Then return and continue uphill on the trail.

1.4 The trail joins the dirt road along the canal at the water tunnel.

1.7 Come to a fork and go left down road.

1.8 Arrive back at the picnic ground.

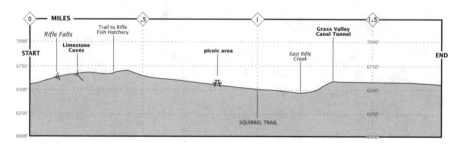

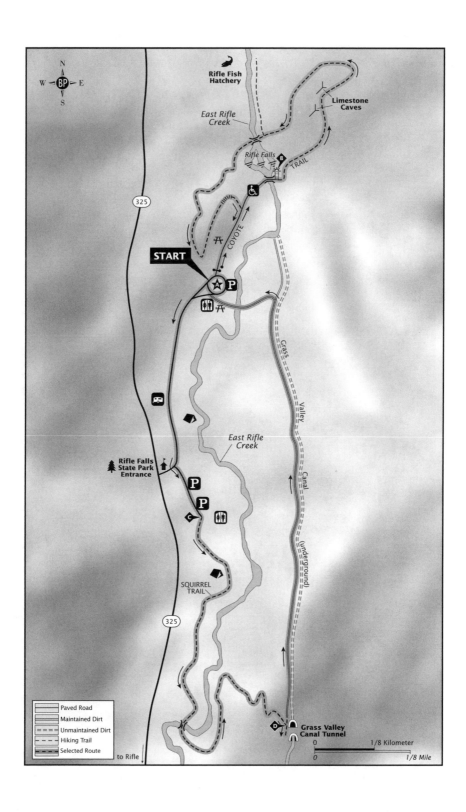

N W E S BP

325

Rifle Fish
Hatchery

*East Rifle
Creek*

Limestone
Caves

Rifle Falls

B

TRAIL

COYOTE

START

☆ P

P

*East Rifle
Creek*

Rifle Falls
State Park
Entrance

P

P

C

SQUIRREL
TRAIL

Grass
Valley
Canal
(underground)

Paved Road
Maintained Dirt
Unmaintained Dirt
Hiking Trail
Selected Route

to Rifle

D

Grass Valley
Canal Tunnel

0   1/8 Kilometer

0   1/8 Mile

Limestone cave near Rifle Falls.

water from East Rifle Creek to Harvey Gap Reservoir, which stores irrigation water for farms and ranches. The reservoir is in Harvey Gap State Park.

Squirrel Trail follows the creek through the walk-in campground then crosses it on a swinging bridge. The Gambel oak on the other side creates a thick forest, a cool treat on a hot day. The trail twists and climbs up the side of the canyon to the base of the cliff. A T-intersection appears after one steep stretch. First head right and climb up the metal ladder to see the canal exit a tunnel. Then climb down the ladder and go straight then uphill to where the trail meets the canal before it enters the tunnel. The water is clear and deep. The dirt road along the canal takes you back to the picnic ground by going downhill at the left-hand curve.

Rifle Falls has attracted visitors since the 1880s. Many people consider this area the Hawaii or Costa Rica of Colorado. The swank Zerbe Resort housed tourists for a number of years starting around 1903 until it unfortunately burned down in 1922.

Hike Information

● Trail Contact:
Rifle Falls State Park, Rifle, CO (970) 625–1607 or *www.parks.state.co.us/ rifle_falls*

● Schedule:
Year round, except after snowstorms. Call first for winter trail conditions

● Fees/Permits:
Daily fee or annual park pass required

● Local Information:
Rifle Area Chamber of Commerce, Rifle, CO (970) 625–2085 or *www.riflecham ber.com*

● Local Events/Attractions:
Garfield County Fair, Rifle, CO (970) 625–2085 • **Cheatin' Woodchuck Chase,** Rifle Recreation, Rifle, CO (970) 625–2151

● Accommodations:
Rifle Falls State Park campground, Rifle, CO (970) 625–1607

● Restaurants:
Shanghai Garden Chinese & American, Rifle, CO (970) 625–4430 • **Sammy's,** Rifle, CO (970) 625–8008

● Other Resources:
Rifle Shots: The Story of Rifle, Colorado, by the Rifle Reading Club • *Roadside Geology of Colorado,* by Halka Chronic, Mountain Press Publishing Co. • *Geology of Colorado Illustrated,* by Dell R. Foutz, Your Geologist • *Exploring Colorado State Parks,* by Martin G. Kleinsorge, University Press of Colorado • *Colorado State Parks A Complete Recreation Guide,* by Philip Ferranti, The Mountaineers

● Local Outdoor Retailer:
Local retailers cater to hunters and fishermen, not hikers • **Timberline Sporting Goods,** Rifle, CO (970) 625–4868 or 1–800–625–HUNT

● Maps:
USGS maps: Rifle Falls, CO • *Trails Illustrated®* maps: #125, Flat Tops SW/Rifle Gap

East Marvine Trail

Hike Specs

Start: From the East Marvine Trail (Trail 1822) trailhead

Length: 16.0-mile out-and-back with back-packing options

Approximate Hiking Time: 3 days minimum (with an option to explore the Flat Tops)

Difficulty Rating: Most difficult due to length, elevation gain, and steep sections

Elevations: 8,160–11,160 feet

Elevation Gain: 3,000 feet

Seasons: Best from late June to mid-October

Terrain: Dirt trail with some muddy sections and several bridgeless creek crossings

Land Status: National forest and wilderness area

Nearest Town: Meeker, CO

Other Trail Users: Equestrians, anglers, and hunters (in season)

Canine Compatibility: Controlled dogs permitted

Getting There

From Meeker: Drive east on CO 13 to where it curves north, and turn right onto CR 8. Follow the sign toward Buford and Trappers Lake. In about 28.5 miles, turn right onto a dirt road by the Marvine Campgrounds sign. There are various residences and a restaurant here. In 0.2 mile, turn left onto CR 12, which later becomes FS 12. Trailhead parking is 5.1 miles down FS 12 on the left. Park away from the corrals reserved for outfitters. There is no water or outhouse at the trailhead. Both are available at the two nearby campgrounds (fee areas). *DeLorme: Colorado Atlas & Gazetteer:* Page 25 D6 and 35 A6

W hile hiking up the trail, notice the pockmarked rocks. The White River Plateau is capped with dark basalt from volcanic eruptions that started around 25 million years ago. These eruptions lasted about 17 million years. After cooling off for another 7 million years, the ice age took hold. An ice cap formed over the plateau between 18,000 and 12,000 years ago. Melting glaciers left numerous little lakes and ponds below and on top of the plateau.

Many years later Ute Indians, also called the People of the Shining Mountains, camped in the Flat Tops on the northern end of the White River Plateau during the summer. Deer, elk, buffalos, and rabbits provided meat. Berries, wild onions, and the root of the yampa rounded out their diet.

As white settlers moved into the area, grazing and timber harvesting ran rampant and forest fires raged. Concerned citizens lobbied to protect western public resources. In 1891, President Benjamin Harrison set aside the White River Timber Land Reserve. White River is the second oldest national forest in the United States. The Flat Tops area earned another special place in history in 1919. The U.S. Forest Service sent landscape architect Arthur Carhart to Trappers Lake at the base of the Flat Tops to survey the area for summer cabins. Instead, Carhart recommended that this beautiful area be set aside and protected from development. He noted: "There are a number of places with scenic values of such great worth that they are rightfully

property of all people. They should be preserved for all time for the people of the Nation and the world. Trappers Lake is unquestionably a candidate for that classification."

Carhart later joined Aldo Leopold and began the movement that created the Wilderness Preservation System. The Flat Tops Primitive Area was established in 1932 with special protections. After many years of negotiation President Lyndon B. Johnson signed the Wilderness Act of 1964. Congress elevated the Primitive Area to the Flat Tops Wilderness in 1975. The second

When hiking on muddy trails, get muddy! Walking around the mud destroys the trail edge, making the bog bigger. By wearing waterproof boots and gaiters, walking through the mud is less painful. Gaiters help keep water out of your boots when rock hopping or wading shallow creeks, too.

East Marvine Trail.

193

largest wilderness area in Colorado is home to the largest elk herd in the state. Keep an eye open for deer and elk while you're hiking. Other wildlife you might encounter includes black bears, bobcats, pine martens, foxes, coyotes, marmots, and pikas.

The trail follows East Marvine Creek through aspen, Gambel oak, and lodgepole pine forests. Occasional grassy meadows provide views of the Flat Tops escarpment and Little Marvine Peaks. Follow along a small stream and past the two-mile mark where ponds and small lakes start to appear. The trail climbs steadily up through aspens, Engelmann spruces, and subalpine firs. Numerous creeks intersect the trail, and some can be tricky to cross depending on water level. Most creeks have muddy edges and no log bridges, so you'll have to rock hop across. After contouring around a ridge, Rainbow Lake lies to the left. A few campsites can be found on the ridge above it. Beyond Rainbow Lake, the trail levels off and loses some elevation across meadows and tiny creeks. It finally rejoins East Marvine Creek and passes an energetic cascade before climbing steeply up the side of the Flat Tops. The spruce-fir forest is thick and dark here. Bark beetles infested the forest in the 1940s and many dead

MilesDirections

0.0 START the hike at Marvine trailheads making sure to take the left trailhead signed as "East Marvine" (Trail 1822). ☆ 40˚00'29"N 107˚25'27"W

0.1 Cross the sturdy bridge over East Marvine Creek. At the T-intersection, turn right onto the trail and head uphill with the creek on your right.

1.4 The trail leaves East Marvine Creek to follow a small stream.

1.7 The trail splits; stay to the right. *[Note. Left trail has logs over it to discourage use. The trail can get very muddy in this stretch.]*

2.2 Johnson Lake is on the right. ◈ 40˚00'16"N 107˚23'18"W

2.4 Come to the junction with Wild Cow Park Trail (Trail 1820-1B). Stay to the right on East Marvine Trail.

4.2 Reach Rainbow Lake. ◈ 39˚59'36"N 107˚21'42"W

5.4 Reach the East Marvine Creek cascades.

6.1 Reach the first set of switchbacks.

6.5 Reach a set of six switchbacks.

7.2 Reach the third set of switchbacks.

7.8 Reach the plateau edge near a cairn and a lake.

8.0 The trail splits. ◈ 39˚57'57"N 107˚19'26"W *[Option. You can choose your own way and explore. If you hike an additional 2.5 miles on East Marvine Trail you will reach a T-intersection with Oyster Lake Trail (Trail 1825). Several loops or longer out-and-back trips can be made from here.]* Turn around and return the way you came or continue from here to a destination of your choice.

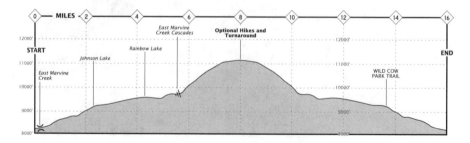

snags make the forest appear ancient. Wood decays slowly in the high, dry Colorado climate. How large animals like elk can maneuver through the tangled dark forest almost defies the imagination.

Two long switchbacks lead to the base of the escarpment. When you find a flat spot, take a breather and enjoy the view. Scan the surrounding cliff bands for silver ribbon waterfalls. Six short switchbacks take you even higher, and two final switchbacks bring you close to the edge of the plateau. The climb is still not quite over, but becomes gentler now. You have gained about 1,000 feet in the last mile.

A large cairn holding up a tree trunk greets you at the top edge. A small lake is just beyond, then another and another. Little Marvine Peaks rise to the north with Big Marvine Peak dominating the southwest view. The subalpine meadows roll

> When meeting horses on the trail, step off on the downhill side until the horses pass. If a horse wants more room, it will move off the trail away from you. It is safer for both the horse and rider if the horse heads uphill. If the trail is narrow, ask the rider for instructions.

along with patches of spruce-fir. After the third little lake, the trail splits. The left branch heads for Twin Lakes and Oyster Lake (Trail 1825), while the right branch (unofficial trail) leads to a good fishing lake and toward Big Marvine Peak. From here you can explore and camp many places. Take a couple of days to enjoy the open high country of the Flat Tops.

Please remember to camp at least 100 feet (about 35 adult steps) away from streams, lakes, and trails. Using a lightweight cookstove instead of a fire will avoid leaving permanent scars on the land. By practicing Leave No Trace techniques, hikers can enjoy a pristine experience and find solitude in the Flat Tops Wilderness for many years.

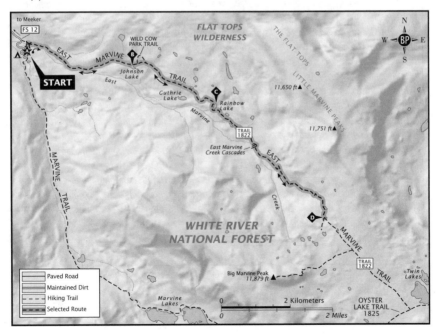

Marvine Valley looking toward the Flat Tops.

A Little Ute Indian History

Ute territory once covered about 150,000 square miles of mountainous Colorado, Utah, and southern Wyoming. The Utes were divided into seven bands, each with its own hunting territory. The White River band called a large area of northwest Colorado their home, including the Flat Tops. For hundreds of years they roamed the huge territory, following game with the seasons. The southern bands had early contact with the Spanish and obtained horses. Accomplished horsemen, their battle skills were feared by whites and other Native American tribes alike.

The Utes tried to live in peace with the new white settlers. Chief Ouray of the Tabeguache band realized that fighting would result in disaster. Although the Utes lived in different bands, Ouray was recognized as the spokesman by the United States government. He crafted treaties very favorable to his people. The treaties, however, were either broken or modified as the pressure for gold and homesteading increased. The treaty of 1868 stipulated that no white man could enter Ute territory, covering the western third of Colorado, without Ute permission. The government created agencies to provide supplies for the Utes and hopefully keep the peace. One agency was located near present day Meeker on the White River. Nathan Meeker became agent in 1878. The next year Meeker decided that the Utes should farm a grassy pasture being used for their prized horses. Farming was not part of the Ute way of life and a disagreement ensued. Meeker requested reinforcements. Led by Major Thornburgh, troops crossed into Ute territory without permission. Who fired the first shot is unknown, but the resulting battle ended in the death of Meeker, many soldiers, and Utes. Angry whites banished all Utes to reservations in 1880 with the White River band going to the Uintah Reservation in Utah.

Hike Information

🕐 Trail Contact:
White River National Forest, Blanco Ranger District, Meeker, CO (970) 878–4039 or *www.fs.fed.us/r2/whiteriver/index.html*

🕐 Schedule:
Access road closed by snow 2.5 miles from trailhead. Ski on road and main Marvine Trail. Trails neither maintained nor marked for winter use.

💲 Fees/Permits:
Group size limited to a combination of 25 people and stock. As this book goes to print, the White River National Forest Plan is undergoing revision. Group sizes and other regulations may change in this process.

❓ Local Information:
Meeker Chamber of Commerce, Meeker, CO (970) 878–5510 or *www.meekerchamber.com* • other helpful websites: *www.colorado-west.com* or *www.meekercolorado.com* or *www.coloradowilderness.com*

🔵 Local Events/Attractions:
Meeker Classic Sheepdog Championship Trials, Meeker, CO (970) 878–5510 or (970) 878–5483 or *www.colorado-west.com/dog.html* • The White River Museum, Meeker, CO (970) 878–9982 or *www.meekercolorado.com/museum.htm#WHITE* • Flat Tops Trail Scenic & Historic Byway, Meeker, CO (970) 878–5510 • Rangecall Rodeo, Meeker, CO (970) 878–5510 or *www.colorado-west.com/rangecal.html*

🍽 Accommodations:
Camping at Meeker City Park, Meeker, CO (970) 878–5344 • Marvine Campgrounds, White River National Forest, Blanco Ranger District, Meeker, CO (970) 878–4039

🍴 Restaurants:
Sleepy Cat Guest Ranch, Meeker, CO (970) 878–4413 • Clark's Big Burger, Meeker, CO (970) 878–3240 • The Bakery, Meeker, CO (970) 878–5500

📖 Other Resources:
A Sierra Club Naturalist's Guide to The Southern Rockies, by Audrey DeLella Benedict, Sierra Club Books • *The Complete Guide to Colorado's Wilderness Areas,* by Mark Pearson and John Fielder, Westcliffe Publishers • *Quiet Revelation,* by Donald H. Baldwin, Pruett Publishing Co. • *People of the Shining Mountains The Utes of Colorado,* by Charles S. Marsh, Pruett Publishing Co.

🛒 Local Outdoor Retailer:
Wyatt's Sport Center, Meeker, CO (970) 878–4428 – *mostly geared to hunting and fishing but has some camping supplies and maps*

Ⓝ Maps:
USGS maps: Big Marvine Peak, CO; Lost Park, CO; Oyster Lake, CO; Ripple Creek Pass, CO • Trails Illustrated® maps: #122, Flat Tops NE/Trappers Lake

Black Mountain (West Summit) Trail

Hike Specs

Start: From the trailhead at the east side of Freeman Reservoir

Length: 6.8-mile out-and-back, (7.6 miles if you include 0.4-mile spur to raptor viewing area)

Approximate Hiking Time: 3.5–5 hours

Difficulty Rating: Difficult due to elevation gain and some rough trail sections

Elevations: 8,750–10,815 feet

Elevation Gain: 2,065 feet

Seasons: Best from late June to mid-October

Terrain: Dirt trail with wet areas and some rocky sections

Land Status: National forest

Nearest Town: Craig, CO

Other Trail Users: Equestrians, mountain bikers, and hunters (in season)

Canine Compatibility: Controlled dogs permitted. Water sparse on trail.

Getting There

From Craig: From the intersection of U.S. 40 and CO 13, head north on CO 13 to just past mile marker 103, about 13 miles. Turn right onto CR 11 (which becomes FS 112) and drive 9.2 miles to Freeman Recreation Area. Remember to pay the day-use fee at the self-service station. You can park on the west side of the reservoir and hike the Aspen Trail (Trail 1183.1A) to Cottonwood Trail (Trail 1183), approximately 0.5 miles. Or you can continue another 0.4 miles to the east end of the reservoir, turn left, and go another 0.1 miles to the parking area at the trailhead near the campground. The hike description starts at the east trailhead. Water and restroom are found at the campground (fee area). Note: Dogs must be on leash at the trailhead, parking lot, and in the campground. **DeLorme: Colorado Atlas & Gazetteer:** Page 15 B6

I n the Elkhead Mountains of northwestern Colorado, Black Mountain forms a 1.75-mile long plateau that rises north of Craig. From a distance, it does indeed look black. The Elkheads were formed by the same volcanic eruptions that shaped the Flat Tops and White River Plateau between 25 and 17 million years ago. At the eastern edge of a desert zone the Elkheads capture enough moisture to feed the Elkhead, Little Snake, and Yampa Rivers. Ute Indians lived and hunted here. Although very popular in fall with hunters because of large elk, deer, and pronghorn antelope herds, summer finds the area less used than the wilderness areas to the east and south. Aspens flourish in the Freeman Reservoir area and the lower part of Black Mountain, making this trail a colorful fall hike.

Aspens and willows growing along Little Cottonwood Creek border the first part of the trail. The lush aspen forest provides a home to many animals and plants. Colorado columbine, the state flower, grows in aspen forests. Pink Wood's rose, white geranium, yellow heartleaf arnica (named for its heart-shaped leaves), pinkish-purple fireweed, dandelion, blue harebells, various paintbrushes, pussytoes, white Mariposa lily, and wild strawberries cover the ground. Larkspur, pearly everlasting, and white to pinkish yarrow are common. In moister areas, tall cow parsnip with its teeny flowers forming a lacey doily and deep purple monkshood grow in profusion. Cow parsnip is often confused with Queen Anne's lace. Monkshood is aptly named with its monk's

View southwest from Black Mountain Trail.

cowl flowers. Listen for the *chick-a-dee-dee-dee* of the mountain chickadee, a small gray and black bird that lives here year round. Elk and deer find ample food in aspen forests including grasses and bushes such as serviceberry, snowberry, twinberry, and chokecherry along with Rocky Mountain maple.

The aspen tree is an interesting plant. Started from seed, expansion of a stand occurs when lateral roots sprout new shoots forming a clone. If you notice how various sets of aspen change color at different times or exhibit different hues, the look-alike bunch is the same plant. Aspens sprout quickly after a fire, mining, logging, or other disturbance has denuded an area. Because they shed leaves that decompose

MilesDirections

0.0 START at trailhead at east end of Freeman Reservoir ☆ 40˚45'51"N 107˚25'21"W—Follow Little Cottonwood Trail (Trail 1183).

0.1 Junction with a trail from the right, but no sign. Keep going straight ahead or you'll end up back at the campground.

0.2 Junction with Aspen Trail (Trail 1183.1A) coming in from left from west trailhead. Keep hiking straight ahead on Little Cottonwood Trail (Trail 1183).

0.5 Cross Little Cottonwood Creek on a bridge.

0.7 Reach a trail junction with no sign. ◆ 40˚46'21"N 107˚24'56"W—Stay on the trail to the left. You are now on the Bears Ears Trail (Trail 1144).

0.8 Reach the trail junction of Bears Ears Trail (Trail 1144) and Black Mountain Trail (Trail 1185). Turn right up Black Mountain Trail.

1.7 *[FYI. Enjoy the views to the south and east as you leave the aspen forest.]*

1.8 Switchback to the left.

2.3 Come to a right switchback and a flat area

near big boulders. *[FYI. This is a good rest stop.]*

3.0 The trail reaches the edge of a plateau.

3.3 Come to a junction with a spur trail to the raptor viewing area. ◆ 40˚47'28"N 107˚23'22"W *[Side-trip. Hike on spur to raptor viewing area will add 0.8-mile out-and-back to your hike. Raptors enjoy the thermals in this area. The viewpoint has an interpretive sign explaining the soaring birds of prey you might be lucky to see. On a clear day, you can see west to Dinosaur National Monument and the Uinta Mountains in Utah.]* Stay right to go to the summit.

3.4 Reach the west summit of Black Mountain (10,815 feet). ◆ 40˚47'29"N 107˚23'14"W *[Side-trip. A hike to the east summit with beautiful views of the Yampa Valley and distant peaks will add three miles out-and-back to your trip.]* Turn around and retrace you tracks back to the start.

3.5 Reach the junction with spur trail to raptor viewing area, on the right.

6.8 Arrive back at the trailhead.

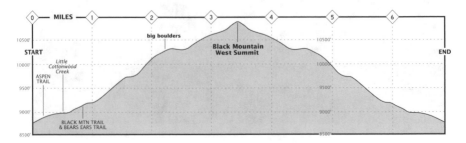

faster than evergreen needles, aspens return nutrients to the soil more rapidly than other trees. The soil is richer, fostering an environment for other plants, which in turn contribute nutrients to the soil. Aspens, however, are susceptible to about 20 different diseases, making one wonder how they survive so well.

Elk depend on aspen trees especially during harsh winters when they cannot uncover buried grasses. Scraping bark off with their lower teeth they feast on the cambium layer just under the bark. Watch for elk teeth marks as you hike. Black bears enjoy many fruits of the aspen forest, from aspen buds and catkins in spring to berries produced by the numerous shrubs. They sometimes climb aspens, leaving claw marks as testimony to their exploits. Avoid surprising bears that are trying to fatten up before winter.

The hike starts along the east shore of Freeman Reservoir, then heads up Little Cottonwood Creek drainage. The trail can be very muddy here. Farther on, one section is very rocky as it climbs to the Bears Ears Trail (Trail 1144). When you reach Black Mountain Trail (Trail 1185), head north to a big aspen stand. Thick forest undergrowth sometimes obscures the trail. Watch your footing as aspen forests are notorious for hidden roots and fallen trees waiting to twist an ankle. Some large boul-

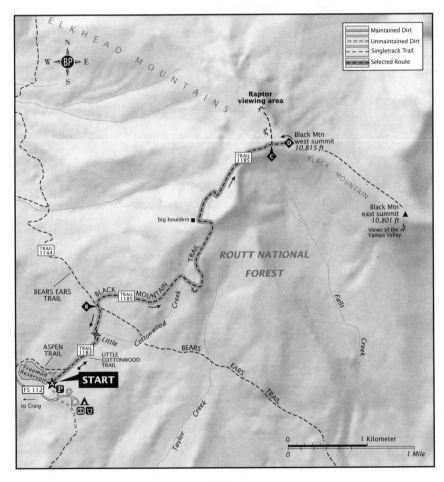

ders lend a rock garden atmosphere along trail sections. A few clearings present views to the south and west, including Freeman Reservoir about 1,000 feet below.

The trail curves up a ridge and enters spruce-fir forest. It climbs steadily to a flat spot below the plateau with views to the north. The big boulders make a nice rest spot. The trail then drops about 60 feet into an open area where a large boulder field on the right lines a thumb of the plateau. After a few tight switchbacks, the trail continues to climb to a saddle on the plateau. After hiking around a boulder field, you come to another open area. A spur trail heads north to the raptor viewing area, where an interpretive sign explains why golden and bald eagles enjoy soaring and playing above the edge of Black Mountain. The west summit is a little farther to the northeast. A sign denotes the summit, barely discernible on the fairly flat plateau top. The trail beyond the west summit continues another 1.5 miles to the east summit (10,801 feet) for views of the Yampa Valley.

Aspens and reflection in Freeman Reservoir.

Hike Information

🔦 Trail Contact:

Medicine Bow–Routt National Forest, Hahns Peak/Bears Ears Ranger District, Steamboat Springs, CO (970) 879–1870 or *www.fs.fed.us/mrnf/hpbe.html*

⏱ Schedule:

Access road closed by snow 2.5 miles from trailhead. Ski on road and main Marvine Trail. Trails neither maintained nor marked for winter use.

💲 Fees/Permits:

Day-use fee required for Freeman Recreation Area

❓ Local Information:

Moffat County Visitors Center, Craig, CO 1–800–864–4405 or (970) 824–5689 or *www.craig-chamber.com* • **Moffat County Lodging Tax Panel,** Craig, CO 1–800–864–4405 or (970) 824–5689 or *www.colorado-go-west.com*

💡 Local Events/Attractions:

Grande Olde West Days, end of May, Craig, CO 1–800–864–4405 • **Museum of Northwest Colorado,** Craig, CO (970) 824–6360 or *www.museumnwco.org* • **ColoWyo Coal Mine,** Craig, CO (970) 824–4451 • **Trappers Mine,** Craig, CO (970) 824–4401 • **Tri-State Generation and Transmission Assn., Inc.** Craig, CO (970) 824–4411 – *Colorado's largest coal-fired electric generating station*

🛏 Accommodations:

National forest campgrounds, Hahns Peak/Bears Ears Ranger District, Steamboat Springs, CO (970) 879–1870

• **Craig KOA,** Craig, CO 1–800–297–6445 or (970) 824–3445 • **Colorado State Parks – Yampa (Elkhead Reservoir),** Hayden, CO (970) 276–2061 or *www.parks.state.co.us/yampa/elkhead/index.asp*

🍴 Restaurants:

The Galaxy, Craig, CO (970) 824–8164 – *Chinese food*

📖 Other Resources:

A Sierra Club Naturalist's Guide to The Southern Rockies, by Audrey DeLella Benedict, Sierra Club Books • *From Grassland to Glacier The Natural History of Colorado and the Surrounding Region,* by Cornelia Fleischer Mutel and John C. Emerick, Johnson Printing

🚶 Hike Tours:

Yampatika, Steamboat Springs, CO (970) 871–9151

🎒 Local Outdoor Retailer:

Cashway Distributors, Craig, CO (970) 824–3035 – *mainly geared to hunting and fishing but some camping gear and maps*

🅝 Maps:

USGS maps: Freeman Reservoir, CO

Gates of Lodore
Nature Trail

Hike Specs

Start: From Gates of Lodore Campground
Length: 1.0-mile out-and-back
Approximate Hiking Time: 30–50 minutes
Difficulty Rating: Easy due to shortness
Elevations: 5,355–5,415 feet
Elevation Gain: 60 feet
Seasons: Year round except after a big snowstorm
Terrain: Dirt trail with some rock steps
Land Status: National monument
Nearest Town: Craig, CO
Other Trail Users: Hikers only
Canine Compatibility: Dogs not permitted

Getting There

From Craig: Drive west out of Craig on U.S. 40 for about 31 miles to Maybell. Turn right onto CO 318. Drive about 40 miles to CR 10 and turn left onto it. This road is dirt, but well maintained. It could get muddy when wet. In 0.6 miles, turn right onto CR 34. Stay on CR 34 for about nine miles, until you reach the Gates of Lodore Campground in Dinosaur National Monument. (Do not turn right onto CR 34N). Drive to the far end of the campground to the trailhead. Water and vault toilets are available at the campground. **DeLorme: Colorado Atlas & Gazetteer:** Page 12 C1

The Uinta Mountains of northeastern Utah and northwestern Colorado are unusual in that the spine runs east-west instead of the typical north-south. Like most of the Rockies, the Uintas are a faulted anticline, meaning that ancient Precambrian rocks have been lifted and the rock layers on top arched. The spectacular walls of Canyon of Lodore are the red sandstones and siltstones of the Uinta Mountain Group formed in Precambrian times over 600 million years ago. Between 65–45 million years ago the land started to rise forming the present Rocky Mountains, including the Uintas. The rising mountains probably caused the Green River to slow its eastern flow. Some geologists believe that Browns Park, to the north of Gates of Lodore, filled with sediments from rivers going nowhere. As the sediments filled Browns Park to the top of the Uintas, the Green River also rose to the top, spilled over the southern edge, and started downcutting the canyon. By about five million years ago, the entire region had been lifted another 5,000 feet higher. The rising land and downcutting action of the river probably worked together to create the great canyon.

In the 1860s and 1870s, several surveys explored the unknown western lands belonging to the United States. John Wesley Powell, a Civil War veteran who had lost his right arm during combat, led one of these surveys. After the war, Powell became a Professor of Geology at Illinois State Normal University. During the summers, he ventured west exploring what is now western Colorado and eastern Utah. He believed the best way to explore the canyons in this area would be by boat. In 1868, he came to the edge of the Uintas with his wife and about 20 students and neighbors. They spent the winter in three small cabins along the White River near

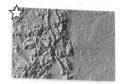

Hike Information

🌜 Trail Contact:

Dinosaur National Monument, Dinosaur, CO (970) 374-3000 or *www.nps.gov/ dino*

🕓 Schedule:

Year round, except after big snowstorm

💲 Fees/Permits:

There is no entrance fee for using the Gates of Lodore area. Campground fee is charged.

❓ Local Information:

Brown's Park Store, Maybell, CO (970) 365-3658 – *has gas and limited supplies, plus interesting locals* • **Moffat County Visitors Center,** Craig, CO 1-800-864-4405 or (970) 824-5689 or *www.craig-chamber.com* • **Moffat County Lodging Tax Panel,** Craig, CO 1-800-864-4405 or (970) 824-5689 or *www.colorado-go-west.com*

💡 Local Events/Attractions:

Browns Park National Wildlife Refuge, Maybell, CO (970) 365-3613 or *mountain-prairie.fws.gov/ refuges/BROWNS* • **Swinging Bridge,** Browns Park National Wildlife Refuge, Maybell, CO (970) 365-3613 • **Lodore Hall National Historic Site,** Browns Park National Wildlife Refuge, Maybell, CO (970) 365-3613 • **John Jarvie Historic Ranch (BLM),** Browns Park, UT (435) 885-3307

🛏 Accommodations:

Gates of Lodore Campground, Dinosaur National Monument, Dinosaur, CO (970) 374-3000 or *www.nps.gov/dino* • **Browns Park NWR campgrounds,** Browns Park National Wildlife Refuge, Maybell, CO (970) 365-3613 • **Craig KOA,** Craig, CO 1-800-297-6445 or (970) 824-3445

🍴 Restaurants:

The Galaxy, Craig, CO (970) 824-8164 – *Chinese restaurant*

🕹 Other Resources:

Powell's trip report can be downloaded in PDF format from: *www.library.unt.edu/ gpo/powell/publications.htm* • *A Sierra Club Naturalist's Guide The Southern Rockies,* by Audrey DeLella Benedict, Sierra Club Books

🎒 Local Outdoor Retailer:

Cashway Distributors, Craig, CO (970) 824-3035 – *mainly geared to hunting and fishing but some camping gear and maps*

🗺 Maps:

USGS maps: Gates of Lodore, CO • *Trails Illustrated®* maps: #220, Dinosaur National Monument

present day Meeker. In the spring Powell headed east and secured four boats and supplies for a six-month trip. On May 24, 1869, Powell and nine other men left Green River City, Wyoming and headed down the Green for the Colorado River.

On June 6, the motley crew had floated the calm Green River through Browns Park and camped near the head of the canyon. The next day he and a few others climbed to the summit of the cliff. In his journal Powell wrote: "The cañon walls are buttressed on a grand scale, with deep alcoves intervening; columned crags crown the cliffs, and the river is rolling below...the sun shines in splendor on vermilion walls, shaded into green and gray, where the rocks are lichened over; the river fills the channel from wall to wall, and the cañon opens, like a beautiful portal, to a region of glory."

On June 9, one of his men suggested they call the canyon "Cañon of Lodore." During the day, one of the boats missed a pullout to examine the next set of rapids.

> *In John Wesley Powell's time, the official Colorado River started at the confluence of the Grand and Green rivers in Utah. The Grand River started in what is now Rocky Mountain National Park. According to Powell: "The Green River is larger than the Grand, and is the upper continuation of the Colorado."*

MilesDirections

0.0 START at the far end of the Gates of Lodore Campground. ☆ 40°43'24"N 108°53'13"W—In 210 feet, the trail switchbacks. After the switchbacks, stay to the left—the right trail heads to an overlook.

0.5 Come to a viewpoint of Gates of Lodore and Canyon of Lodore. Return the way you came.

1.0 Arrive back at the trailhead.

Green River and Gates of Lodore.

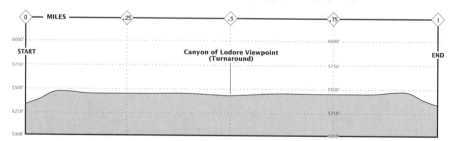

After hitting a few huge rocks, the boat was "dashed to pieces." Luckily the crew survived. A previous party, led by a man named Ashley, had also swamped in this spot and some of his crew drowned. Powell's group decided to christen the rapids Disaster Falls. Barometers (used for determining altitude), a package of thermometers, and a keg of whiskey were rescued from the wreckage of the boat. The group eventually arrived in the Grand Canyon. After many portages, lowering boats down the river, drying out wet food and supplies, and continually being drenched, three men decided to go no farther down the river. They traveled overland, later being killed by Native Americans, who thought the white men had killed a squaw. Powell and the rest of his crew successfully floated through the Grand Canyon, finishing on August 30, 1869. Powell was later funded for a second expedition down the Grand Canyon, which he undertook from 1871 to 1872.

The hike starts at the far end of Gates of Lodore campground. Take a nature trail guide for an introduction to semidesert shrubland, piñon-juniper forests, area history, and geology. After two steep switchbacks, the trail levels off on a bench above the Green River. Take some time to relax on the rocks overlooking the Gates of Lodore. This part of Dinosaur National Monument is less crowded than the Quarry area and has few visitors other than boaters putting in on the Green River. If you have time, take a multi-day raft trip down the Green River to Split Mountain near the Dinosaur Quarry.

The Browns Park area has a classic storybook western history complete with American Indians, wildlife, ranching, and outlaws. Butch Cassidy and the Sundance Kid of the Wild Bunch used this area for a hideout, while other local characters included outlaws Matt Warner, Isom Dart, and Ann Bassett, Queen of the Rustlers. Take time to explore this remote area of Colorado. Make sure to stop at the Browns Park Store for local information and history.

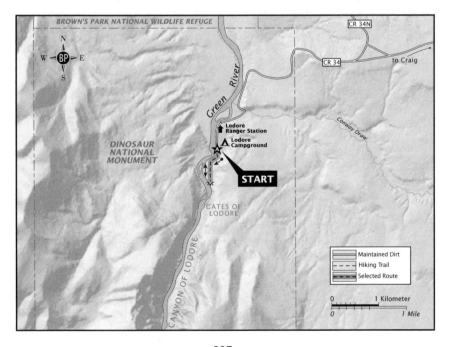

Buckwater Draw

Hike Specs

Start: From the gate to Bull Canyon Wilderness Study Area on a side road off of Harpers Corner Road in Dinosaur National Monument

Length: 10.0-mile out-and-back

Approximate Hiking Time: 4–7 hours

Difficulty Rating: Difficult due to distance and elevation change

Elevations: 6,040–7,640 feet

Elevation Gain: 1,600 feet

Seasons: Best from April through November. Avoid hot summer days.

Terrain: Dirt road and trail, cattle trails, and creek bed

Land Status: BLM land and wilderness study area

Nearest Towns: Rangely, CO and Dinosaur, CO

Other Trail Users: Equestrians and hunters (in season)

Canine Compatibility: Controlled dogs permitted. Little to no water on the trail.

Getting There

From Rangely: Drive north on CO 64 about 18 miles to the town of Dinosaur and U.S. 40. Turn right on U.S. 40 and drive east about 1.8 miles to the Harpers Corner Road (not marked as such) and Dinosaur National Monument Visitor Center. Turn left onto Harpers Corner Road and drive about 6.9 miles north. If you reach the Escalante Overlook, you went about one mile too far. It's easy to zip by the trailhead so watch carefully for the cattle pond on the right and immediately to the left is a dirt road and gate. Turn left onto the dirt road, open the gate, making sure no cattle escape, and pull just inside the fence. Make sure to close the gate behind you and not totally block the road. The BLM says to park just inside the gate to avoid parking on the national monument right-of-way. However, the wilderness study area is closed to motorized vehicles. (The rancher with the grazing permit can drive in here.) There are no facilities here. Vault toilet available at Plug Hat Picnic Area. Bring a lot of water with you. *DeLorme: Colorado Atlas & Gazetteer:* Page 22 B1

I n 1776, Fray Francisco Atanasio Dominguez and Fray Francisco Silvestre Vélez de Escalante embarked on an expedition to find a route from Santa Fe to the California missions near Monterey. Dominguez provided leadership while Vélez de Escalante kept a detailed journal. Andrés Muñiz served as translator with the Utes. While the main purpose of the expedition was route finding, details about native peoples, plants, animals, potential farming areas, terrain, and rivers were recorded.

The expedition left Santa Fe on July 19, 1776, and followed a route north and west through Durango, Mancos, and north to Montrose. They occasionally hired a native to guide them in exchange for goods such as knives and strings of white glass beads. By early September the expedition crossed Grand Mesa. Continuing northwest they noticed pictographs on canyon walls, which they named Cañon Pintado (Painted Canyon). Farther to the north they crossed the White River and Rangely Oil Field area. Just beyond they found an arroyo with running water where the party stayed two nights to rest their thirsty horses. A buffalo was hunted to replenish their

Buckwater Draw.

dwindling supplies. The party named the area El Arroyo del Cibolo meaning Buffalo Arroyo.

You can see this general area while hiking downhill. The K Ranch is about 1.5 miles beyond the rock thumbs protruding skyward in the open area to the west. Dominguez and Escalante's camp at El Arroyo del Cibolo was near the ranch.

The party then headed west into Utah and turned south. From mid-October to early November, the expedition spent much time trying to cross the Colorado River, El Rio Grande, in what is now northern Arizona. But the Grand Canyon and its tributary canyons proved too difficult. They returned to Santa Fe on January 2, 1777.

MilesDirections

0.0 START at the gate to the wilderness study area. ☆ 40˚18'47"N 108˚55'56"W

0.5 A road comes in from the left. Continue walking straight ahead. *[FYI. Watch for ducks in the cattle pond.]*

0.6 A road goes left toward the pond. Continue walking straight ahead.

0.9 Road forks. Turn left. *[FYI. You'll occasionally see little stone outcrops—some are conglomerate and some sandstone.]*

1.3 Road comes in from the right. Continue walking straight ahead. *[FYI. A few junipers grow among the sagebrush.]*

2.2 Pass through an old fence with no gate. *[FYI. You're in a nice juniper forest here.]* The trail drops and levels in this area.

2.5 *[FYI. Enjoy a nice view of sandstone formations to the west.]* The trail descends steeply at times from here.

3.2 *[FYI. Enjoy another nice view of sandstone canyons and outcrops.]*

3.5 *[FYI. There's a view out onto the plain below with rock thumbs protruding.]* The trail descends steeply in places.

4.0 Trail becomes flatter. Buckwater Draw and the creek are to the left. Turn left here and follow cattle trails across sagebrush flats. ◈ 40˚18'20"N 108˚59'57"W

4.2 Arrive at several large cottonwood trees at the edge of the arroyo. Walk along the edge until you find a place to drop to the creek bottom. Follow the creek bottom, sometimes using cattle trails to avoid the willows. *[Note. Avoid walking above the creek because of all the cryptobiotic soil crust that is easily damaged by footsteps.]*

4.8 This area narrows with high colorful cliffs to the left.

5.0 Reach a very narrow canyon. ◈ 40˚18'12"N 108˚58'58"W—Depending on waterholes, you may not be able to walk this far or much farther. Enjoy the coolness. Return the way you came. Remember, it's uphill!

10.0 Arrive back at the trailhead.

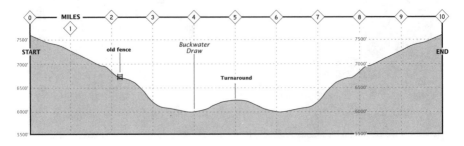

Although Dominguez and Escalante did not find a route to Monterey, the party explored and documented a large area of the west.

Today ranchers and farmers work the land for their living. Bull Canyon Wilderness Study Area (WSA) along with Willow Creek and Skull Creek Wilderness Study Areas to the east form a southern boundary to the canyon section of Dinosaur National Monument. Other

The Escalante Overlook is 1.2 miles north of the trailhead on Harpers Corner Road. The overlook offers an expansive view toward Escalante's historic campsite and Utah. Interpretive posters explain Escalante's camp and why air pollution may be visible in this area.

than a few old ranch roads, there are no trails in these WSAs. Occasionally you can follow cattle or game trails, but they meander everywhere. This area provides outstanding opportunities for solitude and beautiful canyon hiking, but access is difficult and good route finding skills are a must.

If you hike in spring, gnats can be a royal pain. Another interesting insect is the Mormon cricket, actually a katydid, which hatches around April. As you drive to the trailhead, you may run over hundreds of these little things as they cross the road. They can actually make the road very slippery. In the early morning the crickets enjoy the sun for a couple of hours before starting to migrate when temperatures reach about 96°F. They migrate up to 50 miles in a single season, but no one understands why. The crickets are an important food source for peregrine falcons and endangered fish down in the river canyons. Around 1850, Major Howard Egan documented his observations of a Native American cricket roundup. One method used trenches, covered with a thin layer of stiff wheat grass. They would then drive the crickets into the trenches and set the grass on fire. The crickets were gathered into

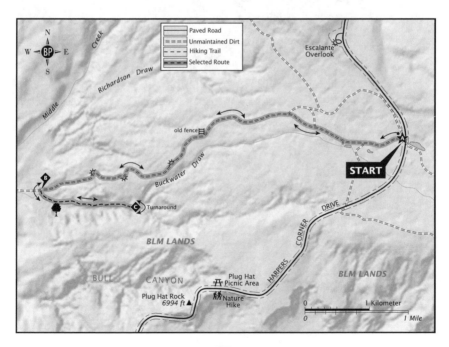

baskets, taken to camp, dried, and ground into fine flour for bread. A Native American companion told Egan: "The crickets make the bread good, the same as sugar used by the white woman in her cakes." Watch for these interesting insects as you hike and drive.

The trail is obvious while it follows the old ranch road. Watch for deer, turkey vultures, and piñon jays. The cattle will move out of your way, please do not harass them. Once at the flatter area where the ranch road and Buckwater Draw converge, head upstream into Buckwater Draw. Follow the Miles/Directions carefully. While traveling cross-country, please avoid walking on the black lumpy cryptobiotic soil crust as it is very fragile (see "Cryptobiotic Soil Crust" on page 218). Colorful sandstone cliffs draw closer and tower above you. The canyon narrows and depending on water pools, you may not be able to walk any farther. Be extremely mindful of the weather in this area and the potential for flash floods. This narrow slot canyon in the midst of sagebrush plains and juniper woodlands is a pleasant and cool surprise. Just remember it's uphill on the return trip!

Narrows in Buckwater Draw.

Hike Information

◔ Trail Contact:

Bureau of Land Management, White River Field Office, Meeker, CO (970) 878-3601 or *www.co.blm.gov/wrra/wrra index.htm*

◔ Schedule:

Access road closed by gate 2.5 miles from trailhead in winter. Call Dinosaur National Monument (970–374–3000) for road information in winter.

ⓢ Fees/Permits:

No fees or permits required

❓ Local Information:

Rangely Area Chamber of Commerce, Rangely, CO (970) 675-5290 or *www.rangely.com* • **Dinosaur Area Chamber of Commerce,** Dinosaur, CO 1-800-864-4405 or (970) 374-2744 or *www.colorado-go-west.com*

ⓘ Local Events/Attractions:

National Hang Gliding Championships, for a week in June, Dinosaur, CO 1-800-864-4405 or *www.colorado-go-west.com* • **Dinosaur Diamond** (driving tour), Dinosaur, CO 1-800-864-4405 or *www.fruita.org/dinod.htm* • **Dinosaur Quarry,** Dinosaur National Monument, Jensen, UT (435) 789-2115 or *www.nps.gov/dino* • **Canyon Pintado** (BLM), Meeker, CO (970) 878-3601 • **Rangely Outdoor Museum,** Rangely, CO (970) 675-2612 • **Raven A1 Memorial Oil Field** Exhibit, Rangely, CO (970) 675-5290

◒ Accommodations:

The 4-Queens, Rangely, CO (970) 675-5035 • **White River Inn,** Rangely, CO (970) 675-5556

ⓘ Restaurant:

Max's Pizza and Grill, Rangely, CO (970) 675-2670

✆ Other Resources:

High Desert Bookstore & Video, Rangely CO (970) 675-2665 • *The Dominguez – Escalante Journal,* by Ted J. (Ed.)Warner, University of Utah Press • **"Some Insect Foods of the American Indians: And How the Early Whites Reacted to Them:"** *www.hollowtop.com/finl_html/ amerindians.htm*

⛓ Local Outdoor Retailer:

Rangely True Value Hardware, Rangely, CO (970) 675-2454

ⓝ Maps:

USGS maps: Plug Hat Rock, CO • **BLM maps:** Rangely

Devils Canyon

Hike Specs

Start: From Devil's Canyon Trail trailhead
Length: 6.7-mile loop
Approximate Hiking Time: 3–5 hours
Difficulty Rating: Moderate due to length and terrain
Elevations: 4,600–5,220 feet
Elevation Gain: 620 feet
Seasons: Year round except after big snowstorms. Avoid hot summer days.
Terrain: Dirt roads (non-motorized) and trails
Land Status: BLM land and wilderness area
Nearest Town: Fruita, CO
Other Trail Users: Equestrians, hunters (in season)
Canine Compatibility: Controlled dogs permitted. Little to no water on trail.

Getting There

From Fruita: From the I-70 interchange (Exit 19) in Fruita, drive south on CO 340 about 1.3 miles to Kingsview Road. Turn right and drive another 1.2 miles to the turnoff to Devil's Canyon. Turn left and drive to the parking lot 0.2 miles down this dirt road. There are no facilities at the trailhead. Bring plenty of water (one gallon per person per day), especially if it's hot. ***DeLorme: Colorado Atlas & Gazetteer:*** Page 42 D2

The Black Ridge Canyons Wilderness Area was approved by Congress on October 5, 2000 and signed into law by President Clinton on October 24, 2000. The wilderness shares its eastern border with Colorado National Monument. The Black Ridge Canyons area includes the second largest collection of arches in the country outside of Arches National Park. Access to the arches is via a long trail or a rough 4WD road. The grandeur of this area can also be seen on an easier hike into Devils Canyon. If you ask how the canyon got its name, locals will simply state: "It's hotter than Hell!"

Devils Canyon lies on the northeastern edge of the Uncompahgre Plateau. Uncompahgre roughly means "rocks that make the water red" in the Ute language. About 300 million years ago forces pushed ancient (over 1.7 billion years old) "basement" rock upward to form Uncompaghria, the forerunner of today's Uncompahgre Plateau. About 65 million years later, Uncompaghria had eroded to a plain barely above the level of an inland sea. A delta or floodplain collected red sand on the coastal plain. As the climate changed, the sea receded and windblown sand filled the area. Visualize tall buff and salmon colored dunes, like those in Great Sand Dunes National Monument and Preserve. Then the climate changed again, becoming moister and streams began to flow across the area. Conglomerate, comprised of mud and pebbles, formed as did other sand deposits. Over the eons, other seas and dunes covered these sediments and under great pressure the dunes and conglomerate became rock. The Kayenta formation of sandstone and conglomerate forms a caprock, or hard-to-erode sandstone, that protects the old dunes, now known as Wingate sandstone. The red floodplain sand changed into the Chinle formation.

Cliffs of Wingate sandstone tower 100 to 200 feet into the sky in Devils Canyon. Look around at the cliffs and try to find the elephant's tail, the coke bottles or ovens, and the Tiki head formations eroded by the elements.

This area is harsh and wild. Temperatures soar in the summer creating an oven effect. In winter, temperatures can drop below freezing. Desert bighorn sheep and mountain lions live here. An interpretive sign near the trailhead explains ways to watch wildlife without disturbing them. Bighorn sheep are especially affected by humans and our pets during lambing season in April and May. Please watch and enjoy from a distance and keep dogs next to you! The cliffs shelter peregrine falcons—keep an eye out for these beautiful birds of prey.

Another area resident that is very fragile is the crypto, a black lumpy growth on the sand. This interesting combination of green algae, bacteria, fungi, lichens, mosses, and cyanobacteria holds the sandy soil together so other plants may grow.

Devils Canyon and trail.

MilesDirections

0.0 START at Devils Canyon Trail trailhead. ★ 39˚08'22"N 108˚45'28"W

0.15 Come to a trail junction. Turn left and continue down the dirt road, which is closed to public motorized vehicles.

0.2 Stop and read the bulletin board, containing interesting area information.

0.4 Come to a trail junction. Turn left and follow the dirt road, passing any singletrack trails.

0.5 Come to a trail junction. Turn right here and follow the dirt road. You'll return via the left road. ◈ 39˚08'09"N 108˚45'33"W

0.8 Come to a trail junction. Turn left here onto the Devil's Canyon Trail. When you reach the creek bed, look carefully for rocks and cairns and cross the creek bed.

1.1 Look carefully for cairns as trail drops down into canyon to the left. ◈ 39˚07'46"N 108˚45'50"W—When you reach the creek bed, turn right and travel upstream. *[**Note.** During thunderstorms, do not enter in case of flash flood!]*

1.4 Reach the wilderness boundary sign. ◈ 39˚07'31"N 108˚45'57"W—The trail turns right and heads steeply uphill here. The trail meanders past various amphitheaters, cliffs, and up and down little gullies.

3.5 Reach the west end of the loop at the old sheepherder's cabin. ◈ 39˚06'13"N

108˚45'56"W—Great lunch spot. Find the trail on the north side of the cabin to finish the loop. The trail drops into Devils Creek then follows the bank on the east side.

4.7 *[**FYI.** Good view of the Grand Valley and Bookcliffs to the north.]*

5.3 The trail drops back down into Devils Creek and starts to retrace the route on which you came.

5.6 Come to a trail junction (same as mile 1.1). You came into the canyon via the left trail. For more variety on the return trip, stay to the right in the creek bed (unless there's danger of flash flood) and make another mini-loop back to the trail junction at mile 0.5 above.

5.9 Come to a trail junction. Take the left trail, which climbs out of the creek bed on a slick-rock ledge to avoid a tight spot but then drops back down to the creek.

6.1 Come to a trail junction with a road. Turn left and walk down the road across a little wooden bridge.

6.2 Come to a trail junction. Turn right here to return to the trailhead. The road to the left is the way you walked into the canyon. Return the way you came.

6.7 Arrive back at the trailhead.

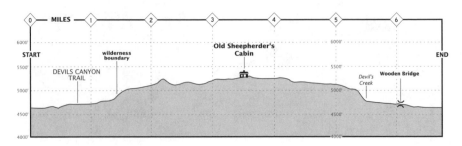

The hike starts out on a road closed to public motorized vehicles. The first part is relatively flat with sparse vegetation of rabbitbrush, sagebrush, some thorny plants, and a few hardy junipers. After traveling along several roads, the hike turns onto a single-track trail. A few places require careful observation to find the cairns that mark the route. The cliffs of the canyon loom ahead. You drop into a creek bed and follow it for a little while among cottonwood and ash trees and some tamarisk. Do not hike here if there are thunderstorms anywhere in the area in case of flash floods.

Just past the wilderness boundary the trail climbs steeply to the right out of the creek bottom. As you hike along, look back down into the canyon bottom to your left to see black rock walls with shiny mica and lots of lichen. These rocks are the "basement" rocks of Uncompaghria. On the right, sandstone cliffs are a colorful parfait of yellow and pink. Continue climbing through black rocks, mica, and white quartz. The trail traverses the Chinle formation at the base of the cliffs, undulating across many little creek gullies. Look to the right into each little amphitheater for alcoves or other interesting rock features. The buzz of cicadas and lyrical song of the canyon wren may fill the air.

Domesticated sheep once grazed in Devils Canyon. At the west end of the loop, an old sheepherder's cabin still stands. The cabin provides a little shade and a great place for lunch. To finish the loop the trail drops, crosses the creek, then climbs to the bench above. Again, the trail undulates across many little dry creek gullies. Near the close of the loop is a great view of the Grand Valley and the Bookcliffs to the north. A little farther downstream, continue along the creek bed to add variety to your hike and another mini-loop back to the trailhead. (See details in *Miles/Directions*.)

Mike, the headless chicken, in Fruita.

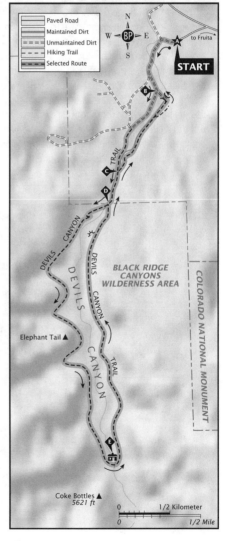

Cryptobiotic Soil Crust

When hiking in Colorado's desert country, notice black lumps in between plants and sand. This cryptobiotic soil crust, sometimes called cryptogamic soil or "crypto," is actually a combination of living creatures! Green algae, bacteria, fungi, lichens, mosses, and cyanobacteria live together in the soil crust. Cyanobacteria are an ancient life form, about 3.5 billion years old. In this area, cyanobacteria is a filament in a sheath that becomes active when moistened. It moves through the soil leaving behind a sticky glue. Soil particles (think sand grains) stick to the gooey sheath. When wet, cyanobacteria swell to as much as ten times their dry size. Plants growing in areas with crypto soils tend to have much higher levels of nutrients than plants in non-crypto soils. In particular, cyanobacteria help the soil obtain nitrogen. This special combination of living creatures binds soil particles together creating the topsoil of the arid West.

Human activity can easily destroy this delicate topsoil. Dry crusts are very brittle and break up easily when crunched under foot. Breakup by tires on bikes or vehicles causes even worse damage, as their continuous strips create a mini-gully for water to carry soil away creating larger channels. Wind also gets in the act by blowing loosened soil around, covering other crypto and preventing it from photosynthesizing. Damaged cryptobiotic soil crusts can take 50 years or more to recover to a well-developed state.

When hiking in drier areas where crypto is common, please watch your step. Walk in gullies, on trails, and on rocks. If you must walk through crypto, walk single file stepping in the leader's footprints to minimize damage. Remember the wonder of these ancient life forms and the important function they provide by holding sandy and silty soil together. Sand dunes are probably not the landscape of preference 100 years from now!

Coke oven or bottle formations in Devils Canyon.

218

Hike Information

Trail Contact:

Bureau of Land Management, Grand Junction, Grand Junction, CO (970) 244–3000 or *www.co.blm.gov/gjra/hiking hp.htm*

Schedule:

Year round, except after major snowstorms. Avoid hot summer days.

Fees/Permits:

No fees or permits required

Local Information:

Fruita Chamber of Commerce, Fruita, CO (970) 858–3894 or 1–877–680–7379 or *www.fruitachamber.org*

Local Events/Attractions:

Mike the Headless Chicken Statue and Festival, Fruita, CO 1–877–680–7379 or *www.miketheheadlesschicken.org* • **Dinosaur Journey,** Fruita, CO 1–888–488–DINO or (970) 858–7282 or *www.dinodigs.org* • **The Museum of Western Colorado,** Grand Junction, CO (970) 242–0971 or *www.wcmuseum.org*

Accommodations:

Colorado National Monument Campground, Fruita, CO (970) 858–3617 or *www.nps.gov/colm* • **Highline Lake State Park,** Loma, CO (970) 858–7208 or 1–800–678–2267 or *http://parks.state.co.us/highline* • From the local mountain bike shop website and Chamber of Commerce: **Stonehaven Bed & Breakfast,** Fruita, CO (970) 858–0898 or 1–800–303–0898 or *www.gj.net/'stonehvn* • **H Motel,** Fruita, CO (970) 858–7198 • **Park Hotel,** Fruita, CO (970) 858–3917 or 1–800–878–3917 – *1898 restoration. No phones or TVs in room, and a shared bath.*

Restaurants:

End Zone Eatery & Pub, Fruita, CO (970) 858–3603 – *If you can eat the 2 lb. burger and 2 lb. fries, you get a t-shirt!* • **Diorio's Pizza of Fruita,** Fruita, CO (970) 858–1117 • **Pancho's Villa II,** Fruita, CO (970) 858–9380 • **Munchies Pizza and Deli,** Fruita, CO (970) 858–1200

Other Resources:

Pages of Stone Geology of Western National Parks and Monuments 4. Grand Canyon and the Plateau Country, by Halka Chronic, The Mountaineers • *Roadside Geology of Colorado,* by Halka Chronic, Mountain Press Publishing Co. • *Geology of Colorado Illustrated,* by Dell R. Foutz, Your Geologist • *Hiking Colorado's Geology,* by Ralph Lee Hopkins and Lindy Birkel, The Mountaineers • *Research Papers* by Jayne Belnap

Clubs and Organizations:

Colorado Mountain Club—West Slope Group, Grand Junction, CO *call the CMC clubroom in Denver at 303–279–3080 , 1–800–633–4417 (Colorado only) to find the current local contact or www.cmc.org*

Hike Tours:

Rimrock Adventures, Fruita, CO (970) 858–9555 or 1–888–712–9555 – *hiking and rafting combination*

Local Outdoor Retailers:

Summit Canyon Mountaineering, Grand Junction, CO (970) 243–2847 • **Recreational Equipment Inc. (REI),** Grand Junction, CO (970) 254–8796 • **Gene Taylors Sporting Goods,** Grand Junction, CO (970) 242–8165

Maps:

USGS maps: Mack, CO; Battleship Rock, CO

Honorable Mentions

Northwest

Compiled here is an index of great hikes in the Northwest region that didn't make the A-list this time around but deserve recognition. Check them out and let us know what you think. You may decide that one or more of these hikes deserves higher status in future editions or, perhaps, you may have a hike of your own that merits some attention.

(N) Hanging Lake

The trail to Hanging Lake is very popular and leads to a beautiful little lake fed by Bridal Veil Falls. The 2.8-mile out-and-back trail gains 1,100 feet in 1.2 miles and is considered most difficult to strenuous (elevation 6,100 to 7,200 feet). Dogs are not allowed on the trail and swimming and fishing are prohibited in the lake to protect it. The trail is very steep in spots, with switchbacks and stairs. Please stay on the boardwalk around the lake to protect the fragile shoreline. The hike is a trip back into geologic history with the area around the lake composed of limestone. Take a little side trip to Spouting Rock, where water spouts from a cliff wall. From Glenwood Springs drive east on I-70 to Hanging Lake, Exit 125. Park in the lot and walk about 0.25 miles east to start up Deadhorse Creek just before a bridge. For more information contact White River National Forest at (970) 328–6388 or visit their website at *www.fs.fed.us/r2/whiteriver*. *DeLorme: Colorado Atlas & Gazetteer*: Page 35 D7

(O) Glenwood Canyon National Recreation Trail

This 18-mile point-to-point paved non-motorized trail travels through beautiful Glenwood Canyon along the Colorado River. You can access the trail from the Art Center just past the hot springs pool in Glenwood Springs or from various I-70 exits: No Name (Exit 119), Grizzly Creek (Exit 121), Shoshone Power Plant (eastbound only Exit 123), Hanging Lake (Exit 125), Bair Ranch (Exit 129), or the east end that's two miles west of Dotsero along the Frontage Road north of I-70 (use Exit 132 for Dotsero). Trail elevation is 5,900 feet at Glenwood Springs and 6,200 feet at Dotsero. Use your imagination and however much energy you have to create your own hike ranging from an 18-mile point-to-point hike to shorter out-and-back hikes. Some sections of the trail are closed during spring runoff because of high water covering the trail. Bicyclists, hikers, joggers, rollerbladers, and anglers all use the trail, so be aware of other trail users. Rest areas are available at Grizzly Creek and Bair Ranch. For more information contact White River National Forest at (970) 328–6388 or visit their website at *www.fs.fed.us/r2/whiteriver*. *DeLorme: Colorado Atlas & Gazetteer*: Page 35 D7

(P) Crag Crest National Recreation Trail

Crag Crest trail, high point 11,189 feet, traverses the backbone of Grand Mesa southeast of Grand Junction. Fantastic scenery to the south, east, and north keeps popping into view. Lone Cone, the San Miguels, La Platas, and San Juan Mountains line the southern skyline. The West Elks are to the east with the Book and Roan Cliffs to the north, an interesting contrast of high peaks and more desert-like formations. Numerous lakes, small and large, dot the landscape below. Wildflowers bloom colorfully and profusely in July and early August along the sometimes narrow

path with steep drop-offs. The trail provides three options: a 9.6-mile loop, 6.5-mile point-to-point, or 6.2-mile out-and-back. The point-to-point and out-and-back are the most scenic. Start your hike at the East Trailhead, 10,150 feet, near Crag Crest Campground, about 3.5 miles east on Forest Road 121 from the Grand Mesa Visitor Center. Starting at the East Trailhead puts the sun to your back in the morning for bet-

ter light. For the point-to-point, leave a second car at the West Trailhead, 10,380 feet, about 1 mile west of the Visitor Center on CO 65. To reach Grand Mesa from Grand Junction, head east on I-70 to exit 49, CO 65, Grand Mesa Scenic Byway. Head south for about 35 miles to the Visitor Center at the intersection of CO 65 and FR 121. Pick up a trail brochure and check the weather. Make sure to bring plenty of water and insect repellant. Grand Mesa cradles over 300 lakes and plenty of mosquitoes. For more information, contact Grand Mesa National Forest at (970) 856-4153 or (970) 874-6600 or check out the website at *www.fs.fed.us/r2/gmug*.

(Q) Harpers Corner Trail

Harpers Corner Trail in Dinosaur National Monument gives you an excellent view of this park's canyon country. It's just up the road about 24 miles from Buckwater Draw, one of the featured hikes in this book. Buy a Harpers Corner Trail guide at the visitor center before you head up. The trail follows a promontory that was once used as a natural corral. While you hike, you'll learn about geology, seashells along the trail, trees and animals living above the canyon, and John Wesley Powell's trip down the Green River. Fremont Indians carved petroglyphs down on the canyon walls, and later the Chew family ranched along Pool Creek. Echo Canyon can be seen from above and is close to the confluence of the Green and Yampa rivers. This enjoyable two-mile out-and-back hike has moderate elevation gains and losses for an easy trip (start at 7,625 feet and end at 7,510 feet). Do watch out for lightning! Remember the binoculars and water. It can be hot on the trail in the summer. From the town of Dinosaur drive east on U.S. 40 about 1.8 miles to the Harpers Corner Road (not marked as such) and Dinosaur National Monument Visitor Center. Turn left onto Harpers Corner Road and drive about 31 miles to the trailhead. A guide to the Harpers Corner Scenic Drive is also available at the Visitor Center. There is no entrance fee to drive the Harpers Corner Scenic Drive. For more information, contact the Dinosaur National Monument Visitor Center at (970) 374–3000 or check out their website at *www.nps.gov/dino*. *DeLorme: Colorado Atlas & Gazetteer*: Page 12 D1

Ⓡ Trail Through Time

Located near the Colorado-Utah border in the Rabbit Valley Research Natural Area, this trail takes you by dinosaur bones still imbedded in rock! The 1.5-mile loop trail is moderate with some steep, slippery sections (elevations from 4,600 to 4,700 feet). You'll first come to a quarry, still worked by paleontologists. A trail guide explains the dinosaur bones and also various geological and plant features. The trail starts at the quarry, about 0.1 miles from the parking lot. Best times to hike are spring and fall because summers can be incredibly hot (over 100°F.). Bring water. There's a restroom near the trailhead. Pets and smoking are discouraged along the trail. Because the area is fragile, please stay on the trail and remember to leave what you find. To reach this unique hike, travel west on I-70 from Grand Junction to Exit 2 (about 30 miles) and turn right. The parking lot is straight ahead of you. Trail guides may be available at the trailhead, or contact the Museum of Western Colorado at (970) 242–0971 or visit their website at *www.wcmuseum.org*, or contact the Bureau of Land Management in Grand Junction at (970) 244–3000 or visit their website at *www.co.blm.gov/gjra/hikinghp.htm*. *DeLorme: Colorado Atlas & Gazetteer*: Page 42 C1

Ⓢ Rattlesnake Canyon

Rattlesnake Canyon contains the largest concentration of natural arches in the nation outside of Arches National Park. Contained in the newly created Black Ridge Canyons Wilderness area (October 2000), the two accesses are both difficult. A third access is gained via the Colorado River and is not included in this description. The area is very dry, so you need to bring water with you. Best time to hike is April through November, but summer can be very hot. The Pollock Bench trail is 14-mile out-and-back with elevations from 4,600 to 5,420 feet. Some sections are steep, with many ups and downs. You'll get a good tour of this canyon country. Watch for desert bighorn, deer, mountain lions, and bald and golden eagles. The BLM requests that dogs stay under control or on leash and do not chase wildlife. From the I-70 interchange (Exit 19) in Fruita, drive south on CO 340 about 1.3 miles to Kingsview Road (Kingsview Estates). Turn right and drive about six miles to the parking area and trailhead on the left side of the road. Follow the cairns to a junction where you take the right branch to go to Rattlesnake Canyon and the arches. For the Upper Trail, which is a three-mile loop through the arches, you need a high clearance 4WD vehicle, and the road is very rough and tricky in spots. From the I-70 interchange (Exit 19) in Fruita, drive south on CO 340 into Colorado National Monument. About 11 miles past the entrance station, turn right at the sign for the Glade Park Store. Travel about 0.2 miles to the Black Ridge Access roads on the right. Make sure to stop and read the signs as there is an upper and lower road, one of which is closed seasonally (they alternate). These roads are impassable when wet, so don't attempt the drive under wet conditions. Both roads are closed mid-February to mid-April. The trailhead is 13 miles from the Glade Park Road. For further information contact the Bureau of Land Management in Grand Junction at (970) 244–3000 or visit their website at *www.co.blm.gov/gjra/hikinghp.htm*. *DeLorme: Colorado Atlas & Gazetteer:* Page 42 C2

(T) Monument Canyon

Monument Canyon trail takes you by some of the famous rock sculptures of Colorado National Monument. To Independence Monument, the crown jewel, the hike is a six-mile out-and-back. As it drops about 600 feet in about 0.5 miles, the hike is rated as difficult to most difficult (elevation from 6,200 to 5,300 feet). Remember to bring water and avoid hiking on really hot summer days. The trail takes you through eons of time past the Kayenta formation (caprock) and Wingate Sandstone (massive cliffs and monuments). At about two miles, you'll find the Kissing Couple followed in about another mile by Independence Monument, a 450-foot high monolith, the largest freestanding rock formation in the park. Dogs are not allowed on park trails. You can make this a six-mile point-to-point hike by parking a second car at the east trailhead along CO 340 to the southeast of the west entrance to Colorado National Monument. To reach the upper (west) trailhead, from the I-70 interchange (Exit 19) in Fruita, drive south on CO 340 into Colorado National Monument (fee area). Drive about 10 miles to the trailhead on the left side of the road just beyond the Coke Ovens Overlook. For further information contact Colorado National Monument at (970) 858–3617 or visit their website at *www.nps.gov/colm*. *DeLorme: Colorado Atlas & Gazetteer:* Page 42 D3

Southeast
MOUNTAINS

An arch in a volcanic dike on Wahatoya Trail.

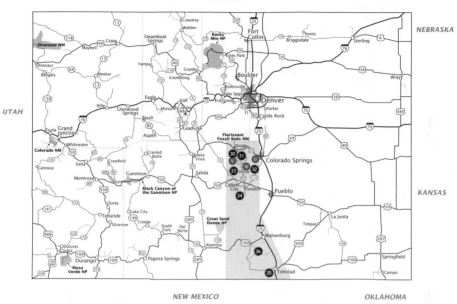

The Hikes

Twin Rock Trail **30.**
Rock Pond to Werley Ranch Loop **31.**
Aiken Canyon **32.**
Thompson Mountain **33.**
Newlin Creek Trail **34.**
Reilly and Levsa Canyons **35.**
Wahatoya Trail **36.**

Honorable Mentions

U. Colorado Springs Area Trails
V. Petrified Forest Loop
W. Vindicator Valley Trail

Southeast Mountains

The geological feature called the Front Range ends at Cheyenne Mountain near Colorado Springs. But to keep things reasonably equal north and south, Colorado Springs and the area immediately west is included in this section.

Colorado Springs at the base of Pikes Peak (14,109 feet) contains an interesting assortment of businesses and attractions. The U.S. Air Force Academy is located to the north, and the Olympic Training Center is in town. El Paso County has developed a system of trails, and the Pike National Forest offers many hiking opportunities as well. By no means the highest of the Fourteeners, Pikes Peak holds the honor of rising the farthest above its base, giving it a formidable profile. Inspired by the view from the top of Pikes Peak in 1893, Katherine Lee Bates wrote the lyrics for "America the Beautiful," which read: "Oh beautiful for spacious skies, for amber waves of grain, for purple mountains majesty, above the fruited plain…"

To the west of "the Springs," Florissant Fossil Beds National Monument holds a treasure trove of petrified giant redwood and a world famous source of fossilized insects. Mueller State Park and Dome Rock State Wildlife Area offer both a refuge for elk and bighorn sheep and a multitude of hiking trails through this former ranching area.

Explore Cripple Creek and Victor by following the Gold Belt Tour Scenic and Historic Byway drive. Fortunes were gained and lost in the gold fields of Cripple Creek and Victor and the tradition continues into the 21st Century at Cripple Creek's casinos. Two hikes in this book are located off this tour route. The new Vindicator Valley Trail, a two-mile loop near Victor, explores mining remnants from the 1890s. In winter the trail is groomed for cross-country skiing.

Cañon City makes a good base of operations for exploring the northern half of this region. Gold fields and the graveyard of famous dinosaurs such as allosaurus, diplodocus, and stegosaurus lie to the north. (There is a dinosaur museum in Cañon City.) Stop at the Museum of Colorado Prisons for a present-day piece of history. The Royal Gorge, an incredible canyon carved by the Arkansas River, lies to the west, and Colorado's oldest oil field to the south. A new trail on Thompson Mountain northwest of Cañon City is featured in this book along with an interesting hike to an old steam boiler.

Follow the Frontier Pathways Scenic & Historic Byway into the Wet Mountain Valley, which contains several historic ranches and farmsteads. The valley provides access to trails on the eastern side of the Sangre de Cristo Range.

The area encircling the Spanish Peaks is steeped in various Indian and Spanish legends. Be sure to drive the Scenic Highway of Legends to learn more. Volcanic dikes radiate from the Spanish Peaks, recently designated as a wilderness area. The Wahatoya Trail was extended in 1999, so you can hike among the dikes on West Spanish Peak's south flank and then continue to cross the saddle between these two majestic mountains.

At the southern end of this region, Trinidad still has streets of cobblestones and beautiful old historic buildings. Once connecting Trinidad with Santa Fe, the Mountain Branch of the Santa Fe Trail over Raton Pass was replaced by railroads. Now cars and trucks move easily on Interstate 25 over the pass where wagons once struggled. A coal miners strike that ended in disaster is memorialized at the Ludlow Massacre site to the north. A few miles farther west on the Highway of Legends you can visit historic Cokedale and the relics of coke ovens near Trinidad Lake State Park.

Petrified stump along the Petrified Forest Loop.

West Spanish Peak from
Cuchara Recreation Area.

Section Overview

Twin Rock Trail

The Twin Rock Trail is a fairly new trail in Florissant Fossil Beds National Monument. It's a gentle hike through ponderosa pine forests and open meadows so scenic you might wonder where the buffalo are. The trail meanders through old ranch lands and across an ancient lakebed. It then turns east and follows an unnamed stream to South Twin Rock. This part of the trail wanders along a riparian area, past open meadows, through a beautiful aspen grove, and past several other rock formations. Summer brings a profusion of wild flowers. *(See page 232.)*

Rock Pond to Werley Ranch Loop

The Rock Pond to Werley Ranch Loop takes you into the heart of Mueller State Park and Dome Rock State Wildlife Area. Descending through forests of aspen, limber pine, and Douglas fir, the trail follows old ranch roads, closed to the motorized public. A side trip brings you to Brook Pond, reflecting big rounded rock forma-tions of Pikes Peak granite. The trail continues through grasslands and meadows, popular with the abundant elk population. The old Werley Ranch is an excellent lunch spot, giving you a chance to reflect on ranch life. The loop continues back, ascending on singletrack and old ranch roads. *(See page 236.)*

Aiken Canyon

Aiken Canyon harbors a rich diversity of life where plains and foothills converge. The nature preserve is home to bear, mountain lion, elk, mule deer, bobcat, fox, squirrels, rattlesnakes, and over 100 species of birds, including the threatened Mexican spotted owl. The canyon also provides a wildlife corridor between the plains of Fort Carson Military Reservation to the east and the higher hills and forests to the west. In an area experiencing housing development pressures, Aiken Canyon preserves a foothills ecosystem that is rapidly disappearing along the Front Range. *(See page 242.)*

Southeast Mountains

Thompson Mountain

This adventurous hike makes a loop on both new trails and old dirt, non-motorized ranch roads through part of the Deer Haven Ranch. Most of the trail is obvious, but some sections are marked by flags or trail markers. Follow the directions carefully. The trail winds through ponderosa pines, Douglas firs, and meadows. Open areas provide nice views of Pikes Peak and the Sangre de Cristo Range. *(See page 248.)*

Newlin Creek Trail

Newlin Creek Trail wanders up a little canyon following the remains of an old logging road. Due to floods and deterioration, it's tough to tell that this trail was once a road. Rocky cliffs loom over the trail in spots, while little waterfalls and cascades dance down the creek. After crossing one wooden bridge, the trail crosses creeks 18 times on logs and rocks. The most interesting features of this hike lie in the destination meadow. An old steam boiler, flywheel, and chimney are all that remain of a sawmill operation. *(See page 254.)*

Reilly and Levsa Canyons

This hike first follows the Levsa Canyon Nature Trail and then about 2.2 miles of the Reilly Canyon Trail. Winding through piñon pine and juniper forest gives you an idea of the land through which early settlers traveled, especially on the Mountain Branch of the Santa Fe Trail (where Interstate 25 now exists). The suggested turnaround point is a bench where the trail approaches the lake and has a good view of the dam. Look for deer in some of the meadows. While hiking

you can catch views of Fishers Peak as well as the old coal mines and town sites on or below the south shore. *(See page 258.)*

Wahatoya Trail

This hike explores a new section of trail through several volcanic dikes on the south side of West Spanish Peak. The dikes are fascinating and the views into New Mexico go forever on a clear day. The trail winds through forests of bristlecone, limber, and lodgepole pine, aspen, spruce, subalpine fir, and white fir with some Gambel oak for good measure. An unmarked overlook by a little dike provides a good view of East Spanish Peak—a good turnaround point for the out-and-back hiker. After the overlook, the hike continues descending to an old Forest Service cabin then climbs to the saddle between the two peaks. It descends a final time along the north side of West Spanish Peak to Forest Service Road 442 and on to County Road 360. The new trail was cut in 1999, and final tread should be finished in 2002. This area was designated official wilderness on November 7, 2000. (*See page 264.*)

Twin Rock Trail

Hike Specs

Start: From the Hornbek Homestead
Length: 6.0-mile out-and-back
Approximate Hiking Time: 2.5–4 hours
Difficulty Rating: Moderate due to length
Elevations: 8,300–8,760 feet
Elevation Gain: 460 feet
Seasons: Best from May through October
Terrain: Dirt trail and old dirt road with one highway crossing
Land Status: National monument
Nearest Town: Florissant, CO
Other Trail Users: Equestrians
Canine Compatibility: Dogs not permitted

Getting There

From Florissant: Head south on CR 1 from its intersection with U.S. 24 at the center of town. First drive 2.3 miles and turn right onto the visitor center road. The parking lot is about 0.3 miles from the highway. Pay the entrance fee to the national monument, check out the displays, and if you have time hike the short and very interesting 1.0-mile Petrified Forest Loop trail. Then, return north to the Hornbek Homestead, which is located 0.9 miles north of the visitor center road on the west side, and park in the parking lot. A vault toilet and picnic tables are available. *DeLorme: Colorado Atlas & Gazetteer:* Page 62 A1

The hike starts at the old Hornbek Homestead. Take a few minutes either before or after the hike to look around at the bunkhouse, carriage shed, barn, and root cellar. Walk inside the main house (when it's open), built in 1878. A single mother with four children, Adeline Hornbek homesteaded this land in 1878 under the 1862 Homestead Act. Grasslands, nearby water and timber, and fertile soil made this an ideal area for ranching. Adeline Hornbek's was the first homestead in the Florissant Valley.

After looking at the restored house, stay to the left and head southeast on the Hornbek Wildlife Loop and cross County Road 1. Keep an eye open for mountain bluebirds. While you hike across the grasslands, picture this area 35 million years ago during the Oligocene epoch. Hickory and sycamore trees were overshadowed by 300-foot giant sequoias. Volcanic activity increased in the nearby Thirtynine Mile volcanic field. Mudflows caused by the volcanoes reached the giant sequoias, smothering them in 15 feet of mud. The upper portions of the trees decayed, while the lower portions, inundated with dissolved silicates and other minerals, started to petrify. Mudflows also blocked a small stream creating a long and skinny lake that occupied the area where you are walking. Airborne ash clouds and poisonous gasses often killed insects and butterflies that dropped into the lake. Over the years, eruptions continued and the ash layer built up in the lake, eventually filling it. Insects, leaves, and fish lay buried under the ash layers. Mudflows continued to cover the old lake. Between 28 and five million years ago, the entire area was uplifted about 5,000 feet. Over the eons, erosion took its toll in the valley, uncovering petrified tree stumps. A treasure of ancient insects, butterflies, leaves, and fish fossils were also discovered.

Hike Information

Trail Contact:
Florissant Fossil Beds National Monument, Florissant, CO (719) 748–3253 or *www.nps.gov/flfo*

Schedule:
Call first for trail conditions November to April. You can cross-country ski or snowshoe in winter. Trail not marked for winter use.

Fees/Permits:
Entrance fee, annual pass, Golden Eagle Pass, or Golden Age Pass required

Local Information:
Florissant-Lake George Chamber of Commerce, Florissant, CO (719) 748–3562

Local Events/Attractions:
Florissant–Seminar Series, Friends of the Florissant Fossil Beds, Inc., Florissant, CO (719) 748–3253 • **Florissant Heritage Museum,** Florissant, CO (719) 748–8259 • **Heritage Days Celebration,** Florissant, CO (719) 748–8259 • **Cripple Creek & Victor Mining Districts, Casinos, Mine Tours, and Narrow Gauge Railroad,** Cripple Creek and Victor, CO (719) 689–3315 or 1–877–858–GOLD • **Gold Belt Tour Scenic Byway,** Bureau of Land Management, Cañon City, CO (719) 275–0631

Accommodations:
Mueller State Park campgrounds, Divide, CO (719) 687–2366 or *parks.state.co.us/mueller* • **National Forest Campgrounds,** Pike National Forest, Colorado Springs, CO (719) 636–1602 or *www.fs.fed.us/r2/ psicc* • **Eleven Mile Motel,** Lake George, CO (719) 748–3931 – *a rustic motel* • **Lake George Cabins & RV Park,** Lake George, CO (719) 748–3822

Restaurants:
One & Oney's Ice Cream & Pizza, Florissant, CO (719) 748–3315 • **Mountain Shadows Rest,** Lake George, CO (719) 748–3833

Other Resources:
Florissant Fossil Bed National Monument: Window to the Past, by Walter Saenger, Rocky Mountain Nature Association, Paragon Press, Inc.

Clubs and Organizations:
Friends of the Florissant Fossil Beds, Inc., Florissant, CO (719) 748–3253

Hike Tours:
Florissant Fossil Beds National Monument, Florissant, CO (719) 748–3253

Local Outdoor Retailers:
Great West Outfitters, Colorado Springs, CO (719) 596–3031 • **Mountain Chalet,** Colorado Springs, CO (719) 633–0732 or *www.mtnchalet.com*

Maps:
USGS maps: Lake George, CO; Divide, CO

> *The fossil insect collection at Florissant Fossil Beds National Monument is a real treat. Insects are very delicate and rarely preserved. Volcanic ash the consistency of talcum powder gently covered the dainty creatures preserving their impressions in shale.*

Be sure to check out the fossil collection in the visitor center. As homesteaders populated the valley, they collected petrified wood and fossilized insects. Scientific investigations were conducted in the 1870s and 1930s. Talk of preserving the area as a national monument began back in 1911, but the designation only occurred in 1966.

Continuing on your hike, the trail meanders along the edge of ponderosa pine forest and grassland. In more recent times buffalo roamed here getting fat on the nutritious grasses. Ute Indians hunted the buffalo for meat and hides. Today the buffalo and Utes are gone, but the grassland remains. Abert squirrels, also known as tassel-eared squirrels, frolic amid the ponderosas.

The trail drops down to a little stream and crosses it on a nice wooden bridge. A riparian area lines the right side of the trail to South Twin Rock. Willow and aspen trees along with cinquefoil (*potentilla*), butter-and-eggs, and sage plants inhabit the area. An old stock pond lies to the right reflecting nearby aspen trees. In the dry cli-

MilesDirections

0.0 START at the parking lot and walk to the Hornbek Homestead entrance gate. ☆ 38˚55'40"N 105˚16'52"W The hike starts here. Take the left trail signed as Hornbek Wildlife loop with mileage to the visitor center.

0.2 Cross CR 1.

0.6 Turn left at the junction of Twin Rock Trail, Shootin' Star Trail, and Hornbek Wildlife Loop. ◈ 38˚55'18"N 105˚16'28"W

0.8 Turn left at the junction of Twin Rock and Shootin' Star trails onto Twin Rock Trail.

1.3 Turn right where the old road goes left but the trail continues to the right. ◈ 38˚55'41"N 105˚16'12"W

1.4 Cross the bridge over an unnamed creek and veer right (east) on the Twin Rock Trail

heading upstream.

1.6 Reach an old stock pond.

2.0 Reach a rock formation with large quartz crystals to the left of the trail. ◈ 38˚55'34"N 105˚15'45"W *[FYI. Look at the band of quartz in the rock. You can see where looser grains eroded into a small fan and gully below the rock.]*

2.1 Reach an open area with lots of thistles.

2.7 Reach South Twin Rock.

3.0 National Monument boundary. ◈ 38˚55'26"N 105˚14'46"W Return the way you came.

6.0 Arrive back at the trailhead.

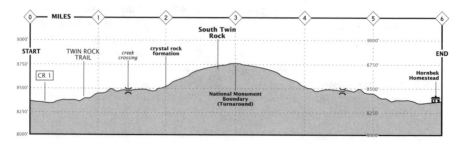

234

Hornbek Homestead.

mate of Colorado, ranchers built little earthen dams across creeks, creating ponds for their cattle. Mountain mahogany bushes grow along the creek, their seeds looking like feathery question marks. Grasshoppers abound and an occasional green-armored locust sits in the trail. When the trail passes next to granitic rocks, look closely at the colorful lichen. Lichens are an interesting combination of algae and fungus that live together synergistically. Colored rusty orange, black, gray, and various greens, they brighten up the granite. Their job is to break rocks into soil. On warmer south-facing slopes, look for yucca and mountain ball cactus. Cross an area filled with this-tles complete with spider webs. The thistles can be very scratchy on bare legs. Look ahead to see South Twin Rock (8,963 feet). One part looks like an elephant head with a long trunk. South Twin Rock is in the Florissant Fossil Beds National Monument and North Twin Rock is on private land. The area just before the mon-ument boundary is a good place for lunch, either sitting on some boulders or a log in a thick stand of aspen. The monument boundary is near a road, so you may hear mod-ern vehicle sounds—quite a contrast with the memory of a volcanic-ash filled lake!

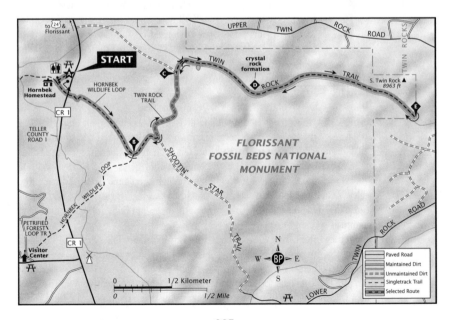

Rock Pond to Werley Ranch Loop

Hike Specs

Start: From Rock Pond Trail trailhead near the visitor center

Length: 7.7-mile loop trip

Approximate Hiking Time: 5 hours

Difficulty Rating: Moderate due to gentle trails and distance

Elevations: 8700–9660 feet

Elevation Gain: 960 feet

Seasons: Best from mid-May to November

Terrain: Dirt trail and old dirt ranch roads

Land Status: State park and state wildlife area

Nearest Town: Divide, CO

Other Trail Users: Equestrians, mountain bikers (in state park only), and hunters (in season)

Canine Compatibility: Dogs not permitted

Getting There

From Divide: Drive 3.9 miles south on CO 67 to the entrance to Mueller State Park. Turn right into Mueller State Park, and pay the fee at the entrance station. The visitor center is about 1.6 miles from CO 67. Turn left into the visitor center parking lot and park. Take a few minutes to check out the many interesting exhibits and interpretive displays at the visitor center. The trailhead is at the south end of the parking lot by a bulletin board. The visitor center has restrooms and water. *DeLorme: Colorado Atlas & Gazetteer:* Page 62 A1

The Mueller family ranched in the meadows and valleys west of Colorado Springs, slowly buying up neighboring ranches. W.E. Mueller envisioned his ranch becoming a wildlife preserve. The Muellers sold the land in 1978 resulting in the creation of two preserves: Mueller State Park, managed by the Colorado Division of Parks and Outdoor Recreation (CDPOR), and the 7,000-acre Dome Rock State Wildlife Area (SWA), managed by the Colorado Division of Wildlife (CDOW). Exhibits and interpretive displays in the visitor center convey more of the area's history.

In 1986, CDOW entered into a lease management agreement with CDPOR, allowing CDPOR to manage the wildlife area under the state park umbrella. The 12,103 acres of the two preserves became known as Mueller State Park. In June 2000, CDOW resumed management of the leased lands, changing the name back to Dome Rock SWA. Mueller State Park now contains 5,121 acres. The Rock Pond and Werley Ranch loop starts in Mueller, loops through the Dome Rock and back into Mueller. Watch for golden eagles, red-tailed hawks, great horned owls, and turkey vultures. Elk, mule deer, coyote, black bear, and mountain lions are some of the larger mammals you might see.

From the visitor center the mountain views are excellent. Pikes Peak (14,110 feet) to the east is the most obvious, but numerous 14,000-foot peaks—Yale, Columbia, Harvard and others—stand out to the west. The Sangre de Cristo Range and Mount Pisgah (10,343 feet) near Cripple Creek rise in the south. Interpretive signs in a gazebo near the trailhead identify the many peaks. Walk down the trail to the right of the

trailhead bulletin board, along a mowed path to the gravel road. Notice the Douglas fir trees along the way and look at a fir cone. They're easy to spot as they have distinctive three-pronged bracts between the scales. Naturalists' stories relate that once upon a time, a hungry fox chased a little mouse, hoping for a tasty meal. Not wanting to be eaten, the little mouse begged a nearby tree for help. The tree kindly told the mouse to jump into its branches where it would protect it from the fox. The mouse took a mighty leap, and to this day the tree's cones reflect the two hind feet and tail of the mouse that reached safety. The Douglas fir is not a true fir as its cones hang down while true fir cones grow upright near the tree's top, although fir trees are usually too tall to easily distinguish upright cones.

A side trail takes you to Brook Pond where rock formations of Pikes Peak granite reflect in the water. A little farther down the main trail Rock Pond shimmers in the sun. The Werley family built these ponds to irrigate the meadows downstream. Continuing down the road, you walk along meadows by a little creek. Turkey Cabin sits just uphill to the right. The Snare family built this little house in the late 1800s

Werley Ranch.

MilesDirections

0.0 START at the Rock Pond Trail (Trail 5) trailhead and walk down the trail to the right of the bulletin board, not the Wapiti Nature Trail to the left. ★ 38°52'46"N 105°10'48"W Turn left onto the gravel road at sign #5.

0.1 At the trail intersection, stay on the road heading downhill.

0.7 Come to the trail intersection with Preacher's Hollow Trail (Trail 4). Continue up the road.

1.1 The trail forks. ◆ 38°52'14"N 105°11'25"W Walk on the trail to the right, Rock Pond Trail (Trail 5). This point is the start/end of your loop.

2.1 The trail forks. *[**Side-trip**. The right fork goes to Brook Pond, an easy 0.4-mile out-and-back walk to a nice little pond. This extra mileage is not included in the hike.]* To continue to Rock Pond and Werley Ranch, take the left fork.

2.2 Arrive at Rock Pond. ◆ 38°52'30"N 105°11'59"W *[**Option**. For a shorter hike, you can return the way you came.]*

2.9 Turkey Cabin sits just uphill.

3.1 Rock Pond Trail (Trail 5) ends at its intersection with Werley Ponds Trail. Turn left here to go to Werley Ranch.

3.4 Werley Ponds are on your left. These ponds also provided water for fields and cattle.

3.8 Reach the junction with the road into Werley Ranch. Turn right to see the old ranch buildings and have a rest.

3.9 Reach Werley Ranch. ◉ 38°52'06"N 105°13'20"w Return back to Werley Ponds Trail.

4.0 Turn right at the road (Werley Ponds Trail) to continue the loop back to the visitor center.

4.2 Turn left at the junction with Cabin Creek Trail and walk down an overgrown road to cross the dam to the northeast.

4.4 Go through a gate and follow the trail across the dam. Continue on the trail through a fence, heading for the aspen and a drainage. The trail wanders up the drainage.

4.6 The trail crosses from the right to the left side of the creek.

4.8 Come to the trail junction with Fourmile Overlook Trail (Trail 44). Turn left and walk uphill on Trail 44, an old ranch road.

5.4 Trail junction with Hammer Homestead Trail. ◆ 38°51'54"N 105°12'19"W Continue to the left on Fourmile Overlook Trail.

5.8 *[**FYI**. Check out the view to the west (left) from this area—rolling hills of conifer to purple mountain majesties!]*

5.9 The trail descends steeply here on a couple of switchbacks.

6.1 Arrive at a low point. *[**FYI**. The trail to the left is closed. This is a good spot for a rest break.]*

6.6 Come to the trail junction with Rock Pond Trail (Trail 5) and Fourmile Overlook Trail (Trail 44). Go straight ahead on Trail 5 to return to the visitor center the way you came.

7.7 Arrive back at the trailhead.

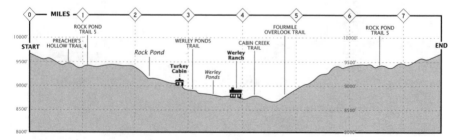

or early 1900s. After the Mueller family bought the land, they reintroduced wild turkeys. They used the cabin to acclimate the turkeys before releasing them, hence the name. Less than a mile after turning left onto Werley Ponds Trail, you come to the Werley Ranch buildings (circa 1930s) up a road to the right. Check out the dilapidated two-hole outhouse, with one hole smaller and a seat cover! Large ponderosa pines grow near the old ranch.

From Werley Ranch, follow the road to Cabin Creek Trail and turn left onto the overgrown road and cross the dam below the pond. The large rock hill to the right is Sheep Rock. Rocky Mountain bighorn sheep, Colorado's state animal, are another resident of this area. The trail climbs up a drainage through a nice aspen forest. While hiking past aspen, look for telltale teeth marks made by elk with their lower teeth. Elk mainly eat grasses, but when snows are deep elk will supplement their diet by scraping the bark off aspen trees and eating shrubs. Black bears also leave claw marks in aspen bark from climbing their favorite tree. The trail joins an old road, Fourmile Overlook Trail, and undulates up and down and around until it rejoins Rock Pond Trail (Trail 5).

This loop is an excellent way to see diverse vegetation and terrain and some ranching history. With luck you might see some wildlife, the best viewing being in early morning or late evening. Mueller State Park has many excellent trails—take time to investigate some others.

> *Colorado State Parks manages Mueller State Park for outdoor recreation. The Colorado Division of Wildlife's primary purpose at Dome Rock State Wildlife Area is to maintain and enhance wildlife habitat. The area and trails around Dome Rock are closed seasonally from December 1 to July 15 each year to protect the bighorn sheep population.*

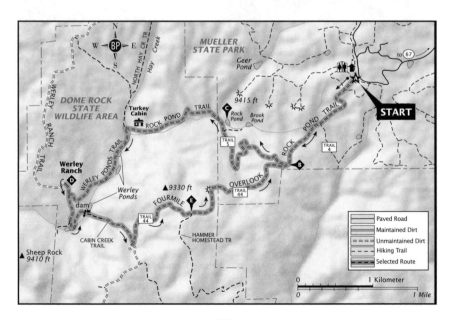

Rock Pond.

Hike Information

📞 Trail Contacts:

Mueller State Park, Divide, CO (719) 687–2366 or *parks.state.co.us/mueller* • **Dome Rock State Wildlife Area,** Colorado Division of Wildlife, Colorado Springs, CO (719) 227–5200 or *wildlife.state.co.us*

🕐 Schedule:

Open year round. Call first for trail conditions in winter. Trails used by cross-country skiers and snowshoers

💲 Fees/Permits:

Daily fee or annual parks pass required for Mueller State Park

❓ Local Information:

Manitou Springs Chamber of Commerce & Visitors Bureau, Manitou Springs, CO 1–800–642–2567 or *www.manitou springs.org*

💡 Local Events/Attractions:

Cripple Creek and Victor, CO, 1–877–858–GOLD or *www.cripple-creek.co.us – old mining towns* • **Florissant Fossil Beds National Monument,** Florissant, CO (719) 748–3253 or *www.nps.gov/flfo* • **Pikes Peak Cog Railway or Road,** Manitou Springs, CO (719) 685 5401 or *www.cograil way.com/default.asp*

🛏 Accommodations:

Mueller State Park campgrounds, Divide, CO (719) 687–2366 or *parks.state.co.us/mueller* • **National Forest Campgrounds,** Pike National Forest, Colorado Springs, CO (719) 636–1602 or *www.fs.fed.us/r2/psicc*

🍴 Restaurants:

Rocky Mountain Joe's, Divide, CO (719) 686–1500 • **Hungry Bear,** Woodland Park, CO (719) 687–5912 • **Swiss Chalet Restaurant & Lounge,** Woodland Park, CO (719) 687–2001

📖 Other Resources:

The Chinook Bookshop, Colorado Springs, CO (719) 635–1195 or 1–800–999–1195 or *www.chinookbook.com* • *A Sierra Club Naturalist's Guide to The Southern Rockies,* by Audrey DeLella Benedict, Sierra Club Books • *From Grassland to Glacier The Natural of History of Colorado and the Surrounding Region,* by John C. Emerick and Cornelia Fleischer Mutel, Johnson Printing • *Shrubs and Trees of the Southwest Uplands,* by Francis H. Elmore, Southwest Parks and Monuments Association

👥 Clubs and Organizations:

Friends of Mueller State Park, Divide, CO (719) 687–2366 · **Colorado Mountain Club – Pikes Peak Group,** Colorado Springs, CO (719) 635–5330 or *www.cmc.org/cmc*

🚶 Hike Tours:

Mueller State Park, Divide, CO (719) 687–2366

🏔 Local Outdoor Retailers:

Great Outdoor Sporting Goods Company, Woodland Park, CO (719) 687–0401 • **Great West Outfitters,** Colorado Springs, CO (719) 596–3031 • **Mountain Chalet,** Colorado Springs, CO (719) 633–0732 or *www.mtnchalet.com* • **REI,** Colorado Springs, CO (719) 260–1455 or *www.rei.com* • **EMS,** Colorado Springs, CO (719) 574–8207 or *www.emsonline.com*

🅽 Maps:

USGS maps: Cripple Creek North (20 foot contours), CO; Divide (40 foot contours), CO • *Trails Illustrated®* maps: #137, Pikes Peak/Cañon City

Aiken Canyon

Hike Specs

Start: From behind the bulletin board near Aiken Canyon Preserve's visitor center

Length: 4.0-mile loop (5.6 miles if you include the out-and-back canyon spur)

Approximate Hiking Time: 2.5–4 hours

Difficulty Rating: Moderate due to one steep stretch with loose footing

Elevations: 6,480–6,840 feet (optional spur reaches 7,160 feet)

Elevation Gain: 360 feet (loop only); 680 feet (with spur)

Seasons: Year round except after big snow

Terrain: Dirt trail with some rocks and tree roots, and a creek bed

Land Status: Nature preserve

Nearest Town: Colorado Springs, CO

Other Trail Users: Hikers only

Canine Compatibility: Dogs not permitted

Getting There

From Colorado Springs: From its exit on I-25, drive south on Nevada Avenue (CO 115) for 15.8 miles to just beyond mile marker 32. Turn right onto Turkey Canyon Ranch Road. Drive another 0.1 miles and turn right into the parking lot for Aiken Canyon Preserve. The preserve is open to hikers on Saturday, Sunday, and Monday from sunrise to sunset. Vault toilets are available at the visitor center.

DeLorme: Colorado Atlas & Gazetteer: Page 62 D3

Back in the 1870s, ornithologist Charles Aiken first surveyed this area and identified two globally rare plant communities: the piñon pine, one-seeded juniper/Scribner needlegrass woodland and the Gambel oak-mountain mahogany shrubland. When a quarry was proposed on state land in Aiken Canyon in the 1980s, strong local outcry prompted protection of the area. The Nature Conservancy and the Colorado State Land Board formed a partnership in 1991 allowing the Conservancy to lease and manage the state land, thus saving it from the mining operation. Aiken Canyon Preserve consists of 1,080 acres of state land and another 541 acres owned by The Nature Conservancy. In 1993, volunteers with Volunteers for Outdoor Colorado built the current trail.

The loop trail passes through an amazing number of plant communities in a small area. Big bluestem grass with its trident or turkey-track heads grows over five feet tall. Watch for spiny yucca, a cactus-like plant that is really a member of the lily family. Pincushion and prickly pear cactus grow here, too. The trail crosses a seasonal creek numerous times. When the creek is running you can easily cross using stones. The creek is usually dry in summer, but thick vegetation grows along the banks fed by spring runoff. In some places the creek disappears underground, and the trail and creek continuously wind together and apart giving the impression of crossing many creeks over a long distance instead of one creek over a relatively short distance.

The red rocks of the Fountain formation rise in interesting shapes or just lean against the area's foothills. The Fountain formation, commonly found along the

Front Range, is a combination of sandstone and conglomerate, the latter being a mixture of pebbles and sand cemented together. About 300 million years ago, the Ancestral Rockies, also known as Frontrangia, slowly rose above the surrounding land parallel to today's Front Range, but about 30 to 50 miles west. Frontrangia eroded into red-colored gravel and sand that reached depths of 7,000 to 12,000 feet. Over time, the sand became sandstone and the gravel turned into conglomerate. Fountain formation can also be seen in other places west and north of Colorado Springs at Garden of the Gods, Roxborough State Park, Red Rocks Park, and the Boulder Flatirons.

The trail winds in and out of meadow, creek bed, and forest. Trees and bushes intermix to form an interesting mosaic. Interpretive signs along the first 0.7 miles explain the vegetation and wildlife. It's easy to understand why so many animals and birds are attracted to life in the canyon as the area offers deluxe habitat and a cornucopia of food. Ponderosa pines tower over an assortment of currant bushes. The great

Big bluestem grass along Aiken Canyon Trail.

variety of grasses are identified by the different seed heads. As you approach the hills, the trail gets rockier. Cairns direct you, but sometimes blend in with the trail, so take care to stay on course. Green lichens cover the trunks of one particular patch of piñon pine. Most people associate lichens with rocks, but many varieties exist, some of which live on trees.

In one spot, the trail slips between two closely spaced trees and can be a tight squeeze. Soon you reach a meadow where a spur trail to the right heads up a side canyon. If you have time, explore this 1.6-mile out-and-back. The spur trail takes you farther up the narrowing canyon where Douglas firs start to appear in the cooler, moister environment. Take note that it's easy to confuse the creek bed and the trail in some places. When you come to a big pile of boulders between you and the creek bed, step on over and continue up the canyon. A sign near the remains of an old rock cabin signals the spur trail's end.

Returning to the loop trail, turn right (or continue straight if you skipped the canyon spur) and climb up a somewhat steep ridge. Near the top of the climb to the right of the trail is a boulder that's an excellent example of conglomerate rock. The trail drops steeply and has loose pebbles that can be slippery. On these south facing slopes, Gambel oak, mountain mahogany, sagebrush, and cactus predominate, a noticeable change from the first half of the hike. Little lizards zip along the rocks. Ridges run down the sides of the foothills. Gambel oak, reaching about ten to twelve feet tall, form a canopy over the trail. The trail crosses several arroyos, where the deep, narrow gullies cut by flash floods remind you of the power of water. Flash floods occur infrequently here, but be mindful of lightning, which signals a storm upstream. Cross a final meadow to complete the loop part of the trail. Head back the way you came.

MilesDirections

0.0 START near the visitor center ★
38°37'08"N 104°53'11"W

0.1 The trail drops into streambed for several hundred feet.

0.7 The loop section of the trail starts. Turn onto the right branch. ◈ 38°37'35"N 104°53'10"W

1.9 Come to the junction with the canyon spur trail. ◈ 38°38'07"N 104°53'33"W Stay on the trail straight ahead. [Side-trip. If you have time to explore the canyon spur, turn right and hike about 0.8 mile to the End of Trail sign. Return the same way back to the loop trail and take the right branch. This side-trip will add 1.6 miles to your overall trip.]

3.3 Come to the junction with the loop trail. Turn onto the right branch and retrace your steps.

4.0 Arrive back at the trailhead.

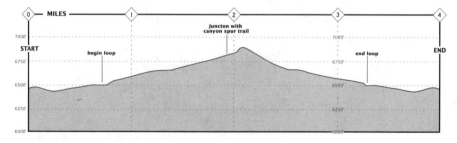

244

Gambel oak with piñon-juniper forest in Aiken Canyon.

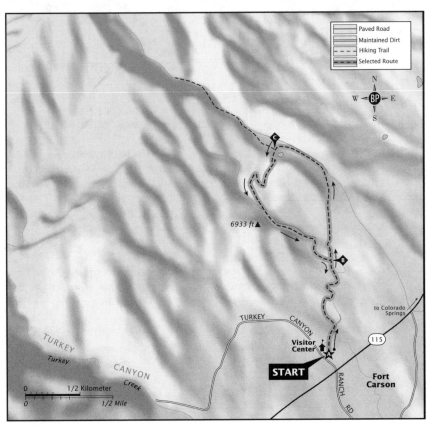

Hike Information

📞 Trail Contact:

Aiken Canyon Preserve, The Nature Conservancy, Colorado Springs, CO (719) 576–4336 or *nature.org*

🕐 Schedule:

Open year round on Saturdays, Sundays, and Mondays from dawn to dusk. Call first to check conditions after big snowstorms.

💲 Fees/Permits:

No fees or permits required

❓ Local Information:

Colorado Springs Convention & Visitors Bureau, Colorado Springs, CO 1–800–745–3773 or *www.coloradosprings-travel. com*

📍 Local Events/Attractions:

U.S. Air Force Academy, U.S. Air Force Academy, CO (719) 333–7746 • **Cheyenne Mountain Zoo,** Colorado Springs, CO (719) 633–0917 • **U.S. Olympic Visitors Center,** Colorado Springs, CO 719–578–4618 • **Pikes Peak Cog Railway,** Manitou Springs, CO (719) 685–5401 • **Pro Rodeo Hall of Fame,** Colorado Springs, CO (719) 528–4764 • **Garden of the Gods,** Colorado Springs, CO (719) 385–5940

🛏 Accommodations:

KOA, Colorado Springs, CO 1–800–562–8609 or (719) 382–7575 • **Golden Eagle Campground,** c/o May Natural History Museum, Colorado Springs, CO (719) 576–0450

🍴 Restaurants:

The Blue Star, Colorado Springs, CO (719) 632–1086 • **La Casita Patio Café,** Colorado Springs, CO (719) 633–9616 • **Il Vicino,** Colorado Springs, CO (719) 475–9224

📖 Other Resources:

The Chinook Bookshop, Colorado Springs, CO (719) 635–1195 or 1–800–999–1195 or *www.chinookbook.com* • *A Sierra Club Naturalist's Guide to The Southern Rockies,* by Audrey DeLella Benedict, Sierra Club Books • *From Grassland to Glacier The Natural of History of Colorado and the Surrounding Region,* by John C. Emerick and Cornelia Fleischer Mutel, 1992. Johnson Printing

👥 Clubs and Organizations:

Colorado Mountain Club, Pikes Peak Group, Colorado Springs, CO (719) 635–5330 or (303) 279–3080 (state office) or *www.cmc.org/cmc* • **Volunteers for Outdoor Colorado,** Denver, CO (303) 715–1010 or 1–800–925–2220 or *www.voc.org*

🚶 Hike Tours:

Aiken Canyon Preserve, Colorado Springs, CO (719) 576–4336

🎒 Local Outdoor Retailers:

Grand West Outfitters, Colorado Springs, CO (719) 596–3031 • **Mountain Chalet,** Colorado Springs, CO (719) 633–0732 or *www.mtnchalet.com* • **REI,** Colorado Springs, CO (719) 260–1455 or *www.rei.com* • **EMS,** Colorado Springs, CO (719) 574–8207 or *www.ems online.com*

🗺 Maps:

USGS maps: Mt. Pittsburg, CO; Mt. Big Chief, CO • *Trails Illustrated®* maps: #137, Pikes Peak/Cañon City

The Nature Conservancy

The Nature Conservancy (TNC) is a nonprofit organization. Its mission is "to preserve the plants, animals and natural communities that represent the diversity of life on Earth by protecting the lands and waters they need to survive." Several ecologists, who wanted to use their knowledge to conserve endangered areas, founded TNC in 1951. Their first accomplishment in 1955 protected a small area in New York State. Since then TNC has grown to be an international organization, preserving more than 1,500 areas just in the United States.

When evaluating a property, TNC first conducts scientific studies of the imperiled species of plants, animals, and natural communities. These areas are ranked based on rarity of the species. Using money contributed by individuals and corporations around the world, TNC works with willing landowners to preserve the lands by either purchasing the land outright or forming management partnerships. Management of the preserves is accomplished using the latest ecological techniques. With some restrictions most areas are open to the public activity for the purpose of nature study, wildlife watching, photography, and hiking. Ongoing projects include inventorying of species and review of habitat health.

For more information about supporting or getting involved with The Nature Conservancy, please contact the Colorado Field Office in Boulder at (303) 444–2950 or nature.org.

Thompson Mountain

Hike Specs

Start: From Wilson Creek Trail (Trail 5827) trailhead

Length: 7.2-mile out-and-back with a loop

Approximate Hiking Time: 3–5 hours

Difficulty Rating: Moderate due to length and unclear sections of trail

Elevations: 7,640–8,620 feet

Elevation Gain: 980 feet

Seasons: Open year round except after big snowstorms

Terrain: Dirt trail, singletrack and doubletrack; some sections not obvious and others marked with flags

Land Status: BLM land

Nearest Town: Cañon City, CO

Other Trail Users: Equestrians, mountain bikers, and hunters (in season)

Canine Compatibility: Leashed dogs permitted. Minimal water on trail

Getting There

From Cañon City: From the intersection of CO 115 and U.S. 50 in Cañon City, drive west on U.S. 50 about 9.5 miles past the Royal Gorge turnoff (restaurants, motels here) to CO 9. Turn right on CO 9 and head north approximately 8.7 miles to CR 11. Turn right onto CR 11, watching for deer along this twisty paved road. (You're on the Gold Belt Scenic Byway.) At the Deer Haven sign, just past mile marker 5, turn right onto CR 69, a well-graded narrow dirt road. Drive slowly to avoid collisions with oncoming traffic or cattle because this area is open range. Drive about 3.3 miles to the Wilson Creek Trail (Trail 5827) sign and turn right. Park immediately in the meadow. Do not attempt to drive the extra 0.2 miles to the bulletin board. The road can be extremely wet and muddy, driving around on the dry grass only makes the muddy area larger, and even the BLM has been known to get stuck on this road. Do not be surprised to find your vehicle surrounded by cattle upon your return. There are no facilities at the trailhead. Bring water!

DeLorme: Colorado Atlas & Gazetteer: Page 61 D7

Charlie and Lee Switzer first started cattle ranching in the Thompson Mountain area back in the 1870s. Their 640 acres covered open range, rolling hills, and bunch grass. During the Cripple Creek-Victor gold rush, they supplied beef to the miners. Around 1900, Toll Witcher bought the ranch from the Switzers then sold it to Lon Gribble in 1914 or 1915. During World War I the price of cattle rose. With his profit, Gribble built a new house in 1917. While digging the basement, he struck solid rock in one corner. After digging four feet into the rock, he struck water. Gribble built a water tank of sorts and built the kitchen right above it. The two-story house had two bedrooms downstairs and four upstairs, a big fireplace, and a full basement. Lumber for the house was hauled from Cañon City with a four-horse team. The house cost $12,000 to build, a substantial sum in those days. You passed the historic house (still a private residence) on the way to the trailhead.

Pikes Peak.

MilesDirections

Note: *Trail work and signage continues on this trail so some of the following directions may change over time.*

0.0 START in meadow near the Wilson Creek Trail (Trail 5827) sign. ★ 38˚36'38"N 105˚21'00"W—Hike up the dirt road.

0.2 Bulletin Board for the trail. Please stop and read the area information and regulations.

0.4 Look for an old rock fence to your right.

0.6 The trail forks at directional sign. Continue to the left on the trail.

0.7 Reach the remains of an old one-room house with corrugated siding.

1.1 The trail reaches a saddle and turns right up the ridge. *[FYI. During the next 0.2 miles, look to the right for views of Pikes Peak through the trees.]*

1.8 *[FYI. Good views of the plains south of Cañon City and the Wet Mountains.]*

2.0 *[FYI. Nice views to the southwest of the Sangre de Cristo Range.]* Reach a fence. Use the metal gate to the left—remember to close the gate behind you. The trail practically disappears as you descend the meadow. Head downhill until you reach a trail junction sign.

2.2 Reach the junction of Water Tank Trail and Thompson Mtn. Trail. Turn left onto Water Tank Trail and follow the trail through the trees, turning right to cross the little dam. The trail comes to a T-intersection. The loop in the trail starts here. Turn left and follow the trail to a meadow. The trail disappears here. Head

south around the head of a little gully that's on your left. Don't go down the gully. Head about 155˚ magnetic north.

2.3 Try to find a ponderosa pine and a piñon pine growing very close to each other. ◈ 38˚36'02"N 105˚22'41"W—Head about 130˚ magnetic north and look to the right for the trail. Just down the trail between rocks is a carsonite trail marker.

2.5 The trail curves left to head around a ridge. If you go straight here, you'll lose the trail at the edge of the ridge. After curving around the ridge, the trail heads down a gully.

2.8 Enter a meadow where the trail and markers disappear. Start downhill but stay a little to the right and look downhill. You'll see a circular water tank, a narrow water trough, and a creek. Head to the water tank.

2.9 Drop down past the metal water tank and cross the creek. ◈ 38˚35'41"N 105˚22'34"W You'll find a trail on the other side that takes you up and around into a grassy open meadow and drainage. Follow the faint old non-motorized ranch road on the left. (Don't head up the gully.) Head uphill toward a saddle.

3.4 Reach the saddle. *[Side-trip. If you'd like to hike up to Thompson Point, follow the ridge to the rocky outcrop up on your left. The Gambel oak can be vicious to walk through. Out-and-back distance to Thompson Point is about 0.6 miles.]* Turn right and follow the non-motorized ranch road uphill. *[FYI. Look to your left for some interesting rock formations.]*

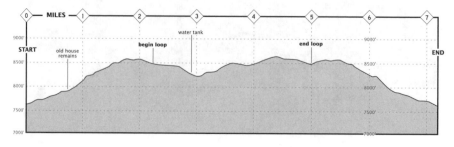

3.6 Follow the non-motorized road downhill to the right. As you approach a gully, the road turns left and starts heading uphill again. Pass a metal corrugated water tank and trough.

3.9 Enter an open area with a rusted barrel stuck in the ground to your right. The trail forks here at a trail marker. Take the trail to the right up a little hill to a check dam at mile 4.0. Continue along the trail to the left of the dam.

4.2 Enter an open, flat area. ✛ 38˚36'05"N 105˚23'16"W *[FYI. There are great views of various hills ahead with Thompson Point and the Sangre de Cristos and Wet Mountains behind you.]* The trail turns right before the road starts heading slightly downhill. A trail marker is on your far right. Turn right here and find the road. Follow this road as it curves right then left then right again.

4.6 Arrive in an open meadow. A big rock outcropping will be on your left. The non-motorized road splits, but either trail takes you where you want to go. Once across the meadow, if you can't see the trail, keep heading downhill. A check dam will be on your left and a gully in front of you.

4.8 When you come to the gully, turn right and follow a faint trail back to the dam you crossed at the start of the loop. Cross the dam and turn left to reach the trail junction sign.

5.0 Reach the trail junction sign for Water Tank Trail and Thompson Mtn. Trail. Turn right, head uphill, and return the way you came.

7.2 Arrive back at the trailhead.

Gribble also established a sawmill with a Case tractor to run it. He hired a worker to run the mill and others to cut the timber. He sold the lumber for mine props to the coal mines south of Cañon City. By 1932, cattle prices had fallen and a hard winter took its toll on Gribble's ability to pay his loans, resulting in foreclosure on Gribble's ranch.

The *Frontier Times* (June-July 1976) contained a story entitled, "Last Wilson Creek Roundup." Dud Van Buskirk, who was Lon Gribble's brother-in-law, bet Gribble that Fred Short could hold a cow by the tail for five minutes. Short walked into the herd of cattle and grabbed the tail of a two-year old heifer. The heifer ran as

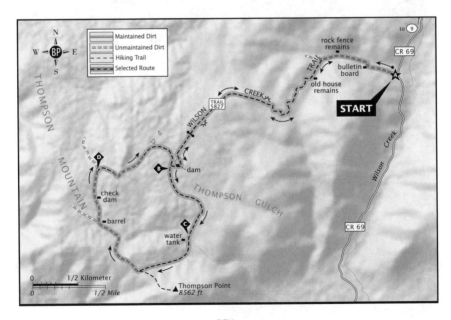

fast as she could, out of the herd of cattle, up along the fence. Fred was hanging on. After about 100 feet, the heifer decided to head back to the herd, "stopped right quick and turned back down the fence. Fred, however, just kept going—about 10 feet to a step—till he fell and lit on his face."

In 1940, Floyd Murphy bought the old Switzer Ranch and actually made it profitable. He grazed a string of relay horses and was one of the best relay riders in America. He also grazed cattle. He sold the ranch about 10 years later at $10 per acre.

After several other owners, The Richard King Mellon Foundation and the Conservation Fund of Arlington, Virginia bought the land and donated it to the U.S. Bureau of Land Management (BLM) in 1992 to "provide significant wildlife habitat, riparian, and wetland habitat, recreation opportunities, protect scenic quality and to improve stewardship and access to adjoining public land." The donation amounted to 4,900 acres. On National Trails Day in 1993, a groundbreaking ceremony was held to initiate the current trail. The Rocky Mountain Back Country Horsemen and the Medicine Wheel Bicycle Club have steadily worked on the trail. As of fall 2001, much of the trail was finished with the rest roughed out and marked. The trail is still a work in progress. Follow the directions carefully.

The hike starts up a drainage then turns up another drainage at a check dam. The first part climbs steadily through the forest then up a ridge. As you gain elevation, keep an eye open to the right for views of Pikes Peak. In a beautiful ponderosa pine forest, the trail is marked with brown carsonite signs. Mica flecks sparkle in the trail.

About two miles in, descend a meadow to a pond where the loop part of the trail begins. Take the left fork first. The trail follows occasional trail markers. It heads down another drainage to a metal cattle trough. From the descending trail you can see the rocky knob of Thompson Point. After the cattle trough, the trail heads up a broad drainage to a saddle. From here, the BLM would like to create a trail to Thompson

Mountain ball cactus in bloom.

Point in the future. At the saddle the trail turns right onto an old non-motorized dirt road and eventually climbs, descends, and climbs again to an open area with views of Cap Rock. Turn right here and follow an old non-motorized road that winds through forest and meadow and back to a gully. Turn right at the gully and walk back to the first pond and dam to end the loop. Head back to your vehicle the way you came.

Thompson Mountain covers a large area, its gentle ridges surrounding drainages and meadows. It's definitely not the typical Colorado pointy-topped mountain.

Hike Information

○ Trail Contact:
Bureau of Land Management, Royal Gorge Field Office, Cañon City, CO, (719) 269–8500 or *www.co.blm.gov/ccdo/ canon.htm*

○ Schedule:
Open year round, except after a big snowstorm

○ Fees/Permits:
No fees or permits required

○ Local Information:
Cañon City Chamber of Commerce, Cañon City, CO, (719) 275–2331, or 1–800–876–7922 or *www.canoncitycolo rado.com*

○ Local Events/Attractions:
Royal Gorge Bridge & Park, Royal Gorge, CO, (719) 275–7507 or *www.royalgorge bridge.com* • **Museum of Colorado Prisons,** Cañon City, CO, (719) 269–3015 • **Dinosaur Depot,** Cañon City, CO, 1–800–987–6379, or (719) 269–7150 or *www.dinosaurdepot.com* • **Royal Gorge Route** (train ride), Cañon City, CO, 1–888–724–5748, or (303) 569–2403 or *www.royalgorgeroute.com* • **Fiddler's on the Gorge Western Festival,** Royal Gorge, CO, (719) 275–7507 • **Music and Blossom Festival,** Cañon City, CO, 1–800–794–8702, or (719) 275–7234 • **Holy Cross Abbey,** Cañon City, CO, (719) 275–8631 or *www.holycrossabbey.org*

○ Accommodations:
St. Cloud Hotel, Cañon City, CO, 1–800–405–9666, or (719) 276–2000 or *www.stcloudhotel.com .*

○ Restaurants:
Janey's Chili Wagon, Cañon City, CO, (719) 275–4885 – *Mexican food* • **Santa Fe Depot Restaurant,** Cañon City, CO, (719) 269–7076 • **The Old Mission Deli,** Cañon City, CO, (719) 275–6780 • **Gourmet Chef Chinese Restaurant,** Cañon City, CO, (719) 269–1818

○ Organizations:
Rocky Mountain Back Country Horse-men, P.O. Box 312, Cotopaxi, CO 81223

○ Other Resources:
The Book Corral, Cañon City, CO, (719) 275–8923 • **Cañon City Public Library,** Local History Center, Cañon City, CO, (719) 269–9036 or *www.ccpl.lib.co. us/lhc* • **"Last Wilson Creek Roundup,"** June-July 1976. Frontier Times • *100 Years on the Switzer Ranch,* by Paul L. Huntley, Master Printers

○ Local Outdoor Retailers:
None that cater to hikers. Closest hiking oriented stores seem to be in Colorado Springs or Pueblo.

○ Maps:
USGS maps: Gribble Mountain, CO; Rice Mountain, CO • *Trails Illustrated®* maps: #137, Pikes Peak/Cañon City

Newlin Creek Trail

Hike Specs

Start: From the Newlin Creek Trail (Trail 1335) trailhead near Florence Mountain Park

Length: 5.4-mile out-and-back

Approximate Hiking Time: 2.25–4 hours

Difficulty Rating: Moderate due to distance and elevation gain

Elevations: 7,000–8,360 feet

Elevation Gain: 1,360 feet

Seasons: Best from mid-May to early November

Terrain: Dirt trail with numerous creek crossings

Land Status: National forest

Nearest Town: Florence, CO

Other Trail Users: Equestrians and hunters (in season)

Canine Compatibility: Controlled dogs permitted

Getting There

From Florence: From the intersection of CO 115 and CO 67 in the middle of Florence, drive south on CO 67 for 4.6 miles to CR 15. The intersection is marked as National Forest access, Newlin Creek Trail trailhead. Turn right onto the CR 15. The road forks in 2.6 miles; stay on CR 15 by driving on the right fork. The road turns to dirt in another 0.9 miles—it can be very muddy and slippery when wet. The road forks in another 0.8 miles; stay right following the sign to Florence Mountain Park. The entrance to the mountain park is designated by a big log frame over the road in another 1.1 miles. At the junction in another 0.1 miles marked "amphitheater," go straight. In another 0.2 miles, there's an intersection where you continue straight followed by the caretaker's house on the left. Follow the signs to Newlin Creek Trail trailhead. The road continues to deteriorate. About 0.2 miles past the house is some parking if the road is too rough for your vehicle. In another 0.2 miles is the national forest boundary sign. There's some parking just past here near a little pond. Drive or walk another 0.1 miles to the trailhead. The trailhead is about 10.9 miles from the middle of Florence. There are no facilities here. Bring water in case the creek is low. *DeLorme: Colorado Atlas & Gazetteer:* Page 72 B1

ewlin Creek is nestled in the northeastern end of the Wet Mountains. Early explorers such as the Gunnison Expedition of 1853–1854 observed that rain constantly fell on this mountain range and named it accordingly. Streams ran high in late winter and early spring, and summer thunderstorms flooded creek beds. Newlin Creek was probably named after a local by the same name who lived in Locke Park to the west.

Oil was discovered near the town of Florence in 1881 and some wells are still producing oil today. Coal mining also became a big industry in the late 1800s. Coal Creek lies just north of Newlin Creek. The discovery of silver on the west side of the Wet Mountains created booming mining towns such as Silver Cliff and Westcliffe. Coal and silver mines needed much timber for shoring up mine shafts

and for residential and commercial buildings. The forests of the Wet Mountains provided an opportunity for an entrepreneur to provide lumber to industries on both sides of the range.

Nathaniel F. Herrick, originally from Canada, lived in Galena near Locke Park southwest of Cañon City and a few miles west of Newlin Creek with his wife and children. He grabbed at the opportunity to build a lumber mill and built a road and sawmill up Newlin Creek. The hand-built road measured about five feet in width and in places was supported with rock walls. Herrick hauled a huge steam boiler and flywheel to a nice meadow where he also built a cabin, complete with stone chimney. The boiler used water from Newlin Creek to run the flywheel and power a saw to cut lumber. On November 28, 1887, Herrick signed a chattel mortgage with W. D. McGee and W. F. Hasidy for $900. The "chattel" involved the sawmill, including the engine, boiler fixtures, and tools; five horses and one mule with their harnesses; and two log wagons and a Studebaker wagon along with the log chains. According to the mortgage record, the sawmill was "situated on Newland Creek in said County of Fremont, 23 or 24 miles from Cañon City." Unfortunately, after Herrick had all the equipment set up and mortgaged, he died the very next month at the age of 61. The lumber mill was apparently abandoned soon thereafter. Between floods and rockslides, the road was destroyed and the equipment remained in place.

Today the steam boiler lies rusting amidst aspen trees next to Newlin Creek. Some bricks lie near its base. Pipes point in different directions, and the flywheel sits forlorn and disconnected. Exactly how much time it took to haul this equipment from

Old steam boiler by Newlin Creek.

Cañon City or Florence is unknown, but it must have been quite an effort. Look carefully at the boiler for interesting gargoyle-type faces and other inscriptions.

The hike follows Newlin Creek up to the steam boiler meadow. Between rockslides and floods, it's hard to tell today that any type of wagon road existed along the creek. The trail twists through forests of Douglas fir, ponderosa pine, and Gambel oak. A picnic table sits just before the trail slips between steep canyon walls. Enjoy the fancy wooden bridge that crosses Newlin Creek since you'll be using rocks and logs to cross creeks 18 more times over the duration of the hike. Watch the creek for miniwaterfalls and cascades. Look up occasionally for interesting pointy cliffs and rocks. After 11 creek crossings, you'll hike along an open slope with Gambel oak above. Then head back into the trees dotted with red columbine, heart-leafed arnica, Wood's rose, strawberries, pussytoes, and some nice aspen.

A few creek crossings later, you enter a little meadow on the left (west) side of the creek. Look carefully for a faint trail heading off to the right to some aspen. The old boiler and other equipment lie among the trees. Return to the main trail and continue a little farther up the creek, keeping an eye open to the left for the chimney remains. Remember the equipment and chimney are protected as historical items under the Antiquities Act. Please do not climb on or disrupt the remains. The meadow is a wonderful picnic spot. Enjoy and return the way you came.

MilesDirections

0.0 START at upper trailhead parking area for Newlin Creek Trail (Trail 1335). If you parked lower down add the appropriate mileage from your vehicle to the trailhead. ☆ 38˙16'00"N 105˙11'18"W

0.5 Come to a picnic table.

0.7 The trail crosses Newlin Creek on a wooden bridge with handrails. ◈ 38˙15'38"N 105˙11'42"W

1.0 The trail goes through an area of big boulders with rocks in the trail.

1.1 Come to the first of many creek crossings without a bridge.

1.6 Reach a nice four-foot-high waterfall off to the right of this creek crossing.

1.8 The trail and creek join in one spot. There's a tricky creek crossing on slopey rock (like slickrock). Look about three feet upstream for an easier spot to cross.

2.5 Arrive in a little meadow. Look for the faint trail at about 1 o'clock, heading to some aspen. The old boiler and flywheel are hidden in the trees near the creek. ◈ 38˙15'42"N 105˙13'00"W

2.7 After following the trail through the meadow and looking to the left, you'll hopefully find the chimney remains. ◈ 38˙15'46"N 105˙13'00"W Return the way you came.

5.4 Arrive back at the trailhead.

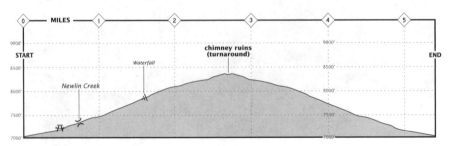

256

Hike Information

Trail Contact:

San Isabel National Forest, San Carlos Ranger District, Cañon City, CO (719) 269–8500 or *www.fs.fed.us/r2/psicc*

Schedule:

Open year round,. Access road closed 0.5 miles from trailhead in winter.

Fees/Permits:

No fees or permits required

Local Information:

Florence Chamber of Commerce, Florence, CO (719) 784–3544

Local Events/Attractions:

Annual Pioneers Days Celebration, Florence, CO (719) 784–3544 • **The Price Pioneer Museum,** Florence, CO (no phone) – *open Memorial Day to Labor Day • (See Hike 33: Thompson Mountain.)*

Accommodations:

Riviera Motel, Florence, CO (719)

784–6716 • **River Valley Inn,** Florence, CO (719) 784–4800

Restaurants:

Walker's Sports Bar & Deli, Florence, CO (719) 784–2202 • **Golden Pheasant Grill,** Florence, CO (719) 784–4432

Other Resources:

Cañon City Public Library, Local History Center, Cañon City, CO (719) 269–9036, or *www.ccpl.lib.co.us/lhc* • *From Trappers to Tourists Fremont County,* Colorado 1830–1950, by Rosemae Wells Campbell, Filter Press • *Southern Front Range Trail Guide,* by Nadia N. Brelje, Master Printers

Local Outdoor Retailers:

None that cater to hikers. Closest hiking oriented stores seem to be in Colorado Springs or Pueblo.

Maps:

USGS maps: Rockvale, CO

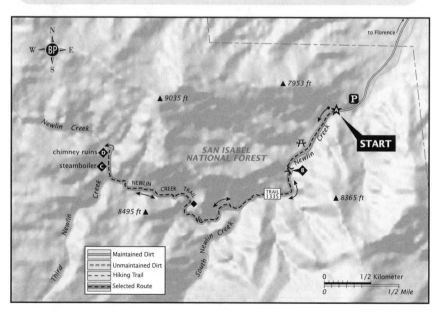

Reilly and Levsa Canyons

Hike Specs

Start: From the Trinidad Lake State Park campground
Length: 5.5-mile out-and-back with a loop
Approximate Hiking Time: 2.5–4.0 hours
Difficulty Rating: Moderate due to length and a few steep sections
Elevations: 6,260–6,500 feet
Elevation Gain: 240 feet
Seasons: Open year round except after big snowstorms
Terrain: Dirt trail with a few steep sections
Land Status: State park
Nearest Town: Trinidad, CO
Other Trail Users: Hunters (in season)
Canine Compatibility: Leashed dogs permitted

Getting There

From Trinidad: Drive 3.9 miles southwest on CO 12 from its intersection with I-25 to the Trinidad Lake State Park Entrance. CO 12 is the Scenic Highway of Legends, so follow the scenic byway signs. Turn left onto the Park road. The entrance station is about 0.5-mile on the left. Stop and pay the entrance fee. Drive less than 0.1 miles and turn right at the campground entrance. At the fork in the road, turn left and drive to the restrooms. The trailhead is across from the restrooms. Parking is available here as well as restrooms and water. Take water with you. *DeLorme: Colorado Atlas & Gazetteer:* Page 93 C6

T
he Mountain Branch of the Santa Fe Trail passed nearby what is today Trinidad Lake State Park. Interstate 25 basically follows the old trail over Raton Pass, just south of the city of Trinidad. These lands were home to many Native American tribes: Comanche, Kiowa, Cheyenne, Arapaho, Jicarilla Apache, and Ute. They traveled over the plains, hunting bison, elk, antelope, and deer and creating trails that lay the foundation of the Santa Fe Trail.

What we now know as New Mexico belonged to Mexico and the Spanish in the early 1800s. Spain prohibited trade between the United States and Santa Fe. In 1821, the Mexican people revolted against Spanish rule and gained their independence.

One entrepreneur, William Becknell, left Franklin, Missouri in August of 1821 and headed to Santa Fe with trade goods on pack animals. He traveled over Raton Pass, taking two days to roll boulders out of the way so his pack animals could pass. This route later became the Mountain Branch of the Santa Fe Trail. Becknell reached Santa Fe in mid-December and quickly sold his goods. In exchange for manufactured goods and supplies the Mexicans traded gold, silver, fur, and mules. Becknell returned to Missouri by an overland route that avoided Raton Pass, arriving home in January 1822. Later that year Becknell traveled back to Santa Fe with trade goods using wagons along the 780-mile over-land route, which became known as the Cimarron Cutoff. Round trip between Missouri and Santa Fe took two to three months.

For the next 25 years, the Cimarron Cutoff was the preferred route, being 100 miles shorter with rolling plains and no mountain obstacles. Two disadvantages were a lack of water along one 60-mile stretch and travel through the hunting grounds of unpredictable Comanche, Kiowa, and Apache tribes. In 1846, two events caused the

Sangre de Cristos from Levsa Canyon National Trail.

Mountain Branch over Raton Pass to become the preferred route. First a bad drought occurred in 1846, drying out the few springs and streams along the Cimarron Cutoff. The Mountain Branch followed the Arkansas River, which always had some water, even if one had to dig in the streambed to find it. Bent's Fort was also located on this route. General Stephen Kearney moved his army along the Mountain Branch to run military excursions into Mexico. Kearney also drove his wagon supply trains over Raton Pass after improving the trail. The Mexican-American War started in 1846 and resulted in New Mexico becoming part of the United States in 1848.

Raton Pass provided many challenges to early trail users. Before crossing the pass, people camped along the Purgatoire River on the east side, a welcome relief after the endless dry prairies. The town of Trinidad was founded here around 1862. From a travel account written in 1846, progress could be as little as 600–800 yards a day as men hauled wagons by hand over the great rocks. It took five days to cross the pass, a distance of about 30 miles. One place was so narrow that one little slip sent mules, wagons, and people to a certain death. In 1865, the legislatures of Colorado and New Mexico granted "Uncle Dick" Wooton a charter to build a toll road over Raton Pass. Wooton blasted away the rocks and widened the road. Tolls ranged from five cents per head of cattle to $1.50 per wagon. In one 15-month period, the toll road collected

MilesDirections

0.0 START at trailhead near restrooms in campground. ☆ 37˚08'39"N 104˚34'11"W

0.05 At the fork, take right fork to follow Levsa Canyon Nature Trail.

0.1 At the fork, take right branch of Levsa Canyon Nature Trail and head uphill.

0.3 Arrive at the intersection of Reilly Canyon Trail and Levsa Canyon Nature Trail. Turn right onto Reilly Canyon Trail. ◆ 37˚08'41"N 104˚34'25"W

1.3 Cross the wooden bridge in Levsa Canyon. ◆ 37˚08'44"N 104˚35'01"W

2.2 There's a slickrock slab on the right.

2.5 Reach a bench and a view of the dam. Return the way you came. ◆ 37˚08'11"N 104˚35'36"W

4.7 Come to the trail intersection of Reilly Canyon Trail and Levsa Canyon Nature Trail. Turn right (more like straight) onto Levsa Canyon Nature Trail.

5.0 Reach a bench with a view.

5.25 Reach a bench with a view.

5.3 Reach a bench.

5.4 Reach the other end of the Levsa Canyon Nature Trail loop. Take the trail on the right. At the next intersection, go straight.

5.5 Arrive back at the trailhead.

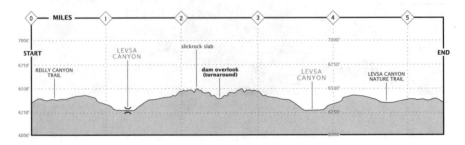

Trinidad Lake (reservoir) from Levsa Canyon Nature Trail.

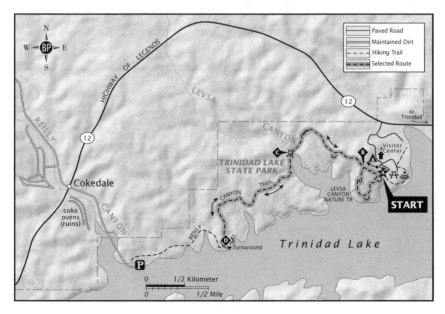

$9,193! The completion of a railroad line from Trinidad to Santa Fe in 1880 eliminated the need for the Santa Fe Trail.

As you hike the Reilly Canyon trail, imagine driving a horse drawn wagon through the area. Some of the trail appears fairly negotiable while other sections dropping into the canyons and ravines would be a bit dicey. The suggested hiking route starts at the trailhead near the campground.

Horno Cooking

If you stay at the campground, try your hand at horno (pronounced OR-no) cooking. The horno is a beehive shaped oven made of adobe used by Spanish settlers and still in use in the southwest today. One is available for use at Trinidad Lake State Park near the amphitheater. Inquire at the visitor center for details.

Hike up the first part of Levsa Canyon Nature Trail, then take the right fork and follow the Reilly Canyon Trail for about 2.2 more miles (the mileage noted on the bulletin board starts at this intersection). The trail drops into Levsa Canyon then climbs out and wanders across a high stretch. Dropping down another little canyon to a flat stretch, the trail climbs to a big slab of slickrock then descends to Trinidad Lake. A bench to rest your feet awaits you. From here you can see the dam at the east end of the lake.

If you want to add some mileage, you can hike another 1.8 miles west to Reilly Canyon itself, for a nine-mile round trip. Otherwise, on the way back, take the right fork at the Levsa Canyon Nature Trail/Reilly Canyon intersection and continue back along the nature trail. It drops, climbs, and drops providing good views of the area across the lake where coal mines and towns resided before the dam was built, plus Fishers Peak (9,655 feet) to the south. Watch for blue piñon jays and deer as you hike.

Old coke ovens in Reilly Canyon near Cokedale.

Hike Information

🌑 Trail Contact:
Trinidad Lake State Park, Trinidad, CO (719) 846–6951 or *www.parks.state. co.us/trinidad*

🕐 Schedule:
Open year round, except after a big snowstorm.

💲 Fees/Permits:
Daily fee or annual parks pass required

❓ Local Information:
Colorado Welcome Center, Trinidad, CO (719) 846–9512 • **Trinidad/Las Animas County Chamber of Commerce,** Trinidad, CO (719) 846–9285, *www.trinidadco.com*

📍 Local Events/Attractions:
Colorado's Scenic Highway of Legends, 120-mile loop including Trinidad, CO (719) 846–9412 • **Corazon De Trinidad National Historic District,** Trinidad, CO 1–800–748–1970 • **Trinidad History Museums,** Trinidad, CO (719) 846–7217

• **Louden-Henritze Museum of Archaeology,** Trinidad, CO (719) 846–5508 • **A. R. Mitchell Museum of Western Art,** Trinidad, CO (719) 846–4224 • **Santa Fe Trail Festival,** Trinidad, CO (719) 846–9285

🛏 Accommodations:
Trinidad Lake State Park campground, Trinidad, CO (719) 846–6951

🍴 Restaurants:
El Capitan Restaurant & Lounge, Trinidad, CO (719) 846–9903 • **Main Street Bakery Café,** Trinidad, CO (719) 846–8779 • **Nana & Nano's Pasta House,** Trinidad, CO (719) 846–2696 • **Mission at the Bell Restaurant,** Trinidad, CO (719) 845–1513

📖 Other Resources:
Bob's Books, Trinidad, CO (719) 846–4273

🅝 Maps:
USGS maps: Trinidad West, CO

Wahatoya Trail

Hike Specs

Start: From the Apishapa (a-PISH-a-pa) Trail trailhead

Length: 11.8-mile point-to-point (with a 9.6-mile out-and-back option)

Approximate Hiking Time: 5–8 hours (4–6.5 hours for out-and back option)

Difficulty Rating: Most difficult due to length and elevation gain and loss

Elevations: 8,420–10,960 feet (9,440–10,960 feet for out-and-back option)

Elevation Gain: 2,580 feet (2,780 feet for out-and-back option)

Seasons: Best from June to mid-October

Terrain: Dirt trail with some rocky sections across talus fields, and rough dirt road

Land Status: National forest and wilderness area

Nearest Towns: La Veta, CO and Cuchara, CO

Other Trail Users: Equestrians and 4WD vehicles (on last two miles)

Canine Compatibility: Controlled dogs permitted. Little to no water on the trail

Getting There
With Shuttle

From La Veta: Drive to the south end of La Veta on CO 12 to Cuchara Street, next to La Veta Sports Pub & Grub. Turn left on Cuchara Street. In about 0.7 miles Cuchara Street ends but the road curves right, so follow this road, which is supposedly CR 361, but isn't marked. In one mile, turn left at the Huajatolla Valley sign (CR 362—not marked). In 0.5 miles, turn right where the road lazy "Ts" onto

CR 360. There is no road sign here, but the road straight ahead says "Dead End." Drive about five miles on this somewhat twisty but maintained dirt road to the Wahatoya Trail (Trail 1304), FS 442 sign. There's a good place to park in about 0.1 miles down the hill. With a high clearance vehicle, you can drive about two miles up FS 442. Set up a car shuttle here. Return to La Veta the way you came. Drive south on CO 12 about 17 miles to the top of Cucharas Pass. Turn left onto the Cordova Pass road (FS 46—not marked) and drive another 10.8 miles, driving left at two intersections that are well marked. Pass through the Apishapa Arch, which was cut through a dike by the Civilian Conservation Corps. A little farther down the road, the Apishapa Trail trailhead will be on your left. There are no facilities here. Bring water with you.

Without Shuttle

From La Veta: Drive south on CO 12 about 17 miles to the top of Cucharas Pass. Turn left onto the Cordova Pass road (FS 46—not marked) and drive another 10.8 miles, driving left at two intersections that are well marked. Pass through the Apishapa Arch, which was cut through a dike by the Civilian Conservation Corps. A little farther down the road, the Apishapa Trail trailhead will be on your left. There are no facilities here. Bring water with you. *DeLorme: Colorado Atlas & Gazetteer: Page* 92 B2 *(start point);* Page 92 A3 *(shuttle point)*

Seeing rain clouds gather over what are today known as Spanish Peaks, Indians named them Wahatoya, "Breasts of the World." Rain provided drinking water and helped crops grow—both essential to life. You might also see spellings of Huajatolla or Guajatolla. Over the years, the peaks have been named Twin Peaks, the Mexican Mountains, and Dos Hermanos (Two Brothers).

The first documented sighting of these peaks came in 1706, when Juan de Ulibarri explored this area for Spain. The peaks, long a landmark for Native Americans, trappers, and explorers, became a welcome sight for travelers on the Mountain Branch of the Santa Fe Trail, indicating an end to the dry, open plains.

Apishapa Arch built through a volcanic dike on Cordova Pass Road.

265

The peaks are also important in the world of geology. About 100 million years ago, an inland sea covered much of North America. Sediments were deposited as the sea rose and fell then turned into rock over eons. About 35 million years ago, after the present Rockies had risen, and while volcanic eruptions were creating the San Juan

MilesDirections

0.0 START at the Apishapa Trail trailhead. (Elevation: 9,720 feet.) ✪ 37°20'38"N 104°59'27"W

1.3 Turn right onto the Wahatoya Trail (Trail 1304) ✪ 37°21'25"N 104°59'32"W *[FYI. The Apishapa Trail continues to the left and intersects with West Peak Trail (Trail 1392) which in turn heads up West Spanish Peak.]*

1.4 *[FYI. Enjoy nice views to the south and east toward Trinidad and into New Mexico.]*

1.5 *[FYI. Here's another good viewpoint of many dikes and the Sangre de Cristo Range.]*

1.9 Pass through a little dike.

2.3 Come to a flat area. Follow the cairns into the trees.

2.5 Cross a boulder field with a creek running underneath.

3.0 Come to another boulder field.

3.8 Cross through a passageway (gap) in a large dike.

4.8 Reach an unmarked overlook at a dike. The trail curves right here and continues downhill. Walk ahead and uphill about 90 feet. Good view of East Spanish Peak. (Elevation: 9,440 feet.) *[Option. This is an excellent turnaround point for a 9.6-mile out-and-back hike. Simply return the way you*

came.] Continue on the trail as it heads downhill. ✪ 37°21'53"N 104°56'40"W

5.0 The new Wahatoya Trail intersects with the old Wahatoya Trail. *[FYI. To the right, the old trail headed south to dead-end in private property.]* This junction ends the new section of the Wahatoya Trail. Turn left and hike on the original Wahatoya Trail to the north trailhead.

5.4 Reach an old Forest Service cabin. ✪ 37°22'02"N 104°56'16"W Continue on the trail downstream about 0.1 miles to the crossing of South Fork Trujillo Creek. (Elevation: 8,980 feet.)

7.9 Reach the saddle between East Spanish and West Spanish peaks and the Huerfano and Las Animas County line. (Elevation: 10,320 feet.) ✪ 37°23'24"N 104°57'01"W

9.7 The Wahatoya Trail joins FS 442. ✪ 37°23'56"N 104°58'30"W Continue heading downhill on the road.

10.4 *[FYI. There's a great view of a big dike to west from an imbedded dike to the left of the trail.]*

10.9 *[FYI. Enjoy a good view of East Spanish Peak and the Wahatoya drainage from an unmarked viewpoint to the right of the trail.]*

11.8 Arrive at the north Wahatoya Trail trailhead. (Elevation: 8,420 feet.) ✪ 37°25'21"N 104°54'37"W

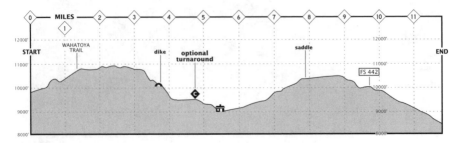

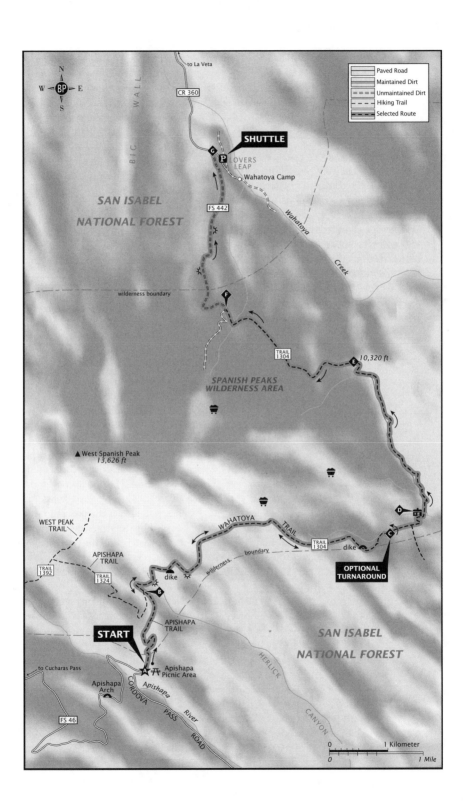

Paved Road
Maintained Dirt
Unmaintained Dirt
Hiking Trail
Selected Route

to La Veta

CR 360

SHUTTLE

G

P

LOVERS
LEAP

Wahatoya Camp

BIG WALL

SAN ISABEL

NATIONAL FOREST

FS 442

Wahatoya Creek

wilderness boundary

F

SPANISH PEAKS
WILDERNESS AREA

TRAIL
1304

E

10,320 ft

▲ West Spanish Peak
13,626 ft

WEST PEAK
TRAIL

WAHATOYA   TRAIL

D

TRAIL
1392

APISHAPA
TRAIL

TRAIL
1324

dike

boundary

wilderness

TRAIL
1304

dike

C

**OPTIONAL
TURNAROUND**

B

APISHAPA
TRAIL

START

Apishapa
Picnic Area

SAN ISABEL

NATIONAL FOREST

to Cucharas Pass

Apishapa
Arch

CORDOVA

Apishapa

River

PASS

HERLICK CANYON

FS 46

ROAD

0   1 Kilometer

0   1 Mile

Mountains to the west, molten magma pushed its way up into the sedimentary rocks, which cracked and buckled from the pressure. The magma oozed into vertical cracks still below the earth's surface, then cooled and hardened. When the entire region was uplifted about 5,000 feet some five million years ago, these volcanic intrusions rose also. Erosion washed away the softer sedimentary rocks, leaving behind two peaks and many dikes. Geologists have identified over 400 dikes around the Spanish Peaks. Looking like huge stone fences, they have been given colorful names like Devils Stairsteps.

Volunteers for Outdoor Colorado (VOC) is "a nonprofit organization formed in 1984, dedicated to promoting and fostering a sense of personal responsibility for Colorado's public lands among its citizens and visitors." VOC sponsors work projects throughout Colorado from April to October, partnering with various land management agencies. For more information contact (303) 715-1010 or 1-800-925-2220 or www.voc.org.

Circumnavigating the peaks is the Scenic Highway of Legends, commemorating the many legends that surround the peaks. One legend tells of a tribe of giants who once lived around Wahatoya. They quarreled amongst themselves and built rock walls about chest high for protection. They hurled huge boulders at each other. The gods of Wahatoya, angered by the wars, stopped the rains. The giants stopped fighting and left in search of water. One warrior remained behind to guard the valley, but the others never returned. The guard grew tired and sat to rest. The gods turned him to stone for his dedication. The rock is now known as Goemmer's Butte, a volcanic plug south of La Veta.

In pre-Spanish days, a legend told of gold being used as offerings to the Aztec deities. One of the Aztec rulers established a dazzling court and "the gods of the Mountain Huajatolla became envious of the magnificence of his court and they placed demons on the double mountain and forbade all men further approach." Years later, in the mid-1500s, when Coronado returned to Mexico after abandoning his search for the fabled cities of gold, three monks remained behind to convert the natives. Legend has it that two were killed while the third monk, Juan de la Cruz, found the gold mines. He forced Native Americans to extract the precious metal from the mines. Ready to return to Mexico, he killed the tribesmen, and left with the gold carried by pack animals. The demons became angry, and the priest and his treasure disappeared. According to some versions, a settler found gold nuggets years later. In any case, the lost treasure drew people to the area in search of the lost gold and mines.

Designated an official wilderness area in November 2000, hiking around the Spanish Peaks and through the dikes is a trip through geologic time. The Wahatoya and Apishapa trails used to be connected via the Peaks Trail, which crossed private property. The U.S. Forest Service, with the assistance of Volunteers for Outdoor Colorado, built a new four-mile section of trail higher on the south slope of West Spanish Peak. The new trail crosses several boulder fields below the peak. Many different types of trees line the trail, including ancient bristlecone pine. You can see west to the Sangre de Cristos, south to the mesas near Trinidad, and farther yet to the volcanoes in northeastern New Mexico. The most interesting parts are the little passages through the volcanic dikes.

The featured hike is a roller coaster ride, climbing about 1,240 feet in elevation, then losing about 1,980 feet, only to climb another 1,340 feet to the saddle between the two peaks. Finally the trail traverses the north flank of West Spanish Peak descending another 1,900 feet to the north trailhead in the Wahatoya Valley. The longer hike between the two peaks gives you an intimate view of the Spanish Peaks Wilderness, but those looking to make an equally enjoyable out-and back of the hike can turn around at a little dike with a viewpoint of East Spanish Peak after dropping only 1,540 feet. The shorter hike allows you to experience the large variety of trees and the area's geology without the roller coaster effect.

Hike Information

📞 Trail Contact:

Pike/San Isabel National Forest, San Carlos Ranger District, Cañon City, CO (719) 269–8500 or *www.fs.fed.us/r2/ psicc*

🕐 Schedule:

Open year round. FS 46 closed by snow 9.3 miles from trailhead. Trail crosses several avalanche paths on south side of West Spanish Peak. Trail neither maintained nor marked for winter use from either trailhead.

💲 Fees/Permits:

No fees or permits required. Call for group size limits

❓ Local Information:

La Veta/Cuchara Chamber, La Veta, CO (719) 742–3676 or *www.ruralwide web.com/lvcc.htm* • **Huerfano County Chamber,** Walsenburg, CO (719) 738–1065

💡 Local Events/Attractions:

Fort Francisco Museum, La Veta, CO (719) 742–5501 or *www.ruralwideweb. com/fofag.htm#tffm* • **Scenic Highway of Legends,** La Veta CO, *www.highway oflegends.org* • **Fort Francisco Days,** La Veta, CO (719) 742–5501 or *www.rural wid>web.com/ffdays.html* • **Oktoberfest,** La Veta, CO (719) 742–5501

🛏 Accommodations:

National forest campgrounds, Pike/San Isabel National Forest, San Carlos Ranger District, Cañon City, CO (719) 269–8500 or *www.fs.fed.us/r2/psicc*

🍴 Restaurants:

La Veta Inn, La Veta, CO (719) 742–3700 • **The Timbers,** Cuchara, CO (719) 742–3838 • **Covered Wagon,** La Veta, CO (719) 742–5280 – *burger joint* • **Pat McMahon Fine Art Gallery & Café,** La Veta, CO (719) 742–3150 • **Boardwalk Saloon & Restaurant,** Cuchara, CO (719) 742–3450 – *pizza restaurant*

🚶 Hike Tours:

Wahatoya Base Camp, La Veta, CO (719) 742–5597 – *guided hikes and nature trips*

🔄 Other Resources:

Little La Veta Bookshop, La Veta, CO (719) 742–3776

🎣 Local Outdoor Retailer:

Hollowpoint Sporting Goods, Walsenburg, CO (719) 738–3426 – *hunting, fishing, and camping supplies*

Ⓝ Maps:

USGS maps: Spanish Peaks, CO; Herlick Canyon, CO

Honorable Mentions

Southeast Mountains

Compiled here is an index of great hikes in the Southeast Mountain region that didn't make the A-list this time around but deserve recognition. Check them out and let us know what you think. You may decide that one or more of these hikes deserves higher status in future editions or, perhaps, you may have a hike of your own that merits some attention.

(U) Colorado Springs Area Trails

The Colorado Springs area has numerous trails ranging from paved and flat to a long and strenuous hike up Pikes Peak. Of course, there are many trails in between for just the right hike. Contact The Trails and Open Space Coalition at (719) 633–6884 or visit their website at *www.trailsandopenspaces.org/index.htm*. You'll find a listing of trails and their descriptions. *DeLorme: Colorado Atlas & Gazetteer:* Page 63 B4

(V) Petrified Forest Loop

The one-mile easy Petrified Forest Loop takes you past several petrified giant redwood stumps, once 200 to 250 feet tall. Buried by volcanic ash, it's an amazing reminder of how old the earth is and of things that lived long before humans arrived on the scene. At the end of the loop are posts that indicate time since the earth was formed to present, noting such events as the reign of the dinosaurs to how long humans have been on earth. It's very eye opening! You can combine this loop with the easy 0.5-mile Walk Through Time loop. Both start near the visitor center at Florissant Fossil Beds National Monument. To reach the visitor center from Florissant on U.S. 24, drive south on CR 1 about 2.3 miles and turn right into the visitor center, about 0.3 miles from CR 1. For more information , contact Florissant Fossil Beds National Monument at (719) 748–3253 or visit their website at *www.nps.gov/flfo*. *DeLorme: Colorado Atlas & Gazetteer:* Page 62 A1

(W) Vindicator Valley Trail

This two-mile loop trail winds through historic gold mining areas near Victor. A series of interpretive signs explain the history of the area. The trail is also packed for cross-country skiing or hiking in the winter. Two trailheads access the trail, both off of CR 81. Drive north from Victor on CR 81 (Diamond Avenue). The first trailhead is 1.7 miles north of Goldfield on the left side of the road. The second trailhead is 0.4 miles farther north, then left on CR 831. For more information contact the Southern Teller County Focus Group at P. O. Box 328,Victor, CO 80860 or visit their website at *www.web-xpres.com/stcfgtrail.htm*. *DeLorme: Colorado Atlas & Gazetteer:* Page 62 C2

Devils Stairsteps.

South Central
MOUNTAINS

Gothic Mountain from Washington Gulch Trail.

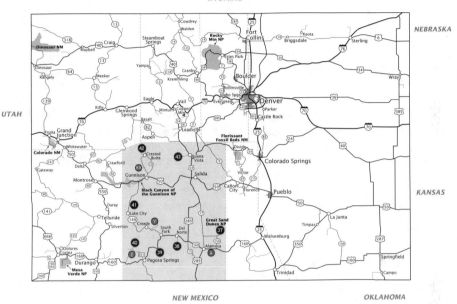

WYOMING

NEBRASKA

UTAH

KANSAS

NEW MEXICO

OKLAHOMA

The Hikes

Dunes Hiking **37.**

Middle Frisco Trail **38.**

Alberta Peak: Continental Divide Trail **39.**

Williams Creek Trail **40.**

Devils Creek and Lake **41.**

Washington Gulch Trail **42.**

Ptarmigan Lake **43.**

Honorable Mentions

X. Alamosa National Wildlife Refuge

Y. Wheeler Geologic Area (East Bellows Trail)

Z. Piedra River

AA. Mill Castle Trail

South Central Mountains

The great rift valley of the Rio Grande cuts right through the heart of the South Central Mountains. To the west, the San Juan Mountains contain some of the most rugged country in Colorado. The last grizzly was killed here and some may still hang out undercover. Farther north, the Collegiate Peaks are 14,000-foot summits named after Ivy League universities. To the east, the jagged crest of the Sangre de Cristo Range rises above the sand dunes it helps create. An unusual geological feature, the Great Sand Dunes National Monument and Preserve encompasses a 39-square-mile area in the San Luis Valley with 700-foot-high sand dunes. From Native American tribes to Spanish explorers and settlers to miners all searching for their own riches, the South Central Mountains region has a rich and diverse history.

The Spanish first journeyed into the San Luis Valley in the late 1500s. Their legacy remains in the town of San Luis, the oldest permanent settlement (established 1851), and Our Lady of Guadalupe in Conejos, the oldest parish in Colorado. The state's Spanish history is also reflected in many place names such as Del Norte, Costilla County, and Antonito. Most streams flowing into the San Luis Valley, one of the highest alpine valleys in the world, sink into its sandy and gravelly floor. The Alamosa and Monte Vista national wildlife refuges, San Luis Lakes State Park and Blanca Wetlands provide a welcome resting spot for migrating waterfowl and shore birds. Surprisingly, potatoes are the main farm crop in the San Luis Valley. Even more surprising, an unusual farm and tourist attraction north of Alamosa called Colorado Gators harbors alligators and raises tilapia (a tropical freshwater fish) in 87°F water flowing from a 2,000-foot-deep geothermal well.

One of Colorado's historic narrow gauge railroads still carries visitors back in time to the late 1800s when trains transported silver and gold. Leaving from Antonito, the Cumbres-Toltec Scenic Railroad heads west and south through beautiful country, a spectacular fall trip when the aspens turn gold. Crossing the Colorado–New Mexico border 11 times, the trip ends in Chama, New Mexico.

Crested Butte, north of Gunnison, hosts a wildflower festival each summer in early July and the incredible flowers are truly worthy of the celebration. An area known for mountain biking, it's also a hikers' paradise with the Raggeds and Maroon Bells–Snowmass Wilderness areas nearby. The former mining town of Gothic now hosts scientists and students at the Rocky Mountain Biological Institute instead of rowdy miners.

Twenty-one of Colorado's 54 peaks over 14,000 feet are located in this region. A long section of the Colorado Trail winds through the South Central Mountains region, mostly following the Continental Divide and sometimes joining its cousin, the Continental Divide Trail. Wheeler Geologic Area, located northeast of Creede, is famous for its pinnacles and domes eroded from lava and ash.

The Buena Vista and Salida areas access the Collegiate Peaks as well as exciting whitewater rafting on the Arkansas River. The Alpine Tunnel, a marvel of railroad engineering, can be visited via Saint Elmo. Mount Princeton and Cottonwood Hot Springs soothe muscles and weary bones after a long day hiking or peak bagging.

Mining touched this region, too, with Crested Butte, Creede, Lake City, and Summitville being founded after rich strikes were discovered. Del Norte, once a major mining supply town, now supplies area farms and ranches. A few surprise trails are located here if you poke around a little. Middle Frisco Trail, near Del Norte, is featured in this book.

Scenic and historic byways exploring the riches of this area include Los Caminos Antiguos, West Elk, and Silver Thread.

Treasure Falls by Wolf Creek Pass.

Section Overview

Dunes Hiking

This is a make-your-own hike through the Great Sand Dunes National Monument and Preserve. Starting and exit points are suggested for a hike across the east side of the dune mass and back along Medano Creek. A few plants and various insects live in the dunes. Making footprints and seeing the patterns are great fun, as is sliding down the dunes. Hiking in the sand takes a lot of energy, but it's an experience you won't soon forget! Fall is a beautiful time to visit. Watch out for thunderstorms—lightning is extremely dangerous on the dunes! (*See page 280.*)

Middle Frisco Trail

Middle Frisco Trail follows sparkling, gurgling Middle San Francisco Creek and its tributaries up to Frisco Lakes. Starting among stands of ponderosa pine and Douglas fir, the trail slowly gains elevation, eventually switchbacking up to a nice spruce-fir forest and sub-alpine meadows. Wildflowers are abundant along the trail in July. Keep an eye open for elk and cattle. Near the upper lake, there is an ancient bristlecone pine forest. The lower part of the trail is fantastic when the aspen are golden yellow and orange. The lakes are snuggled in high basins between Bennett Peak and Pintada Mountain. (*See page 286.*)

Alberta Peak: Continental Divide Trail

This hike follows the Continental Divide Trail south from Wolf Creek Pass to Alberta Peak. It climbs through a pleasant spruce-fir forest and passes a ski lift at Wolf Creek Ski Area. Past the ski lift the trail winds through the forest then out on the edge of a ridge with great views to the south and west. Passing through willows, the trail ascends above treeline with views in all directions and beautiful alpine wildflowers. A short scramble takes you to the top of Alberta Peak (11,870 feet) with its resident pikas. (*See page 292.*)

Williams Creek Trail

The Williams Creek Trail in the Weminuche Wilderness reaches the Continental Divide in 14 miles. This hike description takes you to the first crossing of Williams Creek. Traveling above the creek, you'll see various volcanic rock shapes from eroded fins to fluted cliffs. The trail progresses through forests of Douglas and white fir, limber pine, Gambel oak, aspen, and some beautiful wildflowers. Watch for deer. At the creek crossing, a little area to the right makes a great lunch stop. You can continue on the trail for a long day hike or a multi-day backpack. Crossing Williams Creek can be challenging or unsafe during spring runoff. (See page 298.)

Devils Creek and Lake

The hike to Devils Lake is a great warm-up or trial hike for anyone wanting to climb the 14,000-foot peaks near Lake City. The elevation gain is similar, but at lower altitude. For those wishing a shorter hike, the old cow camp at mile 2.6 is a good turnaround point. The Devils Creek Trail into the Powderhorn Wilderness was constructed in 1994. The relatively undisturbed Cannibal and Calf Creek plateaus contain one of the largest, relatively flat alpine tundra areas in the lower United States. The Cannibal Plateau is named after the area's famous cannibal, Alferd Packer. (See page 304.)

Washington Gulch Trail

Washington Gulch Trail offers several options. The main goal is the ridge at 11,400 feet with spectacular views of the Maroon Bells–Snowmass Wilderness and the Raggeds Wilderness. The flowers are spectacular during July. The hike starts at the Gothic side trailhead, climbing through fields of wildflowers and spruce-fir forest to the ridge. The out-and-back option returns from here. The point-to-point option descends to the Washington Gulch side passing an old mine with relics. A high-clearance vehicle is required to reach the west side trailhead. Be mindful of mountain bikers the entire way. (See page 310.)

278

Ptarmigan Lake

The hike to Ptarmigan Lake winds through spruce-fir forest, gently climbing into an area of beautiful sub-alpine meadows dotted with tarns and little lakes. For flower aficionados the meadows show off beautiful wild-flowers in July. After a little climb up the side of a cirque, you arrive at crystal clear Ptarmigan Lake. Another 0.3 miles leads to a saddle with a view down into South Cottonwood Creek. This hike travels above treeline, so if the weather is threatening a thunderstorm, stay at the lower lakes. *(See page 316.)*

Dunes Hiking

Hike Specs

Start: From Dunes parking area

Length: Create your own hike or suggested route is approximately 4.3-mile loop

Approximate Hiking Time: Allow 3–6 hours for suggested route

Difficulty Rating: Difficult because of sand and steepness

Elevations: 8,040–8,690 feet (trailhead to top of highest dune)

Elevation Gain: Varies depending on route

Seasons: Open year round, but sands can be extremely hot in summer

Terrain: Mostly loose sand, with some pockets of firmer sand

Land Status: National monument and wilderness area

Nearest Town: Alamosa, CO

Other Trail Users: Hikers only (in dune mass) and equestrians (along Medano Creek)

Canine Compatibility: Leashed dogs permitted. No water in dunes and summer sand temperatures can be extremely hot in summer.

Getting There

From Alamosa: Drive east on U.S. 160 to CO 150 at mile marker 248. Turn left (north) onto CO 150 and drive about 20 miles to Great Sand Dunes National Monument & Preserve. If no one is at the entrance station, stop at the visitor center and pay the entrance fee. Take a few minutes to browse through the displays and watch the video. Check the latest on the status of this special area. From the visitor center, turn left onto the main park road and drive 0.3 miles to the road to the Dunes Parking Area. Turn left and drive 0.6 miles to the parking lot. Restrooms and water are available. *DeLorme: Colorado Atlas & Gazetteer:* Page 81 C6

These sand dunes, the tallest in North America, cover about 39 square miles of the San Luis Valley. Hiking up and around them is a real treat and a lot of exercise with fun slides down. After leaving the trees at the trailhead and wading across Medano Creek, enter the Great Sand Dunes Wilderness. By designating the dune field and western sand shield a wilderness area in 1976, Congress provided extra environmental protection to this unique area. Medano (Spanish for sand dune) Creek fluctuates throughout the year, depending on season and recent moisture and may be a damp streambed or ankle deep. Even during a single day, the water levels vary because thirsty trees upstream absorb water during the day. As the creek flows downhill, it eventually disappears into the sand. Medano Creek starts 13 miles upstream in the Sangre de Cristo Range.

While crossing the first flat area, some green plants may surprise you. Scurfpea, blowout grass, and Indian ricegrass manage to survive here. Sunflowers and rabbitbrush bloom yellow against the dunes in fall. The wind makes interesting patterns in the sand. You can see who or what passed this way recently by the different tracks—that is until the wind wipes them out.

At the first dune start climbing and sometimes sinking in the sand. There is no formal trail; just cruise around wherever it looks interesting to you. Watch for other footprints as their patterns will tell you if the surface is firm or very soft. The hike

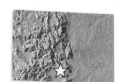

Crossing the dunes.

becomes an exercise of finding the path of least resistance. Climbing up a dune ridge in the steep sand you take three steps forward only to slide back two! Once on top of the ridge, look behind at the patterns you made, especially if you're the first to pass that way. Keep an eye open for sand avalanches. Sand grains tumble down when the surface angle reaches 34 degrees. Of course, try hiking up these slipfaces, and you'll swear they're even steeper!

> If a dunes hike isn't appealing, try Little Medano Creek Trail. Starting from the Pinyon Flats Campground, this 5.5-mile point-to-point trail wanders north past "escape dunes" (small dunes created by sand that escaped from the main dune mass). Return via the trail, the 4WD road, or along Medano Creek.

The dunes are deceiving. A path that looks easy becomes a steep descent followed by an equally steep ascent to get up the next ridge. Some low spots display an amazing amount of green plant life. Sand stays moist about five inches below the surface. Where sand doesn't cover and snuff out life, plants hang on. Little bugs, perhaps blown by the wind, struggle to climb in the sand. A ladybug may fight mightily, its little legs moving quickly and going nowhere. Four new insect species have been found in the dunes since 1990, some of which are found nowhere else in the world! Insects, kangaroo rats, and ravens leave telltale tracks in interesting patterns. A dust devil may swirl by, rearranging sand grains into new patterns.

The sand itself comes in different colors. The black grains that streak the dunes are magnetite from the once volcanic San Juan Mountains to the west. Tan grains also come from the San Juans, having been stranded over the years as the Rio Grande changed course along the San Luis Valley to the west. Coarser grains come from the Sangre de Cristos to the east. The dunes are kept in place by southwesterly winds blowing the sand against the Sangre de Cristos, followed by northeasterly wind blowing them back. Meanwhile, Medano Creek carries grains downstream and deposits them where the wind can spit them back into the dune mass.

Two joys of dune hiking are playing in a big sandbox and sliding down the sandy dune slopes. Listen for the jet engine roar as your feet slide with each step—the sand

MilesDirections

START at the trailhead at the Dunes Parking Area and cross Medano Creek. ✖ 37°44'21"N 105°31'00"W After crossing Medano Creek and entering the dune field, a nice loop hike can be made by hiking up the dune of your choice heading north then curving east along dune ridges or whatever path you desire until you drop into Medano Creek. Hike back along the creek to the Dunes Parking Area.

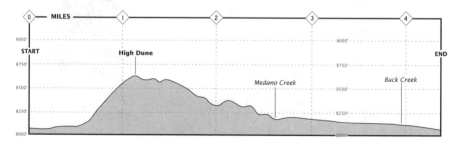

View of San Luis Valley looking southeast from dune mass.

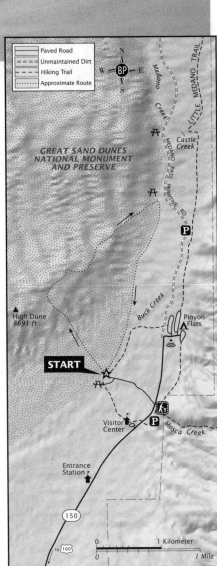

grains sing their song when rubbing against each other. Some disadvantages include biting gnat-like bugs in early summer and biting housefly types in the fall. Nearby Mosca (fly in Spanish) Pass is aptly named.

Once you've slid back down to Medano Creek, if water is flowing, sit and watch the surges for a while. Little dunes build up beneath the water, only to break down. Waves become mini-breakers, and the process begins again. A mountain bluebird or piñon jay may flutter by. Dragonflies dart their way through the air. Parts of the wide creek bottom are filled with ankle-twisting rocks. Willows and other plants send sprouts to the sky. As you proceed downstream, the creek slowly diminishes. Footsteps fill with water as you pull your foot from moist sand. Tracks of larger animals tell who visited overnight. Mule deer, coyote, and bobcat tracks may be seen.

No one knows for sure how long the dunes have been here. They probably formed after the glaciers started melting around 12,000 years ago. In millions of years, will they be exposed as petrified dunes in some sandstone formation? In the meantime, have fun playing in the sand!

Sand dunes and Mount Herard.

The Sangre de Cristo Range, according to legend, received its name when a dying Spanish priest watched sunset color the mountains brilliant red and uttered his last words, "Sangre de Cristo" (Blood of Christ).

Great Sand Dunes National Monument (38,659 acres in 2000) was authorized to be expanded when President Clinton signed the Great Sand Dunes National Park & Preserve Act on November 22, 2000. This act transferred public land lying between the dunes and the crest of the Sangre de Cristo Range from the U.S. Forest Service to the National Park Service. This land is now called Great Sand Dunes National Preserve. Another provision in the act enables procurement of the 100,000-acre Baca Ranch that adjoins the national monument's northwest boundary. After the ranch is procured, the national monument will be renamed Great Sand Dunes National Park. The entire area will be called Great Sand Dunes National Park & Preserve, totaling over 150,000 acres. From the land procurement, the Baca National Wildlife Refuge will be created. Kit Carson Peak (14,165 feet) and surrounding lands will be added to the Rio Grande National Forest. Check at the visitor center for updates on boundaries and hiking trails.

Summer hiking requires some type of shoes to prevent burning your feet on the hot sand. Other times of year bare feet and sandals may work. To avoid large quantities of sand in shoes and boots, wear short gaiters. Protect your camera! Blowing sand gets in everything.

Hike Information

🕐 Trail Contact:
Great Sand Dunes National Monument and Preserve, Mosca, CO (719) 378–2312 or www.nps.gov/grsa

🕐 Schedule:
Open year round, but in summer the sand can reach 140°F.

💲 Fees/Permits:
Per person entrance fee, annual pass, Golden Eagle, Golden Access, or Golden Age pass required. Overnight camping requires a free backcountry permit. Note that some regulations may change with the new designation of Great Sand Dunes National Monument & Preserve, and then in the future when it becomes a national park.

❓ Local Information:
Alamosa County Tourism Development Board, Alamosa, CO 1–800–258–7597 or www.alamosa.org • **San Luis Valley Information Center,** Monte Vista, CO (719) 852–0660 or 1–800–214–1240

📍 Local Events/Attractions:
Cumbres-Toltec Railroad, Antonito, CO 1–888–286–2737 or 1–800–724–5428 or www.cumbrestoltec.com • **Ft. Garland Museum,** Ft. Garland, CO (719) 379–3512 • **Trail of the Ancients Scenic Byway,** Ft. Garland, CO (719) 379–3512 or www.loscaminos.com • **San Luis Visitor Center,** San Luis, CO (719) 672–3002 – *the oldest town in Colorado* • **Shrine of the Stations of the Cross,** San Luis, CO (719) 672–3685 • **San Luis Lake State Park & Wildlife Area,** Mosca, CO (719) 378–2020 or www.parks.state.co.us/san_luis • **Zapata Falls and Picnic Area,** Bureau of Land Management, La Jara, CO (719) 274–8971 • **Colorado Gators285,** Mosca, CO (719) 378–2612 • **Alamosa-Monte Vista National Wildlife Refuges,** Alamosa, CO (719) 589–4021

🛏 Accommodations:
Campground at Great Sand Dunes National Monument and Preserve, Mosca, CO (719) 378–2312 • **Great Sand Dunes Oasis,** Mosca, CO (719) 378–2222 or www.coloradodirectory.com/greatsanddunesoasis • **San Luis Lake State Park campground,** Mosca, CO (719) 378–2020 parks.state.co.us/san_luis • **KOA,** Alamosa, CO or (719) 589–9757 or 1–800–562–9157

🍴 Restaurant:
Sands Restaurant, Alamosa, CO (719) 589–2242

🥾 Hike Tours:
Great Sand Dunes National Monument and Preserve, Mosca, CO (719) 378–2312

👥 Clubs and Organizations:
Friends of the Dunes, Mosca, CO (719) 378–2312

📖 Other Resources:
Narrow Gauge Bookstore, Alamosa, CO (719) 589–6712 • **Autumn Harvest Bookstore,** Alamosa, CO (719) 586–4987

🎒 Local Outdoor Retailer:
Kristi Mountain Sports, Alamosa, CO (719) 589–9759

🗺 Maps:
USGS maps: Liberty, CO; Zapata Ranch, CO

Middle Frisco Trail

Hike Specs

Start: From Middle Frisco Trail (Trail 801) trailhead

Length: 12.4-mile out-and-back

Approximate Hiking Time: 6–8.5 hours

Difficulty Rating: Difficult due to length and elevation gain

Elevations: 9,000–11,500 feet

Elevation Gain: 2,500 feet

Seasons: Best from mid-June to mid-October

Terrain: Dirt trail

Land Status: National forest

Nearest Town: Del Norte, CO

Other Trail Users: Equestrians, mountain bikers, and hunters (in season)

Canine Compatibility: Controlled dogs permitted

Getting There

From Del Norte: Toward the east end of town, find French Street (CR 13). There's a big green and white sign stating NATIONAL FOREST ACCESS SAN FRANCISCO CREEK. Turn south onto French Street. In about 1.8 miles the pavement ends and becomes a good gravel road. Stop and read the bulletin board on the right side of the road in another 1.9 miles. The trailhead is another 6.1 miles down the dirt road (total 9.8 miles from Del Norte). The trail starts on the left after passing the cattle guard/fence where FS 320 starts. There's a large parking area with no facilities. Cattle graze in the area. Bring your own water or be sure to have a water treatment system with you. *DeLorme: Colorado Atlas & Gazetteer:* Page 79 D7

L ocals and several signs call these trails, creeks, and lakes by the nickname of "Frisco." The official name on topo maps is "San Francisco." So, you're in the correct spot at Middle Frisco trailhead. A little farther down the road is West Frisco Trail, open to all-terrain vehicles (ATVs) and dirt bikes.

San Francisco Creek is a tributary of the mighty Rio Grande del Norte (Great River of the North) named by Spanish explorers. On the western edge of the San Luis Valley, the town of Del Norte took its name from the river. Early native peoples of the Folsom culture lived in the valley over 10,000 years ago. Starting around 1300, the Moache and Tabeguache bands of Utes called this area home. Chief Ouray, of the Tabeguache band, often camped near present-day Del Norte. Juan Bautista de Anza headed north from Santa Fe in 1779 to quiet the Comanches who were causing trouble for the Spanish. He commanded an army of 700 men from Santa Fe and 200 Ute-Apaches.

The Spanish divided parts of southern Colorado into land grants. These huge tracts were normally given to individuals or small groups. The Guadalupe Land Grant on the west side of the Rio Grande was designated for 100 families and their descendants. In 1859, Juan Bautista Silva led fourteen families 200 miles from New Mexico to the fertile pastures along San Francisco Creek, just south of Del Norte, to settle part of this land grant. It took one month to travel that distance! The newcomers named their town La Loma de San Jose, planted crops, and raised livestock.

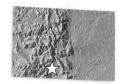

Then in 1870, gold was discovered in the San Juan Mountains southwest of La Loma, and Summitville became the major gold camp. Del Norte, founded in 1871, developed into a major mining supply center for Lake City, Silverton, Summitville, and others. Del Norte was so prosperous that one rich mine owner proposed a separate state called San Juan with Del Norte as its capital!

In the 1880s, cattlemen and sheepherders disputed over ranges, but actually agreed to boundaries. Sheep grazed between the Rio Grande and San Francisco Creek while cattle ruled the grasses from San Francisco Creek south to Rock Creek. Today, cattle graze near Frisco Lakes.

The trail heads off through aspen groves and meadows and is soon surrounded by forests of limber pine, ponderosa pine, and Douglas fir. Middle Frisco Creek is tiny and lively, a pleasant hiking companion. Aspen becomes the dominant tree species, occasionally alternating with conifers. The trail breaks out of the woods into a meadow area with Pintada Mountain (12,840 feet) to the left, a large ridge delineating the drainage's east side. A few bristlecone pines have stood guardian here for centuries. A series of twelve switchbacks soon take you ever higher. Colorful wildflowers like cinquefoil, death camus, Indian paintbrush, stonecrop, and columbine brighten the climb. As you hike up the ridge, the cliffs above the upper lake resemble the edge of a volcanic crater. The mountains here are part of one of the ancient volcanic calderas

Upper Frisco Lake.

that formed the San Juan Mountains. Glaciers carved the upper cirques. A stand of ancient bristlecone pines grows west of the trail.

If you want to hike up the peak above the cliffs, walk past the upper lake, up the grassy bowl to the ridge. You'll join West Frisco Trail just below the summit of 13,203-foot Bennett Peak.

To either overlook the lower lake or hike down to it, cross the creek below the upper lake, wander through a field of old-man-of-the-mountain (alpine sunflowers), then descend a little. There are some good campsites along the hike in and near the lakes. Remember to camp at least 100 feet away from streams, lakes, and trails. The area around the lakes is high subalpine, and trees take years to grow. Wildlife and

MilesDirections

0.0 START at Middle Frisco Trail (Trail 801) trailhead. ★ 37°33'24"N 106°23'45"W—Head toward the creek on Middle Frisco Trail. Reach a brown carsonite post shortly after the trailhead. Go past this post to the left. At the creek's edge, look right. You'll see a little bridge that looks like a flat ladder. Walk across the bridge to find the trail on the other side, which climbs up through aspen and into a meadow. It's easy to follow from here.

3.4 The trail enters a large meadow area with a view of Pintada Mountain to the left. ◆ 37°30'46"N 106°24'49"W *[FYI. Look for some bristlecone pines here.]*

3.5 The trail makes a big U-curve. Follow the curve and not a spur trail.

4.0 The trail starts a series of switchbacks. *[FYI. Look north occasionally for good views of the San Luis Valley and the Sangre de Cristo Range.]* Occasionally a spur trail leads off a switchback but stick to the main trail unless you're looking for a campsite.

4.9 The trail crosses a flatter area with a nice view of the cliffs above upper San Francisco

Lake. More switchbacks to come!

5.7 The switchbacks are finished, and the trail follows a little creek down to the left. There are many cattle trails in this area. Stay on the trail heading toward the cliffs.

6.0 Arrive at the outlet to upper San Francisco Lake. ◆ 37°29'24"N 106°25'31"W *[**Side-trip.** You can continue on to Bennett Peak from here (watch out for lightning). For the peak, continue up to the right of the upper lake, climb up the bowl to the right and follow the ridge up to the West Frisco Trail then left to the peak.]* Continue left across the outlet toward the lower lake.

6.2 Enjoy a nice overlook of the lower lake. ◆ 37°29'22"N 106°25'22"W *[FYI. This area makes a good lunch spot if you don't want to hike down and back up again. Watch for white-crowned sparrows nearby and elk in the high meadows to the east and south.]* Return the way you came.

12.4 Arrive back at the trailhead.

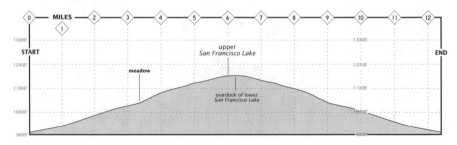

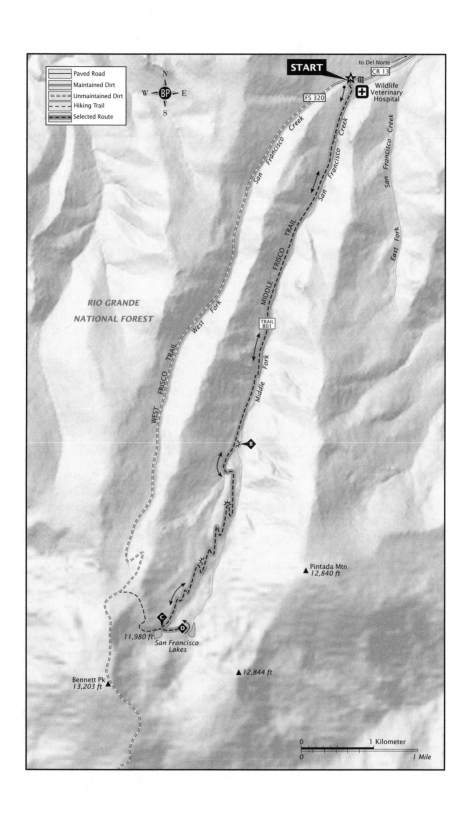

START

to Del Norte

CR 13

FS 320

Wildlife
Veterinary
Hospital

San Francisco Creek

San Francisco Creek

San Francisco Creek

East Fork

MIDDLE FRISCO TRAIL

West Fork

WEST FRISCO TRAIL

Middle Fork

TRAIL 801

RIO GRANDE
NATIONAL FOREST

B

C

D

11,980 ft

San Francisco
Lakes

▲ Pintada Mtn
12,840 ft

▲ 12,844 ft

Bennett Pk
13,203 ft ▲

Paved Road
Maintained Dirt
Unmaintained Dirt
Hiking Trail
Selected Route

N
W BP E
S

0   1 Kilometer

0   1 Mile

birds depend on the trees and dead branches. If you camp up high, bring a stove and candles and forego the campfire to protect the fragile ecosystem.

A little bird you may notice flying around is the white-crowned sparrow. It indeed looks like a sparrow, but has white around its eyes and a black cap. Watch for a while if you catch sight of one. They pick insects off dead branches near the lake. These little sparrows winter as far south as Mexico. When spring arrives, they fly north to mate and nest in the tundra. Their nests are hidden beneath willows, which pro-

According to records in Del Norte, in 1932 during the Depression, calves sold for $0.03 per pound and two-dozen eggs cost $0.15.

vide both shelter and the proper temperature to hatch their tiny eggs.

Middle Frisco Trail is an enjoyable hike in a pretty area. The Trail Wise Back Country Horsemen help maintain the trail. The area shows little sign of human use, so please practice zero-impact outdoor skills.

Colorado Outdoor Recreation Search and Rescue (CORSAR) Card

In Colorado over 1,000 search and rescue missions are conducted each year for overdue hikers, lost hunters, and other outdoor enthusiasts who run into some problem in the backcountry. Colorado has many well-trained volunteer Search and Rescue (SAR) groups. They devote numerous hours to training and to actual rescues. SAR groups have to raise funds for equipment such as climbing gear, radios, rescue vehicles, and snowmobiles. In 1987, the Colorado Legislature created the Colorado Search and Rescue Fund (CSRF). A $0.25 fee from hunting licenses, fishing licenses, and snowmobile and off-highway vehicle registrations finance this fund. The fund's purpose is to help sheriffs recover costs of SAR operations and to provide funding for SAR equipment and training.

As more hikers, skiers, mountain bikers, and climbers required rescue, the legislature created the Colorado Hiking Certificate for other outdoor recreationists in 1997. Effective July 1, 2001, the Colorado Outdoor Recreation Search and Rescue (CORSAR) card replaced the hiking certificate. The CORSAR card costs $3 per year with $2 going to the search and rescue fund and $1 going to the vendor. SAR groups and outdoor organizations can sell the card as a fundraiser.

If you need rescue in the backcountry, a SAR team will come (depending on where you are), CORSAR card or not. The card is NOT insurance. SAR missions can cost money typically when a helicopter is used in the search effort or if a SAR group's equipment is damaged during the mission. If the rescuee has a CORSAR card, certain expenses the SAR group or sheriff encounters during your rescue can be immediately refunded from the CSRF. If the rescuee does not have a CORSAR card, sheriffs must wait until the end of the year, apply for a grant to replace damaged SAR equipment, and hopefully receive enough money.

The CORSAR card does not pay for medical helicopter evacuation. Sheriffs will not charge for rescue effort except in cases of extreme negligence.

Do buy a CORSAR card and help our Search and Rescue groups stay equipped and prepared!

For more information: www.dola.state.co.us/LGS/FA/sar.htm

Hike Information

☎ Trail Contact:

Rio Grande National Forest, Divide Ranger District, Del Norte, CO (719) 657–3321 or *www.fs.fed.us/r2/ riogrande*

🕐 Schedule:

Open year round. Trail not marked for winter use.

$ Fees/Permits:

No fees or permits required

❓ Local Information:

Del Norte Chamber of Commerce, Del Norte, CO (719) 657–2845 or 1–888–616–4638 or *www.delnorte chamber.com*

💡 Local Events/Attractions:

Rio Grande County Museum and Cultural Center, Del Norte, CO (719) 657–2847 • **Covered Wagon Days,** Del Norte, CO (719) 657–2845 or 1–888–616–4638 • **La Ventana Natural Arch,** Del Norte, CO (719) 657–3321 or *www.fs.fed.us/r2/ riogrande – check with the U.S. Forest Service* • **Cumbres-Toltec Railroad,** Antonito, CO 1–888–286–2737 or 1–800–724–5428 or *www.cumbres toltec.com* • **Colorado Gators,** Mosca, CO (719) 378–2612 • **Monte Vista and Alamosa National Wildlife Refuges,** Monte Vista and Alamosa, CO (719) 589–4021 or *www.alamosa.fws.gov*

🛏 Accommodations:

Wiley Bed & Breakfast, Del Norte, CO (719) 657–0507 or 1–877–999–4539 • **El Rancho Motel,** Del Norte, CO (719) 657–3332

🍴 Restaurants:

Stone Quarry Pizza & BBQ, Del Norte, CO (719) 657–9115 • **Boogie's Restaurant,** Del Norte, CO (719) 657–2905

ℓ Other Resources:

Del Norte Colorado, by Ruth Marie Colville, Hackman Printing • *The San Luis Valley Land of the six armed cross,* by Virginia McConnell Simmons, Pruett Publishing Co.

👥 Clubs and Organizations:

Trail Wise Back Country Horsemen, Monte Vista, CO (719) 852–4786

🚶 Hike Tours:

Trail Skills Inc., Monte Vista, CO (719) 852–3277 - *offers backpack trips in San Juans and some in Sangres*

🎒 Local Outdoor Retailer:

Casa de Madera Sports, Del Norte, CO (719) 657–2723

N Maps:

USGS maps: Jasper, CO; Horseshoe Mountain, CO • *Trails Illustrated®* maps: #142, South San Juan Wilderness/Del Norte – *Middle Frisco Creek is on this map, but the trail isn't.*

Alberta Peak:
Continental Divide Trail

Hike Specs

Start: From the top of Wolf Creek Pass, south side by the interpretive signs

Length: 5.5-mile out-and-back

Approximate Hiking Time: 2–3.5 hours

Difficulty Rating: Moderate due to mostly gentle trail and distance

Elevations: 10,850–11,870 feet

Elevation Gain: 1,020 feet

Seasons: Best from July to October

Terrain: Dirt trail

Land Status: National forest

Nearest Town: South Fork, CO

Other Trail Users: Equestrians, mountain bikers, and hunters (in season)

Canine Compatibility: Controlled dogs permitted

Getting There

From South Fork: Drive west on U.S. 160 about 19 miles to the top of Wolf Creek Pass. Park on the south side by the interpretive sign. There are no facilities here. Bring water as there's none on the trail. The last part of this trail is above treeline. Do not hike there if a thunderstorm and lightning are in the vicinity! *DeLorme: Colorado Atlas & Gazetteer:* Page 88 A3

In 1978, Congress designated a National Scenic Trail along the Continental Divide, snaking from the Canadian border across Montana, Wyoming, Colorado, and New Mexico to the Mexican border. Because some ridges on the actual Divide might be difficult or dangerous, a 50-mile wide corridor on either side could be used for the trail. Approximately 1,900 miles of trails and seldom-used roads shaped the initial configuration of the 3,100-mile trail. Ultimately designated the Continental Divide National Scenic Trail (CDNST), most of the trail is closed to motor vehicles.

Benton Mackaye, founder of the Appalachian Trail, first proposed the idea for the CDNST in 1966. Congress authorized a study of his idea under the National Trails System Act of 1968. The study reported that trail users would access great scenery, various ecosystems and life zones, and historical areas while crossing 25 national forests and three national parks (Glacier, Yellowstone, and Rocky Mountain). In 1971, Baltimore attorney Jim Wolf finished hiking the Appalachian Trail and looked for another such adventure. He started hiking the Divide Trail from the Canadian border and became a strong proponent for the CDNST.

The CDNST legislation gave the U.S. Forest Service (USFS) responsibility for coordinating the completion of the trail. Congress, however, did not appropriate funding to finish it. The corridor crosses National Park Service and Bureau of Land Management lands and even though existing trails would be used in places, many miles needed maintenance or improvement. Proposed routes also crossed private property in some areas, requiring negotiations with landowners for either purchase or access of the trail corridor.

Two organizations formed to aid the CDNST. First, Jim Wolf founded the Continental Divide Trail Society (CDTS) in 1978. Today the CDTS continues with its mission: "Dedicated to the planning, development, and maintenance of the Trail as a silent trail. The Society stresses each person's responsibility to be a good steward, with respect for fellow travelers, for proprietors of the land, and for the creatures of the earth." CDTS's efforts focus on the selection and development of the best possible route and in providing reliable information to trail users. Check out *www.gorp.com/cdts* for more information.

Alberta Peak (11,870 feet) along the Continental Divide.

The second organization, Continental Divide Trail Alliance (CDTA), was founded by Bruce and Paula Ward in 1995. CDTA is "dedicated to helping the federal land managers complete, manage and preserve the Trail." They organize volunteer efforts to build and maintain new and old sections of trail, coordinate an Adopt-a-Trail program, and work with legislators to appropriate funding. Find more information at *www.cdtrail.org*.

By the late 1990s, about 70 percent of the CDNST had been completed, mostly in Montana and Colorado. An estimated $10 million is still required to complete the trail on public lands. Congress earmarked $750,000 to the project in the USFS's 1998 budget.

The trail to Alberta Peak travels across a meadow to the south of Wolf Creek Pass. After you cross the bridge and enter the trees, the trail splits in several directions. Turn left to follow the official trail, which then curves right and up. The trail climbs

MilesDirections

0.0 START at the trailhead at the top of Wolf Creek Pass, south side. The Continental Divide National Scenic Trail continues south from the left side of the interpretive sign. ☆ 37°28'59"N 106°48'05"W

0.1 Cross a bridge and turn left at the T-intersection.

0.4 The trail comes to a lazy T-intersection. Turn right and continue uphill. (The branch straight ahead takes you to a ski run.)

1.0 The trail makes several switchbacks with great views to the west and northwest.

1.4 The trail arrives at a ski area road near a chairlift to the left and a boulder field to the right. Stay to the right above the boulder field and you'll see the trail. ◈ 37°28'11"N 106°48'20"W

1.6 The trail opens up to the right with a view of Treasure Mountain.

1.8 The trail travels the edge of a ridge with a steep drop-off. There are several unreadable old signs. *[FYI. You might notice a big green box with the warning DANGER EXPLOSIVES KEEP AWAY. Might be used for ski area avalanche control explosives.]*

2.3 The trail drops slightly to a saddle with good views in most directions. You can readily see Alberta Peak from here. ◈ 37°27'30"N 106°47'59"W

2.6 The Continental Divide Trail continues along the steep south side of Alberta Peak. You can continue on from here for as long as you like. *[Note. Just be aware of any lightning danger!]* Turn left here and scramble up the gentle northwest side of Alberta Peak.

2.75 Reach the top of Alberta Peak with wonderful panoramic views. ◈ 37°27'21"N 106°47'39"W Return the way you came.

5.5 Arrive back at the trailhead.

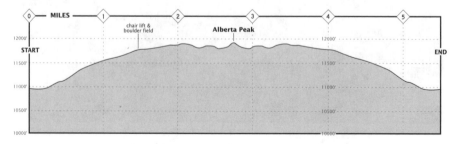

gently along the west side of the ridge. The Wolf Creek Ski Area's ski runs are on the east side. People from the San Luis Valley have skied on Wolf Creek Pass since the 1930s. In 1937, they formed the Wolf Creek Association and installed rope tows in 1938 on the north side of the highway. In 1956, another corporation formed and built a poma at the existing site. In 1976, the Pitcher family purchased Wolf Creek Ski Area and continues to own and manage it today. You can get a first-hand view of what a ski area looks like without snow at about 1.4 miles into the hike where a ski lift stands silently waiting for snow to give it a life again.

After another patch of forest, you arrive at an expansive view of Treasure Mountain (11,120 feet) and points to the southwest. Treasure Mountain earned its name from several legends about a chest full of gold that was buried in the area. Unfortunately, no one ever found the gold. The trail follows the edge of the ridge, which drops steeply to the west. Curving left, it sneaks between willow bushes and emerges above treeline. The lake to the east is Alberta Park Reservoir. The snowshed to the northeast protects the highway from frequent avalanches. Wolf Creek Pass typically receives the most snowfall in Colorado, averaging 460 inches of snow annually. Colorful alpine wildflowers bloom along the trail. From this section, Alberta Peak, the hike's destination, rises meekly to the southeast. It's an easy scramble up the boulder field and grassy slopes to the top. The 360-degree view is worth the extra effort. Resident pikas sun themselves between hasty trips collecting grass and flowers for their winter hay piles. Continue farther along the Continental Divide Trail if you wish. Watch out for lightning!

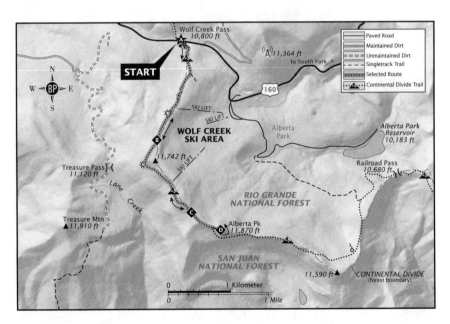

Thunderstorms forming over the San Juan Mountains west of Alberta Peak.

Hike Information

Trail Contacts:

San Juan National Forest, Pagosa Ranger District, Pagosa Springs, CO (970) 264–2268 or *www.fs.fed.us/r2/ sanjuan* • **Rio Grande National Forest,** Divide Ranger District, Del Norte and Creede, CO (719) 657–3321 or (719) 658–2556 or *www.fs.fed.us/r2/ riogrande*

Schedule:

Open year round. Trail neither maintained nor marked for winter use.

Fees/Permits:

No fees or permits required

Local Information:

South Fork Visitor Center, South Fork, CO 1–800–571–0881 or (719) 873–5512 or *www.southfork.org* • **South Fork website:** *www.southfork co.com*

Local Events/Attractions:

Logger Days Festival, South Fork, CO 1–800–571–0881 or (719) 873–5512 • **Wildflower & Mushroom Forays,** South Fork, CO 1–800–571–0881 or (719) 873–5512 • **Wolf Creek Ski Area,** Pagosa Springs, CO (970) 264–5639 or *www.wolfcreekski.com* • **Creede Repertory Theatre,** Creede, CO (719) 658–2540 or *www.creederep.com*

Accommodations:

National forest campgrounds, San Juan or Rio Grande National Forests, Pagosa Springs or Creede, CO (970) 264–2268 or (719) 658–2556 • **The Inn Motel & Cabins,** South Fork, CO 1–800– 233–9723 or (719) 873–5514 • **Wolf**

Creek Ski Lodge, South Fork, CO 1–800–874–0416 or (719) 873–5547 or *www.southforkco.com/wclodge* • **Chinook Lodge & Smokehouse** (cabins), South Fork, CO 1–888–890–9110 or (719) 873–9993

Restaurants:

Hungry Logger, South Fork, CO (719) 873–5504 • **Brown's Country Store,** South Fork, CO (719) 873–5582 • **Chalet Swiss,** South Fork, CO (719) 873–1100

Hike Tours:

Trail Skills, Inc., Creede, CO (719) 852–5194

Clubs and Organizations:

Continental Divide Trail Alliance, Pine, CO 1–888–909–CDTA or (303) 838–3760 or *www.cdtrail.org* • **Continental Divide Trail Society,** Baltimore, MD (410) 235–9610 or *www.gorp. com/cdts*

Other Resources:

Colorado's Continental Divide Trail: The Official Guide, by Tom Lorang Jones, Westcliffe Publishers, Inc.

Local Outdoor Retailers:

The Great Divide Outdoor Store, South Fork, CO (719) 873–5858 • **Rainbow Sports Headquarters,** South Fork, CO (719) 873–5545

Maps:

USGS maps: Wolf Creek Pass, CO • *Trails Illustrated®* maps: #142, South San Juan Wilderness/Del Norte

Williams Creek Trail

Hike Specs

Start: From Williams Creek Trail (Trail 587) trailhead

Length: 6.0-mile out-and-back

Approximate Hiking Time: 2.5–4 hours

Difficulty Rating: Moderate due to mostly gentle trail

Elevations: 8,360–9,100 feet

Elevation Gain: 740 feet

Seasons: Best from mid-June to mid-October

Terrain: Dirt trail, sometimes rocky

Land Status: National forest and wilderness area

Nearest Town: Pagosa Springs, CO

Other Trail Users: Equestrians and hunters (in season)

Canine Compatibility: Controlled dogs permitted

Getting There

From Pagosa Springs: The goal is to reach Williams Creek trailhead just past Cimarrona Campground, about 27 miles total from Pagosa Springs. The road intersections are well marked. On the west side of Pagosa Springs, turn north onto Piedra Road (CR 600) from U.S. 160. In about 6.2 miles the road becomes dirt (FS 631). At about 13 miles, the road forks; stay to the left (right fork is FS 633). The road crosses Piedra Bridge at about 16 miles; continue straight ahead on FS 631. The road forks again at about 21 miles; take the left fork (right fork is FS 636). At about mile 21.7, the road forks, but this time take the right fork onto FS 640. In a little over one mile, Williams Creek Reservoir is on the right. When the road forks again at about mile 25.5, take the right fork (the left fork goes to Poison Park). Drive about another 1.3 miles to the Williams Creek Trail (Trail 587) trailhead. There is an outhouse here, but no water. Bring water with you. *DeLorme: Colorado Atlas & Gazetteer:* Page 77 D7 and 78 D1

The Williams Creek Trail is one of many gateways into the Weminuche Wilderness. Multi-day loop trips can be designed starting at Williams Creek trailhead and returning via Indian Creek or Cimarrona Creek. Hikers can also traverse the wilderness and exit in the Rio Grande Valley to the north.

The Weminuche Wilderness is the largest designated wilderness area in Colorado. The process started back in 1927, when the concept of preserving land in its natural state started to become popular. In 1932, the U.S. Forest Service (USFS) established the San Juan Primitive Area, which covered the southern slopes of the San Juans. The Rio Grande Primitive Area was also created on the eastern San Juan slopes. In 1964, Congress passed the Wilderness Act; however, the Weminuche was not one of the initial wilderness areas. This area was considered for wilderness status starting in 1968, causing both alarm and enthusiasm among locals. Sheep and cattle had grazed in the area for many years. Ranchers feared they might lose their grazing permits and the predator population would increase. Mining interests in the

A woman and friends in Williams Creek.

western part of the San Juans became a hot topic, too. Existing mining claims were not immediately impacted by the Wilderness Act nor were grazing permits.

According to *Walking in Wildness A Guide to the Weminuche Wilderness* by B.J. Boucher, during the early efforts for wilderness designation in the 1960s, Ian M. Thompson, then editor of *The Durango Herald*, was an avid wilderness advocate. Thompson wrote in a special wilderness supplement to the newspaper: "The 'Wilderness' effort we are engaged in at this time is, in one respect, a pitifully futile struggle. Earth's total atmosphere is man-changed beyond redemption. Earth's waters would not be recognizable to the Pilgrims. Earth's creatures will never again know what it is to be truly 'wild.' The sonic thunder of man's aircraft will increasingly descend in destructive shock waves upon any 'wilderness area' no matter how remote or how large. We are attempting to save the battered remnants of the original work of a Creator. To engage in this effort is the last hope of religious men."

A proposal to create the Weminuche Wilderness by combining the San Juan and Rio Grande Primitive Areas and adding some additional land was submitted to Congress in 1971. Recreational opportunities were emphasized, as were water quality and quantity. Water is the *liquid gold* of Colorado, and disputes over water rights and control are a never-ending battle in the state. For three years the proposal suffered through political haggling and boundary adjustments. Finally in 1975, Colorado Senators Peter H. Dominick and Floyd K. Haskell sponsored the bill that created the 405,031-acre Weminuche Wilderness. The name came from the Weeminuche band of Utes, who once thrived here.

MilesDirections

0.0 START at the Williams Creek Trail (Trail 587) trailhead. ★ 37°32'28"N 107°11'54"W Please remember to sign the register.

0.3 Cross a creek with a lot of boulders in it, which may be dry.

1.2 Trail switchbacks above eroded features in cliff along Williams Creek. ◆ 37°33'18"N 107°11'08"W

2.1 Reach the junction with Indian Creek Trail. ◆ 37°33'50"N 107°10'58"W Stay left on Williams Creek Trail.

2.6 Enter a large meadow with fluted cliffs to the left. ◆ 37°34'06"N 107°10'52"W

2.8 Cross a ridge and drop down to Williams Creek.

3.0 Arrive at the creek crossing. ◆ 37°34'20"N 107°10'30"W *[FYI. There's a nice lunch spot to the right along the creek.]* Return the way you came.

6.0 Arrive back at the trailhead.

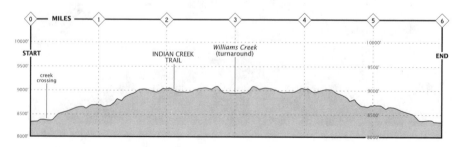

Congress expanded the Weminuche in 1980 and again in 1993. Today the total area stands at approximately 499,771 acres in both the San Juan National Forest (Pacific drainage) and the Rio Grande National Forest (Atlantic drainage). A wilderness team comprised of land managers from both forests provides consistent management for the Weminuche Wilderness.

The hike starts along an old road that quickly becomes a trail. After crossing a boulder-filled waterway, which is often dry, the trail gradually ascends. The large pinecones on the ground belong to the limber pine. Limber pines have five needles to a packet on very flexible branches that give the species its moniker. As the trail becomes steeper, it narrows considerably, so watch for oncoming horse traffic and ask what to do. Usually the hiker steps off the trail on the downhill side, but this could prove difficult in one stretch. Along with the first view of Williams Creek, notice an interesting area with eroded volcanic rock to your right. From here the trail winds up and down around little creek drainages while slowly gaining elevation. The undergrowth thickens in several places with ferns, geraniums, subalpine larkspur, Wood's rose, and aspen trees. In some areas, subalpine larkspur and cow parsnip stand about five feet tall. The Spanish called Williams Creek *huerto*, meaning "garden-like" or

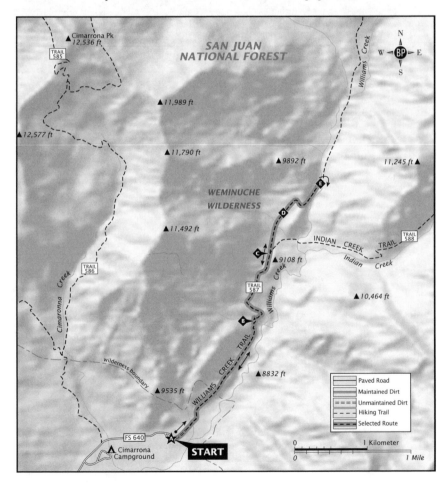

"orchard." About 2.5 miles in, you cross a nice meadow with cliffs to the left that appear fluted. Cross over a ridge and drop to the Williams Creek crossing for lunch.

If you are backpacking, please remember to camp at least 100 feet away from streams, lakes, and trails per USFS regulations for this area. By practicing zero-impact techniques, the Weminuche will remain pristine for your next visit and for future generations.

Fluted volcanic cliffs along Williams Creek.

Hike Information

🕭 Trail Contact:
San Juan National Forest, Pagosa Ranger District, Pagosa Springs, CO (970) 264–2268 or *www.fs.fed.us/r2/ sanjuan*

🕙 Schedule:
Open year round. Access road typically closed in the winter after boat ramp at Williams Creek Reservoir about three miles from trailhead. Trail neither maintained nor marked for winter use.

💲 Fees/Permits:
Maximum number of people in one group is 15 with a maximum combination of 25 people and stock in the Wilderness area. Check with the U.S. Forest Service for up-to-date camping restrictions around certain lakes and hot springs and fire restrictions in certain drainages. Also check on the latest information about bears and protecting food if you're backpacking.

❓ Local Information:
Pagosa Springs Area Chamber of Commerce, Pagosa Springs, CO 1–800–252–2204 or (970) 264–2360 or *www.pagosa-springs.com*

💡 Local Events/Attractions:
Four Corners Folk Festival, Pagosa Springs, CO 1–877–472–4672 or (970) 731–5582 or *www.folkwest.com/ four.htm* • **Spanish Fiesta,** Pagosa Springs, CO (970) 264–5020 • **Hot Springs,** Pagosa Springs, CO 1–800–252–2204 or (970) 264–2360 • **San Juan Historical Museum,** Pagosa Springs, CO (970) 264–4424 • **Chimney Rock Archaeological Area,** Pagosa Springs, CO (970) 883–5359 (between 5/15–9/30) or (970)

385–1210 (between 10/1–5/14) • **Southern Ute Indian Cultural Center,** Ignacio, CO (970) 563–9583 • **Cumbres & Toltec Scenic Railroad,** Antonito, CO, and Chama, NM 1–888–286–2737 or *www.cumbres toltec.com* • **Red Ryder Roundup Rodeo,** Pagosa Springs, CO (970) 264–5332

🍴 Restaurants:
Hogs Breath Saloon, Pagosa Springs, CO (970) 731–2626 • **Loredana's Italian Restaurant,** Pagosa Springs, CO (970) 731–5135 • **JJ's Upstream Restaurant,** Pagosa Springs, CO (970) 264–9100 • **The Greenhouse Restaurant & Bar,** Pagosa Springs, CO (970) 731–2021 • **Paradise Brew Pub & Grill,** Pagosa Springs, CO (970) 731–9101

👥 Clubs and Organizations:
San Juan Mountain Association, Durango, CO (970) 385–1210

🕗 Other Resources:
Moonlight Books, Pagosa Springs, CO (970) 264–5666 • *Walking in Wildness a Guide to the Weminuche Wilderness,* by B.J. Boucher, The Herald Press • *People of the Shining Mountains,* by Charles S. Marsh, Pruett Publishing Co.

🎒 Local Outdoor Retailer:
Switchback Mountain Gear & Apparel, Pagosa Springs, CO (970) 264–2225 or 1–888–425–4322

🅝 Maps:
USGS maps: Cimarrona Peak, CO • *Trails Illustrated®* maps: #140, Weminuche Wilderness

Devils Creek and Lake

Hike Specs

Start: From the Devils Creek Trail trailhead

Length: 13.6-mile out-and-back (with a 5.2-mile out-and-back option)

Approximate Hiking Time: 7–12 hours (recommended 2–3 day backpack)

Difficulty Rating: Strenuous due to elevation gain and altitude

Elevations: 8,480–12,080 feet

Elevation Gain: 3,600 feet

Seasons: Best from mid-June to mid-October; closed April to mid-June to protect elk calving areas.

Terrain: Dirt trail and old non-motorized ranch road, steep in places, through alpine tundra

Land Status: BLM land and wilderness area

Nearest Town: Lake City, CO

Other Trail Users: Equestrians and hunters (in season)

Canine Compatibility: Controlled dogs permitted

Getting There

From Lake City: Drive north on CO 149 for about seven miles, from the post office, to a dirt road heading northeast. The turn is about 0.5 miles north of mile marker 79. Turn right onto the next road, which drops steeply to the river, and follow it 0.5 miles across the Lake Fork River and up a hill to a dirt road marked TRAILHEADS. Turn left onto this road and continue about 0.4 miles to the Devils Creek Trail trailhead. With slow, careful driving, most 2WD cars should be able to reach the trailhead. *[Note. The road along the creek is mostly one vehicle wide, so be very careful.]* There are no facilities at the trailhead, and camping is not allowed. Bring your own water! *[Note. The bridge over the Lake Fork River is closed from April to June 15th each year to protect elk calving areas.]* **DeLorme: Colorado Atlas & Gazetteer:** Page 67 D7

igh peaks and high plateaus surround Lake City. The plateaus were formed by both lava and ash flows, estimated to be as thick as 5,000 feet. More recently, ice age glaciers scraped and molded the land, leaving U-shaped valleys, moraines, lakes, and tarns (ponds).

Volcanic activity also deposited gold, silver, and other precious metals in cracks and crevices. In 1871, J. K. Mullen and Henry Henson found the Ute-Ulay veins west of Lake City. This treasure, however, lay in Ute Territory guaranteed by the Treaty of 1868.

In fall 1873, Alferd Packer was serving a jail sentence in Salt Lake City, Utah Territory for counterfeiting. Hearing of gold discoveries in Colorado Territory, Packer bragged of his knowledge of the area. A group from Provo heard his boasts, paid his fine, and hired him to guide them to the Breckenridge area. The group of 21 men left Provo in November 1873. By mid January, they arrived at the winter camp of Chief Ouray, the Ute's spokesman. Chief Ouray warned them against proceeding, especially with the unusually severe winter. But gold blinds wisdom, and five men plus Packer left Ouray's camp in early February. They headed to Los Pinos Indian Agency southeast of Gunnison via a shortcut across the mountains.

Alferd Packer arrived alone at the agency on April 16, 1874. Apparently healthy, his first request was for a drink of whiskey. He also started spending money on drinks and games in nearby Saguache, although he was known to have little money when he left Utah. Packer's various stories conflicted, and local Utes reported finding strips of human flesh along his trail. At one point Packer agreed to lead a party to the bod-

Old cow camp.

MilesDirections

0.0 START at the Devils Creek Trail trailhead. ☆ 38°08'03"N 107°17'03"W—Remember to sign the trail register.

0.6 The trail makes a left "L" by a big rock thumb.

0.8 The trail comes to a T-intersection with an old road. ◆ 38°07'54"N 107°16'39"W—Turn left and continue uphill on the road.

1.0 The road enters a long sagebrush meadow and continues in the open for 0.5 miles. *[Note. Be careful of lightning.]*

1.5 The road curves left above the aspen grove.

1.8 Reach the wilderness boundary sign. ◆ 38°08'13"N 107°15'57"W

2.0 The trail turns right and leaves the road. Please follow the trail and do not return to the road as the trail crosses it a few more times. *[Note. The BLM requests visitors stay on the trail when it departs from the old road to avoid creating areas where erosion will occur.]*

2.6 The old cow camp appears on the left side of the trail. ◆ 38°08'23"N 107°15'16"W *[FYI. There's a big flat rock that's ideal for a break. Option. For a day hike (three to five hours), return the way you came, arriving back at the trailhead at 5.2 miles.]*

3.1 Pass some huge Douglas firs. *[FYI. In an open spot, look back to the west for a view of Uncompahgre Peak, which at 14,309 feet is Colorado's sixth highest peak. The Cannibal Plateau is above on your right.]*

3.4 The trail is finally next to the creek, and you can see it!

4.4 The trees thin as you enter an old burned area. The trail follows a little ridge. *[Note. Be careful of lightning.]*

5.3 The trail leaves the forest and enters a colorful meadow. Follow the cairns along the right side of the meadow until you see some crossing the meadow. Cross and enter another patch of trees (the trail is faint here), across another meadow, and then follow the cairns.

5.5 The trail is now above treeline. ◆ 38°07'15"N 107°12'50"W—Follow the cairns across the alpine tundra and rocks.

6.5 Reach the intersection with Calf Creek Plateau Trail (Trail 460). ◆ 38°06'31"N 107°12'28"W—Turn right and continue ahead toward Devils Lake. *[FYI. The Calf Creek Plateau Trail is not maintained and may not be visible in places—watch for cairns.]*

6.8 Reach Devils Lake. Return the way you came. *[Option. You can make a longer trip by connecting with other trails in the area.]*

13.6 Arrive back at the trailhead.

From Devils Lake, hike northeast on the North Calf Creek Trail (Trail 460) then north to the top of Calf Creek Plateau for an overlook into beautiful Powderhorn Lakes.

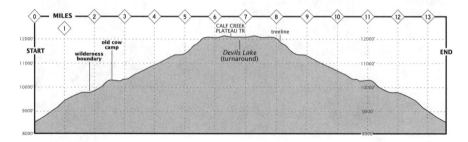

ies, but then became disoriented and refused to go farther. Artist J.A. Randolph found five skeletons near Lake City during the summer and sketched the gruesome site. Another story credits Captain C. H. Graham, a prospector, with the discovery. All five had been shot, and one body was headless. Packer was jailed in August 1874, but soon escaped. He was recaptured in 1883.

Packer was found guilty of premeditated murder and sentenced to execution on May 19, 1883 in Lake City. The execution was overturned because the murders occurred on Ute territory. Packer was tried again in Gunnison in 1886, found guilty of five counts of murder, and sentenced to 40 years in the state penitentiary at Cañon City. In 1900, the owners of the *Denver Post* requested parole for Packer as part of a publicity maneuver for the paper. After several interesting incidents, Governor Thomas paroled Packer in 1901. Packer died in 1907 and is buried in a Littleton cemetery. Just south of Lake City local citizens established a memorial to Packer's victims.

The Devils Creek Trail was completed in 1994 as a western access to the Powderhorn Wilderness. The area sees relatively little use (more during hunting season), so take care to keep it pristine. The trail climbs steadily and fairly steeply to an old cow camp through forests of ponderosa pine, Douglas fir, juniper, aspen, and sage. The trail also crosses a large meadow. Be careful during thunderstorms—this section is very exposed to lightning. The historic cow camp is protected as an antiquity, so please be respectful and leave it untouched. No camping is allowed inside or within 50 feet of the cabins. For a shorter 5.2-mile out-and-back hike, return the way you came from here. To reach Devils Lake in another 4.2 miles, continue hiking up the trail.

The trail then winds more gently up along Devils Creek, through aspen groves and into thick spruce-fir forest, finally traveling along the creek at times.

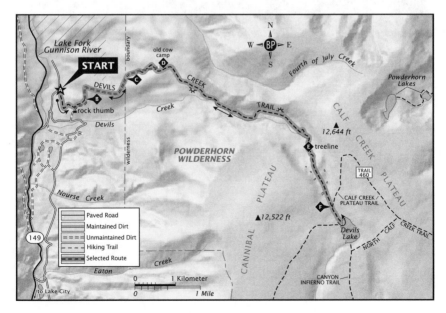

307

Switchbacking away from the creek, the trail enters another open meadow where a forest fire raged over 20 years ago. Several steep switchbacks through thick forest bring you to a beautiful subalpine meadow, full of colorful wildflowers in July. Cairns mark the trail. Enter a final patch of forest where you need to look closely to find the path. After another flower meadow, the trail reaches treeline at about 12,000 feet. Follow the cairns while climbing through open alpine tundra and rocks. The trail then flattens, crossing more alpine tundra and rocks that reflect the area's volcanic history. Head south across the alpine tundra to Devils Lake.

If you are backpacking, please camp below treeline during thunderstorm season for your own safety. Water is usually available in Devils Creek to about the fire meadow. If you camp near the lake, please follow BLM's regulations and camp at least 150 feet away, out of sight of other visitors, and use only camp stoves to protect the fragile tundra. Several grassy bluffs above the lake provide excellent camping spots and are more resistant to damage than the alpine tundra near the lake.

As you hike, think of the volcanic flows and seas of ice that have been replaced with fragile alpine tundra plants. Imagine Alferd Packer's party, trudging through snow and meeting its gruesome death.

Cannibal Plateau from the old cow camp.

Hike Information

🕿 Trail Contacts:
Bureau of Land Management – Gunnison Field Office, Gunnison, CO (970) 641–0471 or *www.co.blm.gov/gra/gra hmepge.htm* • **Gunnison National Forest,** Gunnison Ranger District, Lake City, CO (970) 641–0471 or (970) 944–2500 or *www.fs.fed.us/r2/gmug*

🕐 Schedule:
Area closed April to mid-June to protect elk calving areas. Access road may be closed by snow in winter. Trail neither maintained nor marked for winter use.

💲 Fees/Permits:
No fees or permits required

❓ Local Information:
Lake City Chamber of Commerce, Lake City, CO 1–800–569–1874 or *www.lakecityco.com*

💡 Local Events/Attractions:
Hinsdale County Museum, Lake City, CO (970) 944–2050 • **Hard Tack Mine Tours & Museum,** Lake City, CO (970) 944–2506 • **Alferd Packer Massacre Site,** Lake City, CO (970) 944–2050 • **Slumgullion Slide,** Lake City, CO 1–800–569–1874 or (970) 641–0471 • **Black Crooke Theatre,** Lake City, CO (970) 944–2706 • **Mountaineer Theatre,** Lake City, CO (970) 944–2298

🛏 Accommodations:
National forest and BLM campgrounds, Gunnison Ranger District/Gunnison Field Office, Lake City, CO (970) 641–0471 or (970) 944–2527 or *www.fs.fed.us/ r2/gmug* or *www.co.blm.gov/gra/gra hmepge.htm*

🍴 Restaurants:
Poker Alice, Lake City, CO (970) 944–4100 • **Charlie P's Mountain** **Harvest Restaurant,** Lake City, CO (970) 944–2332 • **Mother Lode,** Lake City, CO (970) 944–5044 • **Mammy's Kitchen & Whisky Bar,** Lake City, CO (970) 944–4142

🏃 Hike Tours:
Cannibal Outdoors, Lake City, CO (970) 944–2559 or 1–877–226–6422 or *www.cannibaloutdoors.com*

👫 Clubs and Organizations:
Lake City Nordic Association, Lake City, CO (970) 944–2732

📖 Other Resources:
Back Country Navigator, Lake City, CO (970) 944–6277 or 1–888–700–4174 or *www.bcnavigator.com* • **John Wagner Public Library,** Lake City, CO (970) 944–2615 • *Alferd Packer: Fact, Legend, Myth* (special newspaper), Silver World Publishing Co. • *Quick History of Lake City, Colorado,* by Margaret Bates, Little London Press • *Stampede to Timberline,* by Muriel Sibell Wolle, Sage Books, The Swallow Press, Inc. • *Ouray Chief of the Utes,* by P. David Smith, Wayfinder Press

🚲 Local Outdoor Retailers:
Cannibal Outdoors, Lake City, CO (970) 944–2559 or 1–877–226–6422 or *www.cannibaloutdoors.com* • **San Juan Mountain Bikes,** Lake City, CO (970) 944–2274 or *www.sanjuanmountain bikes.tripod.com/sjmbIndex.htm* – has hiking supplies, too

🅝 Maps:
USGS maps: Alpine Plateau, CO; Cannibal Plateau, CO; Powderhorn Lakes, CO • *Trails Illustrated®* maps: #141, Silverton/Ouray/Telluride/Lake City; #139, La Garita Wilderness/Cochetopa Hills

42 Washington Gulch Trail

Hike Specs

Start: From the Washington Gulch Trail (Trail 403) trailhead near Gothic Campground on Gothic Road

Length: 3.9-mile point-to-point (with an optional 5.4-mile out-and-back)

Approximate Hiking Time: 1.5–2.6 hours (2.2–3.7 hours for out-and-back option)

Difficulty Rating: Difficult due to elevation gain

Elevations: 9,630–11,400 feet

Elevation Gain: 1,770 feet

Seasons: Best from mid-June through September

Terrain: Dirt trail with some steep sections

Land Status: National forest

Nearest Towns: Crested Butte, CO, and Mt. Crested Butte, CO

Other Trail Users: Equestrians, mountain bikers, and hunters (in season)

Canine Compatibility: Leashed dogs permitted. Popular mountain bike trail so keep dogs leashed for their safety as well as bikers' safety.

Getting There

With Shuttle *(requires high clearance vehicle)*

From Crested Butte: Drive north and east on Gothic Road from the Crested Butte Chamber of Commerce (located in the old train station at the corner of Elk Avenue and Gothic Road) toward the town of Mount Crested Butte, but turn left at Washington Gulch Road (FS 811) in about 1.7 miles. From this intersection drive about eight miles up Washington Gulch. The trailhead is on the right side of the road,

just up the hill after a very sharp and steep left switchback above the cabins at Elkton by the Painter Boy Mine. Drop one vehicle off here and return to Gothic Road. Turn left at this intersection continuing north on Gothic Road (CR 317). The pavement ends at mile 3.7. Drive down the dirt road, which becomes FS 317 just past Gothic and the Rocky Mountain Biological Laboratory. The Washington Gulch Trail trailhead is located on the left side of the road about 10 miles from Crested Butte or 6.4 miles from where the pavement ends.

Without Shuttle

From Crested Butte: To reach the Washington Gulch Trail trailhead on Gothic Road, accessible by all vehicles, start at the Crested Butte Chamber of Commerce (located in the old train station on the corner of Elk Avenue and Gothic Road) and drive on Gothic Road through the town of Mount Crested Butte. Continue north on Gothic Road (CR 317). The pavement ends at mile 3.7. Drive down the dirt road, which becomes FS 317 just past Gothic and the Rocky Mountain Biological Laboratory. The Washington Gulch Trail trailhead is located on the left side of the road about 10 miles from Crested Butte or 6.4 miles from where the pavement ends.

There are no facilities at either trailhead. Gothic Campground is about 0.1 miles south of the Gothic side trailhead. ***DeLorme: Colorado Atlas & Gazetteer:*** Page 58 A2 (start point); Page 58 A1 (shuttle point)

Gothic Mountain (12,625 feet), south of the Washington Gulch Trail, received its name from the interesting rock formations on its east side that resemble Gothic cathedral spires. In May 1879, John and David Jennings discovered silver at the head of Copper Creek east of Gothic Mountain and named their discovery the Sylvanite. The deposit of silver in wire form was so rich that it often brought in over $15,000 per ton. From 1880 to 1910, the Sylvanite Mine produced over $1 million worth of silver.

Hopeful miners arrived in droves, searching the surrounding hills and valleys for ore, praying to strike it rich. A few months later the town of Gothic was laid out at the confluence of East River and Copper Creek. In one week's time, 100 tents and cabins reportedly sprang up. Two sawmills were set up and had a hard time keeping up with the demand for lumber. By the end of 1879, more than 200 buildings had been constructed and over 500 people lived in the area. The next summer the town boasted five law firms, four grocery stores, three restaurants, two general mercantile stores, a bank, three doctors, two hotels, and the usual assortment of saloons, gambling halls, and dance halls. A nightly bonfire on Main Street allowed the locals to

Ruby Range, Raggeds Wilderness, and Washington Gulch.

tell stories and smoke their tobacco. Gothic became the supply center for the area's various small camps and mines.

Transporting ore out of and goods into town was a challenge. The East River Toll Road was the main route in 1879. Eventually another road was built around the west side of Crested Butte (12,162 feet) saving several miles. Gothic even supplied Aspen via a road up Copper Creek over East Maroon Pass and down Maroon Creek. Gothic eventually boasted a population of 8,000 people until the Silver Panic of 1893 signaled the end of the "City of Silver Wires."

In 1928, the Rocky Mountain Biological Laboratory (RMBL) moved into the remaining buildings at Gothic, tearing down some and remodeling others. RMBL was the dream of Dr. John C. Johnson, a biology professor at Western State College at Gunnison. Johnson purchased land and old buildings to create a research and training facility for field biologists. Scientists use the surrounding national forest, wilderness area, and Gothic Research Natural Area to hone their investigative and research skills.

The hike description starts at the Gothic side of Washington Gulch Trail as it is more accessible and easy to find. The trail starts by climbing up switchbacks through a field of cornhusk lily and tall larkspur. As the trail winds higher, the Elk Mountains expand into view to the east. Columbine, Indian paintbrush and varieties of sunflowers add color along the trail. Rock Creek rumbles downhill to the left. At times the vegetation is so tall and hanging over the trail that you might feel a machete

MilesDirections

0.0 START at Washington Gulch Trail (Trail 403) trailhead north of Gothic. ★ 38°58'56"N 107°00'24"W

1.3 Reach a meadow with a view of Mount Baldy.

1.5 Cross Rock Creek. ◆ 38°58'37"N 107°01'33"W

1.7 Encounter steep switchbacks.

2.1 Reach a marshy meadow with a view of Gothic Mountain.

2.5 Encounter more steep switchbacks. Views of Ruby Range are to left and Elk Mountains is to right.

2.7 Reach a scenic overlook. ◆ 38°58'13"N 107°01'52"W—Great place for lunch! Make sure to see the spectacular views both east and west. *[Option. For a 5.4-mile out-and-back without a shuttle, turn around here and return the way you came.]* Continue.

3.7 Reach an old mine and relics. ◆ 38°58'11"N 107°02'34"W

3.9 Arrive at the Washington Gulch side trailhead. ◆ 38°58'03"N 107°02'32"W *[FYI. This trailhead is an optional starting point. It can also be the turnaround point for a 7.8-mile out-and-back hike.]*

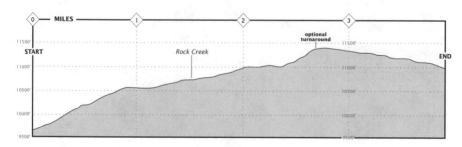

would be useful. In about one mile, a cirque on Gothic Mountain comes into view. The mountain will dominate the southern view for most of the hike. Keep an eye out for deer. The trail enters a relatively flat meadow with a red mountain looming just beyond. This is Mount Baldy (12,805 feet).

After crossing Rock Creek, the trail meanders a long way through spruce-fir forest and meadows before making a final steep zigzag climb to a fantastic scenic overlook. There's even a "scenic pullout" to the right of the main trail, a great place for lunch. Looking east, you can see into the Maroon Bells–Snowmass

> An amazing toll road was built over Schofield Pass connecting the towns of Marble and Aspen with Gothic and Crested Butte. The road was only seven to eight feet wide in places instead of the usual 10 feet. Freight traffic normally negotiated an 8 percent grade, with 12 percent being the maximum. Schofield Pass, near the Devil's Punchbowl, however, is a steep 27 percent grade!

Wilderness, including the top of one of the Bells. Notice how the rock is folded on one ridge of Avery Peak across Gothic Road. Tremendous uplifting forces created these mountains. Walk west across the trail to a field of beautiful flowers. Looking west to the Raggeds Wilderness and Ruby Range, you can see Daisy Pass (11,600 feet) snaking upward to the ridge. Washington Gulch lies below. From here, the trail gently descends about one mile to the Washington Gulch Road near the Painter Boy

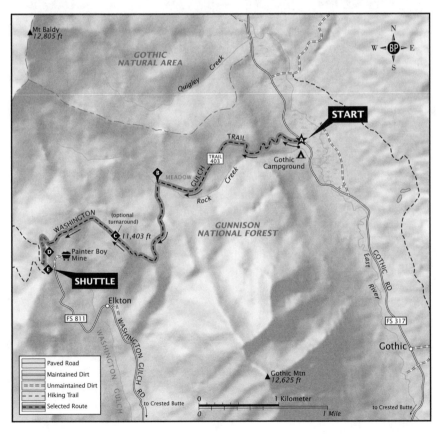

Mine, another great ore producer in its day. Remember, old mines can be extremely dangerous—stay out!

As you hike along enjoying the fabulous views and fantastic wildflower show, visualize the miners streaming through the area, searching for the strike that would make them rich.

Wildflowers adorn the Washington Gulch Trail in early July.

Hike Information

🕻 Trail Contact:

Gunnison National Forest, Gunnison, CO (970) 641–0471 or *www.fs.fed.us/ r2/gmug*

🕘 Schedule:

Open year round. Call first for winter trail conditions

💲 Fees/Permits:

No fees or permits required

❓ Local Information:

Crested Butte/Mt. Crested Butte Chamber of Commerce, Crested Butte, CO, (970) 349–6438, 1–800–545–4505 or *www.crestedbuttechamber.com*

💡 Local Events/Attractions:

Wildflower Festival, Crested Butte, CO (970) 349–2571 or *www.visitcrested butte.com/wildflower* • **Wild Mushroom Festival,** Crested Butte, CO (970) 349–7487 • **Crested Butte Mountain Heritage Museum,** Inc., Crested Butte, CO (970) 349–1880 • **Mountain Bike Hall of Fame & Museum,** Crested Butte, CO 1–800–454–4505 or (970) 349–6817

🛏 Accommodations:

National Forest Campgrounds, Gunnison National Forest, Gunnison, CO (970) 641–0471 • **The Forest Queen Hotel & Restaurant,** Crested Butte, CO (970) 349–5336 or 1–800–937–1788 – *some hostel facilities* • **Crested Butte International Hostel,** Crested Butte, CO (970) 349–0588 or 1–888–389–0588 or *www.crestedbuttehostel.com*

🍴 Restaurants:

Donita's Cantine, Crested Butte, CO (970) 349–6674 – *Mexican restaurant* • **Brick Oven Pizzeria,** Crested Butte, CO (970) 349–5044 • **Teocalli Tamales,** Crested Butte, CO (970) 349–2005 – *Mexican restaurant* • **Pitas in Paradise,** Crested Butte, CO (970) 349–0897 – *Mediterranean café restaurant* • **Lil's Land and Sea,** Crested Butte, CO (970) 349–5457

🥾 Hike Tours:

Columbine Hiking Mountaineering, Crested Butte, CO (970) 349–1323 or *www.troutfitter.com* • **Crested Butte Mountain Guides,** Crested Butte, CO (970) 349–5430 • **Alpine Meadows Hiking and Backpacking,** Crested Butte, CO (970) 349–0800 or *www.visitcrested butte.com/alpinemeadowshiking* • **Adventure Experiences,** Inc., Almont, CO (970) 641–4708 or *www.advexp.com*

👫 Clubs and Organizations:

High Country Citizens Alliance, Crested Butte, CO (970) 349–7104 • **Rocky Mountain Biological Laboratory,** Crested Butte, CO (970) 349–7231 or *www.rmbl.org/index.html*

📖 Other Resources:

The Book Store, Crested Butte, CO (970) 349–0504 • **Bookworm,** Crested Butte, CO (970) 349–6245 • *The Gunnison Country,* by Duane Vandenbusche, B&B Printers • *Stampede to Timberline,* by Muriel Sibell Wolle, Sage Books

🎒 Local Outdoor Retailers:

The Alpineer, Crested Butte, CO (970) 349–5210 or *www.alpineer.com* • **High Mountain Drifter,** Gunnison, CO (970) 641–4243

Ⓝ Maps:

USGS maps: Oh-Be-Joyful, CO • *Trails Illustrated®* maps: #131, Crested Butte/Pearl Pass

43

Ptarmigan Lake

Hike Specs

Start: From Ptarmigan Lake trailhead off Cottonwood Pass Road

Length: 6.6-mile out-and-back (7.2 miles if you include out-and-back to saddle)

Approximate Hiking Time: 3–4.5 hours

Difficulty Rating: Difficult due to elevation gain and altitude

Elevations: 10,660–12,132 feet (12,260 feet at saddle)

Elevation Gain: 1,472 feet

Seasons: Best from July through September

Terrain: Dirt trail with some boulders and rocks

Land Status: National forest

Nearest Town: Buena Vista, CO

Other Trail Users: Equestrians, anglers, mountain bikers, and hunters (in season)

Canine Compatibility: Controlled dogs permitted

Getting There

From Buena Vista: Drive about 14.5 miles west on CR 306, which later becomes FS 306, heading to Cottonwood Pass. The trailhead is on the south (left) side of the road about 0.1 miles in. There's a vault toilet but no water. *DeLorme: Colorado Atlas & Gazetteer:* Page 59 B7

The raspberries found along the trail are edible. Because animals, including bears, depend on the berries for food, please take no more than one berry in 10 from a raspberry patch for your group.

Cottonwood Pass was originally a toll road from Buena Vista connecting with other roads leading to Crested Butte, Gothic, and eventually Aspen in the 1870s. Harvard City, which you pass on the way from Buena Vista to the trailhead, boomed for a couple of years as placer claims were located along Cottonwood Creek and later lode mines were discovered and developed in 1874. Freighters also stopped at Harvard City to repack their loads for the long and difficult climb over the Continental Divide. Times changed, and the road connecting Aspen and Leadville over Independence Pass that opened in 1881 drew traffic away from Cottonwood Pass. The mines in the area couldn't match new mines farther west, and the miners moved on.

Cottonwood Pass, named after the many trees lining the creek alongside the road, fell into disrepair. The U.S. Forest Service repaired and improved the road for automobile travel in the late 1950s. Several trailheads and good fishing are all accessible via the road today. The pass is closed during the winter, but is open to various winter sports.

Several lakes in Colorado bear the name Ptarmigan. The white-tailed ptarmigan, *Lagopus leucurus*, is a member of the grouse family that lives year round above treeline and in the *krummholz* just below. *Krummholz* refers to the stunted twisted tree hedges growing at the edge of treeline. It's usually made up of subalpine fir, Engelmann spruce, or limber pine. Ptarmigans are masters of disguise, with snow

white feathers in the winter, which turn mottled brown and white in the summer. It's easy to almost step on one because they blend in so well with the rocks. As you hike, look for these birds. Little chicks follow after mom in the summer. If approached, the mother pretends to have a broken wing to draw predators away from her chicks. Please do not harass ptarmigans to see if they'll play injured, and please do not let your dogs chase them.

Winter finds the male ptarmigan still above treeline, sometimes in the shelter of the *krummholz* and sometimes in willow thickets hidden below the snow. Females winter in willows below treeline. The ptarmigan is one animal that may gain or maintain weight during harsh Colorado mountain winters by eating the energy rich buds of the willow bushes. To save energy in the spring, willows set their leaf buds during the prior autumn.

White-tailed ptarmigan appear to be monogamous, although after the chicks hatch, the female raises them alone. Mating time in the spring, like molting, is triggered by lengthening daylight and other changes in climate.

If you head around the lake on the trail to the little saddle, look up to the left and notice the streams of rocks heading down toward the lake. Freezing and thawing, which occurs most of the year, can force rocks buried underground up to the surface. On steep slopes the unearthed rocks roll into depressions. If one rock stops, others may roll into it or along a small water depression causing a stream-like appearance.

Looking toward the cirque containing Ptarmigan Lake.

In more level places, the rocks may form polygons or garlands. This "patterned ground" is common in Colorado's alpine tundra.

The hike starts in thick spruce-fir forest, opening occasionally as two boulder fields flow over the trail. Watch for raspberry bushes among the boulders. Although you can hear Ptarmigan Creek in the distance, the trail keeps a good distance until you are almost to the lake. The hike continues through spruce-fir forest without much of a view. At about mile 1.2, cross a dirt road (FS 346—4WD access to trail). Go straight and don't turn onto the road. The trail continues to wind and switchback gently through the forest. About 2.4 miles in, the trees are less dense and more flowers appear. Some possible campsites come into view away from the trail. (Camp at least 200 feet from the trail, lakes, and streams.) Then the world opens with Jones Mountain on the right and Gladstone Ridge on the left. You can see the edge of the cirque that contains Ptarmigan Lake. Flower-filled meadows dotted with little ponds and a lake line the trail. Continue hiking through the meadows, jump across Ptarmigan Creek, and two switchbacks later arrive at the lake. Mount Yale (14,196 feet) looms large to the northeast. Two other high peaks rise above other ridges. Those high points are Mount Harvard (14,420 feet) and Mount Columbia (14,073 feet). The pointy peak between you and the Fourteeners is Turner Peak (13,233 feet).

If the weather is good, continue another 0.3 miles to the saddle for views down Grassy Gulch and South Cottonwood Creek. The views to the east and northeast of the Collegiate Peaks are worth the short climb.

MilesDirections

0.0 START at Ptarmigan Lake Trail (Trail 1444) trailhead. ☆ 38°48'13"N 106°22'27"W In 350 feet cross a bridge over Middle Cottonwood Creek. The trail register is on the other side—please sign in.

0.2 Reach the first boulder field.

0.7 Reach the second boulder field.

1.2 Cross a dirt road. ◆ 38°47'32"N 106°22'09"W—The trail is clearly marked. (FS 346—can access the trail, but only by 4WD vehicle.)

2.5 Reach the first little kettle pond on right and lake down to left.

2.9 Cross Ptarmigan Creek.

3.2 Arrive at Ptarmigan Lake. ◆ 38°46'41"N 106°22'56"W—Hike another 0.1 miles to the other side of lake.

3.3 Reach the south side of the lake. Return the way you came. *[**Side-trip.** Continue another 0.3 miles to the saddle between Middle Cottonwood and South Cottonwood drainages. This side trip will add 0.6 miles to the hike.]*

6.6 Arrive back at the trailhead.

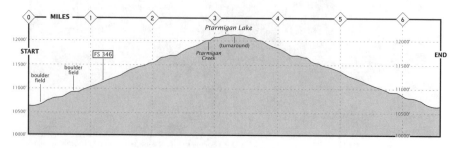

Ptarmigan Lake from the saddle.

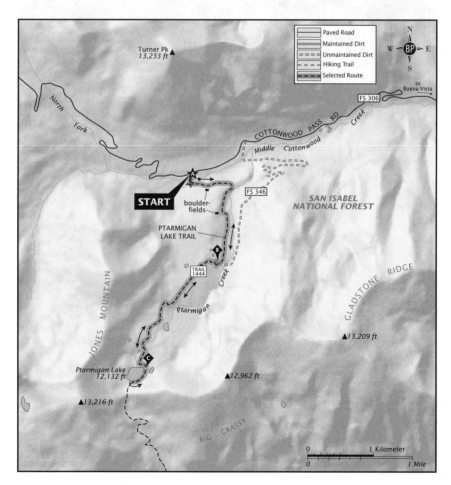

319

A little tarn along Ptarmigan Lake Trail.

Hike Information

🕭 Trail Contact:

San Isabel National Forest, Salida Ranger District, Salida, CO (719) 539–3591 or *www.fs.fed.us/r2/psicc*

🕘 Schedule:

Open year round. Trail neither maintained nor marked for winter use.

🅢 Fees/Permits:

No fees or permits required

❓ Local Information:

Buena Vista Chamber of Commerce, Buena Vista, CO (719) 395–6612 or *www.fourteenernet.com/buenavista* • **Buena Vista Heritage Society,** Buena Vista, CO (719) 395–8458

🕯 Local Events/Attractions:

Gold Rush Days, Buena Vista, CO (719) 395–6612 or *www.fourteenernet.com/goldrush/* • **Annual King Boletus Mushroom Festival,** Buena Vista, CO (719) 395–8458 • **Salida Steam Plant Theater,** Salida, CO 1–877–772–5432 • **Colorado Brewers Rendezvous,** Salida, CO 1–877–772–5432

🍴 Restaurants:

Casa del Sol, Buena Vista, CO (719) 395–8810 • **Buffalo Bar & Grill,** Buena Vista, CO (719) 395–6472 • **River Valley Inn,** Buena Vista, CO (719) 395–0977 • **Jan's Restaurant & Lounge,** Buena Vista, CO (719) 395–6940

🚶 Hike Tours:

Mountain Spirit Adventures, Salida, CO (719) 530–0914 or *www.coloradovacation.com/tours/spirit* • **American Adventure Expeditions,** Salida, CO 1–800–288–0675 or *www.americanadventure.com* • **Noah's Ark Whitewater Rafting Co. and Adventure Program, Ltd.,** Buena Vista, CO (719) 395–2158 or *www.noahsark.com*

📖 Other Resources:

Creekside Books & Arts, Buena Vista, CO (719) 395–6416 • *Stampede to Timberline,* by Muriel Sibell Wolle, Sage Books • *A Sierra Club Naturalist's Guide to The Southern Rockies,* by Audrey DeLella Benedict, Sierra Club Books • *From Grassland to Glacier The Natural of History of Colorado and the Surrounding Region,* by John C. and Mutel Emerick, Johnson Printing • *Land Above the Trees A Guide to American Alpine Tundra,* by Ann H. Zwinger and Beatrice E. Willard, Johnson Books

🔧 Local Outdoor Retailer:

The Trailhead, Buena Vista, CO (719) 395–8001

🅝 Maps:

USGS maps: Mt. Yale, CO; Tincup, CO • *Trails Illustrated®* maps: #129, Buena Vista/Collegiate Peaks

Honorable Mentions

South Central Mountains

Compiled here is an index of great hikes in the South Central Mountains region that didn't make the A-list this time around but deserve recognition. Check them out and let us know what you think. You may decide that one or more of these hikes deserves higher status in future editions or, perhaps, you may have a hike of your own that merits some attention.

(X) Alamosa National Wildlife Refuge

A 4.0-mile out-and-back doubletrack trail follows the Rio Grande River and various canals/ditches in the wildlife refuge. The Rio Grande lazily meanders along here. Various ponds as well as the river host numerous waterfowl. The Sangre de Cristo Mountains, especially the 14,000-foot summits of Little Bear, Ellingwood, and Blanca, rise to the northeast. Located in the San Luis Valley southeast of Alamosa, the wildlife refuge seems out of place in this high desert basin. The trail starts at the headquarters/visitor center, which has interesting displays. From Alamosa, drive about 3 miles east on U.S. 160 to El Rancho Lane just past mile marker 236. A sign for Alamosa National Wildlife Refuge marks the intersection. Turn right and drive about 2.4 miles to the headquarters/visitor center and park. The trail is called the River Road Walk and is open from sunrise to sunset. Dogs must be on leash. The trail provides an interesting look at a riparian area along a major river. For more information contact Alamosa National Wildlife Refuge at (719) 589–4021 or visit their website at *www.r6.fws.gov/alamosanwr*. Another interesting area to visit (and camp) is San Luis Lakes State Park, a fantastic wildlife viewing area. Contact the park at (719) 378–2020 or visit their website at *parks.state.co.us/san_luis*. *DeLorme: Colorado Atlas & Gazetteer:* Page 91 A5

(Y) Wheeler Geologic Area (East Bellows Trail)

Wheeler Geologic Area is well known for its unusual, colorful, and picturesque formations, eroded from volcanic ash. The East Bellows Trail provides a difficult 16.8-mile out-and-back hike. Camping spots can be found along the trail. From Creede, drive south on CO 149 for 7.3 miles to FS 600, Pool Table Road. Turn left and drive about 9.5 miles to Hanson's Mill Trailhead. Park here. Hike down the 4WD road about 0.25 miles toward East Bellows Creek, take the left fork for about 1.0 mile to where the foot trail starts. Crossing East Bellows Creek can be difficult during spring runoff because there is no bridge, so be very careful. After crossing the creek, take the west fork at mile 0.5. The trail will join the 4WD road. Turn left and walk up the road to the foot trail then another 0.5 miles into the area. Follow the signs. The pinnacles and domes are very fragile, so please stay on the trail and don't climb on the formations. The formations lie within the La Garita Wilderness area. For more information contact Rio Grande National Forest at (719) 658–2556 or check the website at *www.fs.fed.us/r2/riogrande*. *DeLorme: Colorado Atlas & Gazetteer:* Page 78 A3

(Z) Piedra River

The Piedra Area is one of those pristine places that earned wilderness protection except for water rights. It's a beautiful little canyon that you can explore from either the north or south end or traverse the entire length of about 12 miles. Being lower in elevation, this area is a good place to hike when the high country is still covered with snow. Old-growth forests surround the river where you might catch a glimpse of river otters at play. The Piedra forms an important wildlife corridor between the Weminuche Wilderness and winter range to the south. To reach the north trailhead, drive about 16 miles north of Pagosa Springs on Piedra Road, CR 600, which becomes FS 631. After you cross the Piedra River bridge, the parking lot is up on your left at 7,700 feet. The south trailhead is called First Fork trailhead. Drive about 22 miles west of Pagosa Springs on U.S. 160 to First Fork Road (FS 622). Turn right onto FS 622 and drive about 12 miles to the trailhead at 7,200 feet. For more information contact the Rio Grande National Forest at (970) 264–2268 or visit their website at *www.fs.fed.us/r2/riogrande*. **DeLorme: Colorado Atlas & Gazetteer:** Page 87 A7

(AA) Mill Castle Trail

This trail climbs up Storm Pass for a view of the incredible castles (rock formations). However, you must earn the great views. The trail climbs 3,300 feet in about eight miles one way to the top of Storm Pass. The trail is extremely scenic and rugged, taking you into the heart of the West Elk Wilderness area. From Storm Pass you can either return the way you came, or drop down into Castle Creek for a longer backpack. From Gunnison, drive 3 miles north on CO 135 to Ohio Creek Road and turn left. Drive about 9 more miles to Mill Creek Road (FS 727) and turn left. The trailhead is another 4 miles. For more information contact Gunnison National Forest at (970) 641–0471 or check their website at *www.fs.fed.us/gmug*. **DeLorme: Colorado Atlas & Gazetteer:** Page 58 C1

Southwest

Spruce Tree House.

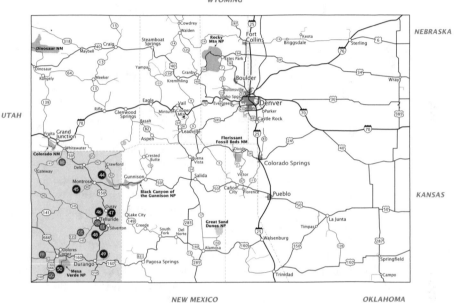

WYOMING

NEBRASKA

UTAH

KANSAS

NEW MEXICO

OKLAHOMA

The Hikes

North Vista Trail **44.**
Upper Roubideau Area Loop **45.**
Jud Wiebe Memorial Trail #432 **46.**
Cascade and Portland Loop **47.**
Pass and Coal Creek Loop **48.**
First Fork and Red Creek Loop **49.**
Petroglyph Point Trail **50.**

Honorable Mentions

BB. Dominguez Canyon
CC. Geyser Spring
DD. Wasatch Trail
EE. Ice Lake Trail
FF. Sand Canyon/East Rock Creek
GG. Ute Mountain Tribal Park

Southwest

L and of the Ute and the Ancestral Puebloans (formerly called Anasazi), the Four Corners area and San Juan Mountains are rich in culture, history, and beauty. Hiking opportunities abound in both canyons and on rugged mountain trails. Twelve of Colorado's 54 peaks over 14,000 feet are located in this region.

Ouray has long been known as the Little Switzerland of America and also boasts of hot springs for those weary bones and muscles. Telluride is just ten miles away from Ouray as the crow flies, about 18 miles on 4WD roads, or 49 miles by twisty highway. The feats of miners and road builders from Ouray to Durango and Telluride to Lake City take on a new meaning after touring and hiking the steep, rough terrain of this region. The San Juan Mountains, born of explosive volcanoes and later carved into sharp pinnacles and cirques by several glacial periods, provide years of exploring for any hiker. The Million Dollar Highway through the San Juans, connecting Ouray and Silverton, is another accomplishment of stubborn humans who had to get from Point A to Point B through horrendously rugged country. Avalanches still claim lives today on this highway.

To the west lies the Uncompahgre Plateau, an interesting geological uplift between mountains and canyons. To its east and west, rivers have carved canyons through its back and along its edges. Farther east, the Gunnison River has carved its skinny canyon through ancient Precambrian bedrock, now preserved by the Black Canyon of the Gunnison National Park and the Gunnison Gorge National Conservation Area.

Mesa Verde National Park, world-renowned for its superb cliff dwellings, lies in the southwest corner. Here you can visit mesa-top pueblo sites or take a guided tour of the cliff dwellings. The lesser-known Ute Mountain Tribal Park just south of Mesa Verde also contains ancient treasures. The Utes offer tours on their reservation for a less developed view of the ancient world. The new Canyons of the Ancients National Monument, designated in June 2000, adds to the cultural, natural, and historical offerings. Ancient sites are hidden in and around the many little canyons west and northwest of Cortez.

Telluride, an old mining town turned ritzy ski resort, offers strong hikers interesting loops over steep ridges with a few easier hikes to get acclimated. The Bluegrass Festival in mid June draws people from all over while other music, outdoor activities, and arts events keep the town hopping all summer.

The Durango-Silverton Narrow Gauge Railroad is a ride not to be missed. Connecting Durango and Silverton, the railroad has been operating since 1882. You can even depart/board at two points (Elk Park and Needleton) for a spectacular 35-mile loop hike in the Weminuche Wilderness northeast of Durango. Colorado's largest wilderness, the Weminuche contains jagged peaks, high alpine lakes, and many miles of trails. Durango is also the western terminus of the 470-mile long Colorado Trail.

The scenic and historic byways in this area are San Juan Skyway, Unaweep-Tabeguache, Trail of the Ancients, and Alpine Loop (4WD required).

Downtown Telluride.

Aspen along Red Creek Trail.

Section Overview

North Vista Trail

The North Vista Trail follows the north rim of the Black Canyon of the Gunnison, traveling through Gambel oak and piñon-juniper forest. Dramatic canyon views appear along the trail and at two unprotected overlooks accessed by short spur trails. A third and longer spur loops out to the accurately named Exclamation Point with an incredible view into the canyon. From here, the trail continues along the north rim then switchbacks up to the top of Green Mountain (8,563 feet). The spectacular, aerial view of the Black

Canyon is almost surrealistic. A short loop takes you around the top of Green Mountain, offering a 360-degree view of western Colorado. *(See page 332.)*

Upper Roubideau Area Loop

This hike explores the upper section of the Roubideau Area, a special part of the Uncompahgre Plateau. First descend on Roubideau Trail from Cobb (Gray) Cow Camp to Pool Creek. Aspen trees abound for a beautiful fall hike. After reaching Pool Creek Trail, the trail ascends along tiny Pool Creek through forests of aspen and spruce-fir. A bit of the Old West remains here with cattle driven to their grassy fields by cowboys on horses. The point-to-point hike ends at Pool Creek trailhead or you can loop back to Roubideau Trail trailhead via FS 406 and FS 546. *(See page 338.)*

Jud Wiebe Memorial Trail #432

The Jud Wiebe Trail climbs up and across the hill north of Telluride between Butcher and Cornet Creeks. Although short, it has its steep moments as very precipitous mountains surround Telluride. This trail is a good early season south-facing hike and a great warm-up for other longer, more difficult trails in the area. From various points, Bridal Veil and Ingram Falls, the ski area, spectacular craggy peaks, and the town below come into view. The trail was completed in 1987 in memory of Jud Wiebe, a Forest Service employee who designed the trail. *(See page 344.)*

Cascade and Portland Loop

This pleasant hike loops along Cascade Trail and Portland Trail in Ouray's Amphitheater area. The trail offers nice views of surrounding mountains, jagged cliffs, and mining operations. The hike includes the trail to Upper Cascade Falls. This spur trail switchbacks its way past cliffs for great views of surrounding mountains. After enjoying the falls, you can walk to the Chief Ouray Mine's bunkhouse and machinery building. (*See page 350.*)

Pass and Coal Creek Loop

This hike makes a loop above Coal Bank Pass via Pass Creek Trail to the foot of impressive Engineer Mountain then north to return on Coal Creek Trail. You can also climb Engineer Mountain via Pass Creek Trail. The wildflowers are spectacular in many sections of this hike during July and early August. Several places offer great views of the West Needle Mountains in the Weminuche Wilderness to the east and north to the mountains between Silverton and Telluride. The final 1.3 miles of the hike are along U.S. Route 550 and can be avoided with a car shuttle. (*See page 356.*)

First Fork and Red Creek Loop

The First Fork Trail follows a sparkling little creek up to Missionary Ridge northeast of Durango. Watch for elk and deer. The trail travels through forests of Douglas fir, ponderosa pine, Gambel oak, and aspen. After joining the Missionary Ridge Trail, head northeast through mixed conifer and aspen forests and several beautiful meadows with occasional views north to the craggy San Juan Mountains. Return via Red Creek Trail, which drops down several steep switchbacks, then past huge aspens. The trail intersects the road on which you park, about 0.3 miles above First Fork Trail trailhead. A beautiful hike when aspens are golden! (*See page 362.*)

Petroglyph Point Trail

This hike takes you below the rim of Spruce Canyon along a self-guided trail, up and down various steps, between huge rocks through skinny cracks to a wonderful petroglyph panel. Petroglyph Point, unfortunately misnamed Pictograph Point on topo maps, is the largest and best-known group of petroglyphs in Mesa Verde National Park. The hike gives you a glimpse of what it was like to live in this area, including climbing up a little cliff using big toeholds and handholds, much larger than the Ancestral Puebloans used. You must register at the trailhead (about 0.1 miles down the Spruce Tree Trail) before hiking this trail. No water is available along the trail. (*See page 368.*)

North Vista Trail

Hike Specs

Start: From North Rim Ranger Station
Length: 6.7-mile out-and back (with a 2.8-mile out-and-back option to Exclamation Point)
Approximate Hiking Time: 3–5 hours
Difficulty Rating: Moderate due to length and terrain
Elevations: 7,600–8,563 feet
Elevation Gain: 963 feet
Seasons: Best from May through October
Terrain: Dirt trail
Land Status: National park
Nearest Town: Crawford, CO
Other Trail Users: Hikers only
Canine Compatibility: Dogs not permitted

> The juniper is a member of the cypress family. For years it has been misnamed as a cedar in many parts of Colorado and Utah.

Getting There

From Crawford: Head south on CO 92 about 3.2 miles to Black Canyon (BC) Road. Turn right onto BC Road and follow it to the North Rim. The way is well marked but here are some details. From CO 92, drive about 4 miles, then BC Road turns right. In 0.7 miles, BC Road turns left by the Black Canyon Gallery. In another 0.8 mile the paved road becomes a good dirt road. In 1.1 miles, turn right to stay on BC Road. The park boundary is in another 1.7 miles. Cattle can graze here, so watch for them on the road. At the fork 3.3 miles into the park, turn right to the North Rim Ranger Station, which is another 0.5 miles. Total distance from Crawford is about 15 miles. There is a vault toilet by the ranger station. Water is available at the North Rim Campground, 0.5 miles down the road, between mid-May and mid-September. Be sure to bring your own water at other times. The North Rim access road is typically closed by snow from November to May. **DeLorme: Colorado Atlas & Gazetteer:** Page 56 D4

Gazing into the shadowy depths of the Black Canyon of the Gunnison, the name makes sense. The shadows alone would earn the moniker, but the canyon walls really are black. They are comprised of metamorphic "basement" rock, over 1.7 billion years old, pressed and heated into schist and gneiss (pronounced nice). White and pink stripes of granite and pegmatite snake across the black cliffs. They formed when hot magma worked its way into cracks in the metamorphic rocks and slowly cooled. After the present Rocky Mountains rose and the San Juan and West Elk mountains erupted, the Gunnison River slowly carved the Black Canyon during the last two million years. Without major tributaries eroding away its sides, the canyon has remained narrow, only 40 feet wide at the bottom of "The Narrows." The Gunnison River used to surge 12,000 cubic feet per second (cfs) during spring runoff. Imagine what force that amount of water created raging through this narrow spot. Today, with three dams upstream slowing the flow, the mighty Gunnison rarely rushes above 4,000 cfs.

Due to the efforts of local citizens, particularly Reverend Mark Warner, President Herbert Hoover created Black Canyon of the Gunnison National Monument on March 2, 1933, preserving the most spectacular 12 miles of the 53-mile-long canyon. In October 1976, 11,180 acres in the national monument were designated as wilderness under the Wilderness Act of 1964 further protecting the impressive canyon. The northern side of the monument was expanded in 1984. In October 1999, Congress upgraded the Black Canyon to National Park status while adding approximately 10,000 new acres to protect a valuable view corridor along the southern boundary and expand the wilderness to include two additional river miles (for a total of 14 miles). An additional 12 miles of the Gunnison River is protected in the Gunnison Gorge National Conservation Area just downstream. The visitor center on the South Rim offers interesting interpretive displays and an excellent movie about the history of Black Canyon.

The North Rim attracts fewer visitors than the South Rim, and thus offers quieter hiking opportunities. The North Vista Trail, built in 1991 and 1992 by the Volunteers for Outdoor Colorado (VOC), provides impressive views not only down into the canyon from various angles, but also 360 degrees of the surrounding area. Starting near the North Rim Ranger Station, the trail winds its way through Gambel oak, piñon pine, and juniper forest. You'll first encounter dense oak thickets and sagebrush as the trail drops slightly to cross S.O.B. Draw. Gambel oaks produce nutritious acorns that bears, chipmunks, and squirrels love, and deer browse on the lobed

Black Canyon of the Gunnison from Green Mountain.

leaves. The thickets also provide shelter for smaller animals and their young. Gambel oak can be extremely flammable during a wildfire, but nature provided it with underground rhizomes (roots), which house dormant buds that sprout readily. Another bush along the trail is serviceberry, an important food source for the local critters.

Two little side trails lead down to overlooks between 0.6 and 0.7 miles. These overlooks don't have any type of protective barriers, so watch where you walk and make sure your children don't wander. At 1.2 miles, be sure to take the 0.2-mile spur trail to Exclamation Point, which rightly earns its name by providing a fantastic view down into the canyon. When you reach the viewpoint, walk down to the next little level spot among the rocks. The view is best here because you can see the river 1,900 feet below. Violet-green swallows and white-throated swifts enjoy soaring on the thermals along the cliff edge.

MilesDirections

0.0 START at the trailhead by the North Rim Ranger Station (near the vault toilet). ★ 38°35'12"N 107°42'16"W

0.1 Open the gate in the fence and be sure to close it behind you. The fence keeps cattle out of visitor-use areas, such as the ranger station and the campground. Just beyond here there are some good views of the canyon walls.

0.6 Come to a scenic overlook on a trail to the left. *[Side-trip. A 0.1-mile out-and-back will lead you to the actual overlook.]*

0.7 Come to a scenic overlook on a trail to the left.

1.2 Reach the turnoff for Exclamation Point loop. Turn left here for a spectacular view ❺ 38°35'21"N 107°43'15"W

1.4 Arrive at Exclamation Point via west branch of loop. ❺ 38°35'13"N 107°43'13"W

1.5 Arrive back at North Vista Trail via east branch of loop. Turn left to continue up Green Mountain. *[Option. For a shorter trip, 2.7 miles, return from here to the trailhead.]*

1.8 Cross a barbed-wire fence via a wooden stepladder (another cattle fence).

2.5 Enjoy good views to the south. The trail begins to switchback.

3.4 Reach the top of Green Mountain. ❻ 38°35'41"N 107°44'04"W Go either right or left for a loop of panoramic views.

3.6 Arrive at the start of the top loop. Return the way you came. *[Side-trip. Consider going back out to Exclamation Point for another view with a different sun angle. Remember to add 0.4 miles to your overall hike.]*

6.7 Arrive back at the trailhead.

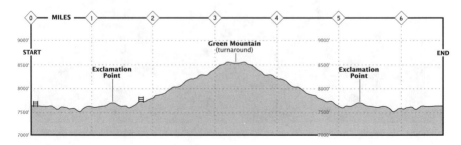

From here, the North Vista Trail continues along the canyon's edge for a little way. Some huge piñon pines grow here. Piñon pine is well known for the large tasty nuts it produces. Keep an eye open for piñon jays, a blue bird without a black crest. The jays love piñon nuts and can store up to 20 seeds in their throats. Considering the appetite of the jays, you'd be lucky to find a pinecone with a nut still inside. Porcupines enjoy the bark and leave large wounds on the pines. Utah juniper is the other common tree along the trail. Its stringy bark has been used by Native Americans for everything from sandals to baby diapers. The berries are an important food source for the local animal and bird populations.

Watch for an interesting step the trail crew created using an imbedded juniper log. The trail and the top of Green Mountain provide great views. Mount Sneffels (14,150 feet) and the Dallas Divide along with several 14,000-foot peaks in the San Juans to the east tower above the other landscape. Miniature looking cars drive along the South Rim road across the canyon. Needle Rock near Crawford points to the West Elk Mountains to the north and east. The Grand Mesa rises in the north like a ship's prow. On a clear day, Utah's La Sal Mountains may be visible to the west. The Black Canyon lies below, trenched into the landscape.

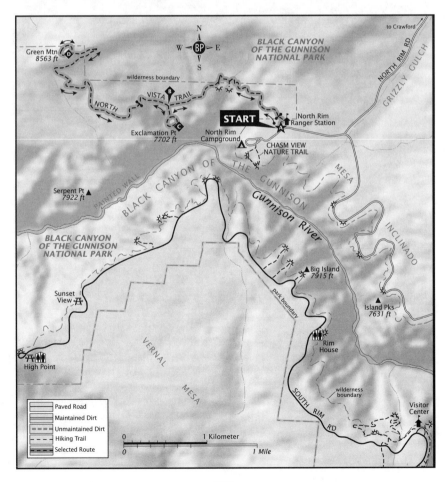

Black Canyon of the Gunnison from
Exclamation Point.

You can hike (slide and scramble) into
the canyon to the river via six different gullies or draws. These difficult routes are not
really trails, usually dropping at least
1,800 feet in one mile. You must obtain a
backcountry permit to travel these routes.
Contact the South Rim visitor center for
information.

Hike Information

📞 Trail Contact:

Black Canyon of the Gunnison National Park (visitor center), Montrose, CO (970) 249–1914, ext. 23 or www.nps.gov/blca

🕐 Schedule:

Open year round. Trails neither maintained nor marked for winter use.

💲 Fees/Permits:

Entrance fee for Black Canyon of the Gunnison National Park (pay at North Rim Ranger Station). Camping fee for developed campgrounds. Free backcountry permits are required for backcountry camping or inner-canyon travel.

❓ Local Information:

Crawford Area Chamber of Commerce, Crawford, CO (970) 921–4000 or www.crawfordcountry.org • Delta Chamber of Commerce, Delta, CO (970 874–8616 or www.deltacolorado.org • Delta Country Tourism, Delta, CO 1–800–436–3041 or www.deltacolorado.org/tourism • Montrose Visitor & Convention Bureau, Montrose, CO 1–800–873–0244 or (970) 249–1726 or www.montrose-colo.com

💡 Local Events/Attractions:

Pioneer Days, Crawford, CO (970) 921–4000 • Olathe Sweet Corn Festival, Olathe, CO 1–877–858–6006 or (970) 323–6006 or www.olathesweet cornfest.com • Council Tree Pow Wow, Delta, CO (970) 874–8616 or www.coun ciltreepowwow.org • The Ute Indian Museum and Ouray Memorial Park, Montrose, CO (970) 249–3098 • Cherry Days, Paonia, CO 970–527–3886 • Summerfest and Arts Festival, Hotchkiss, CO 1–800–436–3041

🛏 Accommodations:

Black Canyon National Park campgrounds, Montrose, CO (970) 249–1914, ext. 23 (visitor center) or www.nps.gov/blca

• Crawford State Park campgrounds, Crawford, CO (970) 921–5721 or http://parks.state.co.us/crawford

🍴 Restaurants:

Mad Dog Ranch Fountain Café, Crawford, CO (970) 921–7632 or www.cocker.com/ mdrfc • Boardwalk Restaurant, Crawford, CO (970) 921–4905 • Red Barn Restaurant & Lounge, Montrose, CO (970) 249–9202 • Camp Robber Café, Montrose, CO (970) 240–1590

🚶 Hike Tours:

Black Canyon of the Gunnison National Park (visitor center), Montrose, CO (970) 249–1914, ext. 23 or www.nps.gov/blca – summer guided walks on South Rim

👥 Clubs and Organizations:

Colorado Mountain Club – West Slope Group, Grand Junction, CO – Call the CMC clubroom in Denver at (303) 279–3080 or 1–800–633–4417 (Colorado only) to find the current local contact or visit www.cmc.org/cmc.

✏ Other Resources:

Shrubs and Trees of the Southwest Uplands, by Francis H. Elmore, Southwest Parks and Monuments Association • Black Canyon of the Gunnison, by Houk Rose, Southwest Parks and Monuments Association

🛍 Local Outdoor Retailers:

Jeans Westerner, Inc., Montrose, CO (970) 249–3600 or www.jeanswesterner. com • Cimarron Creek, Montrose, CO (970) 249–0408

🗺 Maps:

USGS maps: Grizzly Ridge, CO • Trails Illustrated® maps: #245, Black Canyon of the Gunnison (scale 1:28,000)

Upper Roubideau Area Loop

Hike Specs

Start: From the Roubideau Trail (Trail 105) trailhead

Length: 8.1-mile loop (with an optional 5.4-mile point-to-point)

Approximate Hiking Time: 3.5–5.5 hours (2.5–4 hours for point-to-point)

Difficulty Rating: Difficult due to elevation gain on the way back and route finding challenges

Elevations: 8,440–9,711 feet

Elevation Gain: 1,360 feet

Seasons: Best from June through October

Terrain: Dirt trail

Land Status: National forest and special area

Nearest Town: Montrose, CO

Other Trail Users: Equestrians and hunters (in season)

Canine Compatibility: Controlled dogs permitted. Elk bed and graze along this trail. Best to keep dogs leashed to avoid conflicts with wildlife.

Getting There

From Montrose: Head west on CO 90 from its intersection with U.S. 550 and U.S. 50. In 2 miles, CO 90 turns left; in another 0.3 miles, it turns left again. In 1 more mile, CO 90 turns right. At Oak Grove Elementary, another 0.8 miles, CO 90 turns left. In another 4.4 miles,

stay to the left on CO 90 heading to Nucla, by a sign that reads No WINTER MAINTENANCE. In another 0.2 miles, the road becomes an all-weather gravel road, but it might be full of washboards. The Uncompahgre National Forest Boundary is in another 11.9 miles, where CO 90 becomes FS 540. There's a T-intersection (FS 402) 2.7 miles farther where you go straight ahead, staying on FS 540 toward Columbine Pass. At the next fork 1 mile up the road, take the right branch, FS 402. (Do NOT go to Nucla.) Continue on FS 402 past several roads coming in from either the right or left. *[Optional shuttle point. If you're doing a shuttle, turn right in 5.4 miles where the sign reads "Pool Creek Trailhead." The trailhead and shuttle drop-off is 0.2 miles in. Park one car here and drive the second back to FS 402 and turn right, resuming where you left off.]* At mile 7.0 on FS 402, turn right onto FS 546 (East Bull). Go right at the fork to Cobb Cow Camp (called Gray Cow Camp on the USGS topo map) at mile 0.9, and park off the dirt road. The Roubideau Trail is on your right about 0.1 miles down the road past the building. There are no facilities at the trailhead. Bring your own water or water purification system. Cattle graze in the area. ***DeLorme: Colorado Atlas & Gazetteer:*** Page 65 A7

The Uncompahgre Plateau extends about 100 miles running north-south from the San Miguel River to the Colorado River. Rising like a submarine west of Montrose, the plateau is quite rugged. It's a land of multiple uses: hiking trails, 4WD roads, and a long mountain bike route—the *Tabeguache* Trail. Ute Indians hunted this area as local names attest. Tabeguache means "place where the snow melts first." As noted in a journal kept by the 1776 Dominquez-Escalante expedition, the Utes called the river to the east the "*Ancapagari* (which, according to our interpreter,

Pool Creek drainage.

means Red Lake), because they say that near its source there is a spring of red-colored water, hot and ill-tasting."

The Roubideau (roo-bi-doe) Area was created by the 1993 Colorado Wilderness Bill. Because the headwaters of its creeks start outside its designated boundaries, Congress denied it full wilderness protection. Water rights in Colorado create many hotly contested arguments and lawsuits. To avoid potential conflicts, the "Roubideau Area" designation protects its wilderness character, but not its water. Some people call it a *baby* wilderness. The area is closed to motorized and mechanized use, logging, and mining.

Antoine Robidoux headed to Santa Fe from St. Louis in 1824. His family, long involved in the fur trade, wanted to take advantage of trading with newly independent Mexico. Robidoux and an old family friend explored regions northwest of Santa Fe in what became western Colorado and eastern Utah. Beaver were plentiful, and

MilesDirections

0.0 START at Roubideau Trail (Trail 105) trailhead. ⭐ 38°22'22"N 108°14'35"W

0.5 Reach the Roubideau Area boundary. The trail switchbacks down into Goddard Creek.

1.2 Cross Goddard Creek. ◈ 38°22'17"N 108°13'66"W

1.9 Cross another drainage. The trail contours along hill through pleasant aspen forest.

2.2 The trail curves left and descends about 100 feet before contouring again.

2.8 The trail drops more steeply to its intersection with Pool Creek Trail. If you lose the trail, find the easiest way to walk down to Pool Creek. Many cattle trails crisscross this area.

3.0 Reach the intersection with Pool Creek Trail. ◈ 38°21'80"N 108°12'30"W *[Side-trip. Turn left here for a 0.6-mile out-and-back spur to Roubideau Creek. Good spot for lunch.]* Turn right to hike to the Pool Creek trailhead.

3.7 Trail crosses a gooey gully, which can be a little tricky. You might need to walk down the dry creek a few feet to find an easy place to walk across.

5.1 Cross a little water seep coming from under a boulder to the right side of the trail.

5.4 Arrive at the Pool Creek Trail trailhead. ◈ 38°20'58"N 108°14'13"W *[Optional shuttle point. If you left a shuttle, this is where you'll find it.]* Turn right and walk a few steps to the access road, then left onto the access road.

5.6 Arrive at FS 402 and turn right onto it.

7.2 Arrive at FS 546 (East Bull). Turn right and walk down this road. Turn right when the road forks.

8.1 Arrive back at your vehicle near Cobb Cow Camp.

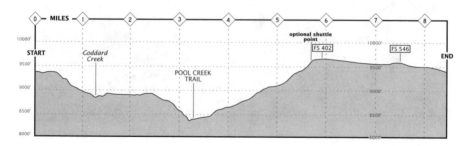

Ute Indians were eager to trade pelts for European tools. Antoine became a Mexican citizen and by 1828 had obtained from the Mexican government an exclusive hunting and trading license to the area he had explored a few years earlier. Rough terrain made for difficult travel on trading routes in those days. Instead of using the established Old Spanish (California) Trail through southwestern Colorado then north into his territory, Robidoux headed north to the San Luis Valley. Turning west he followed an old American Indian trail over Cochetopa Pass into the Gunnison Valley then into the Uncompahgre Valley. Just below the confluence of the Gunnison and Uncompahgre rivers, he built his first trading post, Fort Uncompahgre. For years the Utes had wintered nearby at the Ute Council Tree, a huge 195-year-old cottonwood that still stands. They brought pelts from their lands in exchange for modern conveniences.

Historical documents indicate some of the inventory sold at Fort Uncompahgre included: silk and cotton bandanas, scarves, trousers, shirts, jackets, combs, mirrors, linen thread, needles, blanketing material, scissors, cotton material, steel knives, fire steels, copper cooking pots, tea, coffee, sugar, and leaf tobacco. Food staples also filled the shelves. Modern implements made life easier for the Utes. But as life improved in this tough country, the winds of change started blowing. The Oregon Trail further north became the preferred trading route and more white people settled in Ute territory, creating unrest. The United States won the area during the Mexican-American War. By 1844, Robidoux's trade kingdom crumbled. Angered by a Mexican attack on a Ute village with no reparation from the Mexican government, the Utes went on a rampage in 1844, even attacking Fort Uncompahgre and killing most of the Mexican workers. Two years later, Fort Uncompahgre was in ruins.

Over the years, Fort Uncompahgre's exact location was lost. Perhaps the flooding Gunnison wiped out its traces. Local citizens built a replica of the fort closer to Delta, and opened it to visitors on June 30, 1990.

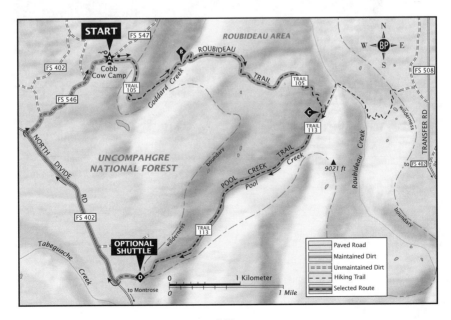

This hike lets you wander in the cool highlands of the Uncompahgre Plateau, away from the bustle of Delta and Montrose. The Roubideau Trail switchbacks down to Goddard Creek drainage, crosses the creek, then climbs up to wander through gently sloping aspen forest. Elk bed and graze in the lush grasses. Approaching the Pool Creek drainage, the trail drops with views down into Roubideau Creek. Cattle enjoy the plentiful grasses in this section and their trails go every which way. Upon reaching Pool Creek, a 0.3-mile jaunt downhill (left) on the trail brings you to Roubideau Creek, a pleasant place for lunch. The hike up Pool Creek Trail gains 1,360 feet in 2.7 miles. Cattle trails crisscross at many angles. Stay on the trail paralleling the creek. Occasionally cattle are driven up or down the trail, which makes for an interesting hiking experience! Notice the difference in vegetation. The right side is sunny and grassy, while the left side is steep, cool, and moist with dark spruce-fir forest dominating. Some aspens bear scars of carved names and dates—this practice exposes aspen to various diseases. At Pool Creek Trail trailhead, either meet your shuttle vehicle or return to Roubideau trailhead via Forest Service Road 402 and Forest Service Road 546.

Near the confluence of Pool Creek and Roubideau Creek.

Hike Information

Trail Contact:

Uncompahgre National Forest, Ouray Ranger District, Montrose, CO (970) 240-5400 or *www.fs.fed.us/r2/gmug*

Schedule:

Access road closes in winter 23.5 miles from the trailhead. Road used by snow-mobiles. Trail neither maintained nor marked for winter use.

Fees/Permits:

No fees or permits required

Local Information:

Montrose Visitor & Convention Bureau, Montrose, CO 1-800-873-0244 or (970) 249-1726 or *www.montrose-colo.com*

Local Events/Attractions:

Unaweep/Tabeguache Scenic & Historic Byway, Bureau of Land Management, Montrose, CO (970) 249-6047 • Council Tree Pow Wow, Delta, CO (970) 874-8616, *www.counciltree powwow.org* • Fort Uncompahgre, Delta, CO (970) 874-8721 · The Ute Indian Museum and Ouray Memorial Park, Montrose, CO (970) 249-3098 • Rocky Hill Winery, Montrose, CO (970) 249-3765

Accommodations:

National Forest Campgrounds, Ouray Ranger District, Montrose, CO (970) 240-5400

Restaurants:

Red Barn Restaurant and Lounge, Montrose, CO (970) 249-9202 • Camp Robber Café, Montrose, CO (970) 240-1590 · Backwoods Inn, Montrose, CO (970) 249-1961 • Kokopelli's Southwestern Grille, Montrose, CO (970) 252-8100

Clubs and Organizations:

Colorado Mountain Club – *West Slope Group, Grand Junction, CO – Call the CMC clubroom in Denver at (303) 279-3080 or 1-800-633-4417 (Colorado only) to find the current local contact or visit www.cmc.org/cmc.*

Other Resources:

Antoine Robidoux and Fort Uncompahgre, by Ken Reyher, Western Reflections, Inc. • *Roadside Geology of Colorado,* by Halka Chronic, Mountain Press Publishing Co. • *The Complete Guide to Colorado's Wilderness Areas,* by John Fielder and Mark Pearson, Westcliffe Publishers, Inc.

Local Outdoor Retailers:

Jeans Westerner, Inc., Montrose, CO (970) 249-3600 or *www.jeanswesterner. com* • Cimarron Creek, Montrose, CO (970) 249-0408

Maps:

USGS maps: Antone Spring, CO

Jud Wiebe
Memorial Trail #432

Hike Specs

Start: From the trailhead at top of Aspen Street

Length: 2.7-mile loop

Approximate Hiking Time: 1.5–2.5 hours

Difficulty Rating: Difficult due to some steeper sections

Elevations: 8,876–10,040 feet

Elevation Gain: 1,164 feet

Seasons: Best from June to mid-October

Terrain: Dirt road and dirt trail

Land Status: National forest

Nearest Town: Telluride, CO

Other Trail Users: Equestrians (some trail sections), mountain bikers, and hunters (in season)

Canine Compatibility: Leashed dogs permitted

Getting There

From Telluride: Find a parking place in Telluride or park in the free parking area across from the visitor center and take the Galloping Goose shuttle into downtown. Walk to Aspen Street (0.4 miles east of the visitor center) and walk uphill to the top of the street. The west end of the trail starts here. The other option is to walk to Oak Street and head uphill to the top of the street to the east end of the trail. You then walk along Tomboy Road to the pipe gate and bulletin board and turn left. The hike description starts at the Aspen Street trailhead. *DeLorme: Colorado Atlas & Gazetteer:* Page 76 A3

elluride, an old mining town snuggled at the mouth of a box canyon, is experiencing a second wave of success. The first came with the mining frenzy in the 1870s as miners swarmed over the rugged San Juan Mountains looking for gold, silver, and other precious metals. Today the spectacular mountain scenery has attracted writers and artisans, and the ski area (opened in 1972) has created a new building frenzy.

The San Juan Mountains were born of volcanic fire and ash and sculpted by the scraping of glaciers. Eruptions started about 35 million years ago and lasted over 13 million years. During one phase, the volcanoes were so explosive that they often collapsed into themselves forming *calderas*. Hot mineralized water oozed up through cracks and faults underground and around the calderas leaving behind gold, silver, zinc, copper, and lead. Within the last two million years, various glaciers covered the area. The San Miguel glacier carved the U-shaped valley floor in which Telluride sits. Spectacular Bridal Veil Falls, at the head of the box canyon, drops 365 feet from a hanging valley.

In 1875, John Fallon discovered ore rich in zinc, lead, copper, iron, silver, and gold. Nearby, the Union Mine also started recovering rich ore. J.B. Ingram discovered that Fallon's claim and the Union were bigger than the legal limit by about 500 feet. He laid claim to the area in between, calling it the Smuggler. The Smuggler's ore contained 800 ounces of silver and 18 ounces of gold per ton. The Union and Smuggler merged and became one of the major producers in Telluride. The Tomboy Mine, about five miles up Tomboy Road, started operations in 1880 and continued until 1928. In 1897, it sold for $2 million!

The mountains around Telluride contain over 350 miles of tunnels (think San Francisco to Los Angeles), some going all the way through the mountains to the Million Dollar Highway between Ouray and Silverton. The town itself was established as Columbia in 1878, when 80 acres were laid out and incorporated. It became the county seat of newly established San Miguel County in 1883. The post office, however, had a problem getting mail to Columbia, Colorado, often sending it to Columbia, California instead. A name change was inevitable. Telluride, the name of a gold-bearing tellurium compound, was chosen for the new moniker in the 1880s.

Telluride and Ballard Mountain.

The rich ore-bearing peaks surrounding Telluride hold a lurking danger—the white death. Three hundred inches of annual snowfall combined with steep terrain resulted in fairly regular avalanches. In 1902, an avalanche demolished part of the Liberty Bell Mine (farther up the road you'll hike down), killing seven men and injuring several others. While the rescue party was recovering the bodies, a second avalanche swept through. The rescuers escaped without additional injuries or deaths; however, as they made their way back to Telluride a third avalanche roared down, killing three and injuring five. In one winter (1905–1906) with unusually heavy snows, 100 people died in avalanches in the area. Snow isn't the only thing to go sliding around here. In 1914, Cornet Creek overflowed sending eight feet of mud down Colorado Avenue, Telluride's main street.

> The book Tomboy Bride by Harriet Fish Backus offers an interesting account of life in the mining camp near the Tomboy Mine from 1908 to 1910.

The Jud Wiebe Trail (Trail 432) starts at the bulletin board at the top of Aspen Street. Continue uphill to the bridge over Cornet Creek and turn left. The trail climbs steadily and after a couple of switchbacks comes to a junction labeled Deep Creek Trail (Trail 418). The Jud Wiebe Trail takes off to the right and continues

MilesDirections

0.0 START at the trailhead bulletin board at the top of Aspen Street. ★ 37°56'27"N 107°48'42"W—In a few feet, turn left and walk across the bridge that crosses Cornet Creek.

0.7 Reach a junction with Deep Creek Trail (Trail 418) and Sneffels Highline Loop (Trail 414). ◆ 37°56'51"N 107°49'04"W—Turn right to continue on the Jud Wiebe Trail (Trail 432).

1.1 Come to an open meadow and slope with fantastic views.

1.6 Cross the bridge over Cornet Creek.

1.7 Reach the junction of Jud Wiebe Trail and a non-motorized road, which leads to Liberty Bell Basin. ◆ 37°56'42"N 107°48'22"W—Turn right and walk down the road.

2.1 Look on the right for an old little mining building with wires coming out of it. You'll be hiking near a red rock canyon on your right.

2.2 The town water tank is on the right.

2.6 Reach the junction of Jud Wiebe Trail and Tomboy Road, which leads to Tomboy Mine. At a pipe gate and bulletin board ◆ 37°56'24"N 107°48'40"W turn right and walk down Tomboy Road.

2.7 Arrive at the Oak Street trailhead. Return to wherever you parked your vehicle.

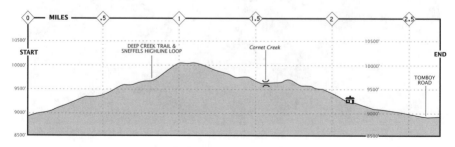

climbing. You soon arrive at a viewpoint, locally called Breakfast Rock, with views of Telluride and the surrounding lofty peaks. A few more switchbacks lead to an open area with more fantastic views. To the west is the San Miguel River heading downstream along a glacial moraine. You might even catch a glimpse of the La Sal Mountains near Moab, Utah. The San Miguel Mountains, home to three 14,000-foot peaks, line up along the horizon. To the south and east, peaks rise dramatically and the gondola climbs the hill from town along ski runs. Ingram and Bridal Veil Falls tumble from cliffs to the east. The trail meanders down through a lush aspen forest and crosses a bridge over Cornet Creek. Climbing further, the trail then intersects the non-motorized road to Liberty Bell Basin. This flat area once served as the local playing field for baseball games between miners and town residents. Turn right and follow the steep road down past the town water tank to Tomboy Road. Turn right and walk down the road to the top of Oak Street and back to town.

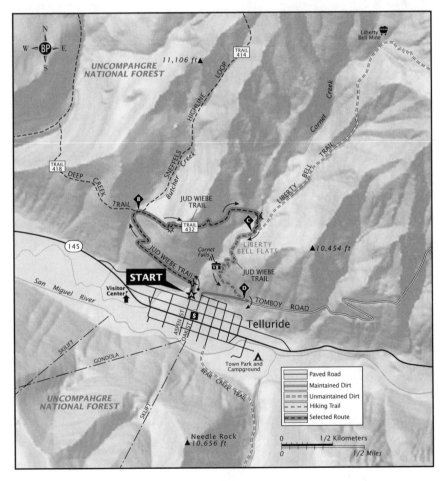

Hike Information

◆ Trail Contact:
Uncompahgre National Forest, Norwood Ranger District, Norwood, CO (970) 327–4261 or *www.fs.fed.us/r2/gmug*

◆ Schedule:
Open year round. Trail is sometimes hikable in winter. Call first for conditions.

◆ Fees/Permits:
No fees or permits required

◆ Local Information:
Telluride & Mountain Village Visitor Information, Telluride, CO (970) 728–3041 or 1–800–525–2717 or *www.telluride.com*

◆ Local Events/Attractions:
Telluride Bluegrass Festival, Telluride, CO 1–800–624–2422 • **Wine Festival,** Telluride, CO (970) 728–3178 • **Jazz Celebration,** Telluride, CO (970) 728–7009 • **Telluride Mushroom Festival,** Telluride, CO (303) 296–9259 • **Telluride Film Festival,** Telluride, CO, (970) 728–4640 • **Telluride Blues & Brews Festival,** Telluride, CO, (970) 728–8037, 1–888–278–1746 or *www.tellurideblues.com*

◆ Accommodations:
National forest campgrounds, Norwood Ranger District, Norwood, CO (970) 327–4261 or *www.fs.fed.us/r2/gmug* • **Town Park Campground,** Telluride, CO (970) 728–2173 • **Johnstone Inn,** Telluride, CO 1–800–725–1901 or (970) 728–3316 • **Victorian Inn,** Telluride, CO 1–800–611–9893

◆ Restaurants:
Fat Alley Barbecue, Telluride, CO (970) 728–3985 • **La Cocina de Luz,** Telluride, CO (970) 728–9355 – *Mexican restaurant* • **Maggie's Hometown Bakery,** Telluride, CO (970) 728–3334 • **Leimgruber's Bierstube,** Telluride, CO (970) 728–4663 • **Blue Jay Café,** Placerville/Sawpit, CO (970) 728–0830 – *breakfast*

◆ Hike Tours:
Herb Walker Tours, Telluride, CO (970) 728–0639 or (970) 728–4538 • **Geology Tours of Telluride,** Telluride, CO (970) 728–3391 • **Telluride Sports,** Telluride, CO 1–800–828–7547 or (970) 728–4477 or *www.telluridesports.com*

◆ Other Resources:
Between the Cover Books, Telluride, CO (970) 728–4504 • **Bookworks,** Telluride, CO (970) 728–0700 • *Telluride A Quick History,* by Rose Weber, Little London Press • *Roadside Geology of Colorado,* by Halka Chronic, Mountain Press Publishing Co. • *Geology of Colorado Illustrated,* by Dell R. Foutz, Your Geologist • *Telluride Hiking Guide,* by Susan Kees, Wayfinder Press • *Hiking Colorado's Geology,* by Ralph Lee Hopkins and Lindy Birkel, The Mountaineers

◆ Local Outdoor Retailers:
Telluride Mountaineer, Telluride, CO (970) 728–6736 • **Telluride Sports,** Telluride, CO (970) 728–4477 or 1–800–828–7547 or *www.telluride sports.com*

◆ Maps:
USGS maps: Telluride, CO • *Trails Illustrated®* maps: #141, Silverton/Ouray/Telluride/Lake City

47

Cascade and Portland Loop

Hike Specs

Start: From the trailhead at the top of the Amphitheater Campground

Length: 6.0-mile loop (with an easier 3.4-mile loop option)

Approximate Hiking Time: 2.5–5.5 hours

Difficulty Rating: Strenuous due to steep trail to Upper Falls

Elevations: 8,360–10,080 feet

Elevation Gain: Up to 1,720 feet

Seasons: Best from May through October

Terrain: Dirt trail, sometimes steep and narrow to Upper Cascade Falls

Land Status: National forest

Nearest Town: Ouray, CO

Other Trail Users: Equestrians, mountain bikers, and hunters (in season)

Canine Compatibility: Leashed dogs permitted

Getting There

From Ouray: Drive south out of town on U.S. 550 to the entrance to Amphitheater Campground. Turn left onto the campground road and drive 1.1 miles to the trailhead at the top of the campground. Dogs must be on leash in the parking lot and in the campground. There's an outhouse in the campground. Bring your own water. ***DeLorme: Colorado Atlas & Gazetteer:*** Page 66 D4

The Ouray area is a jumble of geologic history from ancient bedrock to glacially carved features. Leadville limestone formed in a sea over 325 million years ago. Reddish rock remains from the erosion of Uncompahgria, part of the Ancestral Rockies. Another sea helped form Dakota sandstone. Then the explosions of the San Juan volcanoes started, leaving deep deposits of ash and breccia (broken rocks) called San Juan Tuff of which the Amphitheater seen from the Portland Trail is a good example. Hot mineralized water deposited gold, silver, and other metals in the Leadville limestone during the volcanic era. Ice age glaciers carved craggy peaks and scoured the valley north from Ouray, leaving its moraine by Ridgway.

This combination of geologic events produced a gold and silver bonanza for prospectors. On a hunting and fishing expedition in summer 1875, A.J. Staley and Logan Whitlock meandered up the Uncompahgre River to the headwall by the current site of Ouray and discovered veins of ore, which were subsequently named the Trout and the Fisherman lodes. In August that same year, A.W. Begole and Jack Eckles found the Cedar and Clipper lodes where the hot springs pool is today. As hopeful miners arrived in town, Captain Cline and Judge Long laid out a townsite that they called Uncompahgre City.

The next spring Chief Ouray and his wife, Chipeta, arrived in town to talk with the townspeople. Ouray was chief of the Tabeguache band of Utes, who lived in the Ouray-Montrose area. Although half-Ute and half-Apache, Ouray rose to power as a skilled negotiator. He was friendly to the white man, realizing that fighting could dec-

Chief Ouray mine building from near Upper Cascade Falls.

imate his people. He hoped that through negotiations, his people would survive and perhaps keep some of the land they had called home for hundreds of years. The latter did not happen. The Utes were organized into seven different bands, each with its own leader. Because of his oratorical skill, the U.S. Government regarded Ouray as spokesman for all Utes, a status not always acknowledged by other Ute chiefs. Over time, Chief Ouray gained much respect among white people. Uncompahgre City was renamed in his honor.

MilesDirections

Note. Below trail mileage does not agree with Forest Service signs.

0.0 START at the trailhead at the top of Amphitheater Campground. ★ 38°01'18"N 107°39'35"W

0.1 Reach a trail junction. Turn left and head uphill. (You'll return to this junction later.)

0.2 Reach a trail junction. Turn left and continue uphill.

0.7 Reach the junction of the Cascade Falls Trail (Trail 213) and the Portland Trail (Trail 238). ◈ 38°01'21"N 107°39'15"W *[**Option.** For a shorter easier hike turn right and follow the Portland Trail. This option will make for a 3.4-mile loop.]* Turn left on the Cascade Falls Trail, heading for the Upper Cascade Falls and the Chief Ouray Mine buildings. For an easier hike, stay right on the Portland Trail.

1.8 Round a ridge by some interesting rock formations.

2.0 Reach the Upper Cascade Falls. ◈ 38°01'45"N 107°39'10"W—The Chief Ouray Mine buildings are about 0.1 miles beyond the falls. Return the way you came.

3.3 Arrive back at the junction of the Cascade Falls Trail and the Portland Trail. Turn left here onto the Portland Trail to complete the loop.

3.5 Cross a large gully that shows the power of water.

3.8 Reach the junction of the Portland Trail and the Portland Cutoff Trail (Trail 238.1A). ◈ 38°01'14"N 107°38'57"W—Turn right to stay on the Portland Trail.

3.9 Enjoy the scenic view.

5.4 Reach the junction with the Portland Trail and the Upper Cascade Falls Trail. ◈ 38°01'06"N 107°39'38"W—Turn right onto the Upper Cascade Falls Trail to return to the trailhead. Recross the large gully that you crossed higher up.

5.6 Reach a trail junction. Turn right to return to the trailhead. The trail climbs up here.

5.7 Reach another trail junction. Turn left here.

5.8 Reach another trail junction. Turn left again. This junction completes the loop. The trailhead is just around the ridge.

6.0 Arrive back at the trailhead.

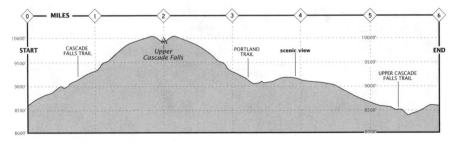

Ouray continued to grow; its mines producing mainly silver. The transportation of ore and supplies was a struggle for many years. In 1887, the Denver and Rio Grande railroad finally reached Ouray, adding to its prosperity. The Silver Crash of 1893, which killed many other mining towns, proved a mere burp to Ouray. A gold discovery on Gold Hill northeast of town saved the day.

Being surrounded by steep mountains poses occasional problems for Ouray. In July 1909, a downpour filled creek channels with tons of water and debris. Portland Creek, above which part of the hiking loop travels, roared into town covering the first floor of the Elks Building with mud. It continued into J.J. Mayer's furniture store carrying carpet rolls and furniture down Main Street. In wintertime the drive south via Red Mountain Pass is very prone to avalanches as witnessed by a marker at one switchback. It commemorates a minister, his two daughters, and three snowplow drivers who met their untimely demise in the "white death."

On the way to the trailhead, stop at the first switchback just south of town. Look to the northeast, and you can see the Chief Ouray Mine buildings perched on a shelf in the cliffs. Believe it or not, the trail to Upper Cascade Falls takes you there without the need for ropes.

The hike starts by contouring around a ridge, then above a drainage. The intersection of Cascade Falls Trail (Trail 213) and Portland Trail (Trail 238) is reached in about 0.7 miles. To do the shorter loop, follow the Portland Trail. The spur trail to Upper Cascade Falls and the Chief Ouray Mine climbs steeply from here, zigzagging its way up a precipitous mountainside. The trail is good, although narrow in a few spots. When you reach a ledge, the walking becomes easier, but can be dangerous in bad weather. Take time to enjoy the fantastic views. The trail rounds a ridge near some interesting rock outcroppings and drops slightly to Upper Cascade Falls. You

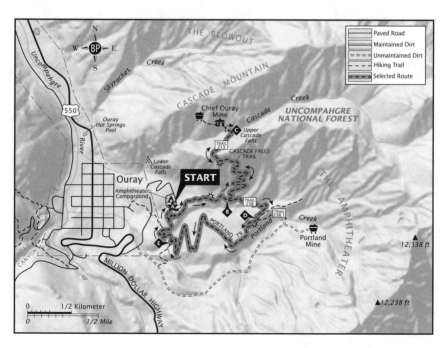

can cross Cascade Creek continuing 0.1 miles to explore the old mine bunkhouse and see Ouray far below. Beyond these buildings the trail to the actual mine can be treacherous.

Return back to the junction of Cascade Falls and the Portland Trail and turn left to continue the loop. When crossing the big gully, you can imagine the force of water that races down the steep cliffs. The hike continues through spruce-fir forest and climbs a little ridge to intersect with the Portland Cutoff Trail (Trail 238.1A) to the Portland Mine. Stay to the right on Portland Trail, enjoy the views into Portland Creek, and continue switchbacking down through a nice forest with aspens. At the next intersection, turn right onto Upper Cascade Falls Trail. After crossing the big gully again, the trail climbs back up to complete its loop and return to the trailhead.

View up Canyon Creek from Cascade Falls Trail.

Hike Information

☎ Trail Contact:

Uncompaghre National Forest, Ouray Ranger District, Montrose, CO (970) 240–5400 or *www.fs.fed.us/r2/gmug*

⏰ Schedule:

Open year round. Call for winter access road and trail conditions

$ Fees/Permits:

No fees or permits required

❓ Local Information:

Ouray Chamber Resort Association, Ouray, CO 1–800–228–1876 or (970) 325–4746 or *www.ouraycolorado.com*

💡 Local Events/Attractions:

Oktoberfest Celebration, Ouray, CO (970) 325–4981 • **Hot Springs Pool & Fitness Center,** Ouray, CO (970) 325–4638 • **Box Cañon Falls Park,** Ouray, CO (970) 325–4464 • **Bachelor-Syracuse Mine Tour,** Ouray, CO (970) 325–0220 • **Highgraders' Holiday,** Ouray, CO (970) 325–4521 • **Ouray County Museum,** Ouray, CO (970) 325–4576

🛏 Accommodations:

National forest campgrounds, Ouray Ranger District, Montrose, CO (970) 240–5400 or 1–877–444–6777 • **Matterhorn Motel,** Ouray, CO 1–800–334–9425 or (970) 325–4938 • **Wiesbaden Hot Springs Spa & Lodgings,** Ouray, CO, (970) 325–4347 – *has underground caves* • **Ouray KOA Campground,** Ouray, CO (970) 325–4736 or *www.koa.com*

🍴 Restaurants:

Buen Tiempo, Ouray, CO (970) 325–4544 – *Mexican restaurant* • **The Outlaw,** Ouray, CO (970) 325–4366 – *good prime rib* • **The Bon Ton,** Ouray, CO (970) 325–4951 or *www.stelmo hotel.com* • **Piñon Restaurant & Tavern,** Ouray, CO (970) 325–4334

👥 Clubs and Organizations:

The Trail Group, Inc., Ouray, CO – *Contact U.S. Forest Service for current group contact at (970) 240–5400.*

🏃 Hike Tours:

San Juan Mountain Guides, Ouray, CO (970) 325–4925 or *www.ouray climbing.com – offers peak hikes & wildflowers along with technical climbing*

📖 Other Resources:

Buckskin Booksellers, Ouray, CO (970) 325–4044 • *Stampede to Timberline,* by Muriel Sibell Wolle, Sage Books • *Roadside Geology of Colorado,* by Halka Chronic, Mountain Press Publishing Co. • *Geology of Colorado Illustrated,* by Dell R. Foutz, Your Geologist • *History of Ouray: A Heritage of Mining & Everlasting Beauty,* by Doris H. Gregory, Cascade Publications • *History of Ouray: Historical Homes, Buildings, People,* by Doris H. Gregory, Cascade Publications • *Ouray Hiking Guide,* by Kevin Kent, Wayfinder Press

🏪 Local Outdoor Retailer:

Ouray Mountain Sports, Ouray, CO (970) 325–4284

🗺 Maps:

USGS maps: Ouray, CO • *Trails Illustrated*® maps: #141, Silverton/Ouray/Telluride/Lake City

Pass and Coal Creek Loop

Hike Specs

Start: From the Pass Creek Trail (Trail 500) trailhead near the top of Coal Bank Pass

Length: 7.0-mile loop (with optional 5.8-mile point-to-point)

Approximate Hiking Time: 3–5 hours

Difficulty Rating: Difficult due to elevation gain and some route finding challenges

Elevations: 10,280–11,840 feet

Elevation Gain: 1,560 feet

Seasons: Best from mid-June through October

Terrain: Dirt trail with some grassy areas, steep in spots

Land Status: National forest

Nearest Town: Silverton, CO

Other Trail Users: Equestrians, mountain bikers, and hunters (in season)

Canine Compatibility: Controlled dogs permitted

Getting There

From Silverton: Drive south about 13.5 miles on U.S. 550 to a dirt road just before the top of Coal Bank Pass. Turn right onto the dirt road and drive about 0.1 mile to park at the Pass Creek Trail trailhead. *[Optional shuttle point. If you're doing a shuttle, leave one car at the dirt parking area on the left side of the road just before a large left switchback by mile marker 58, about 12.4 miles from Silverton.]* There is a vault toilet on the top of Coal Bank Pass. Bring your own water for not much is easily accessible. **DeLorme: Colorado Atlas & Gazetteer:** Page 76 C3

While driving from Silverton to the trailhead, compare the numerous craggy peaks to the south and east with the more rolling terrain and scattered peaks to the west. Engineer Mountain (12,968 feet) and the area of the hike are readily visible from just south of Molas Pass. Engineer Mountain itself is comprised of sandstone and shale that eroded from part of the Ancestral Rockies called Uncompahgria. These sediments add red color to the peak. The lower slopes are limestone formed from marine sediments in an ancient sea. The rolling hills were lava and ash flows, signs of the volcanic origins of the San Juan Mountains. Glaciers placed the final touches on this area. Engineer Mountain once rose above an immense icecap during more recent ice ages, the last of which only ended about 11,000 years ago. Across the highway, craggy Twilight Peak is often seen while hiking down the Coal Creek Trail. Although some geologists say coal doesn't exist near Coal Bank Pass, records in Silverton indicate that people found some type of inefficient coal near here and used it for fuel until the coal mines near Durango were discovered.

Engineer Mountain looms large above the surrounding rolling hills. How the mountain was named is not certain, but historians believe the Hayden Survey (1870–1879) coined the name. "Engineer" most likely commemorates a survey engineer versus a railroad engineer. The San Juan region contains two Engineer Mountains, the other located on the Alpine Loop between Ouray and Lake City.

The Pass Creek Trail starts in a field of cornhusk lily, cow parsnip, sub-alpine larkspur, Indian paintbrush, death camas, geraniums, and columbines. Cornhusk lily (false hellebore) is the large, white-flowered plant with big green leaves resembling cornhusks. Another common name for this member of the lily family is skunk cabbage. The other large plant with clusters of white flowers is cow parsnip, which some people mistakenly call Queen Anne's lace. Both grow in moist areas such as this meadow and are often found with another moisture loving plant, sub-alpine larkspur. These three can grow taller than most hikers forming green walls along the trail. The larkspur is a member of the buttercup family, sporting purple petals with a long spur. Without a close look, it can be mistaken for monkshood, which also loves moist areas. Death camas has six joined petals with a yellow band and red stamens. Both death camas and cornhusk lily are poisonous to humans.

> Lodging in Silverton can fill quickly in summer. Make reservations far in advance if planning a visit in July and August.

Hiking along, the amount and type of flowers change with forest and meadow. The trail enters a spruce-fir forest and wanders around little ridges for about 0.75 miles. A little pond surrounded by elephant heads lies in an open meadow at about 0.9 miles. Elephant head, also called little red elephant, is an appropriate name for

Colorado blue columbine.

MilesDirections

0.0 START at the Pass Creek Trail (Trail 500) trailhead. ☆ 37°41'59"N 107°46'42"W

0.9 A little pond is on the left.

1.3 The trail makes a big right switchback.

1.5 [*FYI. Enter an open area for a great view to the north.*]

2.0 Engineer Mountain comes into view followed by fantastic fields of wildflowers.

2.2 Reach the trail junction with Engineer Mountain Trail. Turn right and follow Engineer Mountain Trail, heading north. [*FYI. A left turn will take you to U.S. 50 in about four miles south of Coal Bank Pass.*]

2.9 Reach the top of the Coal Creek drainage. [*FYI. There's a little saddle to the left for a view to the west. Good lunch spot.*]

3.1 The trail forks. Turn right onto Coal Creek Trail (not marked as such). ◈ 37°43'00"N 107°47'55"W [*FYI. You can also go farther north on Engineer Mountain Trail to intersect with the Colorado Trail.*]

3.4 Watch carefully for a trail to the right just before the trail crosses a small gully. The trail starts in grass before looking like a dirt trail. Follow this trail around to some white rocks where the trail disappears. Walk slowly until you see a trail to the right that goes into a willow patch. If you miss the trail by the small gully, continue to the top of a little ridge with flat rocks and krummholz (stunted trees). Turn right at a little cairn and follow the trail slowly to the clump of white rocks and boulders. Look carefully to the left for the trail through the willow patch.

3.5 The trail dives into the willows. ◈ 37°43'09"N 107°47'31"W—Walk on the trail through the willows and down the ridge.

3.7 The trail disappears at a saddle in the ridge. Do NOT go uphill here Turn right and head downhill in the meadow. Stay to the left along a little gully. Look for a log post in the meadow below. ◈ 7°43'01"N 107°47'18"W If you don't see it, stay close to the little gully and you'll come upon the trail in about 0.1 miles. Turn left onto the trail, which then curves fairly soon to the right.

4.0 The trail comes to a T-intersection. Turn left. (The right branch dead ends.) The trail winds and switchbacks, sometimes steeply, through the forest and some little meadows.

4.5 [*FYI. Enjoy the view of craggy peaks to the east, including Twilight Peak, the closest.*]

5.0 You can see the highway below. After crossing a flatter area, the trail makes several large switchbacks down to the highway.

5.7 Reach Coal Creek Trail trailhead along U.S. 550. ◈ 37°42'30"N 107°46'04"W Turn right, cross the road, and walk about 0.1 miles along the left side up to the parking area at mile marker 58. [*Optional shuttle point. If you left a car here, the hike is finished.*] Continue walking along the road, being mindful of oncoming traffic.

6.9 Cross the highway and turn right onto the dirt road to the Pass Creek Trail trailhead.

7.0 Arrive back at the trailhead.

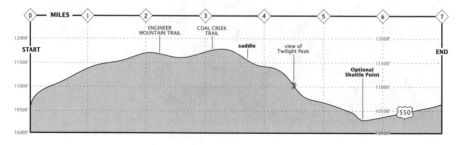

these pink to purple flowers that love boggy areas. The elephant trunk sticks out from the ears as if trumpeting sunny days. Other boggy area plants can be seen along various sections of trail. Globeflowers with their overlapping cream-colored petals, marsh marigolds with their more separated white petals, king's crowns (ruby flowers), occasional queen's crowns (pink flowers), and Parry primroses with magenta to purple flowers line the trail in wetter areas. After about two miles, the hills are covered with yellow, rosy, or magenta paintbrush flowers in a profusion of color. As the trees thin, Colorado blue columbine, the state flower, makes a showy appearance. Engineer Mountain towers above the seas of tiny wildflowers like a castle surrounded by its moat.

When you reach the intersection with Engineer Mountain Trail (Trail 508), turn right and follow Engineer Mountain Trail across the open alpine fields. Willows grow here along with varieties of paintbrush, king's crown, American bistort, Parry primrose, columbine, elephant head, and alpine avens—all commingled as if a higher power had emptied packages of mixed wildflower seeds.

> *Picked wildflowers will only stay fresh for about two hours before fading into oblivion. Please do not pick the wildflowers, but leave them for others to enjoy. The local animals depend on them for food, too.*

The trail proceeds north, crossing the head of Coal Creek. Turn right at an unmarked junction and follow the trail through dense cornhusk lilies. Watch carefully for a little trail off to the right or a cairn at the top of a little ridge. The trail dives into a willow thicket and onto a ridge. At a saddle, the trail disappears completely in the grasses. Turn right and drop down into the Coal Creek drainage where the trail reappears near a wooden post in the meadow. The flowers aren't as spectacular along Coal Creek, but the occasional views of Twilight Peak are. The trail drops, sometimes steeply, above Coal Creek, then makes several switchbacks down to U.S. Highway 550.

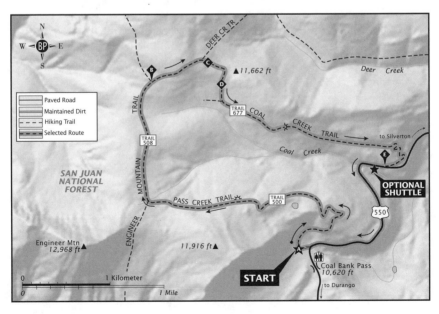

Engineer Mountain from Pass Creek Trail.

Hike Information

Trail Contact:
San Juan National Forest, Columbine Ranger District West, Durango, CO (970) 884–2512 or www.fs.fed.us/r2/sanjuan

Schedule:
Open year round. Trail neither maintained no marked for winter use.

Fees/Permits:
No fees or permits required

Local Information:
Silverton Area Chamber of Commerce, Silverton, CO 1–800–752–4494 or (970) 387–5654 or www.silverton.org • Durango Area Chamber Resort Association, Durango, CO 1–800–525–8855 or (970) 247–0312 or www.durango.org • Go Durango: 1–800–800–7623 or www.godurango.com

Local Events/Attractions:
Silverton Festivals, Silverton, CO (970) 387–5737 or www.silvertonfestivals.org • Blair Street Arts & Crafts Festival, Silverton, CO 1–800–752–4494 or (970) 387–5654 • Durango & Silverton Narrow Gauge Railroad, Durango, CO 1–888–TRAIN–07 or (970) 247–2733 or www.durangotrain.com • Christ of the Miners Shrine, Silverton, CO 1–800–752–4494 or (970) 387–5654 • San Juan County's Museum, Silverton, CO (970) 387–5838 • Mayflower Gold Mill Tour, Silverton, CO (970) 387–0294 • Old Hundred Gold Mine Tour, Silverton, CO 1–800–872–3009 or (970) 387–5444 • A Theatre Group, Silverton, CO 1–800–752–4494 or (970) 387–5337

Accommodations:
National forest campgrounds, San Juan National Forest, Columbine Ranger District West, Durango, CO (970) 884–2512 or www.fs.fed.us/r2/sanjuan • The Grand Imperial Hotel, Silverton, CO 1–800–341–3340 or (970) 387–5527 • The Teller House Hotel, Silverton, CO 1–800–342–4338 or (970) 387–5423

Restaurants:
Pickle Barrel, Silverton, CO (970) 387–5713 • Handlebars Food & Saloon, Silverton, CO (970) 387–5395 • Brown Bear Café, Silverton, CO (970) 387–5630 • Chattanooga Café, Silverton, CO (970) 387–5892 • Avalanche Coffee House, Silverton, CO (970) 387–5828

Hike Tours:
San Juan Backcountry, Silverton, CO 1–800–4X4–TOUR or (970) 387–5565 – by advance arrangements

Clubs and Organizations:
San Juan Mountains Association, Durango, CO (970) 385–1210

Other Resources:
San Juan County Historical Society, Silverton, CO (970) 387–5838 • Guide to Colorado Wildflowers, Volume 2 Mountains, by G.K. Guennel, Westcliffe Publishers Inc. • Walking in Wildness a guide to the Weminuche Wilderness, by B.J. Boucher, The Herald Press • Roadside Geology of Colorado, by Halka Chronic, Mountain Press Publishing Co.

Local Outdoor Retailer:
Outdoor World, Silverton, CO (970) 387–5628

Maps:
USGS maps: Engineer Mountain, CO • Trails Illustrated® maps: #140, Weminuche Wilderness

First Fork and Red Creek Loop

Hike Specs

Start: From First Fork Trail trailhead
Length: 10.3-mile loop
Approximate Hiking Time: 4.5–7.5 hours
Difficulty Rating: Difficult due to distance and some steep spots
Elevations: 7,880–9,860 feet
Elevation Gain: 1,980 feet
Seasons: Best from June through October
Terrain: Dirt trail, sometimes steep
Land Status: National forest
Nearest Town: Durango, CO
Other Trail Users: Equestrians, mountain bikers, and hunters (in season)
Canine Compatibility: Controlled dogs permitted

Durango-Silverton narrow gauge train.

Getting There

From Durango: From the intersection of U.S. 550 and College Drive (near the train station), drive 0.2 mile into downtown on College Drive to E. 3rd Avenue, turn left on E. 3rd and drive 0.7 miles to intersection of E. 3rd Avenue and 15th Street and Florida Road. Turn sort of right onto Florida Road, CR 240, and drive 9.4 miles northeast to the sign Colvig Silver Camps. Turn left here onto dirt CR 247 and drive one mile past the camps. The road gets rougher and bumpier here. In another 0.3 miles, there is a fence, which you may have to open and close to continue. The road beyond is best negotiated with a high clearance vehicle (4WD not necessary). The first parking area is available in about 0.25 miles from the gate. Park here if the road is getting too rough for your vehicle. The trailhead and a small parking area are another 0.35 miles from this point. The trailhead is marked by a lone sign stating TRAIL on the left side of the road. There are no facilities here. Bring your own water. Although water may be available in First Fork and Red Creek, cattle graze in this area so be sure to purify any creek water before drinking. *DeLorme: Colorado Atlas & Gazetteer:* Page 86 B4

Many early settlers to the Animas Valley were Civil War veterans. Legend has it that one morning, fog cloaked a ridge northeast of Durango. The veterans noticed a similarity with Missionary Ridge, site of a famous Civil War battle near Chattanooga, Tennessee. The ridge has since been known as Missionary Ridge.

Today the area surrounding Durango is an outdoor enthusiast's paradise. Mountain biking, hiking, hunting, horseback riding, rafting, skiing, four-wheeling, and fishing are some of the opportunities available. The Durango-Silverton Narrow Gauge Railroad takes people back in time through the Animas River canyon to Silverton, an old mining town that prospers during the summer. Long before white people arrived, the Ancestral Puebloan people lived in the Durango area reaching

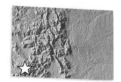

from what is now Mesa Verde National Park, about 36 miles west, to Chimney Rock about 35 miles east.

Summer recreation opportunities attract a high volume of visitors to Durango and nearby San Juan National Forest. In 1988, Bill Sexton, then the Forest Supervisor of the San Juan National Forest, challenged the area's citizens to form an organization to help with public lands education. Citizens responded with enthusiasm, and in 1989 they created the nonprofit San Juan Mountains Association (SJMA). Their mission included developing educational materials about public lands, fostering a sense of community ownership and stewardship, and acting as liaison between the community and local government land agencies, the U.S. Forest Service (USFS) and the Bureau of Land Management (BLM).

Red Creek drainage.

363

SJMA has been very successful. Over 12,500 backpackers in the Weminuche Wilderness area have been given information about backcountry ethics, zero-impact camping, and flora and fauna. Volunteers with Ghost Riders ride horses into the national forest talking with other horseback riders and outfitters. SJMA funded the excellent book, *Walking in Wildness A Guide to the Weminuche Wilderness* by B. J. Boucher. Chimney Rock Archaeological Site tours are conducted by trained SJMA cultural interpreters. Even Missionary Ridge receives their attention.

During 2000, SJMA teamed with Leave No Trace, Inc. (LNT) to conduct a survey of outdoor enthusiasts using Missionary Ridge trails to determine receptivity of

MilesDirections

0.0 START at the First Fork Trail trailhead. ☆ 37°21'18"N 107°44'29"W Immediately cross Red Creek and soon thereafter come to a gate. Remember to close the gate behind you.

2.5 Arrive at an open area filled with bushes. A cliff looms ahead of you. The trail climbs steeply, then drops down and climbs up again.

3.2 The trail arrives at a T-intersection. ◆ 37°22'38"N 107°46'44"W—Turn left here to continue climbing to the Missionary Ridge Trail.

3.4 Reach the junction with Missionary Ridge Trail. ◆ 37°22'37"N 107°46'52"W—Turn right and proceed north, then east along the ridge.

4.3 [**FYI.** *Look through the trees to your left for some good views of the San Juans to the north.]*

4.7 Arrive at a large meadow ringed with aspen and conifers. [**FYI.** *A good spot for lunch.]*

5.1 The trail starts descending, sometimes steeply.

5.4 Cross a fence with an interesting stile.

6.0 After dropping and switchbacking down, arrive at a saddle. ◆ 37°23'22"N 107°45'16"W Red Creek does NOT descend from here. The trail appears to fork. Take the trail to the left that goes around the hill in front of you.

6.5 Reach the intersection with signed Red Creek Trail. ◆ 37°23'44"N 107°44'43"W—Turn right, drop down and follow the steep switchbacks.

6.9 You've completed the dizzying switchbacks. The trail descends, sometimes steeply, through a thick aspen forest. As you go lower, the trail crosses the creek several times.

8.8 Come to a gate. If closed, make sure to close it behind you. Cross the creek to the left. The trail crosses the creek a number of times as you continue down. There are some nice red cliffs along the trail also.

10.0 Arrive at the dirt road. Turn right to head downhill to your vehicle.

10.3 Arrive back at the trailhead.

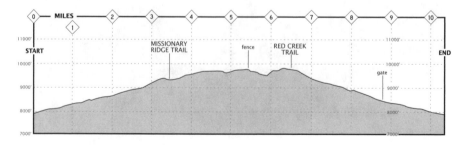

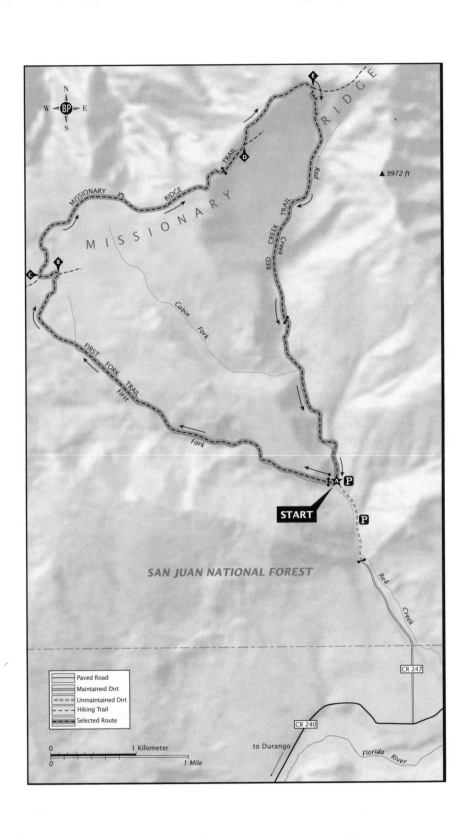

N
W — BP — E
S

MISSIONARY   RIDGE   RIDGE

E

MISSIONARY

▲ 9972 ft

Red

RED   CREEK   TRAIL

Creek

TRAIL

D

C
B

Cabin   Fork

FIRST   FORK   TRAIL

First

Fork

A   P

START   P

SAN JUAN NATIONAL FOREST

Red

Creek

CR 247

Paved Road
Maintained Dirt
Unmaintained Dirt
Hiking Trail
Selected Route

CR 240

to Durango

Florida   River

0   1 Kilometer
0   1 Mile

LNT techniques and perceptions of recreational impacts. In 2000, SJMA merged with Southwest Outdoor Volunteers, which had been providing stewardship opportunities on area trail projects. The expanded organization (still called SJMA) enables citizens to participate in volunteer and stewardship programs. It also provides a more cohesive liaison between the public and land agencies.

SJMA is located in the San Juan Public Lands Center (just west of the intersection of U.S. Highway 550 and U.S. Highway 160) in Durango. Take some time to stop in and ask questions, register concerns, or browse their interpretive bookstore. SJMA sponsors many activities ranging from the Share the Trails Triathlon to various field seminars. Call for the events schedule to see what you might be able to take advantage of while in Durango.

The trailhead to First Fork currently has a wooden TRAIL sign with First Fork scratched into it. After crossing Red Creek, you come upon a gate. (Please close the gate behind you because cattle graze in this area.) The trail follows little First Fork where flowers sometimes grow waist high. Continue climbing as the trail crosses the creek several times. Elk and deer may be hiding in the tall grass or bushes. In a large open area, the trail climbs steeply, drops, and climbs again. Some aspens have telltale elk tooth marks.

When you come to a T-intersection, know that you are not at Missionary Ridge. Turn left and continue up to a second T-intersection with the Missionary Ridge Trail. Along the ridge, Center Stock Driveway metal signs decorate a tree here and there. Ranching has long been a part of the Durango area economy. The trail crosses two large meadows bordered by aspens where wild iris flowers bloom blue-purple in spring. Through the trees to the left, keep looking for glimpses of the craggy San Juans and the red Hermosa Cliffs to the north. After crossing a stile over a fence, the trail becomes a ledge along a steep side slope. At the saddle, stay on the singletrack trail to the left to reach a second saddle. Here you'll find the signed Red Creek Trail. After switchbacking steeply off Missionary Ridge, Red Creek Trail then wanders through a huge aspen forest. Watch for elk and deer in this area. When you come to a road, turn right to return to your vehicle.

The many aspen trees along both creeks make this an excellent fall hike.

Elk tooth marks on aspen along First Fork Trail.

Hike Information

Trail Contact:
San Juan National Forest, Columbine Ranger District West, Durango, CO (970) 884-2512 or www.fs.fed.us/r2/sanjuan

Schedule:
Open year round. Access road closed by snow 0.9 miles from the trailhead. Trail neither maintained nor marked for winter use.

Fees/Permits:
No fees or permits required

Local Information:
Durango Area Chamber Resort Association, Durango, CO 1-800-525-8855 or (970) 247-0312 or www.durango.org • Go Durango: 1-800-800-7623 or www.godurango.com

Local Events/Attractions:
Durango & Silverton Narrow Gauge Railroad, Durango, CO 1-888-TRAIN-07 or (970) 247-2733 or www.durango train.com • Trimble Hot Springs, Durango, CO (970) 247-0111 • Diamond Circle Melodrama, Durango, CO (970) 247-3400 or 1-877-325-3400 • Animas Museum, Durango, CO (970) 259-2402

Accommodations:
National forest campgrounds, San Juan National Forest, Columbine Ranger District West, Durango, CO (970) 884-2512 or www.fs.fed.us/r2/sanjuan

Restaurants:
Tequila's , Durango, CO (970) 259-7655 • Ken and Sue's Place (also called 937 Main), Durango, CO (970) 259-2616 • Carver Brewing Co., Durango, CO (970) 259-2545 • Red Snapper, Durango, CO (970) 259-3417

Hike Tours:
San Juan Mountains Association, Durango, CO (970) 385-1210

Clubs and Organizations:
San Juan Mountains Association, Durango, CO (970) 385-1210 • Colorado Mountain Club, San Juan Group, Durango, CO – Call the state offices at (303) 279-3080 or 1-800-633-4417 (Colorado only) for current contact information or www.cmc.org/cmc.

Other Resources:
Maria's Bookshop, Durango, CO (970) 247-1438 • Walking in Wildness a guide to the Weminuche Wilderness, by B.J. Boucher, The Herald Press

Local Outdoor Retailers:
Pine Needle Mountaineering, Durango, CO (970) 247-8728 or 1-800-607-0364 • Gardenschwartz Outdoors, Durango, CO (970) 259-6696 • Backcountry Experience, Durango, CO (970) 247-5830 or www.bcexp.com

Maps:
USGS maps: Durango East, CO; Hermosa, CO; Lemon Reservoir, CO; Rules Hill, CO

Petroglyph Point Trail

Hike Specs

Start: From the Spruce Tree Trail trailhead between Chapin Mesa Museum and the chief ranger's office
Length: 2.8-mile loop
Approximate Hiking Time: 1.5–3 hours
Difficulty Rating: Moderate due to uneven dirt trail and toeholds in one spot
Elevations: 6,600–6,930 feet
Elevation Gain: 330 feet
Seasons: Best from March through November
Terrain: Paved trail turning to dirt with rock steps, narrow passages, and rock footholds
Land Status: National park
Nearest Towns: Cortez, CO and Mancos, CO
Other Trail Users: Hikers only
Canine Compatibility: Dogs not permitted

Getting There

From Cortez: Drive about 10 miles east on U.S. 160. Turn right at the Mesa Verde National Park interchange. Drive about 21 miles to the parking lot for Spruce Tree House and Chapin Mesa Museum. You will have to pay the entrance fee at the entrance station near the interchange. The visitor center, about 15 miles along the Park road, offers various information and is the only place to purchase tickets for tours of Cliff Palace, Balcony House, and Long House. Water, food, and restrooms are available near the trailhead. *DeLorme: Colorado Atlas & Gazetteer:* Page 85 C5

About A.D. 1200, the sounds of building, farming, grinding corn, and playing children rang through the canyons and mesa tops of Mesa Verde. Spruce Tree House, built between 1200 and 1276, is thought to have housed about 100 people. It is the third largest dwelling at Mesa Verde. The Ancestral Puebloan people lived in this area from about A.D. 550 to 1300. At first they built pit houses partially underground with log, branch, and mud roofs. They farmed the surrounding land and cleared piñons and junipers for their fields using the materials for their structures, clothes, food, and firewood. Water was mainly obtained from winter snows and often meager summer rains. Dryland farming methods were used to grow corn, beans, and squash. Hunting first with atlatls (a spear-throwing device) and then bows and arrows, men brought meat home. Woven baskets were used for storage and cooking. Between A.D. 900 and 1100, pottery and multi-level surface structures called pueblos evolved. Circular ceremonial structures, called kivas, were built completely underground with an entrance from above.

These people progressed and prospered. Pueblos evolved into larger villages, often with several kivas. The Ancestral Puebloan culture covered many square miles of the Four Corners region (where Colorado, Utah, Arizona, and New Mexico meet). Trade routes developed between many villages. Evidence of trade with people in Mexico and California has been found at various sites. By 1100, the Ancestral Puebloans were entering their "golden age." Pottery was decorated with black-on-white designs. Masonry techniques had improved, and structures were built with more regularly shaped stones, resulting in nicer looking buildings. Toward the end of the 1100s, they

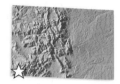

started building their multi-storied dwellings in alcoves in the cliffs. No one knows for sure why the Ancestral Puebloans moved here. Access was difficult, requiring handholds and toeholds to be carved into the solid sandstone and sometimes ladders

Gambel oak and desert varnish stained rock.

had to be constructed. Theories range from protection from enemies to shelter from weather—many populated alcoves face south to benefit from winter sun.

By 1300, the villages and cliff dwellings were abandoned. Possibilities range from environmental problems, severe draught, or religious reasons. According to Hopi culture the various clans were to migrate in four directions then eventually join together again at a common and permanent home. As they lived in, then left their villages, they carved information about their clan, the history of their village and their migration on rock walls. Archaeologists believe the citizens of Mesa Verde moved to pueblos along the Rio Grande to the south and the Hopi mesas to the southwest.

These ancient peoples had no written language. Traditions and knowledge about how to live were passed orally from generation to generation. They did, however, leave stories chipped and scratched on the stone cliffs. Petroglyph Point is one of their storyboards. A *petroglyph* is a drawing pecked into the rock whereas pictographs are painted. The Petroglyph Trail Guide describes a possible interpretation of the panel.

The hike starts on the paved trail to Spruce Tree House. Switchbacks take you down into Spruce Canyon. Before or after your hike, take some time to walk around Spruce Tree House. A ranger is on duty to answer any questions. A self-guided

MilesDirections

Note. If you start on this trail late, you must complete the loop. A gate across the trail is locked at 6:30 PM. (earlier in spring and fall), which prevents you from returning the way you came.

0.0 START at the Spruce Tree Trail trailhead, between the museum/bookstore and the chief ranger's office. ☆ 37°11'03"N 108°29'15"W The trail splits at a left curve. Take the left branch downhill around the left switchback. (The right branch goes behind the chief ranger's office.)

0.1 Pass by a metal chain link gate. This gate is closed and locked at night. The trail forks. Turn right onto Petroglyph Point Trail (a National Historic Trail) and sign the trail regis-

ter. *[FYI. The left trail goes to Spruce Tree House.]* The trail becomes dirt here.

0.3 The trail forks. Turn left and go uphill on Petroglyph Point Trail. The right branch is Spruce Canyon Trail.

0.9 There's a good view of Navajo and Spruce canyons.

1.6 Reach Petroglyph point. ◈ 37°10'23"N 108°29'31"W

1.7 Reach the mesa above Spruce Canyon.

1.9 Come to a slickrock area with views.

2.7 Come to the trail junction with paved Spruce Tree Trail. Turn right and head uphill to trailhead.

2.8 Arrive back at the trailhead.

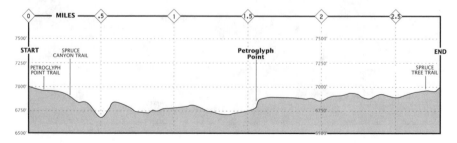

Petroglyph panel.

brochure explains life at the site and some information about preservation.

When you come to the intersection with Petroglyph Point Trail, make sure to sign the trail register. After the intersection with Spruce Canyon Trail, Petroglyph Point Trail climbs up Spruce Canyon, following various ledges. The trail guide explains many plants and geological features of the area. One section of narrow trail can be a challenge with a wide pack or dangling camera. At marker 19, stop and look at the grooves in the rock where axe heads were sharpened. The petroglyph panel is at marker 24. From there, look carefully for the MUSEUM signs with arrows. The trail climbs up a very short rock face, with good steps carved into the rock and handholds that can be easily reached. Just beyond that the trail travels a few feet along a rock ledge. Once on the mesa top, the trail is easy to follow.

Please do not deface or remove any artifacts, or pick any plants. Others will follow you—leave the area clean and unspoiled for the next visitors.

As you hike the trail, envision living here 900 or 1,000 years ago. A people in tune with their environment and skilled in the ways of the land successfully lived here for over 700 years.

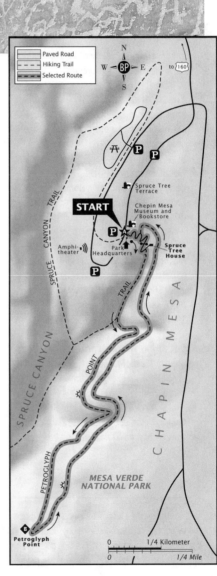

Hike Information

☎ Trail Contact:
Mesa Verde National Park, Mesa Verde, CO (970) 529–4461 or *www.nps.gov/meve*

◷ Schedule:
Open March to November, depending on snow. The trail is open 8:30 A.M. to 6:30 P.M. summer, open 9:00 A.M. to 5:00 P.M. in spring and fall. No visitors can enter ruins without a ranger present.

⑤ Fees/Permits:
Entrance fee, annual pass, Golden Eagle, Golden Access, or Golden Age pass required

❓ Local Information:
Cortez Chamber of Commerce & Colorado Welcome Center, Cortez, CO (970) 565–3414 or (970) 565–4048 or *www.coloradodirectory.com/cortezchamber/* or *subee.com/dir/ctz.html* • **Mancos Valley Visitor Center & Pioneer Museum,** Mancos, CO (970) 533–7434 or 1–800–873–3310 or *www.mancos.org* • **Mesa Verde Country,** Cortez, CO 1–800–253–1616 or *www.swcolo.org*

⚘ Local Events/Attractions:
Chapin Mesa Museum and scheduled special events like Indian dances, Mesa Verde, CO (970) 529–4461 or *www.nps.gov/meve* • **Anasazi Heritage Center,** Dolores, CO (970) 882–4811 or *www.co.blm.gov/ahc/hmepge.htm* •

Crow Canyon Archaeological Center, Cortez, CO (970) 565–8975 or 1–800–422–8975 or *www.crow canyon.org* • **Ute Mountain Tribal Park,** Towaoc, CO 1–800–847–5485 or (970) 565–3751, ext. 282, or *swcolo.org/Tourism/Archaeology/UteMtTribalPark.html* • **Cortez Cultural Center,** Cortez, CO (970) 565–1151 or *www.cortezculturalcenter.org*

⊜ Accommodations:
Morefield Campground, Mesa Verde National Park, CO (970) 565–2133 or 1–800–449–2288 or *www.visitmesa verde.com* • **Far View Lodge,** Mesa Verde National Park, CO (970) 529–4421 or 1–800–449–2288 or *www.visitmesaverde.com* • **Anasazi Motor Inn,** Cortez, CO (970) 565–3773 or 1–800–972–6232 • **Bauer House B & B,** Mancos, CO (970) 533–9707 or 1–800–733–9707 or *www.bauer-house.com*

⊕ Restaurants:
Nero's Italian Restaurant, Cortez, CO (970) 565–7366 • **Main Street Brewery & Restaurant,** Cortez, CO (970) 564–9112 • **Francisca's,** Cortez, CO (970) 565–4093 – *Mexican restaurant* • **Homesteader's Restaurant,** Cortez, CO (970) 565–6253 or *www.thehomesteaders.com*

The Ancestral Puebloan people were formerly called Anasazi. *The descendants of these people are the present-day Pueblo and Hopi people. Anasazi is a Navajo word meaning "enemy ancestors" and is not a term preferred by today's descendants. Mesa Verde is Spanish for "green table," an appropriate name for the mesa when viewed from a distance.*

Hike Tours:
Mesa Verde Tours, Durango and Cortez, CO (970) 247–4161 or (970) 565–1278 or 1–800–626–2066 or *www.mesa verdetours.com – auto tours with some walking to sites* • **Mesa Verde Company,** Mesa Verde National Park, CO 1–800–449–2288 or *www.visitmesa verde.com*

Other Resources:
Earth Song Haven Teahouse & Bookstore, Cortez, CO (970) 565–9125 • **Cortez Books Etc.** Coffeehouse, Cortez, CO (970) 564–0487 • *Those Who Came Before,* by Robert H. and Florence C. Lister, Parks and Monuments Association • *National Parkways*

Photographic and Comprehensive Guide to Rocky Mountain & Mesa Verde National Parks, by Michael D. Yandell (publisher and editor-in-chief), National Parks Division of World-Wide Research and Publishing Co. • *Anasazi Ruins of the Southwest in Color,* by William M. Ferguson and Arthur H. Rohn, The University of New Mexico Press

Local Outdoor Retailer:
Howard's Sporting Goods, Cortez, CO (970) 565–9371 – *more focused on hunting and fishing*

Maps:
USGS maps: Moccasin Mesa, CO

Honorable Mentions

Southwest

Compiled here is an index of great hikes in the Southwest region that didn't make the A-list this time around but deserve recognition. Check them out and let us know what you think. You may decide that one or more of these hikes deserves higher status in future editions or, perhaps, you may have a hike of your own that merits some attention.

(BB) Dominguez Canyon

The Big Dominguez River drains the Uncompahgre Plateau creating a beautiful canyon of sandstone walls, with desert bighorn sheep, raptors soaring in the sky above, and at one spot a seasonal waterfall and petroglyphs. This trail lies within the Dominguez Canyon Wilderness Study Area. You can choose from two trailheads for different hike lengths. For both, start from Grand Junction and drive south on U.S. 50 to Whitewater. At Whitewater turn right onto CO 141 west toward Gateway. Approximately nine miles west of Whitewater, look for the Cactus Park road and turn left onto it. The last two miles of this road requires a 4WD with high-clearance vehicle. Follow the signs to Big Dominguez and Cactus Park trailhead, a total of about seven miles. The trail drops steeply following cairns into the canyon (elevations 6,610 to 5,680 feet), meeting the Big Dominguez Creek trail in about 2.5 miles. The trail can be tricky to follow. You can head downstream to see the waterfall and rock art. Another approach starts the same but travel about 11.5 miles from Whitewater to Divide Road. Turn left, drive about five more miles to the road to the Dominguez Conservation Area sign and turn left. Drive about another five miles to Big Dominguez Campground. (Road not suitable for RVs or travel trailers.) The trail heads downstream to the Gunnison River, about 9.5 miles one way. It meets the Cactus Park trail at about six miles. Please keep your dogs under control in the vicinity of the desert bighorn sheep to avoid stressing them out, especially during hot summer months. For more information, contact the Bureau of Land Management at (970) 244–3000 or visit their website at *www.co.blm.gov/gjra/ hikinghp.htm*. **DeLorme: Colorado Atlas & Gazetteer:** Page 55 B5

ⓒⓒ Geyser Spring

Colorado has one known true geyser located about 1.25 miles (one way) from the West Fork Road (FS 535). The trailhead is not always marked, but a fenced lane leads the way to a blazed spruce tree. Cross the West Dolores River, but if it's running high, it might not be safe to cross. [**Note**: *Do not use the private bridge to cross the creek.*] The first part of the trail crosses private land and is difficult to follow. Follow the fenceline to the creek and stay on the path. The trail stays northeast of Geyser Creek. Climb gradually for about one mile. The spring is fed by the geyser, which has slight, small eruptions every 30 to 40 minutes. The spring's temperature is about 82°F. The trail is easy to moderate after crossing the river (elevations 8,600 to 9,120 feet). From Dolores, drive north on CO 145 about 13 miles to West Fork Road (FS 535). Turn left onto FS 535 and drive about 23.3 miles to the trailhead on the right just below a private residence to the southeast. You can also drive south from Telluride on CO 145 about 18.5 miles to FS 535 and turn right, drive to Dunton. The trailhead is on the left about 2.2 miles south of Dunton. For further information contact the San Juan National Forest in Dolores at (970) 882–7296 or visit their website at *www.fs.fed.us/r2/sanjuan*. *DeLorme: Colorado Atlas & Gazetteer:* Page 76 B1

ⒹⒹ Wasatch Trail

This strenuous hike takes you high above Telluride, past old mines, waterfalls, and beautiful wildflowers in the Wasatch Basin. From town to the Pandora Mill is about 14 miles following the Bear Creek and Wasatch trails and about 4,290 feet elevation gain. Town is about 2.5 miles west of the Pandora Mill, so you might want to leave a car at the mill. Start at the Bear Creek trailhead off of South Pine Street in town at about 7,960 feet. After about two miles up Bear Creek, turn right onto the trail just before the big boulder. This junction is the official start of the Wasatch Trail (Trail 508), which climbs steeply from here. You'll pass the Nellie Mine then reach a fork. Go right here. At the next junction, go left. At the East Fork Trail intersection, you can turn left and head very steeply back downhill for a loop or go right to continue to Bridal Veil Falls power plant. Once you reach the shoulder to the south of Wasatch Mountain (13,050 feet), drop down on the Wasatch Trail and stay right to go to Bridal Veil Basin (going to the left takes you to La Junta Basin). Stay left at the fork to Lewis Mine. The trail comes out at the Bridal Veil power plant on Bridal Veil Road (Trail 647). It's about 1.8 miles down the jeep road to the Pandora Mill. This trail spends a lot of time above treeline, so lightning is a real danger. Wait until the snow melts before making this traverse. For further information, contact the Uncompahgre National Forest at (970) 327–4261 or check their website at *www.fs.fed.us/r2/gmug*. *DeLorme: Colorado Atlas & Gazetteer:* Page 76 A3

(EE) Ice Lake Trail

This popular trail leads to high alpine lakes through aspen and spruce-fir forests to fields of wildflowers in July and August. Spectacular waterfalls roar along the way. To reach upper Ice Lake requires a difficult nine-mile out-and-back hike, climbing from 9,840 to 12,260 feet. Lower Ice Lake is just below treeline. The trail then climbs up a cliff, passing three waterfalls, one close to the trail. Once above treeline, be careful of lightning. Thunderstorms can come in swiftly. Upper Ice Lake is tucked in a spectacular basin. If you explore the area, please remember the tundra is fragile and stay on any trails or rock hop. From Silverton, drive north on U.S. 550 about two miles to South Mineral Creek road (FS 585). Turn left and drive about six miles just past South Mineral Creek Campground and watch for the trailhead sign to the right. For further information contact San Juan National Forest at (970) 884–2512 or check their website at *www.fs.fed.us/r2/sanjuan*. *DeLorme: Colorado Atlas & Gazetteer:* Page 76 B3

(FF) Sand Canyon/East Rock Creek

The Sand Canyon Trail is in the new Canyons of the Ancients National Monument west of Cortez. Several archaeological sites and small cliff dwellings are close to the trail. The trail is 13 miles out-and-back or 6.5 miles point-to-point. You can also make a side trip into East Rock Creek. From Cortez, drive south on U.S. 666 to CR G (McElmo Canyon Road—also the road to the airport). Turn right and drive about 12 miles west to the Sand Canyon trailhead (5,444 feet). Park on the north side of the road on the slickrock. This trail is unimproved and is marked with rock cairns across slickrock. About 1.75 miles a trail takes off to the left to go to East Rock Creek (6.5-mile out-and-back) for a shorter hike. If you continue up Sand Creek, at about 3.6 miles, you'll hike in a very sandy creek bed then come to a 0.5 mile section with 30 switchbacks gaining 680 feet. At the north trailhead is Sand Canyon Pueblo. You can leave a car here by driving north from Cortez on U.S. 666 about 5.3 miles to CR P, turn left and follow CR P. At 8.6 miles, the pavement ends and the road curves right and then left, becoming CR P.5. At a T-intersection, (CR P.5 and CR 18), turn left onto CR 18. CR 18 curves right onto CR P. Turn left on CR 16 at mile 12.7. Turn right on CR N at mile 13.5. Stay on CR N to Sand Canyon Pueblo and the north trailhead (elevation 6,840 feet) at mile 14.7. The trailhead is on the left as you're heading down a hill. There's a tiny sign that's easy to miss. There's a little parking area and no facilities. The left trail goes into Sand Canyon. The right trail goes to the Sand Canyon Pueblo ruin that is not restored. Bring water with you and avoid hiking on hot summer days. Remember all ruins and artifacts are protected by law, so leave what you find for others to enjoy! For further information contact the BLM Anasazi Heritage Center at (970) 882–4811 or visit the Canyons of the Ancients National Monument website at *www.co.blm.gov/canm/canminfo.htm*. *DeLorme: Colorado Atlas & Gazetteer:* Page 84 B2

(GG) Ute Mountain Tribal Park

Hikes in the Ute Mountain Tribal Park are by reservation only with a Ute guide. These hikes are wonderful as you visit cliff dwellings, rock art, and historical sites in small groups. The Tribal Park is just south of Mesa Verde National Park and was also home to many Ancestral Puebloan people. You'll hear about Ute history as well as information about the Wetherill brothers who explored much of this area and the Ancestral Puebloan residents. Some hikes require climbing on ladders to ledges to get to the cliff dwellings (Eagles Nest in particular). Dogs are not allowed on hikes. To reach the hikes, you must provide your own vehicle for an up to 80-mile round trip on gravel roads. One full day tour includes about three miles and five ladders. To reach the Tribal Park Visitor Center, drive south from Cortez on U.S. 160 past Towaoc to the intersection of U.S. 160 and U.S. 666. The visitor center is on the northwest corner in what looks like an old gas station. For further information, contact Ute Mountain Tribal Park at (970) 565–9653 or (970) 749–1452 or 1–800–847–5485 or visit their website at *www.utemountainute.com*. **DeLorme: Colorado Atlas & Gazetteer:** Page 84 D3

The Amphitheater above Ouray.

In Addition

Colorado's
Long Trails:
The Colorado and
Continental Divide Trails

N o Colorado hiking guide would be complete without mentioning two trails that traverse all or most of the state:

The Colorado Trail starts in the east at Waterton Canyon in the foothills southwest of Denver and traverses mountain ranges and valleys to its western end near Durango in the southwest corner of the state. Covering almost 500 miles, it crosses eight mountain ranges, seven national forests, and six wilderness areas. Some people choose to backpack this trail in one summer, while others hike sections of it over many years. Most of the trail is above 10,000 feet with a high point of 13,334 feet. One short section, the Wheeler Trail from Copper Mountain to the top of the Tenmile Range, is a featured hike in this book (see Hike 15 on page 122). For more information on the trail, contact The Colorado Trail Foundation at (303) 384–3729 (ext. 113), or visit their website at *www.coloradotrail.org*. You can buy various hiking guides describing the trail, and the website contains updates to the descriptions.

The Continental Divide Trail in Colorado starts at the Colorado-Wyoming border and travels south across the state to the Colorado–New Mexico border. Work still continues on this trail, but it is hikable. The trail is difficult as much of it is above treeline, and weather is a major factor in hiking this spectacular trail. Some people hike the trail from one end of Colorado to the other in one summer. Unless you have a lot of time, hiking sections is the more practical way to go. The trail covers 759 miles through some of Colorado's most breathtaking high country. Alberta Peak (see Hike 39 on page 292) and Parkview Mountain (see Honorable Mention L on page 170) are along the Continental Divide Trail. *Colorado's Continental Divide Trail The Official Guide* by Tom Lorang Jones breaks the trail into sections, giving excellent descriptions, tips, and other interesting facts and figures. For more information, contact the Continental Divide Trail Alliance at 1–888–909–CDTA or (303) 838–3760 or visit *www.cdtrail.org,* or contact the Continental Divide Trail Society at (410) 235–9610 or visit *www.gorp.com/cdts.*

The Art of Hiking

The Art of Hiking

When standing nose to snout with a grizzly, you're probably not too concerned with the issue of ethical behavior in the wild. No doubt you're just wetting yourself. But let's be honest. How often are you nose to snout with a grizzly? For most of us, a hike into the "wild" means loading up the 4-Runner with everything North Face and driving to a toileted trailhead. Sure, you can mourn how civilized we've become—how GPS units have replaced natural instinct and GORE-TEX, true-grit—but the silly gadgets of civilization aside, we have plenty of reason to take pride in how we've matured. With survival now on the back-burner, we've begun to reason—and it's about time—that we have a responsibility to protect, no longer just conquer, our wild places; that they, not we, are at risk. So please, do what you can. Now, in keeping with our chronic tendency to reduce everything to a list, here are some rules to remember.

Leave no trace. Always leave an area just like you found it—if not better than you found it. Avoid camping in fragile, alpine meadows and along the banks of streams and lakes. Use a lightweight camp stove versus building a wood fire. Pack up all of your trash and extra food and carry it out with you. Bury human waste at least 200 feet from water sources and under six to eight inches of topsoil. Don't bathe with soap (even biodegradable soap) in a lake or stream. Even your body oils (especially if you're wearing sunscreen) can contaminate water sources, so try to take water in a container at least 200 feet from water sources and wash and rinse there. Remember to dump the wastewater away from water sources. Another option is to use prepackaged moistened towels to wipe off sweat and dirt.

Leave no weeds. Noxious weeds tend to out-compete (overtake) our native flora, which in turn affects animals and birds that depend on them for food. Noxious weeds can be harmful to wildlife. Yes, just like birds and furry critters, we humans can carry weed seeds from one place to another. Here are a couple of things hikers can do to minimize the spread of noxious weeds. First, learn to identify noxious weeds and exotic species. You can obtain information pamphlets from the U.S. Forest Service and Colorado State University Cooperative Extension (*www.ext.colostate.edu* then look under Natural Resources). Second, regularly clean your boots, tents, packs, and hiking poles of mud and seeds. Brush your dog to remove any weed seed. Avoid camping and traveling in weed infested areas.

Stay on the trail. It's true, a path anywhere leads nowhere new, but purists will just have to get over it. Paths serve an important purpose; they limit our impact on natural areas. Straying from a designated trail may seem innocent, but it can cause damage to sensitive areas—damage that may take years to recover, if it can recover at all. Even simple shortcuts can be destructive. So, please, stay on the trail.

Keep your dog under control. You can buy a flexi-lead that allows your dog to go exploring along the trail, while allowing you the ability to reel him in should another hiker approach or should he decide to chase a deer or porcupine. Always obey leash laws and be sure to bury your dog's waste or pack it out in resealable plastic bags. In Colorado it is illegal to harass wildlife—that even includes dogs chasing squirrels. A dog on leash may also alert you to nearby wildlife you might otherwise miss.

Respect other trail users. Often you're not the only one on the trail. With the rise in popularity of multi-use trails, you'll have to learn a new kind of respect, beyond the nod and "hello" approach you're used to. You should first investigate whether you're on a multi-use trail, and assume the appropriate precautions. When you encounter motorized vehicles (ATVs, dirt bikes, 4WDs, and snowmobiles), be acutely aware. Though they should always yield to the hiker, often they're going too fast or are lost in the buzz of their engine to react to your presence. If you hear activity ahead, step off the trail just to be safe. Now, you're not likely to hear a mountain biker coming, so the best bet is to know whether you share the trail with them. Cyclists should *always* yield to hikers, but that's of little comfort to the hiker. Be aware. When you approach horses or pack animals on the trail, always step quietly off the trail, preferably on the downhill side, and let them pass. If you're wearing a large backpack, it's often a good idea to sit down. To some animals, a hiker wearing a large backpack might appear threatening. Many national forests allow domesticated grazing, primarily to sheep and cattle. Neither animal will harm you, so don't over-react if you have an encounter. Cattle will normally move out of your way. Make sure your dog(s) don't harass these animals. Respect the ranchers rights while you're enjoying yours.

GETTING INTO SHAPE

Unless you want to be sore—and possibly have to shorten your trip or vacation—be sure to get in shape before a big hike. If you're terribly out of shape, start a walking program early, preferably eight weeks in advance. Start with a 15-minute walk during your lunch hour or after work and gradually increase your walking time to an hour. You should also increase your elevation gain. Walking briskly up hills really strengthens your leg muscles and gets your heart rate up. If you work in a storied office building, take the stairs instead of the elevator. If you prefer going to a gym, walk the treadmill or use a stair-master. You can further increase your strength and endurance by walking with a loaded backpack. Stationary exercises you might consider are squats, leg lifts, sit-ups, and push-ups. Other good ways to get in shape include biking, running, aerobics, and, of course, short hikes.

PREPAREDNESS

It's been said that failing to plan means planning to fail. So do take the necessary time to plan your trip. Whether going on a short day hike or an extended backpack trip, always prepare for the worst. Simply remembering to pack a copy of the *U.S. Army Survival Manual* is not preparedness. Although it's not a bad idea if you plan on entering truly wild places, it's merely the tourniquet answer to a problem. You need to do your best to prevent the problem from arising in the first place. These days the word "survival" is often replaced with the pathetically feeble term "comfort." In order to remain comfortable (and to survive if you really want to push it), you need to concern yourself with the basics: water, food, and shelter. Don't go on a hike without having these bases covered. And don't go on a hike expecting to find these items in the woods.

Water. Even in frigid conditions, you need at least two quarts of water a day to function efficiently. Add heat and/or taxing terrain and you can bump that figure up to one gallon. That's simply a base to work from—your metabolism and your level of conditioning can raise or lower that amount. Unless you know your level, assume that you need one gallon of water a day. Now, where do you plan on getting the water?

Natural water sources can be loaded with intestinal disturbers, such as bacteria and viruses. *Giardia lamblia*, the most common of these disturbers, is a protozoan parasite that lives part of its lifecycle as a cyst in water sources. The parasite spreads when mammals (humans included) defecate in water sources. Once ingested, Giardia can induce cramping, diarrhea, vomiting, and fatigue within two days to two weeks after ingestion. Giarda is treatable with the prescription drug Flagyl. If you believe you've contracted Giardia, see a doctor immediately.

Treating water. The best and easiest solution to avoid polluted water is to carry your water with you. Yet, depending on the nature of your hike and the duration, this may not be an option—seeing as one gallon of water weighs 8.5 pounds. In that case, you'll need to look into treating water. Regardless of which method you choose, you should always carry some water with you, in case of an emergency. Save this reserve until you absolutely need it.

There are three methods of treating water: boiling, chemical treatment, and filtering. Boiling is the safest, if not simplest method because it's not dependent on variables (i.e. brand name or proper dosage). If you boil water, it's recommended that you do so for 10 to 15 minutes, though some will say just bringing the water to a boil is enough. Many may find this method impractical, since you're forced to exhaust a good deal of your fuel supply. You can opt for chemical treatment (e.g. Potable

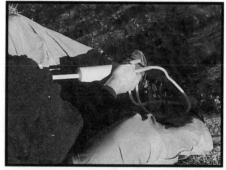

Lizann Dunegan

Aqua), which will kill Giardia but will not take care of other chemical pollutants. Other drawbacks to chemical treatments are the unpleasant taste of the water after it's treated and the length of time it takes for them to be effective, especially in Colorado's cold mountain water. You can remedy the former by adding powdered drink mix to the water. Filters are the preferred method for treating water. Filters (check the instructions to make sure) remove Giardia, organic and inorganic contaminants, and don't leave an aftertaste. Some filters also remove viruses. Water filters are far from perfect as they can easily become clogged or leak if a gasket wears out. It's always a good idea to carry a backup supply of chemical treatment tablets in case your filter decides to quit on you.

Food. If we're talking about "survival," you can go days without food, as long as you have water. But we're talking about "comfort" here. Try to avoid foods that are high in sugar and fat like candy bars and potato chips. These food types are harder to digest and are low in nutritional value. Instead, bring along foods that are easy to pack, nutritious, and high in energy (e.g. bagels, nutrition bars, dehydrated fruit, gorp,

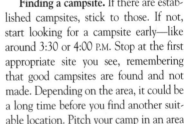

and jerky). Complex carbohydrates and protein are your best food friends. If you are on an overnight trip, easy-to-fix dinners include rice or pasta dinners and soup mixes. A few spices are lightweight and can really perk up a meal. Freeze-dried meals are nice for long trips, but are expensive and bulky. If you do a lot of long backpacks, invest in a dehydrator. For a tasty breakfast, you can fix hot oatmeal with brown sugar and reconstituted milk powder topped off with banana chips. If you like a hot drink in the morning, bring along herbal tea bags or hot chocolate. If you are a coffee junkie, you can purchase coffee that is packaged like tea bags. Pre-package all of your meals in heavy-duty resealable plastic bags to keep food from spilling in your pack. These bags can be reused to pack out trash. Pre-packaging also minimizes extra trash in the form of boxes and cans. Avoid bringing glass containers into the backcountry as broken glass can pose some serious problems. A good book on backcountry cooking is *Wilderness Ranger Cookbook* by Brunell and Swain from Falcon Press, the proceeds of which go to training wilderness rangers.

Shelter. The type of shelter you choose depends less on the conditions than on your tolerance for discomfort. Shelter comes in many forms—tent, tarp, lean-to, bivy sack, cabin, cave, etc. If you're camping in the desert, a bivy sack may suffice, but if you're near treeline and a storm is approaching, a better choice is a three or four season tent. Tents are the logical and most popular choice for most backpackers as they're lightweight and packable—and you can rest assured that you always have

Lizann Dunegan

shelter from the elements. Before you leave on your trip, anticipate what the weather and terrain will be like and bring the type of shelter that will work best for your comfort level.

Finding a campsite. If there are established campsites, stick to those. If not, start looking for a campsite early—like around 3:30 or 4:00 P.M. Stop at the first appropriate site you see, remembering that good campsites are found and not made. Depending on the area, it could be a long time before you find another suitable location. Pitch your camp in an area that's reasonably level and clear of underbrush (which can harbor insects and conceal approaching animals). Make sure the area is at least 200 feet from fragile areas like lakeshores, meadows, and stream banks. Woody stemmed plants like kinnikinnik, blueberry, and whortleberry are easily damaged, so avoid plopping your tent on top of them. Try to avoid camping above treeline, as the tundra is fragile, and you're exposing yourself to possible high winds and lightning.

If you are camping in stormy, rainy weather, look for a rock outcrop or a shelter in the trees to keep the wind from blowing your tent all night. Be sure that you don't camp under trees with dead limbs that might break off on top of you. Also, try to find an area that has an absorbent surface, such as sandy soil or forest duff. This, in addition to camping on a surface with a slight angle, will provide better drainage. By all means, don't dig trenches to provide drainage around your tent—remember you're practicing zero-impact camping.

If you're in bear country, steer clear of creek beds or animal paths. If you see any signs of a bear's presence (i.e. scat, footprints), relocate. You'll need to find a campsite near a tall tree where you can hang your food and other items that may attract bears such as deodorant, toothpaste, or soap. Carry a lightweight nylon rope with which to hang your food. As a rule, you should hang your food at least 15 feet from the ground and four feet away from the tree trunk. Trees at higher elevations don't often have branches longer than five feet so you may need to string rope between two trees or find a leaning snag. You can put food and other items in a waterproof stuff sack or a dry bag and tie one end of the rope to the stuff sack. To get the other end of the rope over the tree branch, tie a good size rock to it and gently toss the rock over the tree branch. Pull the stuff sack up until it reaches the top of the branch and tie it off securely. Don't hang your food near your tent! If possible, hang your food at least 100 feet away from your campsite. Alternatives to hanging your food are bear-proof plastic tubes and metal bear boxes. Chipmunks, ground squirrels, and pine martens will also steal your food if you don't hang it.

Lastly, think of comfort. Lie down on the ground where you intend to sleep and see if it's a good fit. Bring along an insulating pad for warmth and extra comfort. The days of using pine boughs or digging a hip depression in the ground are long gone. And for the final touch, have your tent face east. You'll appreciate the warmth of the morning sun and have a nice view to wake up to.

FIRST AID

If you plan to spend a lot of time outdoors hiking, spend a few hours and bucks to take a good wilderness or mountain-oriented first aid class. You'll not only learn first aid basics, but how to be creative miles from nowhere. The Colorado Mountain Club and specialized companies like Wilderness Medicine Institute (WMI) offer such courses. Check out WMI for course dates and locations at *wmi.nols.edu*.

Now, we know you're tough, but get 10 miles into the woods and develop a blister, and you'll wish you had carried a first aid kit. Face it; it's just plain good sense. Many companies produce lightweight, compact first aid kits. Just make sure yours contains at least the following:

First Aid

- adhesive bandages
- moleskin, duct tape or athletic tape, and/or Band-Aid's Blister Relief Compeed®
- various sterile gauze and dressings
- white surgical tape
- an Ace bandage
- an antihistamine
- aspirin, ibuprofen, or acetaminophen
- Betadine solution
- first aid book
- antacid
- tweezers
- scissors
- anti-bacterial wipes
- triple-antibiotic ointment
- plastic gloves
- sterile cotton tip applicators
- a thermometer

Here are a few tips for dealing with and hopefully preventing certain ailments.

Sunburn. To avoid sunburn, wear sunscreen (SPF 15 or higher), protective clothing, and a wide-brimmed hat when you are hiking in sunny weather. If you do get sunburned, treat the area with aloe vera gel and protect the area from further sun exposure. Protect your eyes by wearing sunglasses with UV protection, too! Colorado's high altitude means there's less atmosphere to protect you from the sun, so you can burn even on a cloudy day.

Blisters. First try to prevent blisters. Break in your boots, wear appropriate socks, and then, if you're prone to blisters, apply moleskin, Compeed, Bodyglide (1–888–263–9454), duct tape, or athletic tape *before* you start hiking to help decrease friction to that area. In case a blister develops despite your careful precautions, an effective way to treat it is to cut out a circle of moleskin and remove the center—like a donut—and place it over the blistered area. Cutting the center out will reduce the pressure applied to the sensitive skin. Then put Second Skin in the hole and tape over the whole mess. Second Skin (made by Spenco) is applied to the blister after it has popped and acts as a "second skin" to help prevent further irritation.

Insect bites and stings. The most troublesome of Colorado's insects are mosquitoes, deer flies, and gnats. Bees live at about every elevation in the state. A simple treatment for most insect bites and stings is to apply hydrocortisone 1% cream topically and to take a pain medication such as ibuprofen or acetaminophen to reduce swelling. If you forgot to pack these items, a cold compress or a paste of mud and ashes can sometimes assuage the itching and discomfort. Remove any stingers by using tweezers or scraping the area with your fingernail or a knife blade. Don't pinch the area as you'll only spread the venom.

Some hikers are highly sensitive to bites and stings and may have a serious allergic reaction that can be life threatening. Symptoms of a serious allergic reaction can include wheezing, an asthmatic attack, and shock. The treatment for this severe type of reaction is epinephrine (Adrenaline). If you know that you are sensitive to bites and stings, carry a pre-packaged kit of epinephrine (e.g. Anakit), which can be obtained only by prescription from your doctor. Also carry an antihistamine such as Benadryl.

Ticks. As you well know, ticks can carry disease, such as Rocky Mountain spotted fever and Lyme disease. The best defense is, of course, prevention. If you know you're going to be hiking through an area littered with ticks, wear long pants and a long sleeved shirt. You can apply a permethrin-based repellent to your clothing and a DEET repellent to exposed skin. During and at the end of your hike, do a spot check for ticks (and insects in general). If you do find a tick, coat the insect with Vaseline or tree sap to cut off its air supply. The tick should release its hold, but if it doesn't, grab the head of the tick firmly—with a pair of tweezers if you have them—and gently pull it away from the skin straight outward. Sometimes the mouthparts linger, embedded in your skin. If this happens, try to remove them with a disinfected needle. Clean the affected area with an anti-bacterial cleanser and then apply triple antibiotic ointment. Monitor the area for a few days. If irritation persists or a white spot develops, see a doctor for possible infection.

In Colorado, you'll want to be on the lookout for the wood tick (*Demacentor andersoni*). About 1/8 inch long with a flat body, these ticks are active from late March into early July. [See Wood Ticks Sidebar on page 103.]

Poison ivy. This skin irritant can be found most anywhere in North America and has leaflets in groups of three. Learn how to spot the plants. The oil it secretes can cause an allergic reaction in the form of blisters, usually about 12 hours after exposure. The itchy rash can last from ten days to several weeks. The best defense against these irritants is to wear protective clothing and to apply a non-prescription product called IvyBlock to exposed skin. This lotion is meant to guard against the affects of poison ivy and can be washed off with soap and water. If you know you've been exposed, wash the area as soon as possible with soap and cool water. Taking a hot shower after

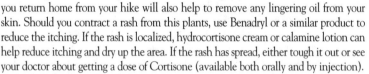

poison ivy

you return home from your hike will also help to remove any lingering oil from your skin. Should you contract a rash from this plants, use Benadryl or a similar product to reduce the itching. If the rash is localized, hydrocortisone cream or calamine lotion can help reduce itching and dry up the area. If the rash has spread, either tough it out or see your doctor about getting a dose of Cortisone (available both orally and by injection).

Snakebites. First off, snakebites are rare in North America. Unless startled or provoked, the majority of snakes will not bite. If you are wise to their habitats and keep a careful eye on the trail, you should be just fine. Though your chances of being struck are slim, it's wise to know what to do in the event you are.

If a *non-poisonous* snake bites you, allow the wound to bleed a small amount and then cleanse the wounded area with a Betadine solution (10% povidone iodine). Rinse the wound with clean water (preferably) or fresh urine (it might sound ugly, but it's sterile). Once the area is clean, cover it with triple antibiotic ointment and a clean bandage. Remember, most residual damage from snakebites, poisonous or otherwise, comes from infection, not the snake's venom. Keep the area as clean as possible and get medical attention immediately.

If you are bitten by a *poisonous* snake, remove the toxin with a suctioning device, found in a snakebite kit (like the Sawyer Extractor). If you do not have such a device, squeeze the wound—don't cut it and do NOT use your mouth for suction as the venom will enter your bloodstream through the vessels under the tongue and head straight for your heart. Then, clean the wound just as you would a nonpoisonous bite. Tie a clean band of cloth snuggly around the afflicted appendage, about an inch or so above the bite (or the rim of the swelling). This is NOT a tourniquet—you want to simply slow the blood flow, not cut it off. Loosen the band if numbness ensues. Remove the band for a minute and re-apply a little higher every ten minutes. (Do NOT try to apply ice to the bite wound to achieve slower blood flow.)

If it is your friend who's been bitten, treat him or her for shock—make him comfortable, have him lie down, elevate the legs, and keep him warm. Immobilize the affected area and remove any constricting items such as rings, watches, or restrictive clothing—swelling may occur. Splint the extremity that was bitten and keep it lower than the heart. Monitor for shock. Keep your friend hydrated but avoid painkillers and alcohol. Once your friend is stable and relatively calm, hike out to get help. The victim should get treatment within 12 hours, ideally, which usually consists of a tetanus shot, antivenin, and antibiotics.

Now, if you are alone and struck by a poisonous snake, stay calm. Hysteria will only quicken the venom's spread. Follow the procedure above and do your best to reach help. When hiking out, don't run—you'll only increase the flow of blood throughout your system. Instead, walk calmly.

In terms of poisonous snakes, only the pit viper group is found in Colorado: western rattlesnake (two subspecies, the prairie and midget faded rattlesnake) and the massasauga. These snakes are identified by a small "pit" found between the eye and nostril. The massasauga, found only in southeastern Colorado, is easily mistaken for the prairie rattler, but don't get close enough to tell them apart! Be especially careful of where you put your hands and feet with rattlers around. They enjoy sunning themselves on rock ledges and outcroppings, and often hang out in old buildings to avoid midday heat. Poisonous snakes tend to live below 8,200 feet in Colorado, a bit of reassuring news.

Dehydration. Have you ever hiked in hot weather and had a roaring headache and felt fatigued after only a few miles? More than likely you were dehydrated. Symptoms of dehydration include fatigue, headache, and decreased coordination and judgment. Dehydration can also make you more susceptible to hypothermia and frostbite. When you are hiking, your body's rate of fluid loss depends on the outside temperature, humidity, altitude, and your activity level. In the high altitude of Colorado, air tends to be dry all year long (especially in winter) and dehydration occurs more quickly with exertion. On average, a hiker walking in warm weather will lose four liters of fluid a day. That fluid loss is easily replaced by normal consumption of liquids and food. However, if a hiker is walking briskly in hot, dry weather and hauling a heavy pack, he can lose one to three liters of water an hour. It's important to always carry plenty of water and to stop often and drink fluids regularly, even if you aren't thirsty. One way to tell if you're adequately hydrated is to check the color of your urine. It should be clear. The darker yellow it is, the more dehydrated you are. With a little creativity, you can check the color in the backcountry. You can also pinch the skin on the back of your hand. If it quickly lowers itself, you're OK. If it remains in a peak, you're dehydrated.

Heat exhaustion is the result of a loss of large amounts of electrolytes and often occurs if a hiker is dehydrated and has been under heavy exertion. Common symptoms of heat exhaustion include cramping, exhaustion, fatigue, lightheadedness, and nausea. You can treat heat exhaustion by getting out of the sun, eating high energy foods, and drinking an electrolyte solution made up of one teaspoon of salt and one tablespoon of sugar dissolved in a liter of water. Drink this solution slowly over a period of one hour. Drinking plenty of fluids (preferably an electrolyte solution like Gatorade) can also prevent heat exhaustion. When drinking a lot of water, remember to snack while you drink. If you don't, you'll disrupt the electrolyte balance as you lose body salt through sweating, and possibly develop hyponatremia (water intoxication). Symptoms include nausea, vomiting, frequent urination, and altered mental states. Avoid hiking during the hottest parts of the day and wear breathable clothing, a wide brimmed hat, and sunglasses.

Hypothermia is one of the biggest dangers in the backcountry—especially for day hikers in the summertime. That may sound strange, but imagine starting out on a hike in midsummer when it's sunny and 70°F out. You're clad in nylon shorts and a cotton T-shirt. About halfway through your hike, the sky begins to cloud up and in the next hour a light drizzle or snow begins to fall, and the wind starts to pick up. Before you know it, you are soaking wet and shivering—the perfect recipe for hypothermia. More advanced signs include uncontrollable, violent shivering, decreased coordination, slurred speech, and blurred vision. When a victim's temperature falls below 91°F, the blood pressure, breathing, and pulse plummet, possibly leading to coma and death.

To avoid hypothermia, always bring a windproof/rainproof shell, a fleece jacket, Capilene tights or rainpants, gloves, and hat when you are hiking in the mountains. Avoid wearing 100 percent cotton clothing as it does not dry easily and provides no warmth when wet. Learn to adjust your clothing layers based on the temperature. If you are climbing uphill at a moderate pace you will stay warm, but when you stop for a break you'll become cold quickly, unless you add more layers of clothing. Keeping hydrated and well nourished are also important in avoiding hypothermia.

If a hiker is showing advanced signs of hypothermia, dress him in dry clothes and make sure he is wearing a hat and gloves. Place him in a sleeping bag in a tent or shelter that will protect him from the wind and other elements. Give him warm fluids (noncaffeinated) to drink and keep him awake. Put water bottles filled with warm water in the crotch and armpits to help warm him.

Frostbite. When the mercury dips below 32°F, your extremities begin to chill. If a persistent chill attacks a localized area, say your hands or your toes, the circulatory system reacts by cutting off blood flow to the affected area—the idea being to protect and preserve the body's overall temperature. And so it's death by attrition for the affected area. Ice crystals start to form from the water in the cells of the neglected tissue. Deprived of heat, nourishment, and now water, the tissue literally starves. This is frostbite.

Prevention is your best defense against this situation. Most prone to frostbite are your face, hands, and feet—so protect these areas well. Wool is the material of choice because it provides ample air space for insulation and draws moisture away from the skin. However, synthetic fabrics have recently made great strides in the cold weather clothing market. Do your research. A pair of light silk or polypro liners under your regular gloves or mittens is a good trick to keeping warm. They afford some additional warmth, but more importantly they'll allow you to remove your mitts for tedious work without exposing the skin.

Now, if your feet or hands start to feel cold or numb due to the elements, warm them as quickly as possible. Place cold hands under your armpits or bury them in your crotch. Carry hand and foot warmers if you can. If your feet are cold, change your socks. If there's plenty of room in your boots, add another pair of socks. Do remember though that constricting your feet in tight boots can restrict blood flow and actually make your feet colder more quickly. Your socks need to have breathing room if they're going to be effective. Dead air provides insulation. If your face is cold, place your warm hands over your face or simply wear a head stocking (called a balaclava).

Should your skin go numb and start to appear white and waxy but is still cold and soft, chances are you've got superficial frostbite. Rewarm as quickly as possible with skin-to-skin contact. No damage should occur. Do NOT let the area get frostbitten again!

If your skin is white and waxy but *dents* when you press on it, you have partial thickness frostbite. Rewarm as you would for superficial frostbite, but expect swelling and blisters to form. Don't massage the affected area, but do take ibuprofen for pain and reduction of tissue damage. If blisters form, you need to leave the backcountry.

If your skin is frozen hard like an ice cube, you have full thickness frostbite. Don't try to thaw the area unless you can maintain the warmth. In other words, don't stop to warm up your frostbitten feet only to head back on the trail. You'll do more damage than good. Tests have shown that hikers who walked on thawed feet did more harm, and endured more pain, than hikers who left the affected areas alone. Do your best to get out of the cold entirely and seek medical attention—which usually consists of performing a rapid rewarming in warm water (104°F–108°F) for 20 to 30 minutes. Get to a doctor as soon as possible!

The overall objective in preventing both hypothermia and frostbite is to keep the body's core warm. Protect key areas where heat escapes, like the top of the head, and maintain the proper nutrition and hydration levels. Foods that are high in calories aid the body in producing heat. Never smoke or drink alcohol when you're in situations where the cold is threatening. By affecting blood flow, these activities ultimately cool the body's core temperature.

Altitude sickness (AMS). The high lofty peaks, clear alpine lakes, and vast mountain views beckon hikers to the high country. Those who like to venture high may become victims of altitude sickness (also known as Acute Mountain Sickness—AMS). Altitude sickness is your body's reaction to insufficient oxygen in the blood due to decreased barometric pressure. While some hikers may feel lightheaded, nauseous, and experience shortness of breath at 7,000 feet, others may not experience these symptoms until they reach 10,000 feet or higher.

Slowing your ascent to high places and giving your body a chance to acclimatize to the higher elevations can prevent altitude sickness. For example, if you live at sea level and are planning a weeklong backpacking trip to elevations between 7,000 and 12,000 feet, start by staying below 7,000 feet for one night, then move to between 7,000 and 10,000 feet for another night or two. Avoid strenuous exertion and alcohol to give your body a chance to adjust to the new altitude. It's also important to eat light food and drink plenty of non-alcoholic fluids, preferably water. Loss of appetite at altitude is common, but you must eat! The prescription drug Diamox can help to prevent altitude sickness, but keep in mind that this drug does nothing to relieve the symptoms of AMS once you get it. Some people find relief from AMS by taking dimethylglycine (DMG). This supplement has been shown in studies to improve oxygen utilization. Look for it in health food stores or alternative pharmacies.

Most hikers who experience mild to moderate AMS develop a headache and/or nausea, grow lethargic, and have problems sleeping. The treatment for AMS is simple: stop heading uphill. Keep eating and drinking water and take meds for the headache. You actually need to take more breaths at altitude than at sea level, so breath a little faster without hyperventilating. If symptoms don't improve over 24 to 48 hours, descend. Once a victim descends about 2,000 to 3,000 feet, his signs will usually begin to diminish.

Severe AMS comes in two forms: High Altitude Pulmonary Edema (HAPE) and High Altitude Cerebral Edema (HACE). HAPE, an accumulation of fluid in the lungs, can also occur above 8,000 feet. Symptoms include rapid heart rate, shortness of breath at rest, AMS symptoms, dry cough developing into a wet cough, gurgling sounds, flu-like or bronchitis symptoms, and lack of muscle coordination. HAPE is life threatening so descend immediately, at least 2,000 to 4,000 feet. HACE usually occurs above 12,000 feet but sometimes occurs above 10,000 feet. Symptoms are similar to HAPE but also include seizures, hallucinations, paralysis, and vision disturbances. You have to descend immediately as HACE is also life threatening.

Hantavirus Pulmonary Syndrome (HPS). Deer mice spread the virus that causes HPS, and humans contract it from breathing it in, usually when they've disturbed an area with dust and mice feces from nests or surfaces with mice droppings or urine. Exposure to large numbers of rodents and their feces or urine presents the greatest risk. As hikers, we sometimes enter old buildings, and often deer mice live in these places. We may not be around long enough to be exposed, but do be aware of this disease. About half the people who develop HPS die. Symptoms are flu-like and appear about two to three weeks after exposure. After initial symptoms, a dry cough and shortness of breath follow. Breathing is difficult. If you even think you might have HPS, see a doctor immediately!

NATURAL HAZARDS

Besides tripping over a rock or tree root on the trail, there are some real hazards to be aware of while hiking. Colorado doesn't have the plethora of poisonous snakes and plants, insects, and grizzly bears found in other parts of the United States, but there are a few weather conditions and predators to take into account.

Lightning. Thunderstorms build over the mountains almost every day during the summer. Lightning is generated by thunderheads and can strike without warning, even several miles away from the nearest overhead cloud. The best rule of thumb is to start leaving exposed peaks, ridges, and canyon rims by about noon. This time can vary a little depending on storm buildup. Keep an eye on cloud formation and don't underestimate how fast a storm can build. The bigger they get, the more likely a thunderstorm will happen. Lightning takes the path of least resistance, so if you're the high point, it might choose you. Ducking under a rock overhang is likewise dangerous as you form the shortest path between the rock and ground. If you dash below treeline, avoid standing under the only or the tallest tree. If you are caught above treeline, stay away from anything metal you might be carrying, Move down off the ridge slightly to a low, treeless point and squat until the storm passes. If you have an insulating pad, squat on it. Avoid having both your hands and feet touching the ground at once and never lay flat. Minimize yourself as a target. If you hear a buzzing sound or feel your hair standing on end, move quickly as an electrical charge is building up. For additional information check out the National Lightning Safety Institute's website at *www.lightningsafety.com*.

Flash floods. On July 31, 1976, a torrential downpour unleashed by a thunderstorm dumped tons of water into the Big Thompson watershed near Estes Park. Within hours, a wall of water moved down the narrow canyon killing 139 people and causing over $30 million in property damage. The spooky thing about flash floods, especially in western canyons, is that they can appear out of nowhere from a storm many miles away. While hiking or driving in canyons, keep an eye on the weather. Always climb to safety if danger threatens. Flash floods usually subside quickly, so be patient and don't cross a swollen stream.

Bears. Colorado theoretically has no grizzly bear population, although some rumors exist about sightings. Black bears are plentiful, especially in Gambel oak and aspen ecosystems. Here are some tips in case you and a bear scare each other. Most of all, avoid scaring a bear. Watch for bear tracks (five toes) and droppings (sizable with leaves, partly digested berries, seeds, and/or animal fur). Talk, clap your hands, or sing where visibility or hearing are limited. Keep a clean camp, hang food, and don't sleep in the clothes you wore while cooking. Be especially careful in spring to avoid getting between a mother and her cubs. In late summer and fall bears are busy eating berries and acorns to fatten up for winter, so be extra careful around berry bushes and Gambel oak. If you do encounter a bear, move away slowly while facing the bear, talk softly, and avoid direct eye contact. Give the bear room to escape. Since bears are very curious, it might stand upright to get a better whiff of you, and it may even charge you to try to intimidate you. Try to stay calm. If a bear does attack you, fight back with anything you have handy. Unleashed dogs have been known to come running back to their owners with a bear close behind. Keep your dog on a leash or leave it at home. (Advice from the Colorado Division of Wildlife.) For more bear information, check out *www.montana.com/rattlesnake/main.htm.*

Mountain lions. Mountain lions appear to be getting more comfortable around humans as long as deer (their favorite prey) are in an area with adequate cover. Usually elusive and quiet, lions rarely attack people, yet Colorado has seen at least two lion-caused deaths in recent years. If you meet a lion, give it a chance to escape. Stay calm and talk firmly to it. Back away slowly while facing the lion. If you run, you'll only encourage the curious cat to chase you. Make yourself look large by opening a jacket, if you have one, or waving your hiking poles. If the lion behaves aggressively throw stones, sticks, or whatever you can while remaining tall. If a lion does attack, fight for your life with anything you can grab. (Advice from the Colorado Division of Wildlife.)

Moose. Because moose have very few natural predators, they don't fear humans like other animals. You might find moose in sagebrush and wetter areas of willow, aspen, pine, or beaver habitats. Mothers with calves, as well as bulls during mating season, can be particularly aggressive. If a moose threatens you, back away slowly and talk calmly to it. Keep your pets away from moose to avoid agitation. (Advice from the Colorado Division of Wildlife.)

Other considerations. Hunting is a popular sport in Colorado, especially during rifle season in October and November. Hiking is still enjoyable in those months in many areas, so just take a few precautions. First, learn when the different hunting seasons start and end in the mountains and on the plains. Hunting in the high country using archery typically starts in late August, joined by muzzleloading season in early September. Hunters using these methods have to be close enough to tell the difference between game and humans. But don't be surprised to see hunters in camo outfits carrying bows or muzzleloading rifles around during their season. Rifle season typically starts in early to mid-October and goes into mid-November in the high country. During this time frame, be sure to wear at least a blaze orange hat, and possibly put an orange vest over your pack. For yearly hunting dates, check hunting literature at sporting goods stores, call the Colorado Division of Wildlife at (303) 297–1192, or check their website at *wildlife.state.co.us/hunt.* If you'd feel more comfortable without hunters around, hike in national parks and monuments and some state parks as well as various local parks where hunting is not allowed.

NAVIGATION

Whether you are going on a short hike in a familiar area or planning a weeklong backpack trip, you should always be equipped with the proper navigational equipment—at the very least a detailed map and a sturdy compass. These tools are only useful if you know how to use them. Courses and books are available, so make sure your skills are up to snuff.

Maps. There are many different types of maps available to help you find your way on the trail. Easiest to find are Forest Service maps and Bureau of Land Management (BLM) maps. These maps tend to cover large areas, so be sure they are detailed enough for your particular trip. You can also obtain national park maps as well as high quality maps from private companies and trail groups. These maps can be obtained from either outdoor stores or ranger stations. Being large, these maps are best used for trip planning and driving, but not to navigate in the backcountry.

U.S. Geological Survey (USGS) topographic maps (topos) are particularly popular with hikers—especially serious backcountry hikers. These maps contain the standard map symbols such as roads, lakes, and rivers, as well as contour lines that show the details of the trail terrain like ridges, valleys, passes, and mountain peaks. The 7.5-minute series (one inch on the map equals approximately two-fifths of a mile on the ground) provides the closest inspection available. USGS maps are available by mail (U.S. Geological Survey, Map Distribution Branch, P.O. Box 25286, Denver, CO 80225), or you can visit them online at *mapping.usgs.gov/esic/to_order.html*.

National Geographic's *Trails Illustrated* covers much of Colorado. Waterproof and tear-proof, these maps are excellent for trip planning. If you need maps for detailed navigation, the scale may not be small enough, as opposed to 7.5-minute quads. Many outdoor stores carry *Trails Illustrated* maps, or you can visit them online at *www.trailsillustrated.com*. These maps often depict trails more accurately than USGS maps because *Trails Illustrated* tries to keep up to date on trail changes and additions.

If you want to check out the high-tech world of maps, you can purchase topographic maps on CD-ROM. These software-mapping programs let you select a route on your computer, print it out, and then take it with you on the trail. Some software mapping programs let you insert symbols and labels, download waypoints from a GPS unit, and export the maps to other software programs. Mapping software programs such as DeLorme's TopoUSA (*www.delorme.com*) and MAPTECH's Terrain Navigator (*www.maptech.com*) let you do all of these things and more. Check out topos on websites such as *www.topozone.com*, too.

The art of map reading is a skill that you can develop by first practicing in an area you are familiar with. To begin, orient the map so it's lined up in the correct direction (i.e. north on the map is lined up with true north). Next, familiarize yourself with the map symbols and try to match them up with terrain features around you such as a high ridge, mountain peak, river, or lake. If you are practicing with a USGS map notice the contour lines. On gentler terrain these contour lines are spaced farther apart, and on steeper terrain they are closer together. Pick a short loop trail and stop frequently to check your position on the map. As you practice map reading, you'll learn how to anticipate a steep section on the trail or a good place to take a rest break.

Compasses. First off, the sun is not a substitute for a compass. So, what kind of compass should you have? Here are some characteristics you should look for: a rectangular base with detailed scales, a liquid-filled housing, protective housing, a sighting line on the mirror, luminous alignment and back-bearing arrows, a luminous north-seeking arrow, and a well-defined bezel ring.

You can learn compass basics by reading the detailed instructions included with your compass. If you want to fine-tune your compass skills, sign up for an orienteering class or purchase a book on compass reading. Once you've learned the basic skills on using a compass, remember to practice these skills before you head into the backcountry.

Courtesy Johnson Outdoors

Because magnetic north keeps moving around the north pole and topo maps use true north, using a map and compass together requires making adjustments for declination (the difference between magnetic and true north). Topo maps show the declination, but if you are looking at a 1970 map, the declination has changed. To determine the declination as of today, you can download shareware for Windows from the USGS (sorry Mac users!). Check out their website *geomag.usgs.gov.*

Global Positioning Systems (GPS). If you are a klutz at using a compass, you may be interested in checking out the technical wizardry of the GPS device. The GPS was developed by the Pentagon and works off 24 NAVSTAR satellites, which were designed to guide missiles to their targets. A GPS device is a handheld unit that calculates your latitude and longitude with the easy press of a button. The Department of Defense used to scramble the satellite signals a bit to prevent civilians (and spies!) from getting extremely accurate readings, but that practice was discontinued in May of 2000, and GPS units now provide nearly pinpoint accuracy (within 30 to 60 feet).

There are many different types of GPS units available, and they range in price from $100 to $400. In general, all GPS units have a display screen and keypad where you input information. In addition to acting as a compass, the unit allows you to plot your route, retrace your path, track your traveling speed, find the mileage between waypoints (straight line distance), and calculate the total mileage of your route. Despite the advances in GPS technology, don't put all of your trust in your GPS. Per the USGS, "GPS units do not replace basic map and compass skills." Keep in mind that these devices don't pick up signals indoors, in heavily wooded areas, or in deep valleys. And most important to remember, they run on batteries.

Pedometers. A pedometer is a handy device that

Magellan GPS unit

Courtesy Magellan Systems

can track your mileage as you hike. This device is a small, clip-on unit with a digital display that calculates your hiking distance in miles or kilometers based on your walking stride. Some units also calculate the calories you burn and your total hiking time. Pedometers are available at most large outdoor stores and range in price from $20 to $40.

TRIP PLANNING

Planning your hiking adventure begins with letting a friend or relative know your trip itinerary so they can call for help if you don't return at your scheduled time. Your next task is to make sure you are outfitted to experience the risks and rewards of the trail. This section highlights gear and clothing you may want to take with you to get the most out of your hike.

EQUIPMENT

With the outdoor market currently flooded with products, many of which are pure gimmickry, it seems impossible to both differentiate and choose. Do I really need a tropical-fish-lined collapsible shower? (No, you don't.) The only defense against the maddening quantity of items thrust in your face is to think practically—and to do so before you go shopping. The worst buys are impulsive buys. Since most of your name brands will differ only slightly in quality, it's best to know what you're looking for in terms of function. Buy only what you need. You will, don't forget, be carrying what you've bought on your back. Here are some things to keep in mind before you go shopping. Your pack should weigh no more than 30 percent of your body weight.

Clothes. Clothing is your armor against Mother Nature's little surprises. Colorado's weather can range from blistering heat to brutal cold, and hikers should

Day Hikes

- daypack
- water and water bottles/water hydration system
- food and high energy snacks
- first aid kit
- headlamp/flashlight with extra batteries and bulbs
- maps and compass/GPS unit
- knife/multi-purpose tool
- sunscreen and sunglasses
- matches in waterproof container and fire starter
- insulating top and bottom layers (fleece, wool, etc.)
- raingear
- winter hat and gloves
- wide-brimmed sun hat
- insect repellant
- backpacker's trowel, toilet paper, and resealable plastic bags
- whistle and/or mirror
- space blanket/bag
- camera/film
- guidebook
- watch
- water treatment tablets
- wet ones or other wet wipes
- Colorado Outdoor Recreation Search & Rescue Card
- hand and foot warmers if hiking high
- duct tape for repairs
- extra socks
- gaiters depending on season

be prepared for any possibility, especially when hiking in mountainous areas. Expect snow any month of the year and afternoon thunderstorms from June into September. The sun may feel hot until a cloud comes along, and instantly the air temperature feels very cool. With the changeable weather and cool temperatures at high altitudes, adequate rain protection and layered clothes are good ideas.

During the summer, your main consideration is protecting your skin from sunburn and having layers to adapt to changeable weather conditions. Wearing long pants and a long sleeve shirt made out of materials such as Supplex nylon will protect your skin from the damaging rays of the sun. Avoid wearing 100 percent cotton, as it does not dry easily and offers no warmth when wet.

Since the weather can change from warm to chilly quickly, if you wear a t-shirt and shorts, make sure you have top and bottom "insulating" layers (see below) in your pack. Aside from keeping you warm, this layer needs to "breathe" so you stay dry while hiking. A fabric that provides insulation and dries quickly is fleece. It's interesting to note that this one-of-a-kind fabric is made out of recycled plastic. Purchasing a zip-up jacket or pullover made of this material is highly recommended.

Another important layer is the "shell" layer. You'll need some type of waterproof, windproof, breathable jacket that'll fit over all of your other layers. It should have a large hood that fits over a hat. You'll also need a good pair of rain pants made from a similar waterproof, breathable fabric. A fabric that easily fits the bill is GORE-TEX. However, while a quality GORE-TEX jacket can range in price from $100 to $450, you should know that there are more affordable fabrics out there that work just as well.

Now that you've learned the basics of layering, you can't forget to protect your hands and face. In cold, windy, rainy, or snowy weather you'll need a hat made of wool or fleece and insulated, waterproof gloves that will keep your hands warm and toasty. Buying a pair of light silk or polypro liners to wear under your regular gloves or mittens is a good idea. They'll allow you to remove your outer-gloves for tedious work without exposing the skin. Even in summer, a light winter hat and gloves can really help, too. Remember over 50 percent of our body heat is lost through our head,

Overnight Trips (also include what's listed for Day Hikes)

- backpack and waterproof rain cover
- bandanna
- biodegradable soap
- collapsible water container (2–3 gallon capacity)
- clothing—extra wool socks, shirt and shorts, long pants
- cook set/utensils and pot scrubber
- stuff sacks to store gear
- extra plastic resealable bags
- garbage bags
- journal/pen
- nylon rope to hang food
- long underwear
- permit (if required)
- repair kit (tent, stove, pack, etc.)
- sandals or running shoes to wear around camp and to ford streams
- sleeping bag
- waterproof stuff sacks (one for hanging food)
- insulating ground pad
- hand towel
- stove and fuel
- tent and ground cloth
- toiletry items
- water filter

so if your extremities are cold, put on that hat! Carry packages of hand and foot warmers if you plan to be above treeline in case it gets really cold or snowy.

A handy item for those hot canyon or plains hikes is the neck cooler. You have to soak it in water for about 20 minutes, but then it stays damp and helps cool your body through your neck. Even wrapping a wet bandanna around your neck helps cool your body.

For winter hiking or snowshoeing, you'll need yet a lower "wicking" layer of long underwear that keeps perspiration away from your skin. Wearing long underwear made from synthetic fibers such as Capilene, Coolmax, or Thermax is an excellent choice. These fabrics wick moisture away from the skin and draw it toward the next layer of clothing where it then evaporates. Avoid wearing long underwear made of cotton as it is slow to dry and keeps moisture next to your skin.

Footwear. If you have any extra money to spend on your trip, put that money into boots or trail shoes. Poor-fitting boots will bring a hike to a halt faster than anything else. To avoid this annoyance, buy boots that provide support and are lightweight and flexible. When you purchase footwear, go to an outdoor store that specializes in backpacking and camping equipment. Knowledgeable salespeople can really help you find the right boot and the right fit for the type of hiking/backpacking you want to do. A lightweight hiking boot that can be waterproofed is usually adequate for most day hikes and short backpacks. Trail running shoes provide a little extra cushion and are made in a high-top style that many people wear for hiking. These running shoes are lighter, more flexible, and more breathable than hiking boots. Sturdier boots may be your best bet for rugged trails and multi-day backpacks. If you know you'll be hiking in wet weather or crossing streams or muddy areas often, purchase boots or shoes with a GORE-TEX liner, which will help keep your feet dry. Especially during spring and early summer when trails are muddy or snowy, make sure you wear waterproofed boots for maximum dryness. Walking around mud holes and snow damages wet ground and makes a bigger muddy mess. Get muddy! It's easier to clean your boots than repair damaged vegetation.

When buying your boots, be sure to wear the same type of socks you'll be wearing on the trail. If the boots you're buying are for heavy-duty or cold weather hiking, try the boots on while wearing two pairs of socks. Speaking of socks, a good sock combination is to wear a thinner sock made of wool or polypro/nylon covered by a heavier outer sock made of wool or wool/acrylic blend. New style socks such as SmartWool or Thorlos are excellent choices. The inner sock protects the foot from the rubbing effects of the outer sock and prevents blisters. Many outdoor stores have some type of ramp to simulate hiking uphill and downhill. Be sure to take advantage of this test, as toe-jamming boot fronts can be very painful and debilitating on the downhill trek.

Once you've purchased your footwear, be sure to break them in before you hit the trail. New footwear is often stiff and needs to be stretched and molded to your foot. A little leather conditioner such as Lexol can help the break-in process without major destruction to your foot in the process.

Hiking poles. Hiking with poles brings interesting comments ranging from "There's no snow now" to "Wow! I wish I had a pair of those on this trail!" Hiking poles help with balance and more importantly take pressure off your knees. With Colorado's non-flat terrain, hiking poles are a smart investment for many years of hiking. The ones with shock absorbers are easier on your elbows and your knees. Some poles even come with a camera attachment to be used as a monopod. And heaven forbid you meet a mountain lion, bear, or unfriendly dog, those poles make you look a lot bigger.

Packs. No matter what type of hiking you do you'll need a pack of some sort to carry the basic trail essentials. There are a variety of backpacks on the market, but let's first discuss what you intend to use it for. Day hikes or overnight trips?

If you plan on doing a day hike, a daypack should have some of the following characteristics: a padded hip belt that's at least two inches in diameter (avoid packs with only a small nylon piece of webbing for a hip belt); a chest strap (the chest strap helps stabilize the pack against your body); external pockets to carry water and other items

Courtesy Johnson Coleman

that you want easy access to; an internal pocket to hold keys, a knife, a wallet, and other miscellaneous items; an external lashing system to hold a jacket; and maybe a hydration pocket for carrying a hydration system (which consists of a water bladder with an attachable drinking hose).

For short hikes, some hikers like to use a fanny pack to store just a camera, food, a compass, a map, and other trail essentials. Most fanny packs have pockets for two water bottles and a padded hip belt.

If you intend to do an extended, overnight trip, there are multiple considerations. First off, you need to decide what kind of framed pack you want. There are two backpack types for backpacking: the internal frame and the external frame. An internal frame pack rests closer to your body, making it more stable and easier to balance when hiking over rough terrain. An external frame pack is just that, an aluminum frame attached to the exterior of the pack. An external frame pack is better for long backpack trips because it distributes the pack weight better, and you can carry heavier loads. It's easier to pack, and your gear is more accessible. It also offers better back ventilation in hot weather.

The most critical measurement for fitting a pack is torso length. The pack needs to rest evenly on your hips without sagging. A good pack will come in two or three sizes and have straps and hip belts that are adjustable according to your body size and characteristics.

When you purchase a backpack, go to an outdoor store with salespeople who are knowledgeable in how to properly fit a pack. Once the pack is fitted for you, load the pack with the amount of weight you plan on taking on the trail. The weight of the pack should be distributed evenly and you should be able to swing your arms and walk briskly without feeling out of balance. Another good technique for evaluating a pack is to walk up and down stairs and make quick turns to the right and to the left to be sure the pack doesn't feel out of balance.

Other features that are nice to have on a backpack include a removable day pack or fanny pack, external pockets for extra water, and extra lash points to attach a jacket or other items. Remember all these extra features add weight to the basic pack, cutting down on the amount of other stuff you can carry.

Sleeping bags and pads. Sleeping bags are rated by temperature. You can purchase a bag made of synthetic fiber such as Polarguard HV or DuPont Hollofil II, or you can buy a goose down bag. Goose down bags are more expensive, but they have a higher insulating capacity by weight and will keep their loft longer. You'll want to purchase a bag with a temperature rating that fits the time of year and conditions you are most likely to camp in. One caveat: the techno-standard for temperature ratings is far from perfect. Ratings vary from manufacturer to manufacturer, so to protect yourself you should purchase a bag rated 10 to 15 degrees below the temperature you expect to be camping in. Synthetic bags are more resistant to water than down bags, but many down bags are now made with a GORE-TEX shell that helps to repel water. Down bags are also more compressible than synthetic bags and take up less room in your pack, which is an important consideration if you are planning a multi-day backpack trip. Make sure to buy a compression stuff sack for your sleeping bag to minimize the space it consumes in your backpack. Features to look for in a sleeping bag include: a mummy style bag, a hood you can cinch down around your head in cold weather, and draft tubes along the zippers that help keep heat in and drafts out. Some sleeping bags are designed especially for a woman's anatomy.

You'll also want a sleeping pad to provide insulation and padding from the cold ground. There are different types of sleeping pads available, from the more expensive self-inflating air mattresses like Therm-a-Rest to the less expensive closed-cell foam pads (e.g., Ridge Rest). Self-inflating air mattresses are usually heavier than closed-cell foam mattresses and are prone to punctures but can be repaired.

Tents. The tent is your home away from home while on the trail. It provides protection from wind, snow, rain, and insects. A three-season tent is a good choice for backpacking and can range in price from $100 to $500. These lightweight and versatile tents provide protection in all types of weather, except heavy snowstorms or high winds, and range in weight from four to eight pounds. Look for a tent that's easy to set up and will easily fit two people with gear. Dome type tents usually offer more headroom and places to store gear. Other tent designs include a vestibule where you can store wet boots. Some nice-to-have items in a tent include interior pockets to store small items and lashing points to hang a clothesline. Most three-season tents also come with stakes so you can secure the tent in high winds. Staking a tent in Colorado is usually a must—winds come up suddenly, and many an unstaked tent has blown down the hill. Before you purchase a tent, set it

Courtesy Eureka

up and take it down a few times to be sure it is easy to handle. Also, sit inside the tent and make sure it has enough room for you and your gear.

Cell phones. Many hikers are carrying their cell phones into the backcountry these days in case of emergency. That's fine and good, but please know that cell phone coverage is often poor to nonexistent in valleys, canyons, and thick forest. More importantly, people have started to call for help because they're tired or lost.

Let's go back to being prepared. You are responsible for yourself in the backcountry. Use your brain to avoid problems, and if you do encounter one, first use your brain to try to correct the situation. Only use your cell phone, if it works, in cases of true emergencies.

HIKING WITH CHILDREN

Hiking with children isn't a matter of how many miles you can cover or how much elevation gain you make in a day; it's about seeing and experiencing nature through their eyes.

Kids like to explore and have fun. They like to stop and point out bugs and plants, look under rocks, jump in puddles, and throw sticks. If you're taking a toddler or young child on a hike, start with a trail that you're familiar with. Trails that have interesting things for kids, like piles of leaves to play in or a small stream to wade through during the summer, will make the hike much more enjoyable for them and will keep them from getting bored.

You can keep your child's attention if you have a strategy before starting on the trail. Using games is not only an effective way to keep a child's attention, it's also a great way to teach him or her about nature. Play hide and seek, where your child is the mouse and you are the hawk. Quiz children on the names of plants and animals.

Courtesy Johnson Outdoors

If your children are old enough, let them carry their own daypack filled with snacks and water. So that you are sure to go at their pace and not yours, let them lead the way. Playing follow the leader works particularly well when you have a group of children. Have each child take a turn at being the leader. *Sharing Nature with Children* by Joseph Cornell, Dawn Publications, describes excellent activities such as those above.

With children, a lot of clothing is key. You always want to bring extra clothing for your children no matter what the season. In the winter, have your children wear wool socks, and warm layers such as long underwear, a polar fleece jacket and hat, wool mittens, and good winter parka. It's not a bad idea to have these along in late fall and early spring as well. Good footwear is also important. A sturdy pair of high top tennis shoes or lightweight hiking boots are the best bet for little ones. If you're hiking in the summer near a lake or stream, bring along a pair of old sneakers that your child can put on when he wants to go exploring in the water. Remember when you're near any type of water, always watch your child at all times. Also, keep a close eye on teething toddlers who may decide a rock or a poison mushroom is an interesting item to put in their mouth.

From spring through fall, you'll want your kids to wear a wide brimmed hat to keep their face, head, and ears protected from the hot sun. Also, make sure your children wear sunscreen at all times. Choose a brand without Paba—children have sensitive skin and may have an allergic reaction to sunscreen that contains Paba. If you are hiking with a child younger than six months, don't use sunscreen or insect repellent.

Instead, be sure that their head, face, neck, and ears are protected from the sun with a wide brimmed hat, and that all other skin exposed to the sun is protected with the appropriate clothing.

Remember that food is fun. Kids like snacks so it's important to bring a lot of munchies for the trail. Stopping often for snack breaks is a fun way to keep the trail interesting. Raisins, apples, granola bars, crackers and cheese, Cheerios, and trail mix all make great snacks. If your child is old enough to carry his/her own backpack, fill it with treats before you leave. If your kids don't like drinking water, you can bring boxes of fruit juice.

Avoid poorly designed child-carrying packs—you don't want to break your back carrying your child. Most child-carrying backpacks designed to hold a 40-pound child will contain a large carrying pocket to hold diapers and other items. Some have an optional rain/sun hood. Tough Traveler (1–800–GO–TOUGH or *www.toughtraveler.com*) is a company that specializes in making backpacks for carrying children and other outdoor gear for children.

HIKING WITH YOUR DOG

Bringing your furry friend with you is always more fun than leaving him behind. Our canine pals make great trail buddies because they never complain and always make good company. Hiking with your dog can be a rewarding experience, especially if you plan ahead.

Getting your dog in shape. Before you plan outdoor adventures with your dog, make sure he's in shape for the trail. Getting your dog into shape takes the same discipline as getting yourself into shape, but luckily, your dog can get in shape with you. Take your dog with you on your daily runs or walks. If there is a park near your house, hit a tennis ball or play Frisbee with your dog.

Swimming is also an excellent way to get your dog into shape. If there is a lake or river near where you live and your dog likes the water, have him retrieve a tennis ball or stick. Gradually build your dog's stamina up over a two to three month period. A good rule of thumb is to assume that your dog will travel twice as far as you will on the trail. If you plan on doing a five-mile hike, be sure your dog is in shape for a ten-mile hike.

Training your dog for the trail. Before you go on your first hiking adventure with your dog, be sure he has a firm grasp on the basics of canine etiquette and behavior. Make sure he can sit, lay down, stay, and come. One of the most important commands you can teach your canine pal is to "come" under any situation. It's easy for your friend's nose to lead him astray or possibly get lost. Another helpful command is the "get behind" command. When you're on a hiking trail that's narrow, you can have your dog follow behind you when other trail users approach. Nothing is more bothersome than an enthusiastic dog that runs back and forth on the trail and disrupts the peace of the trail for others. When you see other trail users approaching you on the trail, give them the right of way by quietly stepping off the trail and making your dog lie down and stay until they pass. The best bet is to keep your dog on a leash to prevent injury to him and to avoid harassing other hikers, horses, and wildlife. Complaints about dogs in the backcountry are on the rise. Be a responsible dog owner to make sure you can keep taking your buddy in the backcountry with you.

Equipment. The most critical pieces of equipment you can invest in for your dog are proper identification and a sturdy leash. Flexi-leads work well for hiking because they give your dog more freedom to explore but still leave you in control. Make sure your dog has identification that includes your name and address and a number for your veterinarian. Other forms of identification for your dog include a tattoo or a microchip. You should consult your veterinarian for more information on these last two options.

The next piece of equipment you'll want to consider is a pack for your dog. By no means should you hold all of your dog's essentials in your pack—let him carry his own gear! Dogs that are in good shape and don't have physical problems can carry up to 25 percent of their own weight for multiple days.

Companies that make good quality packs include RuffWear (1–888–RUFF–WEAR; *www.ruffwear.com*) and Wolf Packs (1–541–482–7669; *www.wolf packs.com*). Most packs are fitted by a dog's weight and girth measurement. Companies that make dog packs generally include guidelines to help you pick out the size that's right for your dog. Some characteristics to look for when purchasing a pack for your dog include: a harness that contains two padded girth straps, a padded chest strap, leash attachments, removable saddle bags, internal water bladders, and external gear cords.

You can introduce your dog to the pack by first placing the empty pack on his back and letting him wear it around the yard. Keep an eye on him during this first introduction. He may decide to chew through the straps if you aren't watching him closely. Once he learns to treat the pack as an object of fun and not a foreign enemy, fill the pack evenly on both sides with a few ounces of dog food in resealable plastic bags. Have your dog wear his pack on your daily walks for a period of two to three weeks. Each week add a little more weight to the pack until your dog will accept carrying the maximum amount of weight he can carry.

You can also purchase collapsible water and dog food bowls for your dog. Plastic storage containers also work well and double to protect your dog's food from getting wet. Some dogs don't like the collapsible bowls, so see what works before heading into the backcountry. These bowls are lightweight and can easily be stashed into your pack or your dog's. If you are hiking on rocky terrain or in the snow, you can purchase footwear for your dog that will protect his feet from cuts and bruises. All of these products can be purchased from RuffWear.

The following is a checklist of items to bring when you take your dog hiking: water bowls, a comb, a collar and a leash, dog food, a dog pack, flea/tick powder, paw protection, water, resealable plastic bags, and a first-aid kit that contains eye ointment, tweezers, scissors, stretchy foot wrap, gauze, antibacterial wash, sterile cotton tip applicators, antibiotic ointment, and cotton wrap. You might consider carrying saline solution for contact lenses or for flushing any doggie wounds. For backpacking, consider bringing a pad or mat to put in your tent for your dog. Never leave your dog tied up in camp unattended. He might become a meal for a predator.

Cleaning up after your dog. In popular areas in Colorado, dog feces are becoming a health problem. Although it sounds awful, use resealable plastic bags to pick up and carry out your dog's waste or bury them like human feces.

Barking dogs. Most people hike and backpack to escape the sounds of the city, including barking dogs. If your dog is a barker, best to leave him at home to avoid dogs getting any more bad raps in the backcountry.

Bears and moose. If a dog discovers and provokes a bear or a moose, and the bear starts chasing him, you'll probably be the destination of this mad chase. In bear and moose country, keep your dog on a leash for his own safety.

Lost dogs. It's not unusual for an unleashed dog to stray from its owner, only to spoil a trip while you hunt for the wayward pooch who may never be seen again. If your dog does not respond well to voice commands, keep it leashed for its own safety.

First aid for your dog. Your dog is just as prone—if not more prone—to getting in trouble on the trail as you are, so be prepared. Here's a run down of the more likely misfortunes that might befall your little friend. A special thanks to Ed Hastain, D.V.M., Breckenridge, for providing insight to potential dog first-aid needs in Colorado.

Bees and wasps. If a bee or wasp stings your dog, remove the stinger with a pair of tweezers and place a mudpack or a cloth dipped in cold water over the affected area.

Porcupines. One good reason to keep your dog on leash is to prevent it from getting a nose full of porcupine quills. You may be able to remove the quills with a pair of pliers, but a vet is the best person to do this nasty job because most dogs need to be sedated.

Heat stroke. Avoid hiking with your dog in really hot weather. Dogs with heat stroke will pant excessively, lie down and refuse to get up, and become lethargic and disoriented. If your dog shows any of these signs on the trail, have him lie down in the shade. If you are near a stream, pour cool water over your dog's entire body to help bring his body temperature back to normal.

Dehydration. Dogs may dehydrate faster than we humans, so make sure your dog is drinking enough water.

Heartworm. Dogs get heartworms from mosquitoes which carry the disease in the prime mosquito months of July and August. Giving your dog a monthly pill prescribed by your veterinarian easily prevents this condition. Heartworm is usually a problem only in warmer areas along rivers in Colorado. If you spend much time in these places, make sure to treat your dog for heartworm.

Plant pitfalls. Plant hazards include burrs, thorns, thistles, and poison ivy. If you find any burrs, foxtails, or thistles on your dog, remove them as soon as possible before they become an unmanageable mat. Thorns can pierce a dog's foot and cause a great deal of pain. If you see that your dog is lame, stop and check his feet for thorns. Dogs are immune to poison ivy but they can pick up the sticky, oily substance from the plant and transfer it to you.

Protect those paws. Be sure to keep your dog's nails trimmed so he avoids getting soft tissue or joint injuries. If your dog slows and refuses to go on, check to see that his paws aren't torn or worn. You can protect your dog's paws from trail hazards such as sharp gravel, talus, ice, snowballs, and thorns by purchasing dog boots.

Ticks and fleas. Dogs can get Rocky Mountain spotted fever from ticks, as well as other diseases, like Lyme disease (though not in Colorado). Before you hit the trail, treat your dog with a flea and tick spray or powder. You can also ask your veterinarian about a once-a-month pour-on treatment that repels fleas and ticks.

Mosquitoes and deer flies. These little flying machines can do a job on your dog's snout and ears. Best bet is to spray your dog with fly repellant for horses to discourage both pests from bothering your dog.

Giardia. Dogs can get giardia, which results in diarrhea. It is usually not debilitating, but definitely messy. Many dogs in Colorado have developed a tolerance to giardia. For dogs coming from other states, a vaccine against giardia is available.

Mushrooms. Make sure your dog doesn't sample mushrooms along the trail. They could be poisonous to him, but he doesn't know that.

Websites. A number of websites have excellent hints about hiking and backpacking with your dog. Suggested sites include: *www.outdoor-dog.com; backpacking.about.com/recreation/backpacking/library/weekly/aa093000a.htm;* and *www.landfield.com/ftp/faqs/dogs-faq/misc/part1.*

Dog regulations. When you and your dog are finally ready to hit the trail, keep in mind that national parks and monuments and some state parks do not allow dogs on trails. Your best bet is to hike in national forests, BLM lands, and canine-friendly state parks. Always call ahead to see what the regulations are as they may change from time to time.

Contact Info
[Local Clubs and Organizations]

COLORADO HIKING CLUBS:

Colorado's main hiking/climbing club is the Colorado Mountain Club. The state offices are located in Golden, but groups exist in many parts of the state. Most other clubs seem connected with places of employment, senior centers, or recreation centers. These clubs may or may not be available to drop-ins and are not listed here. However, if you're wandering through an area, it never hurts to check to see if you can hop on a hike with one of these groups. Check at the local chamber of commerce, visitor center, or land management agency.

Colorado Mountain Club

State Office, 710 10th Street #200, Golden, CO 80401 (303) 279–3080 or 1–800–633–4417 (Colorado only) • *www.cmc.org*

Aspen Group
Call state office for current group contact.

Boulder Group
825 S. Broadway, Suite 40, Boulder, CO 80303 (303) 554–7688 • *www.cmc.org*

Denver Group
Same number as state office.

El Pueblo Group
Call state office for current group contact.

Fort Collins Group
Call state office for current group contact • *members.aol.com/FortCMC/index.html*

Gore Range Group
Call state office for current group contact.

Long's Peak Group
Call state office for current group contact (Longmont area)

Pikes Peak Group
Call state office for current group contact • *www.cmc.org*

San Juan Group
Call state office for current group contact.

Shining Mountain Group
Call state office for current group contact (Estes Park area)

Weld County Group
Call state office for current group contact • *www.homestead.com/weldcmc*

Western Slope Group
Call state office for current group contact.

TRAIL GROUPS (EDUCATION, MAINTENANCE, ADVOCACY)

Aspen Wilderness Workshop, Aspen, CO (970) 963–8684

Indian Peaks Working Group, P.O. Box 2214, Boulder, CO 80306 • *www.gorp.com/nonprof/indpeaks/default.htm*

Friends of the Eagles Nest Wilderness, P.O. Box 4504, Frisco, CO 80443 – contact Dillon Ranger District at (970) 468–5400 for current contact

Poudre Wilderness Volunteers, Contact Canyon Lakes Ranger District at (970) 498–2770 for current contact • *www.fortnet.org/pwv*

Roaring Fork Outdoor Volunteers, P.O. Box 1341, Basalt, CO 81621 (970) 927–8241 or 1–877–662–5220

San Juan Mountains Association, 15 Burnett Court, Durango, CO 81301 (970) 385–1210 • *www.fs.fed.us/r2/sanjuan*

The Trail Group, Inc., P.O. Box 50, Ouray, CO 81427 – contact Ouray Ranger District at (970) 240–5300 for current contact

Volunteers for Outdoor Colorado, 600 South Marion Parkway, Denver, CO 80209 (303) 715–1010 or 1–800–925–2220 or www.voc.org

Colorado Trail Foundation, Golden, CO (303) 384–3729 ext. 113 • www.coloradotrail.org

Continental Divide Trail Alliance, P.O. Box 628, Pine, CO 80470 (303) 838–3760

Continental Divide Trail Society, 3704 N. Charles Street #601, Baltimore, MD 21218 (410) 235–9610

Friends of Dinosaur Ridge, P.O. Box 564, Morrison, CO 80465 (303) 420–0059

Friends of the Dunes, Mosca, CO (719) 378–2312, ext. 227

Friends of Roxborough, Littleton, CO (303) 973–3959

Friends of Mueller State Park, Divide, CO (719) 687–2366

Friends of Lory Trails, Bellvue, CO (970) 493–1623

Friends of Mt. Goliath, Denver Botanic Gardens, Denver, CO (303) 331–4000

Friends of the Florissant Fossil Beds, Inc., Florissant, CO (719) 748–3253

North Fork Trails Network, 1508 Black Canyon Road, Crawford, CO 81415 (970) 921–3340

Pikes Peak Area Trails Coalition, P.O. Box 34, Colorado Springs, CO 80901 (719) 635–4825

CONSERVATION GROUPS

The Colorado Fourteeners Initiative, 710 Tenth Street, Suite 220, Golden, CO 80401 (303) 278–7525 ext. 115

Colorado Wild!, P.O. Box 2434, Durango, CO 81302 • www.coloradowild.org

Colorado Environmental Coalition (also offices in Grand Junction and Durango), 1536 Wynkoop Street #5C, Denver, CO 80202 (303) 534–7066 • www.ourcolorado.org

Colorado Wildlife Federation, P.O. Box 280967, Lakewood, CO 80228 (303) 987–0400 • www.coloradowildlife.org

Leave No Trace, Inc., P.O. Box 997, Boulder, CO 80306 (303) 442–8222, 1–800–332–4100 • www.LNT.org

Nature Conservancy, 1881 Ninth Street, Suite 200, Boulder, CO 80302 (303) 444–2985 • www.tnc.org

Sierra Club, Rocky Mountain Chapter, 1410 Grant Street, Suite B205, Denver CO 80203-1846 (303) 861–8819 • www.rmc.sierraclub.org

Index

Index

Index

Meet the Author

A native of Colorado, Maryann Gaug was born in Denver and spent much of her youth dreaming about living in the mountains. While working on a B.S. degree in Mathematics at Gonzaga University in Spokane, Washington, she started backpacking and downhill skiing. Missing the mountains of Colorado, Maryann returned and earned an M.S. in Computer Science at the University of Colorado Boulder. The Boulder Group of the Colorado Mountain Club and their Mountaineering School provided new friends and a great education about enjoying the Colorado mountains. Between the Colorado Mountain Club and the Rocky Flats Mountaineering Group, Maryann continued to hike, backpack, backcountry ski, and otherwise love doing mountain-oriented activities.

After 20 years at Rocky Flats, Maryann took a voluntary separation plan and moved to Silverthorne, Colorado. Her initial mountain life included working as a cross-country instructor at Copper Mountain Resort, completing a Wilderness Studies Certificate at Colorado Mountain College, becoming a Master of Leave No Trace, and forming About Wilderness, Inc. (*www.aboutwilderness.com*). Maryann also started following another dream: to write about the mountains and canyons that she loves. Her articles—ranging from her outdoor adventures to natural history—have been published in several Summit County newspapers and the e-zine *Cyberwest*. Writing this hiking guide is her latest adventure. Maryann hiked over 400 miles in 10 months, revisiting favorite haunts, and discovering new ones, increasing her love of Colorado.